# What Is Liturgical Theology?

# A Study in Methodology

David W. Fagerberg

# What Is Liturgical Theology?

# A Study in Methodology

**A PUEBLO BOOK**

The Liturgical Press  Collegeville, Minnesota

A Pueblo Book published by The Liturgical Press

Design by Frank Kacmarcik

Library of Congress Cataloging-in-Publication Data

Fagerberg, David W., 1952–
  What is liturgical theology? : a study in methodology / David W.
Fagerberg.
    p.    cm.
  "A Pueblo book."
  Includes bibliographical references.
  ISBN 0-8146-6122-X
  1. Liturgics—Methodology.  I. Title.
  BV178.F34  1992
  264'.001—dc20                                          92-23587
                                                              CIP

# Contents

# Acknowledgments

I wish to place this work between two quotations.

The first comes from Josef Pieper's work on the four cardinal virtues where he reminds a beginning thinker that "In this realm, originality of thought and diction is of small importance—should, in fact, be distrusted" (preface, xii). His point, of course, is not to excuse intellectual sloth but to instill a certain humility in the neophyte as he or she first engages a subject matter which has already exercised both the heart and mind of great thinkers. The following study does, it is true, try to make a distinction in original fashion within the conversation occurring between liturgy and theology, but I beg the reader to believe that I can recognize the difference between shedding light upon the topic liturgical theology, and doing liturgical theology itself. In this latter realm, any originality of thought and diction on my part is of small importance—should, in fact, be distrusted. The challenge is not to come up with yet a new angle, but for me to fit the words which have been used before, and learn to use them rightly myself.

A book such as this gives me the opportunity to thank and acknowledge those teachers in my past who have taught me these words and their use. Simply mentioning their names gives me satisfaction: Bruce Reichenbach, Walter Buschmann, Robert Roth, Paul Sponheim, Rev. Richard Elvee, Fr. Kevin Seasoltz, Fr. Aelred Tegels, Gabriele Winkler, Don Saliers, Hans Frei, David Kelsey, and most especially Paul Holmer, George Lindbeck and Fr. Aidan Kavanagh. If these have trained my head in the grammar of faith, my parents trained my heart, and special gratitude for the nurturing sunlight from my mother and from my father who has since joined the liturgy of the angels.

In nearly twenty years of marriage, dear Elizabeth has only known me as a student. I can put into words my thanks for her patience with me as I followed my ineluctable path, and her willingness to live so long the students' humble life (financial and otherwise), but I cannot put into words what delight she gives! We have grown together over the years, and together, we have grown. Paul Evdokimov cites a conversation in a Russian novel in which someone asks an old peasant what he is doing in his life. "Doing?" he replies. "What am I doing? I am loving Olga." I thank Elizabeth for giving me so much to do.

This book was written when the author was a Lutheran pastor; as it is being published the author is Roman Catholic. Does the reader remember those optical illusions in which if one looks at black on white one sees a vase, but if one blinks and looks at white on black one sees two faces staring at each other? The basis of this book was my dissertation at Yale in which I tried to outline the perimeters of liturgical theology; then I blinked and saw an ecclesiology, one which drew me into the Roman Catholic liturgical tradition. Special thanks to the community of Church of the Nativity which instantiated the liturgical theology I try to write about.

The second quote, which forms the closing parenthesis to the years represented by this work, I received from Paul Holmer. "You cannot peddle truth or happiness. What a thought cost in the first instance, it will also cost in the second." I have happily paid the fee.

## Chapter 1

# Introduction

Ludwig Wittgenstein remarked, with his customary insightfulness, that to know the meaning of a word is not just to know its ostensive definition, it also involves knowing how that word plays in a language game. To illustrate his point, he observes that merely knowing the name of a chess piece, say a knight or a queen, is quite different from knowing how it moves on the chessboard during a game.

Of late, the term "liturgical theology" seems to have been gaining increased usage, but we wonder if the theologians who use the term are moving it on the theological chessboard in the same way, by the same rules, for the same purpose. The simple aim of this book is to gain some perspicuity about the shape and deployment of the term "liturgical theology" by proposing a distinction between theologies of worship, with their assorted forms and purposes, and what alone should properly be called liturgical theology.

To accomplish this we will delineate four possible uses of the term "liturgical theology," but recommend that the title be properly reserved for only one of the approaches, and about this approach two affirmations will be made: (a) liturgical theology recognizes that the liturgical community does genuine theology, although it is of a primary and not secondary sort; (b) liturgical theology is principally what is transacted in historic liturgical rites and secondarily that which can be uncovered by structural analysis of those rites. This understanding is owed to Fr. Alexander Schmemann, Fr. Aidan Kavanagh and Fr. Robert Taft.

One procedural note should be stressed at the outset so that we can remain mindful of it throughout this study and needn't be burdened with mentioning it repeatedly. To defend one approach alone as properly liturgical theology does not correlatively mean that other theological talk about worship is meaningless or mistaken or improper or useless. Other theological treatments of worship and liturgy have their own *raison d'être* and they would need to be judged individually to determine adequacy, truth, or helpfulness. It is not our intention to challenge other approaches as nontheological, but it is our hope to demonstrate that liturgical theology is genuinely theological. The tendency to treat liturgy as devoid of theological content makes this book necessary.

Another of Wittgenstein's imaginative observations is helpful. He considers how manifold are the activities that fall under the title "games"—board games, card games, ball games, Olympic games, etc.—and so disputes that there is a single common essence underlying them all which makes them games. It is impossible to isolate a single, essential factor that defines a game when some are playful and others serious, some require equipment and others do not, some are competitive while others are just for fun, and some are played in teams, some in pairs, and there is even the game of solitaire! But to say that a card game is different from a football game does not mean that one is a game while the other is not. Analogously, when we say that liturgical theology is different from other theological treatments of liturgy or worship, we are not required to say that one is theology and the other is not.

Theology involves words (*logos*) and so any theological task involves a quest for meaning. To reckon liturgical theology genuinely theological we must be able to say that liturgy is itself a stab at intelligibility, a search for understanding and meaning. It cannot be the case that the real search for meaning takes place somewhere else, over there, beyond liturgy in the world of reason and intellect, while liturgical ceremonial takes place in the world of pious feeling. On the other hand, although theology is human activity because it consists of human words, *theos* defines the subject matter. Liturgical theology fulfills a unique role precisely because it is liturgical. The subject matter of liturgical theology is not liturgy, it is God, humanity and the world, and the vortex in which these three existentially entangle is liturgy. If the subject matter of liturgical theology were human ceremony instead of God, it would be sheer self-delusion to call it theology; it would be anthropology, not theology. Liturgy is theological precisely because here is where God's revelation occurs steadfastly. Thus Fr. Schmemann calls liturgy "the ontological condition of theology, of the proper understanding of *kerygma*, of the Word of God, because it is in the Church, of which the *leitourgia* is the expression and the life, that the sources of theology are functioning precisely as sources."[1] So we recognize the usefulness of theologies of worship while nonetheless maintaining a premiere role for liturgical theology because the liturgy is where human words about God (theology) are grounded. Liturgical theology is normative for the larger theological enterprise because it alone, of all the activities that make up the family of theological games, self-consciously examines the vortex where the sources of theology function precisely as sources.

FOUR UNDERSTANDINGS

Four understandings of the relationship between liturgy and theology will be distinguished here. The number could undoubtedly be multiplied if one put one's mind to it because, like any piece of pie, it could be sliced into more pieces if one made the cut finer, but these four distinctions seem to be sufficient to indicate what liturgical theology is, and what it is not. Because each of these four approaches deals with worship and/or liturgy in one way or another it has happened that they are indiscriminately labeled liturgical theology, but it is precisely our thesis that when one discriminates between their methods and presuppositions the label should apply to the third approach alone. The four approaches we label thus: (a) theology *of* worship; (b) theology *from* worship; (c) liturgical theology, as we will specifically define it; and (d) the study of this definition, i.e., the study of the third approach.

As one would lay four white stones side by side in order to notice differences in the shades of white, our procedure in what follows will be to lay representative texts side by side in order to notice differences in shades of meaning. But a preliminary overview of each approach would first be helpful.

The first approach is characterized as theology of worship. The primary topic is worship, and if liturgy is treated at all, it is as an example of the main topic. Christian worship is human response

1. Alexander Schmemann, "Theology and Liturgical Tradition," *Worship in Scripture and Tradition*, ed. Massey H. Shepherd (New York: Oxford University Press, 1963) 175.

11

to the divine action in Jesus of Nazareth, so theology of worship proposes something about the relationship between God and persons, and further claims that the basis of this relationship rests with God's initiative. We refrain from calling it liturgical theology because even if it makes use of liturgy to exemplify and illustrate its discussion, liturgical rite *per se* is insignificant to the project. Two representative works will be examined: the treatment of worship in Regin Prenter's *Creation and Redemption* and Vilmos Vajta's *Luther on Worship*.

The second approach is characterized as theology from worship. It not only wants doctrine to be expressed in liturgical form, it also wants worship to be rooted in doctrine. It therefore has a stake in trying to unify liturgy and doctrine by showing that the worship of the Church has influenced doctrine and the doctrine of the Church has influenced worship. We refrain from calling this liturgical theology as well, because liturgy is treated not as the source of theology but as a resource for theological doctrine. Two representative texts will be examined: Peter Brunner's *Worship in the Name of Jesus* and Geoffrey Wainwright's *Doxology*.

We reserve the title liturgical theology for the third approach. It largely reflects, we believe, an Eastern Orthodox perspective and so we shall devote a critical section (chapter four) to Fr. Alexander Schmemann's understanding of liturgy as the ontological condition for theology before offering our own description (chapter five).

We will not make any explicit treatment of the fourth approach, for a very simple distinction is intended. If liturgical theology is that theology which is found in the structure of a liturgical rite, then it actually happens in liturgies and not on paper. But what, then, shall we call secondary reflections upon liturgical theology's meaning and method? They are observations about liturgical theology, but not liturgical theology itself. Texts such as Fr. Kavanagh's *On Liturgical Theology* or Fr. Schmemann's book *Introduction to Liturgical Theology* fall in this category, as does also this book. These are not cases of liturgical theology, but are an explication, usually in academic form, of the liturgical theological event. This fourth approach must be mentioned because such explanations and defenses are sometimes referred to as liturgical theology, but we would refrain from doing so.

All these four approaches strive to overcome the dichotomy which has grown up between worship and theology, and that, indeed, is what tends to group them in the face of other theological camps (e.g., philosophical theology, systematic theology, biblical theology, historical theology). Yet the door to confusion is thrown open if the term liturgical theology be indiscriminately applied to them all. Entitlement requires more than affirming that worship is an important subject of theology, or that the ecclesiastical theologian should serve the worshiping community, or that the liturgy is a resource for exemplifying doctrines which someone happens to be propounding. In contradiction to this general use of the term for any and every theological discussion of worship, we wish to reserve it for a specific vision of the relationship between liturgy and theology which employs a particular method. Our quarrel with calling either of the first two approaches liturgical theology is not over whether they are talking about worship, but over their starting point and method; our quarrel about so labeling the fourth approach merely concerns its secondary format.

OVERCOMING A DICHOTOMY

When a strict dichotomy is imposed between theology and liturgy, the latter is usually treated as mere expression of faith in pious, esthetic and emotive forms, itself void of theological content. It is as if theology exists for academicians and liturgy exists for pure-hearted (but simple-minded) believers. To their credit, the first two approaches do wish to overcome this false dichotomy. They do suppose that liturgy is more than a particular esthetic expression of faith and this is why they wish to establish a two-way connection between liturgy and theology, so that liturgy can be a resource for theology and theology can inform and correct liturgical practice. However, the definition of theology implicit in this scheme tends toward the prejudice that the theological meaning of a liturgy is in such an inchoate form that additional work is required in order to bring theology to being. Assumed is a two-step procedure to effect the transition from liturgical faith-expression, done by believers, to theological reflection, done by theologians. (Even if the believer and the theologian happen to be the same person—a theologian in the believing community—it still supposes a division of purpose and approach). Our working definition of liturgical theology challenges the supposition that theology exists only after the second step.

Second order, academic theology is a species within the genus theology. It is not the whole genus. It is true that the theological outcome of a liturgy is quite different in form and purpose from the theological outcome of an academic theology (this very difference is what leads us to distinguish between a theology of worship and liturgical theology) but we deny that theology is only really done when one crosses the threshold out of liturgy into academic theology. The liturgical rite is the ontological condition for what is itself a genuine theology, albeit of a different kind: it is primary theology and not secondary theology. It can be translated into secondary theology for certain purposes, but it is not necessary to do so in order to have real theology instead of the mere rudiments of theology.

Overcoming dichotomies as deeply entrenched as this one is very difficult indeed. Permit us to venture two inadequate but we hope illuminating analogies. J. Huizinga offers a useful poetic image. In his work *Homo Ludens* he argues that play is the basis of civilization and that the play-factor, as he calls it, is active in the cultural process and produces fundamental forms of social life (ritual, poetry, music and dancing, philosophy, warfare, conventions of noble living). He concludes, then, with this wonderful statement: "[C]ivilization is, in its earliest phases, played. It does not come *from* play like a babe detaching itself from the womb: it arises *in* and *as* play, and never leaves it."[2] This can be paraphrased in fidelity to our third approach by saying liturgical theology is, in its fundamental phase, liturgical. It does not come from liturgy like a babe detaching itself from the womb: it arises in and as liturgy, and never leaves it. Theology which is liturgical arises in the liturgical structures and does not detach from liturgi-

2. J. Huizinga, *Homo Ludens: A Study of the Play-Element in Culture* (Boston: The Beacon Press, 1950) 173. Aidan Kavanagh expresses the reunification of the dichotomy in remarkably similar terms, using the allegory of language and human community: "In this sense a human community does not merely use a language; it *is* the language it speaks. Similarly, a Christian church does not merely use a liturgy; it *is* the liturgy by which it worships." *On Liturgical Theology* (New York: Pueblo Publishing Company, 1984) 97.

cal rite; liturgy is theology in action, it is not merely a rubrical resource for the allegedly real theologians to rummage through.

We turn to a second image. Gabriel Marcel[3] teaches us how difficult dichotomies are to overcome as he discusses one which is implicit in our language about self and body. Even when trying to unite the two poles by saying "I have a body," a self is posited on the one hand and a body on the other. Marcel suggests that some advance is made by altering the expression to "I am a body," but this shift from a possessive metaphor to an ontological metaphor still supposes an "I" and a "body." Finally he recommends "I am bodily." His suggestion can parallel our efforts to overcome the dichotomy between liturgy and theology. The approach which we called a theology of worship, like the first of Marcel's formulas, supposes that "worship has a theology," but it must be identified by a theologian. An *a priori* theology of worship could be perceived in the liturgical rite if only one knew what it was. The approach which we called theology from worship, like the second of Marcel's formulas, supposes that "worship is theological," that is, buried within the liturgical rite are the rudiments of a theology which academic theologians can release and express in proper form. The two terms are nudged closer, but the theological task is still not studying the liturgical rite itself but unpacking the theology contained within it—and sometimes theology's task is to correct the rite so it gets back on track. Marcel's third formula expresses our vision of the third approach: "liturgical theology." The way this theology is, is liturgical. Liturgical action is theological act.

TWO CHARACTERISTICS OF LITURGICAL THEOLOGY

We have called attention to two characteristics distinctive to this third approach. First, it views liturgy as the condition for primary theology; second, since this theology arises in and as liturgy, even doing secondary work upon it must begin with concrete, historic liturgical structures (rites). Our working definition of liturgical theology cuts in two directions: on the one hand, it is what is

3. Gabriel Marcel, *Mystery of Being*, vols. I and II (Chicago: Gateway Edition, Henry Regnery Company, 1950) cf. 120 ff.

worked out by the corporate liturgical community, and on the other, it is only uncovered when one examines what the liturgical community works out in rite. Precisely these two characteristics will have to be explained in the course of this methodological comparison, but a prefacing is in order here.

Our first affirmation is that liturgical theology is primary theology. "For many this puts us on strange ground indeed, for since the high Middle Ages with the advent of the university and of scientific method, we have become accustomed to the notion that theology is something done in academies out of books by elites with degrees producing theologies of this and that. . . . [D]oing liturgical theology comes closer to doing *theologia prima* than *theologia secunda* or a 'theology of the liturgy'. . . ."[4] It is not as if believers have inchoate experiences which must in turn be formulated by academics to be real theology, nor as if primary theology is amateurish thinking which is better expressed by professionals, nor as if secondary theologians are privy to data which they must transmit to the less informed because theology only occurs in this systematic form. If theology is the struggle for meaning between the terms God, world and humanity, then this struggle goes on in the pew as well as in the study. To acknowledge this might ameliorate the antagonism between faith and theology (really, believers and theologians).

Fr. Aidan Kavanagh discerns three logical moments in the liturgical event. First, the assembly encounters the Holy One; second, by consequence of this encounter the assembly is changed; third, the assembly must adjust to this change, and it is this adjustment which he defines as theological.

" '[T]heology' is not the very first result of an assembly's being brought by the liturgical experience to the edge of chaos. Rather, it seems that what results in the first instance from such an experience is deep change in the very lives of those who participate in the liturgical act. . . . To detect that change in the subsequent liturgical act will be to discover where theology has passed. . . . It is the *adjustment* which is theological in all this. I hold that it is

4. Kavanagh, *On Liturgical Theology*, 74–75.

theology being born, theology in the first instance. It is what tradition has called *theologia prima.*"[5]

It is a truism to say encounter with God precedes reflection upon that encounter. Liturgy is encounter with God, but furthermore it is also a living adjustment, i.e., a theological response, to the Holy One. The division which puts raw experience in the sanctuary but theology in the office is here rejected. The assembly makes response too, in its rite, although this is different in form from the organized, analytic, systematic, researched response which makes up secondary theology. The assembly's response can be truly characterized as theological if our definition of the term is not excessively narrowed by institutional presuppositions, and if their response is ruled activity. The adjustment made by those who encounter God's holy presence in word and sacrament is an instance of *theologia prima.* There may be reasons to reflect in a further, more systematized fashion but such organization of thought does not disqualify primary theology as theology. Secondary theology is but one species in the genus theology.

Because encounter with God precedes reflection upon that encounter, liturgy is the ontological condition for theology. This is what tradition means when it says that the law of prayer (*lex orandi*) establishes (*statuat*) the law of belief (*lex credendi*), and not vice-versa. Thus our second affirmation is that liturgical theology originates and resides in the communal rite. This theology, the one that is liturgical, does not originate and reside in individual minds but is by definition found in the structure of the rite. By virtue of it being *liturgical* theology, it is theology manifested in the liturgy and the only starting point for uncovering liturgical theology, therefore, is to investigate concrete liturgical rites.

Say it this way. Not all worship is liturgical, but there is such a thing as liturgical worship (we mean that not all worship is corporate or ritualized, sometimes it is private and spontaneous). Not all prayer is liturgical, but there is liturgical prayer. Not all space, time, sacrifice or assembly is liturgical; but there is liturgical space, liturgical time, liturgical sacrifice, and there are liturgical assemblies. We are in this case further maintaining that not all theology

5. Ibid., 74.

is liturgical, but there is liturgical theology. It is an instance of corporate theologizing which is done in liturgical community and not in private isolation. The liturgical assembly is a "theological corporation."[6] Thus, as we have said, the corporate theological experience is normative for private theology, and this theological experience is found in concrete liturgical acts and not in abstracted ideas about liturgy.

Fr. Kavanagh writes, "If theology as a whole is critical reflection upon the communion between God and our race . . . then scrutiny of the precise point at which this communion is most overtly deliberated upon and celebrated by us under God's judgment and in God's presence would seem to be crucial to the whole enterprise."[7] The normative character of liturgical theology stems from the fact that it is in the liturgy, under God's judgment and in God's presence, that *theologia prima* is done. It is in the liturgy that the sources of theology function precisely as sources, as Fr. Schmemann put it. Whether the theologian be a monk in the cell, a believer in the pew, or an academic in the study, the subject matter being considered is the Church's corporate theological adjustment to encounter with the Father through Christ in the Holy Spirit.

"This adjustment to God-wrought change is no less critical and reflective an act of theology than any other of the secondary sort. Unlike these, however, it is *proletarian* in the sense that it is not done by academic elites; it is *communitarian* in the sense that it is not undertaken by the scholar alone in his study; and it is *quotidian* in the sense that it is not accomplished occasionally but regularly throughout the daily, weekly, and yearly round of the assembly's life of public liturgical worship."[8]

The term liturgical theology then seems to have two referents. If liturgical theology is done in liturgies, and if one uncovers it only

6. In Kavanagh's response to an address by Wainwright. Wainwright's address was "A Language in Which We Speak to God," and Kavanagh's critique, "Response: Primary Theology and Liturgical Act," both in *Worship* 57 (July 1983) 309–324.

7. Kavanagh, *On Liturgical Theology*, 78.

8. Ibid., 89.

by looking at liturgical structure, then the term means first that which is done by participants in liturgy and second what is uncovered by investigators of liturgical rite. But these two referents are in fact only the same thing looked at from two different perspectives. Liturgical theology is what is done in the church, and it is what is written down in a liturgical theology like Fr. Schmemann's *The Eucharist* or Germanus' *On the Divine Liturgy*. It is not, however, the analytical explanation of liturgical theology's method. An attempted definition of liturgical theology is what we called our fourth approach, but it is not the thing itself nor the thing uncovered by looking at the rite.

To uncover liturgical theology one must begin with the proletarian, quotidian and communitarian liturgical theology of the rite. It has been a mistaken practice of *theologia secunda* to first invent a theory of worship and then search for texts or rubrics to support the *a priori* theory. Thus it happens that academicians first decide what theological principle needs investigation, and then glance about to see whether it can be demonstrated from liturgical evidence or communicated by liturgical practice. Such scholarship may exhibit adroitness in rubric, history and theory, but it is a case of the tail wagging the dog. The starting point must be real liturgies, and they do not exist in the abstract. Only concrete liturgies exist. An analogy presented by both Fr. Kavanagh and Fr. Taft to illustrate this methodological necessity is the relationship between language and grammar. Structural linguistics attempts to uncover the structure and basic laws of how language works, but it does not write these laws nor establish these structures. "Philologists do not set the laws which permit language. They study its acts as formalized in words. Editors do not create language. They arrange its acts as formalized in words. Philosophers do not originate language. They formulate intelligiblity tests to clarify and bring greater precision to the implications of its acts as formalized in concepts and words. All three of these honorable activities represent not first but second order enterprises."[9]

People mean with language. That is, they use language to transact their business with reality, and philologists analyze the structure of a language already in place. People mean with liturgies,

9. Ibid., 84.

and liturgical theologians analyze the structure of a liturgy already in place. The task of writing down a liturgical theology depends upon looking at liturgical theology done.

This is not often the normal procedure, Fr. Taft notes.

"[I]n the history of liturgical *explanation* . . . there has been a contrary shift from structure to symbolic interpretation. Most medieval liturgical commentators attended only to meaning, and their interpretations often did violence to structure. In the Reformation period structure was bent to serve theology. *Legem credendi statuat lex supplicandi* was turned around, and theology determined rather than interpreted liturgical text and form. . . . In my own work I attempt to reverse this process, insisting with the structuralists on the importance of imminent analysis of the structure before relating it to other disciplines such as history, sociology—or even theology. These disciplines are essential for explaining the hows and the whys, but prior structural analysis is necessary to recover the what."[10]

Again the distinctiveness of liturgical theology is revealed. On the one hand, it is distinct from theology about worship because it begins with liturgies; on the other hand, it is distinct from traditional liturgics because it is theology. The subject matter is not liturgy as liturgics, but liturgy as theology. Fr. Schmemann emphasizes this when he distinguishes liturgical theology from what usually appears in the seminary catalogue, and usually under the heading of practical skills.

"What was called liturgics in the religious schools was usually a more or less detailed practical study of ecclesiastical rites, combined with certain symbolical explanations of ceremonies and ornaments. Liturgical study of this kind, known in the West as the study of 'rubrics,' answers the question how: how worship is to be carried out according to the rules i.e., in accordance with the prescriptions of the rubrics and canons. But it does not answer the question what: what is done in worship."[11]

10. Robert Taft, "The Structural Analysis of Liturgical Units: An Essay in Methodology," *Worship*, 52 (July 1978) 315.
11. Alexander Schmemann, *Introduction to Liturgical Theology* (New York: St. Vladimir's Seminary Press, 1975) 9.

If liturgy is an occasion of primary theology because it is adjustment to encounter with God, then liturgical theology will be more than traditional liturgics because it is theological, and it will be different from traditional theologies of worship because it is investigation of liturgical rites. Liturgical theology must begin with liturgies, and it must begin with the meaning of the whole rite, not merely with texts and rubrics.

Thus one is searching not for a symbolic interpretation of liturgy but for its meaning, and the meaning of a liturgy resides in its structure. Structures reveal "how the object works," Fr. Taft suggests. Liturgical theology begins with liturgiology because the latter informs us about the history, but "the purpose of this history is not to recover the past (which is impossible), much less to imitate it (which would be fatuous), but to *understand liturgy* which, because it has a history, can only be understood in motion, just as the only way to understand a top is to spin it."[12]

Our definition of liturgical theology as the third of four possible approaches is thus distinguished by its twofold characteristic of *theologia prima* and *lex orandi*. Encounter with God provokes theological reflection which, while not sharing the reflexive and analytical character of secondary theology, is theological nonetheless; and encounter with God is the ontological condition for the law of prayer which establishes the law of belief, not vice-versa. Liturgy is the ontological condition for theology because here is where primary theology occurs, and here is where the sources of second order theological conversation operate precisely as sources.

If theology is talk about God, humanity and the world, then such talk does indeed occur in all four of our approaches, only differently. That is the reason why all four are called theology. But the burden of adjusting to the divine encounter is assumed not only by professional secondary theologians, but also by each liturgical participant. The latter's adjustment is preserved in the evolving liturgical structures which are bespoken by liturgical theology. The *lex orandi*, as exercised in liturgical rite, establishes *lex credendi*, as expressed in other forms. The relationship is unilateral. Liturgi-

12. Robert Taft, "The Structural Analysis of Liturgical Units," 317.

cal theology is distinct both in its form (it is primary theology) and in its methodology (it begins with concrete liturgies).

What awaits us now is to contrast the third approach with the first two by reviewing some samples of theologies of/from worship in order to note differences in form and methodology. These reviews are an exercise in balance. We will resist the temptation as best we can to frame the comparison in contours of judgment, as if one is right or superior and the other is wrong or inferior. We do not conclude that liturgical theology should be done instead of theologies of worship; we do conclude that because *lex orandi* establishes *lex credendi*, liturgical theology makes a distinctive contribution to the theological enterprise.

Toward this end, we have chosen authors to represent the first two approaches who have been very influential in our own thought: it makes it more difficult to be flippant. In chapter two we will present a theology of worship in the persons of Vilmos Vajta and Regin Prenter, and in chapter three present a theology from worship in the persons of Peter Brunner and Geoffrey Wainwright. Chapter four will examine Fr. Schmemann's vision of liturgical theology in detail. This will put us in a position finally to make some remarks in chapter five about the topography of liturgical theology so defined, and to look at two examples in chapter six.

## Two Theologies of Worship

*a. Regin Prenter,* Creation and Redemption[1]

In this work Prenter explores Christian dogma under a Trinitarian scheme treating creation in part one and redemption in part two. Each is subdivided into a consideration of God's work and the human response, creating the following quadripartite: the God of Creation and the Man of Creation, the God of Redemption (Christology) and the Man of Redemption (Soteriology). It is in the fourth and final section that worship is treated in explicit detail. However, there is a treatment of the relationship between dogmatics and worship prefaced in two propaedeutic chapters, one on the task of dogmatics and the other a prolegomena to dogma.

DOGMATIC PROLEGOMENA

Prenter makes it clear that his is a dogmatic task, and one which he conceives in a particular way. Although the original use of the word was in the plural to denote the doctrinal definitions of the Church councils, he prefers to speak of dogma in the singular.

"Instead of *dogmas* understood as authoritatively established doctrinal statements, we may prefer to speak of *the dogma,* meaning the basic insight into the essential content of the Christian message, an insight which is immediately given in and with faith in the truth of the message, but which cannot be directly equated with faith, inasmuch as the faith which contains the insight is itself more than the insight. . . . This understanding of the word

1. Regin Prenter, *Creation and Redemption,* (Philadelphia: Fortress Press, 1968). References from this work are integrated into the text.

dogma presupposes that the word can appear only in the singular." (4)

Christian dogma differs from secondary formulations on the one hand (dogmas—plural), and from faith itself on the other hand (although dogma is insight given with faith, faith is more than dogma). This is why the work is systematic and not historical. There is but one dogma because there is only one divine revelation which is known Trinitarily: "The light comes *from* the Father, who is the source of revelation. It is mediated *by* the Holy Spirit, who is the power of revelation among sinners. And it shines *upon* Jesus Christ, who is the content of revelation." (5) He further clarifies the characteristics of dogma as (a) singular, (b) able to be put into words, (c) linked to God's revelation by Scripture, (d) conveying to proclamation clarity from the witness of Scripture, and (e) presupposing faith. Dogmatics is therefore defined as "the analysis and development of the insight given in the dogma, with a view to the concrete content of actual proclamation." (8) We may assume that Prenter's theology of worship fits into this scheme as well.

He acknowledges that methodological considerations are necessary because they are demanded by our times, but wishes to distance himself from a certain common type of prolegomena. "An introductory methodology in dogmatics is made necessary by the problem of the trustworthiness of the proclamation, a problem which arises out of the division of the church into mutually opposed confessional bodies. . . ." (5) Although the subject matter of dogmatics is not an entity to be observed but a message to be heard, the fact remains that we live in a world in which the Church proclaims the message of the gospel with many voices, not a unified voice. This state of affairs confronts dogmatics with "dogmatic agnosticism" which is the assumption that a single, genuine Christian dogma is unattainable because different people in different historical circumstances understand differently. Prenter rejects such agnosticism; this was implicit in his affirmation that dogma is singular and not plural. To be sure, the Christian dogma will be expressed in confessionally distinct ways, but he is hopeful of articulating the single Christian dogma which unites the confessional bodies of Christianity. Prenter defines this goal explicitly in his introduction, and we will call attention to this presupposition when we arrive at his treatment of worship.

There are thus two alternatives for dogmatic prolegomena. "The first places the main emphasis on the problems concerning the trustworthiness of the proclamation which are raised from the outside, that is, from the contemporary cultural and scientific consciousness." (19) Such a methodology in dogmatics will assume the character of a philosophical apologetic which defends the truth and validity of the Christian message from attacks without. "The second alternative places the main emphasis on the problems concerning the trustworthiness of the proclamation which are raised from the inside as a result of the division of the church into confessional bodies and factions." (19) Such a methodology in dogmatics will make a critique of authority essential to dogmatic prolegomena, but such a discussion should take place from within and not from without. Thus he rejects the transcendental methodology of Schleiermacher and neo-Protestantism. One cannot establish the category of Christianity (the nature and uniqueness of its message) "prior to and independently of the effort to appropriate its content through the study of biblical writings. . . . The category of Christianity cannot be known prior to, but only together with a knowledge of the content of this category." (28) In other words, the dogmatician must not be a propagandist for his or her confessional body or faction; the dogmatician is to be its theologian.

As one who makes explicit the dogma (singular) of Christianity, the theologian must first establish an authoritative point of departure, and this requires a confessional-ecumenical critique of authority. The point of departure which Prenter adopts is the Trinitarian character reflected in the Nicene creed. "When in the prolegomena we inquire in the light of the Scriptures' own central message into our own confessional body's understanding of the authority of the same Scriptures [i.e. Lutheran], we should also look to the creed confessed in the worship service of the congregation in order that we may see what the center of the biblical witness is for our church." (37) Dogmatics then begins with the Trinity as confessed in the creed of the worshiping congregation. Prenter's consideration and defense of dogmatic method concludes that the basis of our authority is not history, doctrinal points of view, philosophy, or the transcendent anthropology of religion, but revelation. Fundamental to dogmatics (and therefore to a dogma of worship) is the testimony that the God of Christian faith is the God of revelation. The Church knows no other God than God the Father who addresses us through the Son and unites us with himself through the Son and Spirit. There is no relationship with the Father "outside of that congregation where the Holy Spirit reveals the hidden essence of God the Father by uniting his people with him through Jesus Christ the Son, the king of God's people. We underscore here the expression 'living relationship.'" (39)

We thus already begin to see the significance of worship in Prenter's dogmatics. He defends worship as the locus from which will arise our bases for critiquing authority claims (even the authority claim of Scripture) because all dogmatics assumes the self-revelation of God and such divine manifestation occurs within the congregation where the Holy Spirit acts to reveal the Father. Dogmatics, then, is not based upon natural theology[2] but upon revelation. It is not based upon Jesus as a religious genius or ethical leader but upon Jesus as Lord. "We reject, further, all possibilities of finding the right relationship to the living Christ outside that congregation where the Holy Spirit reveals who Jesus Christ is by gathering for God the Father a worshiping people in the Son who is this people's king." (42) Neither is dogmatics based upon the Bible as a mere report of historical facts, but upon Scripture as containing God's self-revealing prophetic and apostolic word.

Prenter is concerned with worship because it is in worship that Jesus functions as Lord, the Bible functions as Scripture, and theology functions as dogma. He affirms this point again in another context. He remarks that the Trinitarian starting point he is advocating understands the threeness revealed in the history of revelation to also belong to God's own eternal essence (Trinitarian theology speaks not only of an economic Trinity but also of an immanent Trinity). Therefore, even though worship language rules

2. By natural theology Prenter means "the attempt to arrive at a preliminary knowledge of God independent of revelation, knowledge which may later be united with that knowledge of God which is gained through revelation." (40)

out independent speculation about God's majesty (*speculatio majestatis*), if Trinitarian theology is divorced from worship it becomes nothing but "logical absurdities." And, he notes, this is not only true of the doctrine of the Trinity but "every theological statement which is not organically connected with worship is a logical absurdity and nothing else." (50)

### DEFINING LITURGY

Prenter states this point even more forcefully in an article, "Liturgy and Theology," and we will tarry here a moment before looking at his discussion of worship in *Creation and Redemption*.

He begins the article by asking, what is liturgy? and answers "Liturgy is service; and every human service, whatever its content, consists in serving God. Thus our whole life may be called a service to God, i.e., a liturgy."[3] As the dominical liturgy is Christ giving himself to the Father in true worship of sacrifice, so the true worship of his believers is our bodily sacrifice of service to our brothers and sisters. We do our priestly worship when we partake in Christ's liturgy of sacrificial love. Prenter seeks to give liturgy a broader definition than merely referring to an order of worship, and if he succeeds then he can also call theology liturgical.

"[L]iturgy is a most comprehensive term consisting of the whole of Christian life. This includes also theology. Theology is a part of the liturgy, part of that sacrifice of our body of which St. Paul speaks. Indeed, when we say this and thereby explain the word 'liturgy' in Pauline terms, we are making a theological statement. But a theological statement of that kind—and this is true of any theological statement—has no meaning at all if it is not considered an essential part of the divine liturgy which it describes and explains."[4]

He has expanded the definition of liturgy to mean more than order of rite, and similarly has expanded theology to mean more than specialized study. In this definition of theology "we are not

---

3. Prenter, "Liturgy and Theology," in *Theologie und Gottesdienst: Gesammelte Aufsatze* (Gottingen: Forlaget Aros Arhus, 1977), 139–151.
4. Ibid., 140.

speaking exclusively of theological research, that is, of the academic theology produced in our seminaries and universities,"[5] but rather theology is human witness to the truth of God's revelation; it is speaking about God (which, he notes, is what the word literally means). And under this definition Prenter can consider theology part of the service about which Paul speaks when he refers to our liturgical life as a sacrifice of our bodies: he calls it our "reasonable service." Reasonable means *logike,* i.e., our logical service. Our reasonable or logical service has to do with words. Our reasonable service would be our witnessing worship which is spoken and proclaimed, our logos-worship. Thus he can paraphrase Paul in the following way: Make your whole life a true liturgy *and* theology by representing your bodies as a living sacrifice, holy, acceptable unto God.

To recap, Prenter unifies liturgy and theology. He calls them identical when taken in the wider sense demanded if we relate both liturgy and theology to our participation in Christ's sacrifice on the cross. Theology is an essential part of any liturgy insofar as all liturgies are reasonable, logical service, expressing sacrificial love through word and action towards God and neighbor in Christ, and liturgy finds its goal in theology insofar as all sacrificial love finds expression in terms of personal relationships which are meaningful words and actions (i.e., logical, reasonable, witnessing). If this is true, then there is the dual danger of separating liturgy from theology or theology from liturgy.

"If liturgy is separated from theology, i.e., if it is no longer in its essence 'theology' or true witness to the revelation of God, it then becomes an end in itself, a 'good work,' [ritualism]. . . . If, on the other hand, theology is separated from liturgy, i.e., if it is no longer seen as a part of the liturgy of the Church, part of the living sacrifice of our bodies in the service of God and our fellow men, it, too, becomes an end in itself, a human wisdom competing with and sometimes even rejecting the revelation of God. . . . We might even say that the main theological task of our day is the reinstatement of theology in its true liturgical function."[6]

5. Ibid.
6. Ibid., 141.

Liturgy is sacrificial service to God and thus we offer our theology liturgically; theology is reasonable service to God and witness to kerygmatic revelation and thus we offer our liturgy theologically.

If this unity is overlooked, as Prenter thinks it often is, then today's theological renaissance is "in danger of becoming a new intellectualism detached from the worship of the congregation," and today's liturgical renaissance is "in danger of becoming a new ritualism in which the theological meaning of worship is neglected for the benefit of reviving beautiful and interesting old customs."[7] The objective of this article, cursory though it is, is to keep the theological and liturgical renewals together, interpreted in the light of the fundamental unity of theology and liturgy.

To this end he offers an interpretation of the structure and liturgy of the Mass, since this ritual liturgy is part of the wider liturgy which comprehends our life in the service of love to God and humanity. However, he here deals with an abstracted skeleton of the ritual liturgy focusing not upon its sequence of moments but offering theological apologetic for the unity of the two moments of word and sacrament. Without explicitly using the terms, he is in fact contrasting the Mass as *sacrificium* with Luther's conception of the Mass as *testamentum*. He explains the representation of the sacrifice of Christ in the Mass not as offering transubstantiated bread and wine to God but as the distribution and reception in faith of the fruits of Christ's perfect sacrifice, and then proposes that such distribution of the fruits of Christ's work happens both in the proclamation of the gospel and in the administration of Holy Communion.

"What is the importance of administering the Holy Communion in the closest possible connection with the preaching of the gospel and vice versa? May I put it this way: Only when the preaching of the gospel is followed by the administration of the Holy Communion is it clearly manifested that the sacrifice of Jesus Christ in history is not simply an important fact of the past, the moral and religious evaluation of which is left to us but, rather, that this sacrifice is God's ultimate dealing with his people and is valid for all places and for all ages."[8]

7. Ibid., 142.
8. Ibid., 145.

The significance of the structure of word and sacrament, united in each ritual liturgy, is that it establishes the theological basis of our lived liturgy.[9] The preached word and the distributed body is the saving presence of Christ, and from this center is interpreted the people's responsive action of receiving both the word and the gifts of the sacrament in faith. Prenter uses Paul's word, "confession," to describe this responsive action in its totality. The Greek word for confession is *homologia* which literally means "to say the same word which has been said before." What God says to the Church in word and sacrament is said back by the people of God in prayer, witness and thanksgiving, which we do in both our ritual liturgy and our lived liturgy. The structure of the liturgy, as Prenter overviews it, underscores the saving event as accomplished by God in Christ's sacrifice, communicated by word and sacrament, and responded to in the confession of prayer, witness and thanksgiving by the community.

"This is the structure of the liturgy of the Church, and it is theological through and through. . . . It is *'theologia,'* a word speaking the truth about God in human, understandable terms, a reasonable service, *latreia logike.* In the theology of the liturgy, any genuine theology of the school, the seminary or the university must be rooted. Academic theology is not a different theology than the theology of the liturgy. They are substantially the same. Academic theology, however, is a reflective unfolding of the content of the theology of the liturgy apart from the worship of the Church, whereas the theology of the liturgy is the unreflected, living

9. We are using the term "lived liturgy" to refer to Prenter's wider definition of liturgy which he proffers at the outset. It is inspired by Jean Corbon's distinction between "the liturgy celebrated" and "the liturgy lived," cf. Jean Corbon, *The Wellspring of Worship* (New York: Paulist Press, 1988), but is a distinction many others also make. Alexander Schmemann, for example, stresses that "leitourgia" refers to all the ministries which manifest the eschatological existence of a believer, both inside and outside the ritual (Schmemann, "Liturgy and Theology," *The Greek Orthodox Review,* 17 [Spring 1972] 89). Joseph Jungmann notes that one cannot make Eucharist without being a *eucharistos* (Jungmann, *The Mass* (Collegeville: The Liturgical Press, 1975). And Robert Taft observes that everything entailed by the liturgical life is summed up by Paul in his phrase "putting on Christ" (Taft, "The Liturgical Year," *Worship* 55 [1981]).

manifestation in the worship of the church of that truth analyzed by academic theology."[10]

We take Prenter to be restating the distinction we preliminarily made in the introduction between primary theology and secondary (academic) theology. In other words (*viz.*, those Prenter used in his prolegomena to dogmatics), academic theology as *theologia secunda* is the dogma of the Church being reflectively unfolded, and *theologia prima* is the dogma of the Church in its unreflected, living manifestation in worship. And the dogma is singular, not plural. The purpose of dogmatics is not to present multiple perspectives but to clarify the single dogma. Thus Prenter can claim that the theology of liturgy and academic theology are "substantially one because both feed upon the same source: the revelation of God historically recorded in the prophetic and apostolic scriptures and actually addressed to the people of God in the preaching of the gospel and the administration of the sacraments."[11]

What makes up this subject matter of academic theology which is the reflective unfolding of dogma? Prenter recognizes three approaches, each of which represents a specific methodology. The first is exegetical theology wherein the revelation of God is approached by studying the historical biblical records using historical methods; the second is systematic theology wherein we approach the revelation of God by reflecting upon it in its relation to the contemporary situation, which would be dogmatics (plural) and ethics; the third is philosophical theology wherein the revelation of God is approached by reflecting upon questions and needs to which this revelation brings the answer. (He does not mention Church history, he says, because it does not represent an independent theological approach like that of exegetical, systematic or philosophical theology and must therefore be considered an auxiliary theological discipline connecting exegetical and doctrinal theology but with no specific approach of its own.) Each approach is an unfolding of the single dogma, though. Since each of these approaches in academic theology is human response to God's revelation, they correspond to the responses which were found in

10. Prenter, "Liturgy and Theology," 147.
11. Ibid.

the structure of the liturgy: witness, thanksgiving and prayer. Exegetical theology correponds to the witness of the Church which unfolds the foundation of the faith; systematic theology corresponds to thanksgiving which unfolds love in doctrine and ethics, making systematic theology primarily doxological; and philosophical theology corresponds to prayer which is the unfolding of our cry for redemption. Prenter says he does not wish to overstate the analogy between the structure of liturgy and the structure of academic theology, not wishing it to appear that he believes the latter can be simply deduced from the former, yet he finds the analogy "significant."

He thus concludes by affirming that the liturgy of the Church is theological, and the theology of the Church is liturgical. On the one hand, because liturgy speaks to God and humanity about God and humanity, it is theological and the liturgical functions of the Church continually need guidance from Scripture; on the other hand, because theology serves God and neighbor, it has no purpose in itself but is part of our sacrifice (our logical sacrifice) when we act as people of God. "This means, then, that theology is real only insofar as it is liturgy, that is, a poor human work attempting to praise God for his mercy and endeavoring to help our neighbor in his need for clarity of thought in his understanding of the gospel."[12]

### WORSHIP IN DOGMATICS

When we now return to Prenter's explicit treatment of worship in the latter pages of *Creation and Redemption*, we can realize the place he accords worship in his dogmatic scheme. "Dogma-in-the-singular," which is then explicated in dogmatics, is rooted in worship for that is where it begins and the point to which it returns. The discussion of worship falls under the dogmatic heading of Soteriology ("The Man of Redemption") but this is only after having explored the divine and human facets of the doctrine of creation and the Christological facet of the doctrine of redemption. What Christ accomplishes for us as savior (atonement) is worked out in our lives through worship (renewal). Atonement and re-

12. Ibid., 151. The reader should note that although Prenter means this remark to be true of all ritual liturgies, it is cast in the abstract.

newal are a unity, which is to say that the *"ordo salutis"* (the way of renewal unto salvation) is "the justified sinner's sacramentally ordered life under faith's struggle against sin (*simul justus et peccator*) on his journey between baptism and death."[13] Standing under the work of atonement, the sinner begins a life of renewal in the Holy Spirit by means of word and sacrament. It is at this juncture that Prenter places his theology of worship.

He offers a tidy schema to speak about this life of renewal. The origin of the renewal is baptism; the growth of the renewal is sanctification which comes about through the proclaimed gospel; the goal of the renewal is the Eucharist; the community of the renewal is the Church; and the fruit of the renewal is eschatological glorification. In fidelity to the prolegomena at the outset of his work where dogmatics was defined as "the analysis and development of the insight given in the dogma," he is trying to explicate the central and singular dogma of the Church: the life of renewal accomplished by Christ and contained in theology and worship. We will conclude our treatment of Prenter by looking briefly at baptism, word, and Eucharist but bypassing the latter two entries.

Baptism is the starting point. It is the "regenerating means of grace by which we are initiated into a participation in the death and resurrection of Jesus Christ through faith." (462) By baptism, the decisive event for an individual in relation to death and resurrection becomes effective already here and now in the midst of the old existence which is marked by death. This, indeed, is the relationship between baptism and faith. In faith's present time, this is a union of the past resurrection of Jesus and the future resurrec-

---

13. *Creation and Redemption,* 441. A debate could occur here, although it is outside of our purview, whether Prenter's adoption of the Lutheran category of *simul justus et peccatur* reflects the common dogma of the Christian faith or a confessionally expressed dogmatic. Consider Roman Catholic treatments of grace transforming nature, such as Karl Rahner's "Concerning the Relationship between Nature and Grace" and "Scholastic Concept of Uncreated Grace" in *Theological Investigations,* vol. I (New York: Seabury Press, 1974) 197–346; or Orthodox treatments of synergy such as Jean Corbon, *The Wellspring of Worship,* John Meyendorff, *Byzantine Theology: Historical Trends and Doctrinal Themes* (New York: Fordham University Press, 1974), or Vladimir Lossky, *Orthodox Theology: An Introduction* (New York: St. Vladimir's Press, 1978).

tion of those who are baptized. This is why baptism has the character of an eschatological covenant. "As an 'earnest' it is faith's anticipation of the promised resurrection. Therefore baptism's bestowal of the Spirit is characterized as a sealing." (465) Regeneration is the operative image throughout Prenter's treatment of the Christian life, and baptism is the genesis of this life of regeneration and worship. That the life of regeneration is lived in the present tense and not the future tense is indicated when Prenter claims that the goal of regenerate life is the Lord's Table, not heaven. Eschatological glorification is a fruit of the Spirit's work, but the goal of the Spirit's regenerating work is to restore communion between humanity and God and this is what Eucharistic worship manifests. Having been delivered from the demonic powers (sin, law, wrath, death and the devil) men and women are initiated by God's Spirit into a life of regeneration which "is born once for all through baptism because the promise which is given there can never be superseded by a greater promise. . . . Therefore there is no Christian life, whether in the process of growth or in its completion, which is not identical with the life which was born through baptism." (466) Baptism bestows nothing less than complete salvation; nothing is to be added, but everything is to follow.

And what follows is growth of the renewal, treated under the category of sanctification. For as long as human beings live on this side of the parousia, the struggle continues between the life of faith and life in the flesh.[14] The impartation of the Spirit is a foretaste and a first fruit, but is not yet the full possession which will belong to the regenerate on the day of glorification, and so throughout this life the Spirit leads disciples forward through death to resurrection. Here is where Prenter fits the role of the Word proclaimed. "The sanctifying means of grace is the gospel, the message concerning God's saving activity in Jesus Christ,

14. In the Pauline sense, not the Platonic sense. See Prenter's treatment in *Spiritus Creator* (Philadelphia: Fortress Press, 1953) or Paul Althaus *The Theology of Martin Luther* (Philadelphia: Fortress Press, 1966) 391 ff., or Rudolf Bultmann *Theology of the New Testament* (New York: Charles Scribner's Sons, 1951) on Pauline anthropology, or Gunther Bornkamm *Paul* (New York: Harper & Row, 1969) on Paul's vocabulary of *sarx*.

34

which is proclaimed in the congregation in the confirmation of baptism, the exposition of Scripture, and the edification of the congregation in the two-fold form of public preaching (*verbum vocale*) and private confession (*absolutio privata*)." (474) Proclamation preserves the life of renewal which baptism bestowed completely and is grasped by faith but which awaits fulfillment at the Last Day.

Sanctification is thus not our own striving, but the work of the Spirit. It is the Holy Spirit's own struggle against the devil, "waged in us only through a means of grace which is indissolubly connected with and which builds upon the means of grace by which we were regenerated." (476) As noted above, this word is proclaimed in several modes: confirmation of baptism, exposition of Scripture, and edification of the congregation. Proclamation of the gospel sanctifies the sinner as it establishes hope resting entirely on the covenant of baptism. It is not an addition to baptism, but the unfolding of the effects of baptism. This churchly proclamation as the sanctifying means of grace appears both as public preaching and as private absolution. "Through the sermon the gospel is proclaimed to all, and takes on a breadth and fullness which it does not have in private absolution. . . . In the confessional, on the other hand, the gospel is proclaimed to the individual in his particular situation. The gospel is thereby concentrated and concretized as it would not be in the sermon." (479–80) In the time between baptism and the parousia the word of sanctification both calls and illuminates the baptized. It elicits the response of confession and prayer, which are the distinctive life manifestations of sanctification. For Prenter, the whole history of sanctification is maintained through confession and prayer under the covenant of baptism. His treatment of the proclamation of the word is cast in broader contours than exclusively the ante-communion of the liturgy.

What was initiated in baptism and struggles under sanctification finds its fruition at the Lord's Table.

"The life of renewal, born as faith through the confession of the triune God at baptism and struggling as hope through prayer under the proclamation, is completed as love through the spiritual sacrifice of praise and the bodily sacrifice of the work of love which are imparted to us when in the Lord's Supper we are united with Jesus Christ in the giving of his body and the shedding of his blood at Calvary." (487)

As previously mentioned, the goal of the life of renewal is communion in love with God, and this is realized at the Lord's Table. It is essential to the theology of worship to remember that this communion is accessible even now; Eucharistic communion between God and humanity is known at the table and not only at post-mortem glorification. This is the Eucharist's eschatological dimension. "The essence of love is the perfect unity between two persons; it is the removal of everything which might separate them from one another. In this sense the love between God and man possesses an eschatological character. . . . This, however, does not mean that love is only a future prospect. Faith, hope, and love are always united." (489)

Such love takes the form of sacrifice. While the perfect sacrificial giving up of oneself is not accomplished by any of the sons of Adam or daughters of Eve, it has been accomplished by the New Adam: Jesus. Between the Father and the Son there is perfect unity; everything which might separate them from one another has been removed, and this is the essence of love. And since we are baptized into Christ, this eschatological consummation of love is already known—in a hidden manner and as a foretaste, true— but it is already known. In baptism one is united with Christ and so taken up into his sacrifice at his table. "The sacrifice of love completes here in time the full unity with the crucified and risen Savior, which faith . . . grasps, and which the repentance and hope struggle to maintain." (489)

Prenter is careful to distinguish the disciples' sacrificial life in Christ from self-reliant sacrifice which would be our work and not Christ's work in us. The work is Christ's. Our sacrifice is not heroism, self-willed and self-chosen. The place and time of the sacrifice is not biographically but sacramentally determined.

"Our death can be a sacrifice to God only if we abandon all thought of our death as having any value in itself. And this giving up of our own life, which is not a matter of our own decision, is given us in the Lord's Supper when the sacrificed body and blood of Jesus are offered us as nourishment on the way to our own

36

death. . . . [In the words of institution] Jesus would say: 'This body which you are now eating becomes your body as you partake of it. The perfect submission of this body in death as a gift of love becomes your sacrifice of love.' And when he says, 'Do this in remembrance of me,' he means: 'You are to find your own death in my death, your own sacrifice in my sacrifice, your own love in my love.' " (490)

A dogmatic treatment of the Eucharist, then, involves a notion of sacrifice and Christ's Real Presence. Prenter is willing to admit straightforwardly that the Lord's Supper is "the constant presence in the church of the sacrifice of Calvary. In fact it must be said that in the Lord's Supper we bring not only communion elements and prayers as a sacrificial gift, but the memorial (*anamnesis*) of [Christ's] one sacrifice, which is the only gift of love we can bring." (491) He acknowledges that these ideas have remained in the background of evangelical theology because of sixteenth-century polemics against the medieval doctrine of the Mass. However, as we have repeatedly pointed out, his goal in dogmatics is to explicate Christian dogma (singular). In other words, he understands his treatment of the Eucharist here not as partisan Lutheranism but as the Lutheran confessional perspective upon the dogma of the Eucharist. As such, something must be said about sacrifice even within confessional Lutheranism because sacrificial categories are part of the dogma.[15]

Prenter provocatively entitles an article on the subject: "Eucharistic Sacrifice According to the Lutheran Tradition."[16] Can we reasonably speak of a Lutheran tradition concerning Eucharistic sacrifice? he asks. At first sight it appears difficult and many Lutheran theologians would dismiss all treatment of sacrifice. But

15. In a second Excursus following this chapter, entitled "The Sacrifice of the Mass and the Real Presence in Confessional Polemics," Prenter writes: "In discussing the sacrificial meal of the consummation in the preceding section we employed a method which is unusual in Lutheran dogmatics. On the basis of New Testament references we tried to develop the content of the Lutheran idea of the real presence in terms of the idea of sacrifice. . . ." (502) (Hereafter: *Excursus II*).

16. *Theologie und Gottesdienst: Gesammelte Aufsatze* (Gottingen: Vandenhoeck & Ruprecht, 1977), 195–206; also published in *Theology*, 67 (New York, 1964) 286–295.

Prenter distinguishes between Luther's condemnation of the Private Mass as a propitiatory sacrifice[17] and the place of sacrifice in the Eucharist. It is true that Luther objected to any formulation which suggested that we offer the sacrament to God. On the contrary, it is God who offers us the sacrament. The consecrated elements are not offered to God as a new or additional propitiatory sacrifice, since the evangelical meaning of the Lord's Supper is that the consecrated bread and wine are received and eaten/drunk as the gifts of God to us. But having said that we do not offer God the sacrament, Luther is willing to say that in the Eucharist we offer Christ to God. "Faith I call the true priestly office which makes of all of us priests and priestesses. Through faith we place ourselves, our misery, our prayer, praise, and thanksgiving in Christ's hands, and through Christ offer it all to God in the sacrament. Thus we offer Christ to God, that is, we give him occasion and move him to offer himself for us, and us with himself."[18]

It is Prenter's purpose to draw attention to the fact that Luther speaks of a Eucharistic sacrifice. What is its content? First, the sacrifice is prayer, praise and thanksgiving; second, Luther mentions that we offer ourselves; but third, we offer Christ. "It is indeed surprising that we do find a text in which Luther himself expressly

17. He cites article 24 of the Augsburg Confession, which reads: "The Scripture teaches that we are justified before God through faith in Christ. But if the Mass deletes the sins of the living and the dead because of the correctly performed rite justification is by the work of the Mass, not by faith. And this the Scripture does not tolerate."

18. Luther's "Sermon on the New Testament" quoted by Prenter, "Eucharistic Sacrifice According to the Lutheran Tradition," 196. In this regard, consider the intriguing suggestion by David Power that the Lutheran-Tridentine squabble was less over doctrine of the Mass than the way in which it was put into practice, i.e., whether Private Mass was possible, in *The Sacrifice We Offer: The Tridentine Dogma and Its Reinterpretation* (New York: Crossroad, 1987). At the first meeting of the Council of Trent seven articles were presented as a list of the Reformer's heresies; four of the seven were matters of practice, piety and tradition, not dogma. "In this listing of alleged errors, the place given to practices is very important. . . . What it was proposed to defend at the Council was traditional Catholic practice and its foundation in the teaching that had been developed about the propitiatory nature of the eucharistic sacrifice. . . . Such practices seemed to stand or fall on the defence of the mass as a priestly offering of propitiation . . ." (52).

says that we offer Christ to God in the Eucharist."[19] We have no right to it, but we venture to pray God for the fulfillment of the promise of Christ because of the righteousness of Christ. And in offering Christ, we pray that he would offer us to the Father. "The entire sacrificial action in the Eucharist comprehending the offertory, the prayer of consecration, the anamnesis and (in some liturgies) the epiclesis, is one indivisible act of imploring Christ and of giving him, as our High Priest and advocate, occasion to present us to God."[20]

The propitiatory character of the Private Mass was rejected because the people did not participate in the priestly act of Jesus Christ by virtue of their personal faith in him. If the sacrifice is offered by virtue of a priestly power to consecrate and offer, such that the Christ's sacrifice made satisfaction for original sin but the Mass functions as a sacrifice of atonement for actual sins, and if such satisfaction can be obtained even if one was absent, then the Mass threatens to become a case of works righteousness. "The error of the particular theory of the mass which is condemned by the Augsburg Confession, is that in separating the sacrifice of the mass for actual sins from Christ's sacrifice on the cross for original sin it turns the sacrifice of the mass into a good work and reliance upon it (especially the private masses) into work-righteousness. . . ."[21] However, if this sacerdotal monopoly is corrected, then the propitiatory quality of the sacrifice is excised and one can unhesitatingly affirm that a sacrifice is offered, as Luther does in his sermon: we offer Christ to God in order that he might offer us to God with himself. The subject of the sacrificial act (the offering priest) is Christ, in union with his people, the Church. The purpose of the sacrifice is to render eucharistia, a sacrifice of thanksgiving.

"The substance of the sacrifice, the gift presented to God, is the people of God itself united with its King and High Priest Jesus Christ, presenting itself to God in the name of Jesus Christ

---

19. Prenter, "Eucharistic Sacrifice According to the Lutheran Tradition," 197.
20. Ibid., 198.
21. Prenter, Excursus II, 503.

through its gifts of bread and wine and through its prayers and thanksgivings, and being presented unto God by the heavenly High Priest, Jesus Christ who, hearing and fulfilling the appeal of his people, through the gift of the sacrament his own body and blood under bread and wine, perfectly unites himself with his people and takes it into his own eternal act of sacrifice."[22]

Prenter considers these ideas of sacrifice altogether biblical. Biblical covenant meals were for the purpose of fellowship with God. Such fellowship was known by the disciples when they sat at table with the Word made flesh dwelling among them, and such fellowship will be known in the parousia when we sit at the messianic table with the Lamb; in the meantime, during this struggle against the flesh, initiated by baptismal regeneration and preserved by confessional struggle under the word, the meal is a sacrificial meal which makes anamnesis of Christ and makes the eschatological petition (epiclesis of God's Spirit) that the communion of love will be known even now. The identity of the bread and wine with Christ's Body and Blood means that the bread and wine are distributed as a sacrificial gift and that the sacrifice of Calvary is really present in the Church's liturgy. In fact, unless our way of thinking includes the idea of sacrifice, Prenter maintains that the idea of Christ's real presence will be perverted into semi-naturalistic speculation about how the heavenly body is miraculously absorbed into the bread. There are thus evangelical elements (doctrines) in the Roman Catholic doctrine of the Mass (our common dogma), namely, that the sacrificing priest is Christ himself, that the ordained priest can bring the sacrifice only on the strength of his participation in Christ's own high priestly office, and that Christ is never without his body so that the Church participates in Christ's priesthood by bringing the sacrifice. What this means is that the Church as body of Christ must be present at and participate in the sacrifice or else, as happened in the abuses of private Mass, the sacrifice threatens to become a case of work righteousness.

". . . [T]he central idea of the original doctrine concerning the eucharistic sacrifice, namely, that through the remembrance

22. Prenter, "Eucharistic Sacrifice According to the Lutheran Tradition," 202.

(anamnesis) in the Lord's Supper the people of Christ present Christ as a prayer that he will incorporate them into his sacrifice is neither unbiblical nor unevangelical. Only theories which make the sacrifice of the mass vicarious instead of representative, that is, theories which exempt man from sacrificing himself and which separate the sacrifice from communion, can be charged with being unbiblical and unevangelical."[23]

Luther's sensitive point was less sacrifice as it was work righteousness.

The sacrifice on the cross lay in the love between God and humanity restored in Christ. "The life of renewal, born as faith and struggling as hope, is consummated in love as the complete giving up of life in death." (500) This life of renewal is given to us in the sacrifice of Jesus Christ at Calvary and is really present in the bread and wine of the Lord's Supper, there given to us as full participation in his sacrificial death and in his victorious resurrection. This participation is the life of the Church. Thus Prenter can say that when he was speaking about renewal as the work of the Holy Spirit he was already speaking about the Church. Nothing can be added to what has already been said, because the Church itself is nothing other than the community of those in whom the Holy Spirit carries out the work of renewal. But five elements of the Church can be made explicit: it is eschatological, it is God's spiritual people, it is hidden in this world while it struggles, it nevertheless manifests the glory of the world to come because it already participates in the gift of the Holy Spirit, and its renewed life is sacramental and liturgical. "The church is . . . the people assembled about baptism, preaching, and the Lord's Supper, and the church's ministers are those who on behalf of Christ administer the gospel and the sacraments to this people." (516) The Church's only visible signs are the means of grace and the office of the ministry; where these signs are, the Church is really present in its hiddenness. As holy, the Church is under the authority of God's word and is not of the world; as catholic, it is in the world because it has been commissioned to serve every human being with the grace it has itself received. "The church is there-

23. Prenter, Excursus II, 504.

fore not identical with the human race, but it is an elected body in the human race. After the judgment, in the state of glory, the church will not be the elect in the human race; it will then be the human race." (517)

Prenter goes on to discuss ministry, and in the next section to discuss our eschatological glorification, but we may conclude here. Prenter's theology of worship dealt with the life of regenerated humanity which is life originating in baptism, sustained by proclaimed word, and fulfilled at the Eucharist.

### b. Vilmos Vajta, Luther on Worship[24]

In the brief four-page introduction to his work, Vajta makes explicitly clear what is his polemic in this study of Luther on worship. He claims that many other treatments of Luther have assumed that Luther had minimal (or marginal) interest in liturgical worship. This is, in Vajta's opinion, a misreading of Luther. He admits that "from a merely historical viewpoint, [Luther's] liturgical output may indeed appear meager and inadequate," and supposes this is why "would-be liturgical reformers are always inclined to bypass the Reformation as they ransack the liturgical treasure chambers of the past." (xi) But Vajta maintains there is actually a deep, inner connection between Luther's theology as a whole and his theology of worship. Far from being tangential to Luther's concerns, worship can be understood as a radical (root) component of his theology. Luther could not avoid coming to grips with the Mass because his theological convictions led to a complete liturgical reorientation. The purpose of Vajta's study is "to link Luther's theology of worship with his teaching on creation, the atonement, the church, and justification. If proof of this connection can be established—and we mean to furnish it—it follows that Luther's theology of worship points to the very center of his whole thought." (xi–xii)

This should not be surprising, notes Vajta, because throughout the history of the Church, worship and doctrine have developed in "mutual dependence." Christian worship of every age reflects

---

24. Vilmos Vajta, *Luther on Worship* (Philadelphia: Muhlenberg Press, 1958). References from this work are integrated into the text.

both confessional struggles and theological differences within denominations. The error committed by previous treatments of Luther on this matter is that they contented themselves with looking at his amendment of liturgical forms without having first sufficiently investigated his theology of worship. "His theology of worship was taken as a matter of course, and scholars asked only how his own practical proposals as well as modern liturgical trends might be evaluated from these premises." (x) Vajta considers this a backward approach. "Their liturgical interest begins where it should end, viz. at the question of liturgical forms. Often they pay scant attention to the theology which underlies these forms. . . ." (xi) Such a backward approach leaves unexamined precisely what is essential in order to understand the Reformer's attitude toward the Mass. Vajta's study is intended to fill that void by outlining the theology of worship in the thought of Martin Luther which is the vantage point from which to see his critique of the liturgical Mass.

Vajta's work is divided into three topics: (1) principles of worship, (2) worship as the work of God, and (3) worship as the work of faith. Within the first section, Vajta examines theology of worship as the relationship between God and human beings, first distinguishing worship and idolatry, and second *beneficium* and *sacrificium*.

PRINCIPLES OF WORSHIP

The relationship between a human being and a god is worship. Luther puts this in a descriptive mode (worship does exist between humanity and its god) and not a prescriptive mode (worship should exist between humanity and its god) because he believes himself to be describing a fundament of human orientation. In Luther's opinion, it is a false question to ask whether or not one worships, because it is impossible not to worship. The true question is whether one worships rightly or idolatrously, i.e., whether one worships the true God or idols. In the Large Catechism Luther asks "What is it to have a god? or what is God?" and Vajta finds the very form of the question significant: Luther equates the question (a) what is it to *have* a god? with (b) what *is* God?

"In answer to his own question, Luther explains: 'To have a god is to trust and believe him from the whole heart, as I have often said that the confidence and faith of the heart alone make both God and an idol (*Gott und Abegott*). If your faith and trust be right, then is your god also true. On the other hand, if your trust be false and wrong, then you have not the true God; for these two belong together, viz. faith and God. That now, I say, upon which you set your heart and put your trust, is properly your god.' "[25]

Human beings cannot not worship. That upon which they set their heart and put their trust is their god. Although this trust may be directed rightly or wrongly, toward the creator or toward the creature, worship itself is written in the heart of man and woman. Indeed, this allows Luther to say that even in idols the name and power of the true God is hidden. "Idolatry, while proving man's perversion, is really an indication of the fact that he belongs to God; for it is a caricature of his natural relation to God." (15) For Luther, relationship with God is unavoidable, although the God to whom one relates will either be a God of wrath who condemns our idolatrous picture of him, or a God of self-revealed mercy.[26]

By this prolegomenon about worship and faith we can see how crucial Vajta thinks worship is to Luther's theology. At least occa-

25. Vajta, 4. Elsewhere in the Large Catechism Luther writes, "Idolatry does not consist merely of erecting an image and praying to it. It is primarily in the heart, which pursues other things and seeks help and consolation from creatures, saints, or devils. It neither cares for God nor expects good things from him sufficiently to trust that he wants to help, nor does it believe that whatever good it receives comes from God." *The Book of Concord*, ed. Theodore G. Tappert (Philadelphia: Fortress Press, 1959) 367.

26. Cf. Paul Althaus: "Man's faith gives God the honor due his deity. Luther summarizes this with the bold assertion that 'faith creates the deity.' Feuerbach referred to such statements to illustrate his thesis that the idea of God is anthropologically derived through man's objectivication of his own being (man created God in his own image) . . . The truth of the matter is, however, that Feuerbach errs in quoting Luther to prove his position. . . . For when Luther says that 'faith creates the deity,' he immediately adds 'not in [God's] person but in us.' " *The Theology of Martin Luther* (Philadelphia: Fortress Press, 1966) 45.

44

sionally, if not frequently, Luther's shibboleths of *sola fides, sola gratia,* and *sola scriptura* have been taken as license for a non-corporate, interior spiritual form of worship, one which opposes worship to justification by faith, but by this discussion of idolatrous versus faithful worship, Vajta would have us realize how intricately connected Luther's remarks about worship are with his protest that humans are justified by faith alone. Any other means of justification is a false relationship with a bogus god, which by definition is idolatry. Worship is intricate not only to the second article of redemption but to the first article of creation as well. Estranged humankind creates false concepts of God (idolatry) which issue in a false relationship (works righteousnes). That which is less than God is worshiped with other than faith. "Worship is inherent in the created nature of man. As man must form a concept of God, so he must worship. Faith breathes worship. Fallen man has not only a false faith and a false confidence in idols, but also false worship. Unbelief results in idolatry. Idolatry is unbelief in action. . . . Man is not free to choose his cult." (12)

If God cannot be had except where God's self-revelation occurs, then worship must not be invented according to our tastes, it can only occur in Christ through faith. The companion of works righteousness is idolatry. In a remark which gainsays subsequent Protestant individualism, Vajta affirms the central role of worship in Luther's thinking by saying "Faith does not belong to a province in the inner soul, but is realized in worship." (14) Vajta is trying to make good on his claim that the Reformer's insistence on justification by faith alone is not independent of a theology of worship but inherent to it. To be in faith is to be in God, which is to relate to God rightly, which is to worship. Furthermore, as faith is not a special province in the inner soul, neither is worship a special cultic behavior. Rather, Luther applies the idea of worship to every phase and province of life, and includes daily work under the term worship: to love the neighbor and so obey the Lord is worship.[27]

27. On worship v. cultic duty, see John E. Burkhart, *Worship* (Philadelphia: Westminster Press, 1982) 18–21. On the reworking of the term sacrifice, see Robert Daly, *The Origins of the Christian Doctrine of Sacrifice* (Philadelphia: Fortress Press, 1978); David N. Power, "Words that Crack: The Uses of 'Sacri-

Other interpretations of Luther on worship made the mistake of competitively contrasting a pedagogical picture of worship against a re-presentative view. The former considers worship to be little more than an institute of the mature in faith for the training of the immature, and the latter considers worship an end in itself, being an expression of the faith of the Church. Vajta, by contrast, claims the dilemma cannot be resolved unless worship is understood in terms staked out by Luther as an institution of God.

"For in this view, worship becomes a means of salvation and an integral part of the work of God. But apart from it, both the 'training school for unbelievers' and the 'believers' sacrifice of praise and thanksgiving' are left in mid-air. . . . The 'pedagogical' view retains the truth that faith is nourished by worship, but forgets that believers need the nourishment as much as unbelievers. The 're-presentative' theory overlooks the fact that the 'believers' sacrifice of praise and thanksgiving' depends on their reception of God's grace through the Word and sacraments." (23–24)

This, then, sets the stage for the distinction between *beneficium* and *sacrificium*. This "copernican revolution" in Luther's view of the Mass is his practical application of these theological insights. At issue for him is not ceremony (although he did critique this) but doctrine. Unlike subsequent Puritan reform movements under the ideal of biblicism, Luther pointed to Christ's institution of the Lord's Supper "not as an example to be copied outwardly, but as a word of God to guide our understanding and faith. He considered the Words of Institution not a law concerning outward ceremonies, but the 'gospel in a nutshell,'. . . . These convictions guided both his criticism and his reform of the mass."[28] In Vajta's opinion, this

fice' in Eucharistic Discourse," *Worship* 53:5 (September 1979) 386–404; and Gordon Lathrop, "Justin, Eucharist and 'Sacrifice': A Case of Metaphor," *Worship* 64:1 (January 1990) 30–48. Of course, the theme of redemption overcoming the divorce which sin caused between the sacred and the profane runs throughout Schmemann's work.

28. Vajta, 28. James White would appear to be correct when on the continuum of Protestant denominations he calls Lutheranism the most conservative, see *Protestant Worship: Traditions in Transition* (Louisville: Westminster/John Knox Press, 1989). White proposes to analyze Protestant worship traditions

shows that Luther's criticism of outward ceremonies did not indicate indifference towards liturgical reform (as has been so often charged) but sprang from his renewed theological fundamentals and his concern for the Christian conscience. Luther's distinction between the Mass as benefaction or sacrifice impinges on the Mass less at the level of ceremonial form than at the level of what is communicated through the external form. External ceremonies do have a place in the Church on earth, but they must never compete with the essential features of Christ's own institution. When they do, ceremonial laws supplant the gospel. But on the other hand, the external form of worship may not be eliminated, as the Enthusiasts desired; the fact that Christ used external things when he gave bread and wine to the disciples and told them to do likewise in remembrance of him was enough for Luther to prove that the Mass must also consist in external actions.[29] "Luther did not oppose the more elaborate liturgical forms as such. He would have tolerated them gladly had they not corrupted the very meaning and message of the mass." (32)

under a political analogy, one which recognizes right, center, and left wings. He says, "I shall refer to the retention of late-medieval forms as characteristically 'right wing' and to moves farther away from medieval worship as 'left wing' " (22). On such a scale, the Lutheran tradition is more right wing than those lying successively to the left: Anglican, Reformed, Methodist, Puritan, Frontier, Anabaptist, Pentecostal and Quaker.

29. For a clear exposition of the differences between Luther and the enthusiasts on this score, see Regin Prenter *Spiritus Creator* (Philadelphia: Fortress Press, 1953), Chapter Five. See also Althaus' claim that Luther's falling out with Zwingli at the Marburg Colloquy regarding the Lord's Supper revolved exactly around their different understanding of what "spiritual" meant. Zwingli understood "spirit v. flesh" in Platonic terms—incorporeal v. corporeal; Luther understood the dialectic in Pauline, biblical terms—of God or of the flesh. Thus for Zwingli, to eat the Lord's Supper "spiritually" meant that Christian worship could disregard external expression. For Luther, "to eat 'spiritually' does not mean that we receive something that is merely spiritual; rather we receive a reality that comes from the Holy Spirit and that must be received and enjoyed in a spiritual way, that is, in faith." Paul Althaus, *The Theology of Martin Luther* (Philadelphia: Fortress Press 1966) 396. Luther is reported to have said, "If God would present me with horse manure to eat, I should eat it spiritually. For wherever the word of God is present, there is spiritual eating."

What animated Luther's reform of the Mass was the picture of God which lay behind the doctrine. He was concerned that God's character be seen as giving and not demanding, for it was the latter picture which led him to admit to Staupitz, his abbot in the monastery, that try as he might to love God, he could not because he hated God for God's demanding righteousness.[30] The picture of God in the Mass should be the God of mercy, not of wrath. If God's character is to give, then the Mass should be called "a benefit, not received, but given (*beneficium, non acceptum sed datum*). . . . What a contrast between God giving his Son for the sins of the world and the pope pretending to offer God his own Son! In the mass of Christ we meet a merciful God reconciling the world to himself, but the mass of Rome reckons with an angry God who must be appeased with sacrifice." (33–34) According to Vajta, Luther was not indifferent toward the liturgy, far from it. His concern for the liturgy was determined by his understanding of the gospel.

That the Mass is a gift (God's benefaction) and not sacrifice explains Luther's explanation of the Lord's Supper as *Testamentum*. The term is drawn from the Words of Institution and Luther made extensive use of it to explain the true meaning of the Mass. "According to Luther, a testament must contain the following elements: There must be, first of all, a testator who prepares for his death and sets up his will, then the testament proper which contains the will of the testator, the seal by which the testator confirms the validity of his will, the inheritance assigned in the testament, and finally, those to whom the estate is bequeathed."[31]

30. In his biography of Luther, Roland Bainton reports Staupitz saying to Luther "Man, God is not angry with you. You are angry with God. Don't you know that God commands you to hope?" but when Luther looks back on his struggles in the confessional he remembers it thus: "I was myself more than once driven to the very abyss of despair so that I wished I had never been created. Love God? I hated him!" *Here I Stand*, (Nashville: Abingdon Press, 1960) 54, 59.

31. Vajta, 39–40. Vajta notes that the prominent Lutheran scholar Yngve Brilioth criticizes Luther on this score, claiming that this category prevented Luther from seeing other equally important moments in the Mass, cf. *Eucharistic Faith and Practice, Evangelical and Catholic* (London: S.P.C.K., 1939). Bryan Spinks critiques those who uncritically accept Brilioth's line of thought

All these elements are found in the Mass. Christ is the testator, the testament is the Words of Institution, the seal is the Body and Blood of Christ in the Eucharist, the inheritance is the forgiveness of sins, and we are the heirs receiving the promise (a *beneficium*). Vajta believes that the metaphor of testament was used by Luther to highlight the biblical concept of covenant whereby the sovereign act of God accepts men and women into fellowship. Priority is placed upon the initiative of God. In Luther's words, ''Whenever man is to deal with God and receive something from him, it is not up to man to take the intiative and lay the first brick. Rather, without man's seeking or desire God must first come with his promise. . . .'' (41)

This makes the Words of Institution the most important part of the Mass, for they are the proclamation of the good news by God—the gospel in a nutshell, as Luther called it. Vajta is again giving evidence that what animates Luther's reform of the external ceremonial form of the Mass is doctrine. His constant criterion for critiquing liturgical worship is the picture of God which is revealed and the response which participants in worship are called to make. Thus Vajta can even say that Luther has room for a sacrificial element in the Mass, so long as it is seen under the light of *beneficium*. ''Luther had no intention of striking the idea of sacrifice from the gospel. On the contrary, he objected to the medieval theology of the mass for the very reason that it corrupted the proper biblical meaning of sacrifice.'' (45) What is at issue is the use made of the Mass, its purpose. Or, we might say, at issue is

in *Luther's Liturgical Criteria and his Reform of the Canon of the Mass* (Grove Liturgical Study, No. 30, 1982). Spinks suggests that the reigning consensus of opinion is that ''in this particular field, the Wittenberg Reformer was conservative, hasty, and singularly inept, and that when he came to reform the canon, his method was one of drastic curtailment, amputation, and displacement'' (7) noting the work of W. D. Maxwell, Raymond Abba, Geoffrey Wainwright, Luther D. Reed, and Louis Bouyer. ''However, a careful examination of the footnotes and bibliographies of these works reveals an interesting fact. All make use of, or cite as authoritative, a single work by the Swedish Lutheran scholar, Bishop Yngve Brilioth. An investigation of Brilioth reveals that we are *not* dealing with the opinions and results of independent investigations by numerous scholars, but simply the constant repetition by successive scholars of the views promulgated by Brilioth'' (11).

discerning the "differing modes of appropriating (*gebrauchen*) the mass." Is it appropriated for faith or for works? "Where the mass is held, there God is always at work. . . . But Luther was concerned with the use of the mass. God's gifts must be used with gratitude. And man cannot prove his thankfulness for them except by faith. The word of promise, the core and center of the mass, requires faith." (47) So long as grace is treated substantially, then the door is left open a crack to saying that the mere celebration of the Mass effects grace in some way. But to Luther, grace is God himself dealing with human beings here and now. To believe is to possess. "The works of God benefit us as long as they are used in faith, for it is only by faith that God's work as a gift of grace enters man as a person." (49) This is why the Mass cannot be participated in vicariously, as in the case of the private Mass when grace is effective even for those absent. Does the Mass please God? Certainly, Luther can reply. But this is not the significance of the Mass. "It is of no benefit as long as it is only *opus operatum*. It must become *opus operantis*. . . . It is not enough for the sacrament to be performed. It must be appropriated in faith." (Luther's words, cited, 48) Vajta believes Luther to have been convinced that the Mass could never have become a sacrifice of the medieval type if the distribution to the people had been retained.[32]

Vajta is relentless in his attempt to indicate that Luther's concerns about the Mass are theological in origin and nature. Traditional Protestant theology has misunderstood this, Vajta charges, and so traditional Protestant polemic about sacrifice "is wont to contrast the continual repetition of the sacrifice in the mass with the uniqueness (*Einmaligkeit*) of the death of Christ. The difference between them is conceived in numerical terms, according to whether the sacrifice is repeated or not." (56) According to Vajta, this is not the salient point of Luther's critique. Luther is not exercised so much over the sacrifice of the Mass—whether it is repeated or remembered, real or figurative, one or many—as he is about the principle behind such repetition. And the principle

---

32. In this Vajta agrees with Brilioth; whether intentionally or not, I do not know. Brilioth writes, "There can be no danger of losing hold of evangelical truth so long as the sacrifice is not separated from the communion." *Eucharistic Faith and Practice*, 48.

which he detects behind the medieval Mass is one of work righteousness, seeking to amass and accumulate ever more good works
in order to appease God rather than accepting God's work on our
behalf. In Luther's eyes, the Mass is rank idolatry because "it pre-
sumes to give to God what man can only receive. . . . What
Luther condemned was not so much the number of worship services, as the tendency behind them and the total disregard of the
work of Christ which they implied. . . . Once and for all the
remission of sins has been procured, but it is offered and distributed again and again." (58) Luther's objection, then, is not directed
toward the form, but toward every self-deceptive presumption to
establish our relationship with God on grounds of our achieve-
ments in which we can boast.[33]

We pause now to remind ourselves that Vajta's intention, enunciated in the introduction, was to establish proof of the connection
between Luther's theology of worship and the very center of his
whole thought. In the contrast between justification and work
righteousness, we encounter this center of Luther's whole
thought. Vajta has attempted to show that Luther's critique of the
Mass stems not from reactionary objection to external form, nor
from simplistic objection to sacrificial categories and repetition of
the Mass, but rather from the fundamental distinction between
righteousness as God's mercy (gift) as opposed to righteousness
as God's justice which humans must fulfill. When applied to worship, this theological distinction plays itself out in two contrasting
concepts, *beneficium* and *sacrificium*. The latter is idolatrous, be-

---

33. Vajta might happily apply to Luther, *mutatis mutandis*, Ernst Käsemann's
words about Paul: "The apostle's real adversary is the devout Jew, not only
as the mirror-image of his own past . . . but as the reality of the religious
man. . . . The real God is the enemy and judge of every human illusion—
especially every pious illusion—which professes to exhibit to God saving
works, to make claims, to glory in one's own achievement and to take comfort in one's own righteousness." "Paul and Israel," in *New Testament Questions of Today* (Philadelphia: Fortress Press, 1969) 184–85. Luther's real
adversary is the medieval structure, not only as the mirror-image of his own
past, but as the reality of the religious person who suffers the illusion, sometimes bolstered with piety, that one can exhibit to God saving works and
make claims on God's grace. Vajta writes: "It is not only with reference to
the mass that Luther rejected the principle of repetition. He detected the
same tendency in every form of work righteousness . . ." (57).

cause the false concept of God (false theology) evokes in human beings a false approach to God (works instead of faith) which results in false worship. Theology and worship are intertwined in Luther's thinking. "We have traced this contrast point by point and now we summarize the result of our inquiry as follows: Worship is the gift of the gracious God through the incarnate and suffering Christ for his congregation which receives the gift by faith and so enters into fellowship with God. Thus worship is a participation in the work of Christ." (63)

Two questions remain for Vajta: (a) what is the gift given by God in worship? and (b) what is meant by participating through faith in worship? He answers these questions in turn by describing worship first as the work of God and second as the work of faith, and this occupies the remainder of his study, but we have cracked the hardest nutshell already.

WORSHIP AS THE WORK OF GOD

Worship as the work of God consists of the proclamation of the Word, the presence of Christ in the Lord's Supper, and the office of the ministry as impartation of the gift of God; worship as the work of faith consists of faith and worship, the priestly sacrifice of believers, and the relationship between freedom and order in worship. We begin with Vajta's opinions about preaching, sacrament and ministry.

It is widely known that Luther was successful at restoring preaching of the Word to liturgical worship. But to Luther the point of preaching is more than pedagogy or exhortation. Say it this way: when the Word is proclaimed it is a divine work, not human theologizing. The word which is preached is not merely commentary on the past activity of God. "[T]o preach is more than to report and comment on certain events of the past. It is to make Christ our contemporary so that his death and resurrection become our own and the redemption which he wrought becomes our righteousness. . . . Thus the proclamation of Christ's work is in itself an integral part of his work."[34]

---

34. Vajta, 73, 74. So long as Christ's death and resurrection remain mere facts of the past, nothing soteriological has occurred. With typical forcefulness Luther affirms this difference vis-à-vis the resurrection: "That Christ had risen

This notion also determines Luther's attitude toward the place of Scripture in worship. Everything is cast in terms of existential relationship between God and humanity. Using Scripture in the pulpit is not tantamount to reading Scripture, for the Word of Scripture is contained in a living and proclaimed Word, not historical texts. Vajta reminds us of the Reformer's insistence that oral proclamation is the proper form of the Word. For Luther, the gospel originally "was not a book but a sermon, and the church is not a *Federhaus* (quill house), but a *Mundhaus* (mouth house)." (77) Vajta speaks of the pulpit as the "battlefield of Christ" because "the sermon is Christ's continued advent, his coming to every generation of men, the means by which he establishes fellowship with his own." (78) The pulpit stands between the lecturn and the pew because the people must hear God's Word proclaimed in the words of Scripture. Luther pushes the bond between word and sacrament to the limit by suggesting that when Christ said in the Words of Institution "This do in remembrance of me," he meant not merely the sacrifice of the Mass but the living remembrance (anamnesis) of Christ's saving work in both sacrament and word. "The difference between Luther and the Middle Ages lies in the exegesis of I Corinthians 11:26. The medieval 'remembrance' consisted in a dramatical representation of the passion of Christ. But to Luther, the sermon itself was the remembrance. . . . Luther identified the remembrance with the sermon because he understood the remembrance as a part of God's redemptive work, rather than as a work of man." (82) As the Sacrament is Christ's work, not our own, so is the public, oral remembering not our own work but Christ's. It is a *beneficium*.

Vajta next turns to consider the presence of Christ in the Lord's Supper. In Luther's theology of worship there are no grounds for

was most certainly a true fact. Yet when the disciples and the women followed their reason alone they concluded, 'They have taken away the Lord.' Behold what reason does, even when the fact is open to the eye. Without the Word, the tomb certainly remains empty." (Luther in footnote, 75). This remark is intelligible only within Luther's doctrine of the Word. Cf. Gustaf Wingren, *The Living Word: A Theological Study of Preaching and the Church* (Philadelphia: Fortress Press, 1960). He affirms that preaching is God's own speech, an objective word subjectively appropriated, not merely speech about God.

disparaging external and earthly forms. Luther proposed a distinction between God's omnipresence and God's presence-for-us. Under the former category, it is affirmed that God is present everywhere, even though this natural presence of God is also an article of faith and not a conclusion of natural theology. As was seen in the earlier discussion of worship and idolatry, God is inescapable and yet God remains invisible to sinful human beings, which means the creation of idols is inevitable without divine self-disclosure. Without God's revelation in the Word, humans will idolatrously claim God's mercy apart from holiness, God's gospel apart from law, and thereby find a false God which is constructed in their own image. "God is indeed present everywhere, but he cannot be found everywhere, at least not as the God of love and mercy. There is a significant difference between his omnipresence and his 'presence-for-us.' The latter is a presence in the Word. God can be found only where he adds the Word to his work. Otherwise he is not presence-for-us, though we must believe his presence as that of the Creator." (87)

Luther's term for God's presence in the Word (which is God's presence in Christ or God's presence-for-us) is "spiritual," but this word must be carefully defined. For Luther it "refers to material realities of this world insofar as they are 'comprehended in God's Word' and accepted in faith." (87) Differing from traditions which use "spiritual" as equivalent to extramundane, incorporeal, or supernatural, Luther affirms that when fallen man and woman are redeemed they are led back to the gifts of creation, not away from them. God's omnipresence is shared by Christ so that since the ascension Christ exercises power over all creation. Thus he has not left the earth, as the Enthusiasts claimed, sitting in splendid isolation on the throne in ethereal heaven but rather comes spiritually through things material. Christ's spiritual presence in things material summons faithful obedience. "The spiritual presence of God through the Word and faith is realized in worship. Through the proclamation of the Word and the administration of the sacraments, God creates the only proper form of worship— faith. His presence cannot be divorced from the church service. Because he is on the right hand of the Father, Christ can be found in the Word and in the sacraments." (89)

In the previous chapter Vajta sought to show that Christ in worship is a presence in the Word proclaimed. The Word is everywhere present, but Christ who was the Word made flesh is now comprehended in his Word. Likewise, Christ presents himself (makes himself present) in the sacrament. Both Luther's theology of preaching and his theology of the sacrament is shaped by the same doctrine of God's prevenient Word addressing itself to humankind with gospel comfort. Because Christ's presence in the Word, comprehended in both preaching and sacrament, is the place of his presence-for-us, "worship may be defined as his presence in Word and sacrament within the communion of saints. His presence is related to his people and cannot be divorced from them." (91) This theology of presence-for-us is worked out in connection with the controversies on the Lord's Supper. Luther affirms that Christ's presence has two characteristics: "1) it is realized in the visible, earthly means of creation and 2) under these means God reveals himself in a hidden manner." (91) The former characteristic stands against the Enthusiasts; the latter characteristic stands against the medieval doctrine of transubstantiation.

The physical nature of the vehicles of Christ's presence is an offense to sinful reason and must be revealed by the Word and received in faith—the same faith required to perceive the Word in Jesus of Nazareth. "To Luther the real presence was a corollary of the incarnation. The incarnation was the real offense, and Christ's presence in worship is no more than a consequence and extension of the revelation of the omnipresent God." (97) Thus Vajta characterizes Luther's opponents on the left as deists whose god is enthroned in lonely majesty, far removed from creation and unable to be present through things of nature.

The incarnation also sets the terms by which Luther abandons the doctrine of transubstantiation which he finds, says Vajta, to be not irrational but too rational. As faith perceives God in Jesus, finding both human and divine nature present without change and without mixture, so natural bread and wine are the vehicles of the presence of Christ. If Jesus' human nature needed no transubstantiation for the divine to dwell in it, the real presence need not depend on transubstantiation.

In what way does God's omnipresence become presence-for-us? It surely cannot be the case that God's omnipresence is simply around and about, leaving to the believer the responsibility of unveiling a hidden God. The presence must be revealed through the Holy Spirit, not by a human work of faith or gnosis.

"Luther understood the Words of Institution as the pledge (*Verheissung, Zusagung*) by which Christ has promised to be present whenever bread and wine are being administered in his name. The celebration of the Eucharist rests on our faith in these words, for it joins them to the elements through which Christ wants to be 'present for us.' This is the liturgical act of consecration. . . . Consecration is the liturgical act in which the omnipresent body and blood of Christ are revealed and promised to man." (99)

In accordance with Christ's command and institution, the bread and wine are received by the Church as God's gift for forgiveness when faith hears the promise of God. The words "this is my body" are called by Luther *Taetelworte* (action words) which create that of which they speak. They make the elements more than signs; the elements become the vehicles of the presence of Christ, attested to by the Word. Luther writes, "It is the Word, I say, that makes the Sacrament and the distinction so that it is not simply bread and wine, but the body and blood of Christ." (103) That Luther insists the bread and wine are more than mere signs can be seen in his statement, "Before I would, with the Enthusiasts, accept mere wine I would rather with the pope accept mere blood."

The place of the office of ministry grows immediately out of the definition of worship which Vajta has supplied. Worship is "God's work of love by which he imparts to us the fruits of the redemption in Jesus Christ. This work is done through the Word and the sacraments." (109) Since the Word is a message it must be preached, and so requires messengers; since the sacrament is a gift, it must be received and so requires administrators. This is the basis for the office of ministry.

Vajta portrays Luther's disagreements with Rome as stemming from confusion over the role of ministers. "The handmaid had become the mistress. . . . Far from serving the work of Christ, the priesthood had abrogated to itself jurisdiction over the means of grace." (110) The accent had moved, Vajta charges, from the office as an institution of God to the officiant as a person of authority.

Instead of a function, the ministry had become a rank. Though Luther admits that the work which God accomplishes in worship is his own work and not the priest's, so that ministers add nothing of their own to worship, he nevertheless insists, unlike other Protestant movements, that we cannot do without ministry (or ministers). The office is indispensable because Christ is known mediately, not directly. In saying this, Luther stands squarely against the Enthusiasts who found the office dispensable and took Luther's words about the priesthood of all believers to mean that the institutional priesthood (and ordination) was unnecessary. Vajta's interpretation of the universal priesthood is thus:

"Certainly all Christians are priests. But not all are pastors, for beyond the fact that a man is a Christian and a priest, he must also have an office and a parish that he has been commanded to serve. It is the call and the command which makes the pastor and preacher. . . . The call which the church extends is a call from God. The people through whom it comes, whether congregation or bishop, are only instruments in the hand of God, for . . . God calls no one directly." (115)

Unlike the Enthusiasts who have recourse to an inner, immediate call from the Holy Spirit, Luther maintains ordination since he understands God to always employ externals as a person is called to ministry through a local congregation. Yet unlike Roman practice, Luther does not see ordination as a consecration, a rite which imparts special sanctity to the candidate. He insists that to ordain is not to consecrate and so it is rejected as a sacrament. Luther writes, "To ordain is not to consecrate. Thus when we have a devout man, we set him aside, and by virtue of the Word which we have, we confer on him the authority of preaching the Word and administering the sacraments. This is to ordain."[35] The call which a candidate receives in ordination does not establish a special priesthood, it only indicates the particular territory where the priesthood common to all may be exercised by the designated individual.

35. Vajta, 119. For an interesting study of the tension in Luther between freedom and institution see Jaroslav Pelikan, *Spirit Versus Structure: Luther and the Institutions of the Church* (New York: Harper & Row, 1968).

Thus far, Vajta admits, his consideration of worship has been somewhat incomplete for he has confined himself to considering worship as the work of God. Since Luther's whole approach is based on the mutual relationship of God and faith, his theology of worship would be incomplete if one neglected to consider what God works in the worshiper by his real presence. Worship is also a work of human beings. Worship is simultaneously the work of God and the work of faith, although logically the former precedes and creates the latter. The complement to the picture drawn thus far is an examination of worship as faith expressing itself in praise and thanksgiving. Luther has written that worship should serve to inspire faith and this has led to what is called the pedagogical theory of worship wherein worship is viewed as a means to the end of faith, a sort of stimulant and tutor. Vajta believes that Luther meant something entirely different when he said worship should inspire faith, and takes exception to the pedagogical view. For that reason, Vajta devotes most of the chapter "Faith and Worship" to defining faith in Luther's thought.

We have already seen that in Luther's understanding of the relationship between God and humanity, non-worship is an impossibility. Human beings are bound to believe and trust by the law implanted by the Creator in his creatures, and this remains true even of fallen humanity. But in our fallen state, when we think we are free of God we are in fact in bondage to a new tyrant. "This is faith in reverse—unbelief. Man is so created that his existence must be marked either by faith or by unbelief, that is either by God for us in Christ, or by the devil against us." (126) No neutrality is possible toward God. Human beings are marked by either faith or unfaith; the Creator is either acknowledged and praised, or God's offer of fellowship is spurned and in bondage to the devil we idolatrously fashion a false God to our pleasing. But in our bondage of the will, we are not free to free ourselves. This is accomplished only by Christ in his humanity and effected in us by Christ only through word and sacrament. Worship/nonworship correlates to faith/unfaith. "We stand here at the intersection of worship and faith. If to believe means to have Christ present within, then faith cannot be without worship, for the church service is the place where Christ meets man through Word and sacraments. On this redemptive work of Christ the believer rests his faith, while unbelievers bypass the activity of God and put their confidence in their own works. As fellowship between the 'God-for-us' and man, faith constitutes the highest form of worship." (127) When Luther said that worship should serve to inspire faith, he did not mean, as the pedagogical school thinks, that worship is a school which faith might eventually outgrow, he meant that faith and worship are inextricably united. Faith cannot be without worship, and faith constitutes the highest form of worship. God's work is the ground and cause of faith; God works in the Church's worship; ergo, faith cannot be without worship and worship finds its highest form where faith is formed by the Word of God.

Since faith is passively received, worship cannot be construed as a self-justifying activity, but must be marked by the same passivity which characterizes the righteousness of faith. "Faith will never reach that degree of maturity where it could live without receiving. A grateful reception of God's gracious gifts will always remain the task of Christian worship, for it is impossible to evolve a church service out of the spiritual assets of the believers."[36] For Luther, the Christian life in its entirety is marked by the passivity of human beings and the activity of God. Christian worship, similarly, is response to God's initiative and cannot be called our own activity. This is clearly evidenced in both of worship's main acts: preaching and the sacrament.

Luther is able to highlight God's activity and faith's passivity when he speaks about hearing the Word proclaimed. "Since faith comes by hearing, it depends on worship. . . . Hearing is not a work of man to prepare himself for grace, but an entirely passive attitude. It is simply being addressed and arrested by the voice of

36. Vajta, 129. In light of this, consider the error in the prevalent idea that purer worship is achieved when crass external things are purged (bread and wine, icons, ceremony, etc.) and instead a precious internal thing alone is offered to God: thankfulness. But wait! Does this not suppose our thanks to be autogenetic? This theory treats thankfulness as the one thing in the universe which is under our autonomous control, which is truly our own, truly does not belong to God. But no part of the universe is autonomous from God. To be capable of thanks-giving is a fruit of the Spirit. In that case, worship is not standing autonomously before God to sing our solo, it is harmonizing ourselves with the tune which God sings to us, sings to himself in the Person of the Son, which creation sings to God.

God." (133) Vajta describes Luther's equation as "sermon-plus-hearing-equals-faith." If the link is broken anywhere in the line, then hearing is in danger of being interpreted as a psychological achievement. Under Luther's doctrine of the Word hearing is a passive response, a continued acceptance of life from God.

The same is true of faith's relationship to the sacrament. Here God's Word is offered in physical form as Christ's presence-for-us and only by faith can we rightly use the Sacrament. Luther's tenacity in construing faith as reception of God's Word, in either preached or sacramental form, permits him to say that even if a person were denied access to the altar, that person could still use the Sacrament simply by faith in the Words of Institution, although normally the Sacrament is to be received not only by the ear but in the mouth as well. In a move common to all the Protestants, Luther admits that eating and drinking without faith is of no avail, but in contradiction to many of the Protestants, Luther also moves the reverse direction: faith cannot be divorced from bread and wine. The Enthusiasts were offended when Luther insisted that Christ is present in the bread and wine to be consumed by the communicant, for they distinguished the inward and outward dimensions as inward faith versus the outward act of eating and drinking while Luther distinguished the inward and outward dimensions as eating and drinking in faith versus eating and drinking without faith.

The point of Luther's argument is to allow him to "strongly stress the connection of faith with the external means of grace and yet refuse simply to identify the external acts of worship with the true worship of faith." (139) Faith is response, not merely hearing and receiving; but faith is response to the Word of God which is heard in the preaching and received in the sacrament. In Vajta's opinion, it is a mistake to think that Luther embraced such a spiritualistic view of the Church that the external ceremonial forms of preaching and sacrament are unnecessary. Even while insisting upon the necessity of faith (thus avoiding a mechanistic or impersonal use of the sacrament), Luther paradoxically insists that God is present-for-us precisely in the outwardly preached word and the outward forms of bread and wine. "Faith is indeed invisible. But it is linked to visible things. It includes a human act as part of God's." (140–41)

Thus on the one hand Church and worship appear to be identical with the proclamation of the Word and the administration of the sacraments; on the other hand, Church and worship appear to be the works of faith, or redeemed humanity. When Vajta says that worship is a work of men and women, he must preliminarily clarify that the work we do is a work of faith, and faith's genesis is God's accosting kerygmatic Word, not an internal capacity. Without faith there is no worship. "Faith or unbelief is the essential. External hearing or receiving is not enough. But a man's personal faith constitutes his worship." (143)

What is true of worship as a whole, that as a human work of faith it depends for its existence and character upon the work of God in Christ, is all the more true about the place of sacrifice in worship.

Sacrifice is a priestly work, but Christ has transformed the priesthood with his coming. His was a unique sacrifice and a unique priesthood. In the New Covenant Christ includes us in his priesthood and so in his sacrifice. The foundation for the universal priesthood of all believers is the incorporation of the Christian into Christ: "As Christ is a priest, so is every Christian who clings to him in faith. Christ and the Christians belong together, and faith is the true priesthood. Christ shares everything with those who believe in him. . . . Sacrifice is an element of faith. Luther never forgot this fact, even in his most violent polemics against the Roman perversion of sacrifice. But as sacrifice is a function of faith, it cannot be without faith." (150–51) Vajta's analysis of Christian sacrifice in worship is more complicated than saying that instead of Christ's sacrifice in the Mass we bring offerings, viz. praise, prayer and material gifts. Sacrifice is associated with death, as Luther notes when he admits "what is to be sacrificed has to be killed." But what must be killed is no longer a creature; nor is it Christ slain again. "The Christian as a priest offers himself. The victim to be sacrificed is he himself, or, to be more correct, the 'old man,' the 'old Adam' within. . . . The Christian as a priest surrenders his own sinful nature into death." (152-53) The sacrifice that is related to faith is the person in totality, men and women in all their relationships. Luther's picture of sacrifice is expressive of the total claim of faith. When we are made one with Christ in baptism, we die to ourselves and this is our sacrifice.

Praise, prayer and material gifts are an expression of our self-sacrifice, not an offering which substitutes for sacrificial death. "Sacrifice as dying with Christ is an expression of that strange work of God by which he grants life through death. . . . [The Christian's] priesthood rests on his baptism, and his baptism in turn is realized by his sacrifice—the death of the old Adam and the daily birth of the new man. Worship is the means by which the Spirit continues this fellowship and conformity with Christ." (154)

True worship is priestly sacrifice which consists in the first place of praise and thanksgiving. Luther often called this the only true worship, claiming that praise is the only work that we may give to God, since God accepts nothing from us but love and praise. The rhythm of worship leads from the gift of God to the faith of the recipient, expressed in denial and death on the one hand, and expressed in grateful thanks and praise on the other. When we make praise, God becomes God. The proper obedience to the first commandment is to let God be God. Our idolatries are swept away when we receive the gifts of God with thanks. Again, this takes two forms: first, to acknowledge the goodness of God and second, to renounce work righteousness by relying upon God's Word of forgiveness. It is essential that the passivity of humanity still be maintained, even in what might appear to be our one and only self-generated act. Praising "is an act of receiving rather than giving on the part of man. . . . Faith as an offering of praise does not create worship. It accepts it through the gospel." (158–59) This response-act is not limited to cultic moments; the Christian life is in its totality a sacrifice when we die to the old Adam and live charitably for our neighbor.

Connected to the sacrifice of praise is the sacrifice of prayer. This too is based on faith since prayer rests on God's initiative and is not an expression of our own initiative. "It was stressed by Luther that the Christian prays solely because of God's command and his promise to hear our prayers. His prayer is not a stab in the dark, nor a search for the unknown, but an exercise of faith, obedience, and hope, based on the mercy and works of God." (162) Luther repeatedly says we pray because God commands it. Prayer is done obediently, and obedience is the essential mark of faith. Without faith, humanity's prayerful devotion amounts to "tempting God." We do not pray in order to render God merciful, we dare to pray because God is merciful. Again, the divine action elicits the human response. The sacrifice of prayer which is done in faith responsively takes God at his word. Our prayer is always made in Christ and through Christ. And as Christ interceded for the world, so the Church's prayer is intercessory. "Prayer as sacrifice implies not only the self-denial and crucifixion of the old man within us, but also a priestly service with and for others . . . Intercession was for Luther the most important part of liturgical prayer. . . . Intercessory prayer is a mark of the church. . . . In the communion of saints, the believers bear each other's burdens in prayer." (165–66) It is not as though we offer prayer instead of sacrifice; prayer is the second form which our sacrifice takes, along with thankful praise.

The third expression of our sacrificial life in Christ is returning earthly gifts to the Lord in the form of material offerings. God does not require such gifts for himself, but the poor and needy do need our material gifts. In Luther's discussion of material offerings Vajta suggests we again see the familiar features of Luther's picture of sacrifice. Sacrifice means the death of the old person and the rising of a person regenerated in Christ. The Christian's whole life becomes a bodily sacrifice. This is the Christian's calling or vocation, and one which although closely connected to the liturgical act is also vastly more because worship includes the whole of Christian life. "Worship is not confined to pious exercises in the sanctuary but includes the whole of Christian life in service and self-surrender to the needs of the world." (169)


THEOLOGY OF WORSHIP AND LITURGICAL FORMS

Now that we have come nearly to the end of our review of Vajta, it should not escape the notice of the reader that nothing has yet been said in this theology of worship about the ceremonies of the Church, i.e., about liturgical forms. Vajta has mentioned preaching and sacraments in order to illumine their significance in Luther's theology of worship, and he has portrayed Luther as contradistinctive to the Enthusiasts for his theoretical defense of God's incarnational use of outward means to work grace, but it is not until the last chapter of Vajta's study that he asks the question, what have liturgical forms to do with worship as a work of faith?

Luther has a paradoxical attitude toward the ceremonies of the Church. On the one hand, he sounds the bell of liberty, extending our freedom from the Law to include liturgical laws too; on the other hand, this should not be mistaken as liberty from God or God's works. Only as men and women partake in Christ can they be free, and Christ is present in the external forms of worship, preaching and sacraments. Luther's concept of liturgical liberty does not mean an anti-ceremonial, spiritualized version of the Mass. Interestingly, then, Luther opposes both papists and Enthusiasts as enemies of Christian liberty, for he perceives both to replace faith with human works. The papists bind a person's conscience to certain ritual works, but the Enthusiasts make a law of evangelical freedom. "Whatever the pope had commanded for salvation, [the Enthusiasts] meant to prohibit. They failed to see that man is justified neither by the performance nor by the neglect of certain rites. They tyrannized the conscience of men as much as the pope and were as slow to grant freedom in the use of liturgical forms."[37]

It is true that we are free from external ceremony, and liturgical forms pose no harm unless they are made an essential tool for salvation, and therefore liturgical rites cannot affect the Christian's conscience since the Christian's faith is an inward thing, not resting on outward things. Yet the world does need order and form. Luther says in other contexts that Christians remain subject to the Law in the first place to discipline themselves, and in the second place in order not offend those who are weaker in faith. In the closing pages of *On the Freedom of a Christian*, for example, he notes that Christians will meet two kinds of people: unyielding, stubborn ceremonialists and simple-minded persons weak in the faith. For the sake of the latter, Luther advises "If you wish to

37. Vajta, 173. The Enthusiasts seemed to think that keeping liturgical form would crush Christian liberty. Luther humorously says, "Thank goodness we have strong enough skulls to wear a tonsure, our stomachs and bellies are healthy enough to fast and eat and digest fish on Friday and Saturday, especially since they allow us to drink good wine with it (doubtless for added chastisement), and we have shoulders and bones strong enough to wear chasubles, surplices, and long robes." Footnote, 174.

use your freedom, do so in secret . . . take care not to offend
. . . yield to their weakness until they are more fully instructed."
But for the salvation of the former, Luther advises, "In the presence of such men it is good to eat meat, break the fasts, and for
the sake of liberty do other things which they regard as the
greatest of sins. . . . Use your freedom constantly and consistently
in the sight of and despite the tyrants and the stubborn so that
they also may learn that they are impious." He applies this same
principle vis-à-vis liturgical law, and Vajta claims it is this sibling
concern for our brothers and sisters which prompts Luther's conservative approach to the question of liturgical reform. Vajta attempts to show "that while the 'inner man' is free from rites and
laws, the 'outer man' for the sake of love is bound to order and
form. . . . The choice of forms is however not a matter of personal preference, but must depend on the need of our fellows."
(177) Liturgical forms are used as a framework for the proclamation of the gospel, and being *simul justus et peccatur* the sinner will
always desperately require rites and forms both for his or her outward life, and as a ministry of love to the neighbor.

From this position Vajta thinks it clear that Luther could not but
reject both the liturgical legalism of the Roman Church and the
anti-liturgical biblicism of the Enthusiasts. His program of liturgical
reform was not an attempt to imitate New Testament worship in
every detail[38] because Christ's example is not binding except by
express command. Alteration of the liturgy was not to be made on
the basis of a pastor's arbitrary change since the liturgy must
serve all who worship.

It is in this context, says Vajta, that Luther's liturgical conserva-
tism must be seen, as well as the liturgical options left to the offi-

---

38. Such was the program of later Puritanism—cf. James White, *Protestant
Worship*, ch. 7 "Separatist and Puritan Worship." "Their most distinctive
mark was a rigorous biblicism. . . . If the worship of God is so important,
then God does not leave to human discretion how God is to be worshiped."
By contrast, Vajta suggests that for Luther "An attempt to imitate [Christ] in
every detail would lead to nonsensical lengths and defeat itself. . . . The
form of worship need not be uniform or unchangeable . . . Luther's views on
liturgical freedom reflect his broadmindedness and pliancy in other matters of
the Christian life. He was done with legalism on the street as well as in the
sanctuary" (177).

ciant in the *Formula Missae* (Vajta insists that the orders of worship which Luther eventually published were reforms made for the actual local congregation in Wittenberg, and not intended to establish an ideal pattern for every Lutheran Church to follow). He reforms the Mass, but does not attempt to reconstruct it anew; in his liturgical work Luther remains within the tradition in which he had been raised. This is not due to disinterest in forms of worship, it is due to his perceived liberty of the Christian. The order of love precludes liturgical uniformity but Vajta believes he has exonerated Luther of the charge of liturgical negligence.

### c. Observations

The purpose of outlining these two authors in detail has not been to evaluate what they say, but to examine what they cover. Our concern at the moment is methodological, not critical, and therefore we do not here wish to ask whether Prenter and Vajta are right about worship, we want to ask how theology of worship differs from liturgical theology. To that end, it has been necessary to present two samples of a theology of worship in order to see what its subject matter covers. The selection of these two texts was more or less random, except for the reason noted earlier that they have exerted an influence on this author, making careless and disparaging remarks more difficult.[39]

Not any and all theological discourse about worship should receive the appellation "liturgical theology." We maintain that the approach of Vajta and Prenter is more accurately called a theology

39. Other possible samples of theologies of worship might have been J.-J. von Allmen, *Worship: Its Theology and Practice* (New York: Oxford University Press, 1965); Gustaf Wingren, *Gospel and Church* (London: Oliver and Boyd, 1964); Gustaf Aulen, *Eucharist and Sacrifice* (Philadelphia: Muhlenberg Press, 1958); John Burkhart, *Worship* (Philadelphia: Westminster Press, 1982); or various studies on the sacraments: Robert Jenson, *Visible Words* (Philadelphia: Fortress Press, 1978), Edward Schillebeeckx, *Christ the Sacrament of the Encounter with God* (New York: Sheed & Ward, 1963), Yngve Brilioth, *Eucharistic Faith and Practice* (London: S.P.C.K., 1939), J. D. Crichton, *Christian Celebration: The Sacraments* (New York: The MacMillan Publishing Co., 1973), Herman Sasse, *This is My Body* (Minneapolis: Augsburg, 1959), etc. Geoffrey Wainwright, as we will see in the next section, offers a lengthy bibliography of what he considers theologies of worship.

of worship. Notice that neither author found it necessary to say much of anything about the particular details of a concrete liturgy. Comments about worship were made without regard to a particular liturgical structure or even a liturgical family or tradition. This is precisely the strength of a theology of worship—and also what makes it different from liturgical theology.

We have claimed that liturgical theology is also genuine theology; it is emphatically not merely an analysis of how a liturgy is conducted. Being theology, it wants to answer not only the question "how" but also "what." However, in the case of liturgical theology the "what" is intimate to the "how," while in the case of Prenter and Vajta a theology has been abstracted from the particulars in order to speak about the theme of worship. This is both permissible and often helpful. Such abstraction is the bread and butter of *theologia secunda,* and its service is to analyze, categorize, unpack, and impose schemata to aid understanding. However, this will cease to be helpful in so far as the abstracted theme reflects the theologian's schemata more than the community's. We are not implying that either Prenter or Vajta should be so charged (to make such a determination would require a different discussion). We are only pointing out that their theology of worship is in fact an abstraction, an attempt to consider worship *qua* worship. The concern of theology of worship is worship, while the concern of liturgical theology is liturgical rite as an instantiation of the Church's *lex orandi.*

Fr. Kavanagh makes the intriguing suggestion that this shift is not just incidental to some theologians, but is endemic to our western tradition.

"I tried to be candid about the difficulties we moderns have when we try to attain so holistic a notion of liturgy and rite. Our minds, it seems, were significantly altered on such matters by various factors which built up a critical mass during and after the Renaissance of the fifteenth and sixteenth centuries in the West. What emerged from this period of immense stress was a rather novel form of endeavor known as 'worship' rather than 'liturgy' in its previously understood sense. The result was that western Christianity as a whole, and the various Protestant churches in particular, embarked upon a hitherto unknown way of dealing with the

Word of God in its written, incarnate, and ecclesial manifestations. This way was, due to the nature of the new 'worship,' increasingly shorn of the witness of the rite as I have tried to describe it. . . . Secondary theological influence increased greatly, primary theology receded."[40]

Perhaps this helps account for the supposition that being Christian means accepting right doctrine (or true doctrine rightly enunciated), a privatized and rationalistic definition of faith which characterizes the modern world. This right belief can then be expressed in various styles, and judged appealing or unappealing according to the tastes of the community. Thus "being liturgical" comes to mean whether or not the presiding minister chants or wears vestments, and is no more than a matter of esthetic preference reckoned adiaphorous to the worship act. To foreshadow a distinction we will try to make clear in chapter five, such a definition treats liturgy and not leitourgia.

Fr. Taft said that because liturgies have histories they "can only be understood in motion, just as the only way to understand a top is to spin it,"[41] but a theology of worship tends to halt the

40. Kavanagh, On Liturgical Theology, 117–118. Fr. Kavanagh does not offer historical detail regarding what these factors were which reached critical mass, but one would believe the disenfranchisement of the people's role is to be counted among them. See any history of the evolution of the western liturgy, including Joseph Jungmann, The Mass of the Roman Rite (Maryland: Christian Classics, 1959), Theodore Klauser, A Short History of the Western Liturgy (New York: Oxford University Press, 1979), Herman Wegman, Christian Worship in East and West (New York: Pueblo Publishing Co., 1985), Johannes Emminghaus, The Eucharist (Collegeville: The Liturgical Press, 1978), Kenneth Stevenson, Eucharist and Offering (New York: Pueblo Publishing Co., 1986). But especially note Nathan Mitchell, Cult and Controversy (New York: Pueblo Publishing Co., 1982) who charts three movements by which the people are disenfranchised from the liturgy: (1) the move from holy meal to sacred food, (2) the move from communal meal to ritual drama, and (3) the priest's relation to the Eucharist becoming estranged from that of the people. The result is a disintegration of participatory rite and the rise of individualized, private and extra-liturgical devotion. Such was the inheritance of the sixteenth century, a time—particularly among Protestants—when Kavanagh says "liturgy waned into a form of doxological education conducted by secondary theologians who possessed academic degrees . . ." (118)

41. Taft, "The Structural Analysis of Liturgical Units," 317.

top's revolution in order to get a clearer picture of it. The object of study is changed when this is done, however. The object of study is no longer the rite in motion, it is a theology in suspended animation. It can often be useful to make abstractions, such as "the liturgy" or "worship," in order to say what one wants to say, but notice should be taken of the category shift. A shift occurs when one speaks about "the American" in order to generalize about the character of certain people, or about "the college student" in order to generalize about the mind-set and activities of a certain student population, and a shift likewise occurs when one speaks about "the liturgy" instead of liturgies. Liturgical theology strives to notice differences, not meld similarities, and the convenience of sameness should not blind it to the structurally unique components of liturgies. The subject matter of liturgical theology is not worship in general, but the theological meaning which derives from the symphony of structures called rite. Fr. Taft insists that particular structures must be dealt with because it has been his "constant observation that liturgies do not grow evenly, like living organisms. Rather, their individual structures possess a life of their own."[42] The meaning of a liturgical action is revealed not merely by its textual content but even more by the structure which abides even after its original intention has been forgotten.

We applaud Prenter's concern to reunify liturgy and theology. He urges that the second order theology of the seminary and academy be connected with what is manifested in a living way in the worship of the Church. Nevertheless, he defines the theological task as "a reflective unfolding of the content of the theology of the liturgy apart from the worship of the Church." Giving expression to a theological content apart from the worship is not the same as giving voice to the *lex orandi* in the rite. Despite his urging that the theologian function as servant to the community, the academic theologian certainly does not do what the community does, *theologia prima*.

In the introduction the analogy was proposed, inspired by Gabriel Marcel, that theology of worship takes the attitude that "worship has a theology." It seems to picture theology as sub-

---

42. Robert Taft, "How Liturgies Grow: the Evolution of the Byzantine 'Divine Liturgy,'" *Orientalia Christiana Periodica*, 43 (1977), 360.

stantial to liturgy: literally, "standing under" liturgy, and thus able to be excised for examination ("under-standing"). Is not such a treatment indicated when Vajta criticizes those whose "liturgical interest begins where it should end, viz. at the question of liturgical forms" because they fail to pay attention to the theology which underlies these forms? True, he claims that this in turn can be expressed in liturgical forms, but his purpose is the systematic presentation of that which "lies under." Is not such a treatment indicated by the fact that Prenter defines his dogmatic task as "the analysis and development of the insight given in the dogma"? True, he goes to lengths to use the term "dogma" in the singular to mean the faith of the Church which originates and has its telos in the worship of the Church, but his purpose is to analyze and develop the insight, not the liturgy. Is not such a treatment indicated by the fact that Vajta does not concern himself with outward liturgical form until the final chapter of his work, and then can conclude that any liturgical form will do so as long as it faithfully expresses the veritable theology?

And what is this true theology? In both cases a polemic is going on, namely the Lutheran agenda of *testamentum* versus *sacrificium*. In both authors, the theological plumb line for worship is God's prevenient action in word and sacrament which elicits faith response. We are not disputing whether this is a good plumb line, we are only pointing out that this seems to be the reason why those elements in the liturgy which are pertinent to this argument receive preponderant treatment, i.e., sermon and communion. The attention of both authors focuses upon evidence for a theology of *testamentum* in worship, and no reference to the liturgical rite is required for this. A theology of worship can speak about the purpose, role and reason for prayer in worship without distinguishing between the Lord's Prayer, the prayer of the Church, and the Eucharistic prayer. A theology of worship can speak about the Eucharist without distinguishing the structural elements of the Eucharist such as anamnesis, eucharistia, epiclesis, and intercession. It can speak about worship in the abstract—as does sacramentology when it debates issues of real presence and transubstantiation and representational presence without mentioning the ritual action of Eucharist.

A stronger and more sarcastic critique, bordering on overkill, may be offered of sacramentology as a subdiscipline of theology of worship. Does the reader share an uneasy sensation when sitting down at a table that has not yet been cleaned up from a meal? Crumbs on the booth chair, dabs of grease on the milk glass rim, knives and forks jumbled. Why is it distasteful? Because one was not in on the activity of which this is an after-the-fact sign. Cleaning up is different if it is the closing act of the activity of dining, but if one was not a participant in the action then the crumbs are a step removed from the human and life-giving activity they signify. This is how much sacramentology feels. It analyzes (abstractly instead of liturgically) the dried wine and the crumbs of bread left behind after the activity in debates about transubstantiation, signification, reconsecration, tabernacling the leftovers or not. A liturgical theology of the sacraments would take into account the meal, the life-giving activity between human and divine, and not simply bus the theological dishes.

We repeat once again that there may be quite valid reasons for dealing with such questions in a rarified atmosphere, but it is different from liturgical theology and care must be exercised when such doctrinal conclusions are mined from the liturgy because they might reflect a specific polemic. Liturgy does not function well as a resourcement for doctrine. In Fr. Kavanagh's words, the liturgy does not

"operate in such a way as to provide doctrinal conclusions. . . . Doctrinal conclusions are lifted from the liturgical engagement of Christians by theologians whose consciousness at the time of the lifting ineluctably affects what is lifted. This means that doctrinal conclusions are selective and may well tell one more about the theologian, and about the state of theological discourse at the time the conclusions are taken, than about the liturgy itself."[43]

This renders the question of the relationship between theology and liturgy in a different manner. Liturgy's normative position to theology is poorly understood if taken in the form of the "chicken or the egg" question: which came first? Yet this is frequently how the relationship between lex orandi and lex credendi is posited. When liturgy is treated as one among other sources for theology,

43. Kavanagh, On Liturgical Theology, 126.

then it is easy to conclude that liturgy sometimes influences theology and theology sometimes influences liturgy. This is precisely Vajta's approach when he says "worship and doctrine have developed in mutual dependence." His tacit assumption is that if doctrinal conclusions may be lifted from liturgy, and if liturgy is one among many expressions of the doctrine belonging to an era or confession, then sometimes *lex orandi* establishes *lex credendi*, and sometimes vice-versa. The mutually transitive influence of theology upon liturgy and of liturgy upon theology justifies his very methodology, which was employed to establish Luther's theology of worship underlying liturgical form, unlike "would-be liturgical reformers" who begin where they should end, viz. at the question of liturgical form.

LITURGY AS EXPRESSION OF DOGMA

Vajta says this explicitly in several passages of an article "Creation and Worship." He writes first that "the liturgy, according to this way of thinking, is the dogma of the Church *as taken into* [emphasis added] the prayer-life of the worshipping congregation. Liturgy is, accordingly, the dogma of the Church viewed in a special dimension—the dimension of prayer."[44] He proposes that the truth of this statement can be proved by the history of Christian worship in which liturgical development has been parallel to the development of Christian dogma. Although we are cautioned not to oversimplify the relationship, as if liturgy is merely the result of dogmatic consideration, nevertheless "dogma was the unconscious background of the beginning of worship in the early Church. There was an interrelationship between dogma and liturgy, and one can hardly give priority to one or the other link."[45] In other words, the apostolic teaching of the Church determines both its dogmatic expression and its liturgical expression. Since liturgy and dogma are expressions of the teaching which stands behind them both, liturgy has influenced dogma and dogma has influenced liturgy.

44. Vajta, "Creation and Worship" in *Studia Liturgica*, 2 (1963) 29.
45. Ibid., 30.

"The dogmatic developments of each age have influenced the liturgical form. This is as true for the early Church as for medieval scholasticism, for the Reformation, for the age of orthodoxy or Pietism, or for modern theological developments.

"The point for our ecumenical discussions on worship can be drawn from the insights in the laws of liturgical development. It could read like this: *the confesssional differences in the interpretation of the dogma of the Church are also reflected in different liturgical forms.*"[46]

Although liturgical orders may receive their final redaction by individuals, Vajta wishes to insist that dogma, as the creative force of the liturgy, is the only source through which the liturgy can get its permanency.

As in the case of Prenter, whose article "Theology and Liturgy" is cited at this point, it is also Vajta's desire to reunify dogmatics and liturgy. Too often dogmatics is done without consideration of the dimension of liturgy, and when this occurs dogmatics becomes excessively intellectual and scholastic. Liturgy would open up new aspects of dogmatic statements which "are more than intellectual exercises but are instead existential in nature. Certainly a *liturgical theology* is a legitimate claim on the work of the basic consideration on the foundation of the Church in God's acts revealed and worshipped."[47] Such a method in dogmatics would not only increase the material of dogmatic interest, he says, but would also definitely contribute to the thorough understanding of the dogma itself, presumably because adding an existential dimension to dogma puts us in concordance with days past when *theologia* included a dimension of worship.

We say again that in this approach it is as if liturgy has a theology as one has a body: *the hypostatized theology is expressed through ceremonial form.* To Vajta, liturgical theology's distinctive mark will be that it expresses this theology in an existential mode. He thinks it good to occasionally leave theology in its existential form and appreciate its worship dimensions because by itself abstracted theology is in danger of becoming intellectual and scholastic. However, the doctrinal backbone of liturgy must not be neg-

46. Ibid. His underscoring.
47. Ibid., 32. His underscoring.

lected and precisely the service provided by the secondary theologian is a critique of forms and practices in worship. This is why although Vajta considers liturgiology important as a discipline, it "cannot be regarded as theological discipline without a consideration of the creative force of all liturgical development in dogma itself."[48] Without a dogmatic dimension, liturgiology will be deprived of its possibility of offering theological evaluation. If Vajta means, as did Fr. Schmemann, that too often liturgiology is relegated to the "how" without consideration of the "what" then we might endorse the above comment, but in fact we suppose Vajta is actually proposing that consideration of the "what" is exclusively the province of secondary theology.

It is at this point that Vajta conjures the theological principle "*lex credendi—lex orandi*" [sic]. "As long as this principle includes only the setting of an interrelationship between liturgy and faith, one cannot object to it. Nevertheless, a critical remark is necessary, especially on the interpretation that development in worship sets a rule for the Christian faith. When men worship God, developments can take place where the critical norm of the divine revelation is called upon to bring about a correction."[49] Since even liturgical areas are not immune to the effects of sin, liturgy too needs the corrective norm of revelation which is enunciated by dogma. He mentions Roman Catholic Marian dogma as proof of the failure which ensues if the law of worship sets the law of belief. Here a custom of prayer was established which he sees as cut off from the roots of divine revelation. The law of prayer has set up a dogma which, when examined by revelatory norms enunciated by theologians, must be rejected. Thus he concludes that the principle *lex orandi—lex credendi* "can only be used in the sense of interrelationship between liturgy and dogma. It is important . . . that the interrelationship between dogma and worship is clearly viewed without giving preference to one or the other factor."[50] The interrelationship seems to be mutually transitive: dogmatics corrects faulty theological expression in worship, and worship opens up an existential dimension to theology. For Vajta the criti-

48. Ibid., 32–33.
49. Ibid., 33.
50. Ibid.

cal norm is expressed in dogma. Secondary theology, not liturgy as primary theology, provides the theological norms.

Vajta's position is persuasive so long as one conceives of liturgy as an expression of worship in ordered form instead of conceiving of it as rite, because in the case of the former a theology must be provided to worship from the outside. Liturgy as ordered esthetic expression needs a substantial theology which it can express. We will argue in chapter five that when leitourgia is taken as rite it can be called theological because it is faith in motion. It does not merely serve as the raw data for theology or the existential expression of theological dictums, for the very reason, claims liturgical theology, that liturgical rite is transaction in the mystery which issues in *theologia prima* which serves as the base for secondary theology. Leitourgia is not a way of saying something, it is a way of becoming something. It is not a way of saying theology, it is how believers become Church. And because it is the Church which theologizes, *lex orandi* establishes *lex credendi*.

The assumption that liturgy and theology are mutually transitive will be met in even stronger form in the persons of Peter Brunner and Geoffrey Wainwright, our two samples of theology from worship.

## Chapter 3

## Two Theologies from Worship

*a. Peter Brunner,* Worship in the Name of Jesus[1]

Save for one fact, Brunner's work could also serve as an example of what we have called theology of worship. In the foreword of the book, Walter Buszin goes so far as to declare that though Christians worshiped throughout the ages and on many occasions "discussed important issues of the Christian religion and its worship" no one until Brunner's 1953 publication "had as yet produced a major literary opus devoted exclusively and profoundly to the significant doctrine of Christian worship. . . . This work paved the way for future generations and gave to the church its first book on the theology of Christian worship." Brunner himself describes his task in this book as a dogmatic one, believing that a dogmatic definition of worship is critical to its proper pneumatic application. "Our task must now be formulated thus: What happens in those assemblies of Christians by virtue of divine institution and as certified by the divine Word, and what must, in consequence, be done in such assemblies by us today? With this question we have formulated our task as a dogmatic one in the strictest sense of the word." (25) The task is dogmatic because the answer to the posed question derives not from an empirical-descriptive approach, nor from a psychological or anthropological orientation, nor is it solved by historicizing eclecticism. Rather, the explanation of what takes place in the Christian assembly, as well as the guide for what should be done, today hinges unconditionally upon the past revelation of God, and this is precisely under the purview of dogmatics. Brunner's concern seems to be to iden-

1. Peter Brunner, *Worship in the Name of Jesus* (St. Louis: Concordia Publishing House, 1968). References from this work are integrated into the text.

tify a plumb line which would permit one to evaluate worship, and thereby also enable one to render prescriptive judgments about what should happen in contemporary worship. In this way dogmatics is in service to the Church.

Dogmatics is no isolated discipline; dogmatics is concerned with "what the fathers of the Reformation termed [worship's] proper *usus*. In our context we may paraphrase this word as 'the pneumatic application of that which takes place in the service.' " (24) That is, the dogmatician (we suppose in contradistinction to a philosopher of religion or a student of religious studies or a theologian in general) is concerned with the life of the Church as a body of believers. To be concerned about worship's proper *usus* is to ask what the person in the pew does with the words she hears, with the song or prayer he voices, with the gifts received at the Lord's table, how proclamation in the pulpit is carried out, in short, with what happens to and for the worshiper. Worship is a critical event, an actual crisis because here men and women encounter God's word and sacrament. "Will this encounter prove salutary? Will a pneumatic appropriation of the gift, a Spirit-filled consummation of the act, and therewith a proper *usus* of worship, result in this encounter? For after all, the proper spiritual implementation by the assembled congregation and its servants is and remains the most important factor in worship." (25) But how is a proper *usus* of worship discerned, defined and maintained? The worshiping community (both the congregation and its servants, the clergy) must be taught in order to arrive at a proper pneumatic application of worship, and this is what makes the correct doctrine of worship so critical.

Of course, the dogmatician does not determine the content of worship. That is determined by the Word. And dogmatics serves the Word generally by making clear the Word which God speaks to humanity, and in this case dogmatics serves the Word specifically by making clear God's Word in the worshiping community. "The basic requirement that must be made of everything called worship reads: God must be able to give assent to everything that happens there; it must be acceptable to Him. And whatever pleases God must be enclosed in His Word and commandment." (25) This is why a doctrine of worship relies not upon empirically, psychologically or historically derived canons, its canon is the apostolic word. A doctrine is dogmatic if in it we hear the voice that belongs to the one, holy, catholic and apostolic Church of Christ. If worship does not express this voice, it is not the worship instituted by God in Christ.

We feel, then, a similarity between Brunner and Prenter and Vajta in that all three distinguish dogmatics from theology in general by defining dogmatics as an intelligible service rendered the Church so that the Word can do its proper work (or, to say it from the bottom side, so the believer can make proper *usus* of worship). If theology speaks not merely of God, and not merely of humanity, but God in relationship to humanity through Christ, then it must include a doctrine of worship. From this perspective Brunner's work might simply be called a theology of worship. But he has made in this study an additional move. He utilizes an additional method, one which prompts us to identify it not as a theology of worship but a theology from worship. In addition to defining the essence of worship in part I of his work, part II treats the meaning of various acts in the worship service itself. It is this which interests us especially, for here is a theology which pays some attention to the liturgical rite. It attempts to extrapolate a theology from the worship. But to understand it we must first see the place which Brunner reserves to worship in the larger scheme.

### THE PLACE OF WORSHIP IN GOD'S PLAN

Brunner identifies three loci for the place of worship: God's universal plan of salvation, the anthropological place of worship, and the cosmological place of worship. A strength of this approach is to fix worship as normative and not treat it merely as corrective surgery. Worship is a fundamental reality, manifesting the right relationship between God and human beings. "As God created man in His image, He created a creature in which His own reality, glory, might, and beauty are reflected within the boundaries implicit in the creatureliness of the foremost creature. . . . Man cannot be God's image without the immediate, adoring word of acknowledgement, of gratitude, of glorification addressed to the Creator. Without prayer and laudation, man would not be the mirror of God's glory, he would not be man." (36) To worship is not to be superhuman; not to worship is to be subhuman. The sons of Adam and the daughters of Eve were intended to worship, for they were intended to be addressed by God and to give personal, conscious and free response to God's love. By the Fall into sin humanity has become less than it was meant to be because "man destroyed the worship given him with his creation and perverted it into the appalling opposite. The bonds of love between God and man were cut asunder by man. The pneumatic reality of being in the image of God, which let man share in God's own life and being, was lost." (41–42) Sin essentially consists of failing to worship, because failing to worship cuts asunder the bond of love between Creator and creature.

It is this state of affairs that must be rectified by Christ's atonement. God has pronounced His judgment of death upon fallen man and woman—not merely biological death, but eternal, judicial death which is repudiation, punishment and execution.

"Adam does not die this bloody death—and yet he dies it, as surely as God abides by His word. Adam will die. All who bear Adam's image will die. . . . God does not break His word. Man actually dies this bloody judicial death of God's rejection—in Jesus Christ. That is the inexpressible miracle of divine compassion. God himself assumes Adam's image and Adam's essence and Adam's guilt and Adam's death in the person of God the Son. This happened in time under Emperor Augustus and under Pontius Pilate, when Jesus was born of the Virgin Mary and was crucified on Golgotha by Jews and Gentiles." (42–43)

This judicial death is suffered by Jesus, the New Adam, in whom the human race also dies to its rebellious egocentricity. And while this took place in history, its effect is not limited to temporal boundaries any more than it is limited to geographical boundaries. In God's sight, the Golgotha judgment was issued on the Adam-Jesus on the day of Adam's fall. The human race receives its gift of life entirely from this sacrifice, and the gift of God's forbearance is founded on the fact that the bloody judicial death intercedes at God's throne in eternity even before Christ's historical execution on Golgotha. "This mysterious presence before God and in God of Jesus' temporally future death on the cross is the fountainhead of God's forbearance and patience, in which all men live and in which all men die from the day of the Fall to the day of Jesus Christ's crucifixion and resurrection." (43)

Like Luther in Vajta's study, Brunner affirms that the phenomena of cult and idol indicate our connection to God, although that relationship is lived as a lie. Worship is ontological to human existence, but the relationship has become a perverted one. "Man robs God of the glory which is due him. Instead of letting the ray of that glory of God which shone upon him beam back upon God in adoration and worship, man holds fast to this ray as a spoil and arbitrarily transfers to the creature what belongs to God. That begets the idol, and with this it begets the pagan cultus." (48)

Having spoken of the foundation for worship, Brunner next turns his attention to God's plan of salvation whereby true worship was restored to man and woman, viz. the history of Israel culminating in Jesus of Nazareth. God's presence withdrew upon our fall into sin, but God's personal and gracious presence began anew with Abraham. Israel, Jesus Christ, and the Church are interconnected; this triple stage in God's plan of salvation presents an interrelated and connected whole. Although God is not present as he was to Adam, God is now present in his Word which selects its charismatic bearers with perfect freedom. In the first covenant the Word-presence was mediated and manifested in theophanies, by the angel of the Lord, in the pillar of cloud, in the ark of the covenant, in Temple cultic worship, in the prophets, and in the writings. But God's presence in the Temple could and did cease, as did also God's prophet-mediated presence. "Then God appeared in the flesh. The eternal Word itself became flesh. . . . [The] Messiah is seated on the right hand of God the Father and is actually and really present solely in the temple of the Holy Spirit, in the *ekklesia* of Jesus Christ . . ."[2] The humanity

2. Brunner, 53. In this connection see Samuel Terrien, *The Elusive Presence* (New York: Harper & Row, 1978). He suggests that the dominant theme throughout the Old Testament is God's elusive presence. "Divine intervention in human affairs is generally, if not exclusively, represented as sudden, unexpected, unwanted, unsettling, and often devastating." The feature of divine disruption is typical of all literary genres in all periods of biblical history. It appears in the primeval legends (Noah), in the patriarch sagas (Abraham), in the national epic (Moses), in the prophetic visions (Amos), in theophanies (Job) and also in the Synoptic traditions on the appearances of the risen Lord. "Biblical man is always 'surprised by God.'" Yet these invasions of human history by the Word are brief and appear to have been the privilege of an ex-

of Jesus is the original eschatological mystery, for what happened in the humanity of Jesus was, in his creatureliness and historical- ness, an event in which God himself acted. During Jesus' sojourn on earth, Jesus—not the cultic institution—was the mediator of sal- vation. After the ascension, when the Lord was no longer present among his disciples either in natural body or in glorified body, the Spirit descended at Pentecost, and at this point "the eschatological transition, which includes the sacrifice on Golgotha's cross, begins to operate on earth in visible events. What happened on the Day of Pentecost was something novel. . . . With the outpouring of the Spirit, the fruit of the suffering and death of Jesus was poured out." (77) The Church as the body of Christ is now the presence of God's abiding Word which had dwelt among humankind as fleshly presence and now dwells among humankind as pneumatic presence in word and sacrament. Baptism propagates the Pente- cost event and creates a place to worship which "is the interim in which the church yearns for the eschatological *transitus*. Sustained by the Word-bound Peneuma and the Word-bound sacrament, the church hastens towards this last epiphany of the Lord and his body. This hastening-toward is carried out principally in its wor- ship." (80)

As a manifestation of humanity's restored likeness to God, wor- ship occupies a cosmological locus. The worship of the foremost creature stands between the worship of angels and the worship of creation. The worship of the angels, Church and earthly creatures

tremely restricted elite. "What sort of access did the average Israelite or Juda- hite have to the presence of Deity? As a member of the cultic community he believed in the real presence of Yahweh at a shrine. . . . A cultic form of presence was sacramentally available. A God who remained historically ab- sent manifested his proximity to the average man through cultic com- munion." (28–29)

Thus Terrien suggests that "the birth of the church lies not in the rein- terpretation of the notion of messiahship but in the appropriation of the temple ideology in the context of the risen Lord." (31) Moses, prophets, priests, psalmists and wise men may have mediated the knowledge of God to the masses, "but their activities were always directly or indirectly related to cultus. It may be said that in Israel there would not have been a knowledge of God without the service of God. Theology was bred in celebration. *The- ologia* could not be separated from *Theolatreia*." (4) We take this to say that *lex orandi* establishes *lex credendi* because theology is bred in liturgy.

all have the same focal point, "namely the One seated on the throne and the crucified and exalted Jesus at His right hand," but the focal point is present to each differently: in heaven above, God's immediate presence on the throne is within immediate view; among men and women, the Word-bound Pneuma-presence and the Word-bound, Pneuma-borne sacramental presence is viewed only by faith; and down below, in the creatural depths, it is in the general intracreatural omnipresence. "But in all three realms it is the Triune God and the one sacrificed and crucified Body that awakens and receives this service offered to God." (106)

Anthropologically, the worship of the Church stands between Christ's ascension and his return, and between baptismal death and our physical death; cosmologically, it stands between the worship of the heavenly creature and the earthly creature. "The worship of the church takes place in a threefold, dawning eschatological *transitus*: in the *transitus* of this world to the kingdom of God; in the *transitus* of this mortal, temptable body to its resurrection from the dead; in the *transitus* which liberates nature for the freedom of the children of God and transforms the children of God into angelic being. Essence and form of worship are bounded by its place in this threefold *transitus*." (106)

This is how Brunner recapitulates the place of worship in God's plan of salvation, and identifies its anthropological and cosmological place. The Church's worship is a manifestation of our restored likeness to God which is what the history of salvation has wrought, and which is being pneumatically worked by God in individual lives and the cosmos as God restores both to their rightful relationship. But why must it be continued? Does humankind require another divine saving act beyond Word and baptism? Or should worship be understood merely as a missionary event wherein unbelievers are addressed by the Word and led to belief and baptism? The latter interpretation would mean that worship as salvation-event has become superfluous for the believer. Brunner acknowledges that in many congregations and in the conception of worship which directs many pastors, worship is exactly thus misperceived, but he himself wishes to correct this misconception and to do so he must move beyond worship's place as a continuation (enactment) of salvation history and speak specifically of ecclesial worship.

It is certainly true that worship which takes place beyond the boundary of baptism adds nothing to the salvation received, however this salvation must be preserved until the believer's physical death. Since its preservation is a pneumatic act, wrought by the Holy Spirit, this can be designated as faith. Preservation of salvation depends on our remaining in the crucified and exalted Christ, and to remain in this saving Word requires that one be addressed by the saving Word. This involves more than private reading of the Bible; the saving Word must continually be addressed to the individual, and this requires a community of faith.

"Since my baptism I am integrated into the people of God of the end time, into the *ekklesia*, which is, in a hidden manner, an epiphany of the body of Jesus Christ on earth. . . . [We] assemble as *ekklesia* to the end that the saving Word may become vital in this assembly and the believers may be preserved in the faith. The worship of the *ekklesia* is necessary because we are unable to preserve the obtained salvation in this earthly life otherwise than by resorting ever anew to the living Word, in which Jesus Christ Himself is present with his acts and fruits of salvation and with which He works on us." (112)

Not only is worship the continuation of the apostolic word as missionary activity, the apostolic word also has an ecclesial function. Brunner must guard himself against a possible misinterpretation which could arise from the way he has thus far framed the discussion. It might appear that his theological investigation of the place of worship reduces worship to a type of continual missionary (apostolic) proclamation of the gospel. Now he must therefore fix attention upon Word and Sacrament as they are vital to the Church. It is surely the same Word, but the missionary form and the ecclesial form are different. This is true for both preaching and the sacrament.

As regards preaching, proclamation which is intended for the believing assembly must be distinguished from that which is not, since ecclesial proclamation bears a specific character and specific forms, even if its substance and content is shared with purely missionary proclamation. But it is the sacrament which most powerfully affirms and safeguards the importance of the Word in its ecclesial form by uniting Word and Sacrament. "The misconcep-

tion of worship as a continuation of missionary activity will arise
with a certain logical force so long as we conceive of this saving
Word in isolation from Holy Communion." (113). The unity of
proclamation and Eucharist establishes the specific character and
form of ecclesial Word. The threshold from sin to salvation has
been crossed in baptism, but this salvation must be preserved.
The Eucharist is the repeated preservation of salvation by the already saved. The Lord's Supper is itself the power which assembles believers as *ekklesia*, and Holy Communion exists only
where the congregation is assembled as *ekklesia*.

Brunner is therefore emphatic about the requirement of the
Lord's Supper, but at the same time he refuses to justify it by
argumentation. He says, on the one hand, ". . . there can be no
theological justification for the worship of the church that is not
centrally based on the command 'This do in remembrance of
Me.' " On the other hand, he admits we are "at a loss for an intelligent answer to the question why we should also receive the
gift of salvation through the Lord's Supper when this has already
been presented through Baptism and the Word" and salvation is
kept alive by the proclaimed apostolic Word. "Any attempt to ascribe the necessity for the reception of salvation in the special
manner of Holy Communion to any other reason than its institution by Christ will miscarry. . . . I do not know why I stand in
need of precisely this gift of Holy Communion. Jesus Christ alone
knows that." (115–16) The Church requires the preservation of the
salvation wrought by Word and conversion and baptism, and this
is worship's ecclesial role. Therefore it behooves a dogmatician
who is enunciating the faith of the Church to examine the
Church's worship. Having described worship's trifold place, Brunner now directs his attention to the theology which can be derived
*from* the assembly's worship. If one could explain this dogmatically then worshipers could make proper *usus* of worship.

TWO MOVEMENTS IN WORSHIP

Brunner discerns in Golgotha two movements: God's service in
Jesus to us, and Jesus' service for us to God. In the liturgy of the
Church he can likewise distinguish "Worship as a service of God
to the congregation" (chapter 7) and "Worship as the congregation's service before God" (chapter 8). The pneumatic event of

worship participates in the twin poles of Christ's action which could be tagged sacrament and sacrifice. In this Brunner is following Melanchthon's *Apology of the Augsburg Confession*, where a sacrament is defined as that external act of worship "in which God presents to us that which the promise annexed to the ceremony offers." (Article 24) Or in Brunner's earlier phrase, a sacrament is God's service in Jesus to us. But one must be cautious about the term "sacrifice," our service to God in Jesus; Melanchthon carefully distinguishes two types: propitiatory and Eucharistic. Brunner straightforwardly invokes this classic Lutheran distinction. The former renders satisfaction for guilt and sin and propitiates God's wrath; the latter is offered by those already reconciled in order to express their gratitude to God for His gift of mercy. While Christ's death is the only propitiatory sacrifice, it may be admitted that some acts of worship are called sacrificial in the second sense, and these consist of faith, prayer, thanksgiving, confession, the afflictions of the saints, and the ceremony of the Mass. These two categories, sacrament and sacrifice, are the twin pillars of all that takes place in Christian worship. "Melanchthon's differentiation between sacrament and sacrifice within the compass of ceremonies reveals the peculiar dual structure of what takes place in a hidden, namely, pneumatic, manner; during the external, perceptible acts of worship: God transmits His gifts of salvation to us, and we present thank offerings to God in prayer, confession, and praise." (123)

Brunner allows that individual acts of worship are pervaded by both sacrament and sacrifice. It is easy to see why this is necessary from what he has said thus far. To supplement God's grace would be to supplant it. Worship is the sustaining presence of the Word which birthed us and now nourishes us. Worship is not a contribution to the salvation event, but rather the continuation of that salvation event, therefore a sacramental component must be discernible in even the most sacrificial action. It would be misleading, for example, to say that the proclamation of the Word (the foremass) is God's service to the congregation, and that Holy Communion (the Mass) is the congregation's service to God because that would tempt us to suppose that Holy Communion is propitiatory sacrifice. As Brunner clusters individual acts of worship around one pillar or the other by discerning which of them are a service of God to the congregation (chapter 7) and which are the congregation's service before God (chapter 8) he does divide the Liturgy of the Word from the Liturgy of the Table, but his distinction between anthropocentric sacrament and theocentric sacrifice is not coterminous with this division. Rather, there are sacramental and sacrificial elements to both the foremass and to the Mass. (The reader may draw his or her own conclusions about which pillar is of more importance to Brunner from the fact that chapter seven is seventy pages long while chapter eight is sixteen pages long.)

THE FIRST PILLAR: A SACRAMENTAL MOVEMENT

In Brunner's doctrine of worship we have already seen a difference between the Word in its missionary form and in its ecclesial form. This is invoked again at the beginning of his treatment of anthropocentric grace in the Liturgy of the Word. The missionary word, he says, has basically but one form because it is always confrontation with the gospel, but the Word spoken to the Church in worship, which Brunner here calls a fundamental and edifying Word, has a multiplicity of forms and bearers. In this way it accomplishes its nurturing and edifying purpose. "The apostles did not only lead Jews and Gentiles to conversion, to faith, to Baptism, to the *ekklesia*, but they also proclaimed their Word in the *ekklesia* and for this *ekklesia* that was called into being by them. In this sense the Word of the apostles was not only fundamental but also edifying, it was not only a planting but also a watering Word." (127)

In ecclesial worship this watering Word takes the forms of Scripture reading, sermon, absolution, salutation and benediction, psalmody and hymns, the Credo, prayers, congregational remembering of the *mirabilia dei*, cultic anamnesis, and forgiveness. Brunner reads his theology from worship by looking at these basic forms of the edifying Word one by one. The doctrine of the Word which he has thus far expounded has been read off the manifold ways in which the edifying Word feeds the congregation and preserves the salvific Word in their hearts. The way dogmatics can identify and urge the proper *usus* of worship is by enunciating the theology from worship.

So Brunner insists that worship will normally include the reading of Scripture and the sermon. In the reading of the apostolic Word, "the apostle of Jesus Christ here and now steps into the midst of the congregation with his church-founding testimony in order to nourish it with this Word," and "an individual arises in the assembled congregation and expounds Scripture in the form of testimony," (129) the sermon. The sermon thus serves the apostolic Word by making it a concretely historical Word for the present moment. The sermonic Word, while preserving substantial identity with the apostolic Word, must be reborn in the preacher by the Holy Spirit, and be exposited in the form of testimony in order for the past Word to become a present apostolic Word. "The sermon is a ministering instrument for [the] inherent power of the Word, placing the salvation-event carried out in Jesus' flesh into the present time and dispensing here and now the salvation effected in that event." (132) In this here and now manifestation, the sermon is related in substance to absolution.

Absolution is a condensation of the gospel as Word. Brunner calls individual (private) confession and individual (private) absolution the most basic forms of the gospel act because forgiveness is actually dispensed in this Word; forgiveness is not merely talked about but actually granted. However, there are other concentrated proclamations of the Word as well, notably the salutation and benediction. Both of these join participants to the salvific action through a gift transmitted. The doctrinal meaning of these condensed gospel words, their *usus* as "pneumatic application of that which takes place in the service," is discerned as one looks at their purpose in the worship service. They are not magic words because the gift received in sermon, absolution, salutation and benediction is received only by faith.

The words of Holy Scripture are also directly proclaimed in psalmody and hymnody. When the choir fulfills its ministering role of presenting the Scriptural words to the congregation, "the singing of psalms represents a prime type of participation in the charismatic-prophetic service of proclamation by nonordained members of the congregation." And when the congregation joins in the action, "this type of presentation of the Word may effect a meditative appropriation, a spiritual 'eating' of the Word such as is achieved in hardly any other form of proclamation in worship."

(137) In congregational hymns the assembly preaches to itself, and so Brunner surprisingly claims that the sacramental element predominates over the sacrificial in the congregation's hymnography.

There are indirect forms of the proclamation of the Word in worship, and the psalm hymn forms a transition to these. Examples include the Credo, the hymn of praise, prayer, Eucharistic prefaces, and doxological acclamations (the Gloria, Sanctus, Benedictus and Maranatha-cry). In these the content of the apostolic proclamation is concentrated as in the focus of a lens. "Although [their] words express devotion to God and praise of God, although this sacrificial side, perhaps, even contains its original and essential function, [they are] nonetheless also a proclaiming word, in which the congregation affirms the great deeds of God to itself and to all the world." (139)

In all this the anamnetic quality of the fundamental and edifying Word proclaimed in worship is evident. We presume Brunner is trying to be intentionally surprising by digressing into a lengthy discussion about anamnesis here, in connection with the Word, and not later, in connection with the Eucharist where anamnesis customarily figures. In the anamnesis of Christ the sacramental function of worship is fulfilled, he says, and this is as true of the Liturgy of the Word as it is of the Liturgy of the Sacrament. The gospel of God proclaimed when the congregation recalls and unfolds that gospel is not a new Word or a different Word; it is the same Word reiterated because it is all-important that the folk in the congregation who have been called and baptized remain in Christ. "The congregation really 'knows' all that is necessary for its salvation. . . . But the congregation must be 'reminded' of what it knows," (142) and so the theology which Brunner reads from worship is pitched in an anamnetic key. This is the proper *usus* of worship which the dogmatic analysis of worship will reveal and protect. When one looks at what happens in a worship service, one sees the anamnetic use of the Word which should not be confused with the missionary use of the Word. If these two uses are ever confused, the result is aimless worship and bad homiletics.

"One does not call the Gospel and Baptism to mind as one recalls a biographical event or a historical date which has escaped the memory and which one tries to recollect. . . . This remembering, rather, implies that man's understanding and thinking and willing and doing are shaped and molded by it in essence, kind, and content. Therefore this remembering is a power decisively determinant for one's existence. It is oriented to the object, to the content of Gospel and Baptism; it is a renewed apprehension, a renewed appropriation, a renewed acceptance of the salvation proferred in the Gospel and in Baptism." (144)

Brunner reminds us that in opposition to Karlstadt, Luther made the bold statement that forgiveness of sins is not to be found at the Cross; the Cross gained forgiveness of sins for us, but does not dispense it. Forgiveness is dispensed in the Word. Of course, by the death and rising of Christ the sovereign and eschatological power of God penetrated the world, but what happened must then be told, and it is in the kerygmatic proclamation, in worship's anamnesis, that the eschatological act of Jesus is rendered present. "God's redemptive act in Jesus is completed in His institution of the means through Jesus by which this history of what happened in Jesus . . . already becomes prehensible, tangible, acceptable, and effectual for us men on this earth in time and space and translates all who participate in it by faith into the eschatological *transitus*. We know that these means are the Gospel, Baptism and Holy Communion." (149) The proclamation of the gospel, in all its manifold forms within worship, is a member in this series of means. This makes proclamation in the worship event not educational and reminiscent, but exhibitive and bestowing. Brunner is outlining a doctrine of the proclaimed Word which parallels the purpose of the doctrine of the Real Presence in Holy Communion. To be sure, Christ's presence in both Word and Sacrament must be apprehended in faith, but it is not faith which makes Christ present. "Whoever would, finally, . . . make the fulfillment of the words of absolution dependent on their acceptance in faith . . . that person did not hear the Bible's message aright, and did not recognize the salvation-event in the proclaimed Word correctly." (152) The twin pillars of sacrifice and sacrament can be logically distinguished, but as is God's way in incarnation, the divine, spiritual or sacramental work is contained in, with and under human, mundane and sacrifical words. He insists that when God bestows faith it is in such a manner that the faith is nonetheless the individual's faith.

In Holy Communion this is even more evident. Indeed, statements on the Lord's Supper will express the most characteristic features of worship done in the name of Jesus because here the doors to the world are closed and the faithful alone participate in the heart of worship.

Brunner writes, "Our task is not primarily to expound a text but to interpret an action. . . . Our interpretation of what takes place in the present-day Holy Communion is doctrine, it is dogma. For the knowledge of what happens in the present Holy Communion of the church is knowledge of doctrine." (157) This dogmatic interpretation will be derived from the worship event, that is, from revelatory event. What interests Brunner is not historical research into the Last Supper, but dogmatic formulation of the power of the Church's Holy Communion. Ask it this way: "Does anything at all take place in our celebration of Holy Communion besides what is clearly open to anyone's view and besides what takes place in the consciousness of every participant: his thoughts, views, inner experiences and convictions? We reply: Yes, indeed! Precisely that which takes place additionally in Holy Communion in, with, and under the visible and psychologically determinable is the salvation-event. . . ." (161–62) This is the doctrine of the Real Presence in brief. Jesus invested the Eucharist with his power to effect that event which constitutes salvation. Our certainty of salvation derives not from historical research, but from the certainty which faith knows when it hears Christ's salvific Word. What has been affirmed about anamnesis regarding the proclaimed gospel word is also affirmed regarding the Meal event. "We have already seen that the real content of the word anamnesis can be understood only from the Israelitic-Jewish, worship-ritual tradition, because this anamnesis-event is possible only where the realization of a redemptive event, emanating from God and tending toward the end, is involved." (166) Brunner said his purpose was to answer the question, what should be taught in the Church relative to that assembly which we call divine service? He formulated a Word-theology by observing the proclaimed Word in the congregation's life, and now he will formulate a sacrament-theology by observing what gifts the assembly receives.

Holy Communion is not our creation, since it is the presence of Jesus which institutes the meal. This is the point of the consecratory prayer which invokes the name of the Lord in concrete obedience to Jesus' command. "Consequently, there must be bread; there must be wine in a cup. Bread and wine must be 'consecrated.' This is not to be an ordinary meal with bread and wine. Bread and wine are to be lifted out of the purpose which they ordinarily serve in a meal and assigned to this special service of rendering Christ's body and blood present." (179) The remembrance of Christ must show a liturgical order, that is, one which reflects compliance with Jesus' command.

What are the gifts bestowed by Holy Communion? The answer to this is already known incipiently. "Holy Communion is a proclamation of the Gospel in the unity of Word and act. Therefore all that was stated before regarding the proclamation of the Word as a means of transmitting salvation and the re-creating Spirit applies to Holy Communion." (182) We may presume this is why Brunner spoke of anamnesis in connection with the Word: what was rendered present in the spoken Word is also rendered present in this visible Word. However, in the Eucharist the redemptive gift is presented in a special manner. Brunner mentions six features of the special manner of the gift's presentation: it is concrete, it is communion with the dying Lord, we are placed into the body of the cross, we are accorded communion with the saints (*communio sanctorum*), and the most particular item of all is the personalized "for-you" character of communion. Holy Communion's gift of salvation is Jesus' atoning sacrifical death which bursts the bonds of sin and guilt, death and the devil. Such a gift is really the end-time gift of God's kingdom and as such is different from the forgiveness granted in absolution. This is eschatological communion with Christ.

As such, the Lord's Supper is an anticipatory participation in the Lamb's wedding feast in glory. Eucharist is not only anamnesis of the foundation of our new life, it is also a "symbolic pregift of Jesus' nuptial meal with His bridal congregation" (188) and is marked with festive joy. This reality is as yet hidden and known only to faith, which is to say that everything remains human and earthly, everything remains symbol, yet the symbol is filled to the brim with the reality of the kingdom of God and it issues in the joy felt when bride and Bridegroom approach each other. Holy Communion with God becomes the mystery of the Church. At this table, the many become one body and the Church as Christ's body is created anew. This creates a crisis—a judgment—in our lives and it leads to the confirmation, preservation, strengthening and perfection of our membership in the Lord's body. It must lead to faith and to love. When the many are made one, they are bound in fraternal responsibility, namely, the responsibility incumbent upon those who feast upon Christ's sacrificial death which is to act in love toward their neighbor.

By humbly accepting God's gracious activity, we enter into the end-time order of salvation quickened by the Spirit so the kingdom may come. The Church is conformed to the Son whose life is glorifying the Father. This is Jesus' service before God, and it is the foundation for worship as the assembly's service before God. "God's glory appears in the Incarnate One. Today and in this world it does not appear otherwise than in the embodiment of His sacrificial love. Every celebration of Holy Communion is—hidden under the veil of the end-time mystery—an epiphany of God's sacrificial love in the sacrificial body of His Son, which is also the pneumatic body of his *ekklesia*." (196)

### THE SECOND PILLAR: A SACRIFICIAL MOVEMENT

Therefore every anamnesis of Christ in Holy Communion materializes the glory of the Triune God. This is the second pillar of worship, the sacrificial component which those assembled in Jesus' name do insofar as their actions are directed to God. Brunner is now prepared to consider this second pillar of worship, the congregation's service before God.

He does not enter into this discussion naively, however. Can our worship ever be considered pure service to God? "[O]ur action addressed to God is questionable from the very beginning. All participants in worship are constrained to concede that their worship is constantly endangered by their old carnal essence." (197) During the interim between the kingdom initiated and the kingdom fulfilled, obedience is imperfect and one's relationship with God depends constantly on God's forgiveness. Therefore, any talk of sacrifice must be rooted in the obedience of faith. In order to preserve proper spiritual conduct of worship and not succumb to the temptation of viewing worship's sacrificial movements as propitiatory, it is absolutely decisive that we approach worship as people living in baptismal obedience, which is the fruit of what God has already performed on us through Word and Sacrament. "Therefore the congregation does not assemble for worship from legal coercion, not from slothful habit, but in the spontaneity of the Spirit. Therefore its service before God does not mark a spasmodic exertion, but a happy privilege. It is true especially of this service designed to praise God that it rests on the gift and the strength which God Himself bestows." (198–99) Worship is our activity, but does not derive from us. God's prevenient sacramental gesture elicits humanity's sacrificial, theocentric gestures in a way which does not exclude human endeavor through words, signs and acts. This is a mystery. "The mystery consists in the fact that our willing, thinking, speaking, and doing no longer derive from ourselves, but are given us, are 'inspired,' and yet are our willing, thinking, speaking, and doing." (199)

What inspired activity does Brunner have in mind? As the congregation's service before God, worship consists of prayer, confession, and glorification.

In considering the first of these Brunner writes, "Prayer presupposes the manifest presence of God. Prayer presupposes that presence of God in which God is present *for us* so that we make speak to Him as He speaks to us. Prayer takes place in the incarnation-presence of God. Prayer takes place in the open door, burst open for us by Christ's cross and resurrection." (200) The sacrificial action of prayer is always responsive to God's sacramental promise, but it is so in two diverse ways, which on first glance may appear contradictory. On the one hand, prayer is elicited from those congregated by God's special presence in proclaimed Word and in Holy Communion. On the other hand, prayer is invoking God for exactly this presence which will in turn elicit prayer. Prayer includes an epicletic address to God wherein God is implored for the gift of this very special presence. The two perspectives are reconciled in that not only prayer elicited from us, but also the very prayer invoking God's presence rests upon God's prior promise. God's incarnation-presence is a pneumatic event, not a mechanical one. Were prayer a mechanical event, then it would function like rubbing Aladdin's lamp to conjure the geni's presence with or without its concord. But as pneumatic event, prayer does not coerce God. In sovereign freedom, God remains free to respond or not, to grant or not—just as God remained free to receive Israel's sacrifice or not, and just as God remains free to receive all of the *ekklesia's* sacrificial movements or not. Worship as prayer includes not only response to God's presence in Word and sacrament, it also includes petition.

True pneumatic prayer is attained when Christ is received through gospel, baptism and Holy Communion. "This prayer is the greatest prerogative of Christians, which God conferred on them as He placed them, justified by faith, into their filial relationship. Prayer is possible only in God's congregational family. Prayer is exercise of the filial privilege in the family of God. . . . Prayer is the permission which God accords His sons to join their voices in the discussion of His affairs." (202)

It would be a misreading of Brunner, although an easy one to make, to suppose that the predominance of the sacramental over the sacrificial pillar means that worship as prayer is exclusively thanksgiving and praise. To the contrary, when Brunner examines prayer he also detects petition as a spirit-filled congregational work which is entirely consonant with the congregation's baptized filial position. The petitionary character of prayer indicates that the congregation is still in *transitus,* still pilgrims. The "not-yet" character of Christian discipleship is indicated distinctively by the fact that the Church's prayer is petition and supplication. As a pilgrim people, the assembly prays for the kingdom of God, prays about the oppression which the Church experiences in its journey, and prays for the world which is the object of God's salvation.

Second, the congregation's service before God includes confession. Confession is related to prayer, but whereas the latter is immediate address to God, the former speaks of God in third person, and it is spoken in public, before others. By confession Brunner means both admission of sin and profession of faith. He notes that the New Testament word *homologein* means simultaneously to confess sin, to profess faith, and to praise God. Before God, before the world, and before itself, the congregation confesses the facts. What are the facts? What is the true situation? That we have sinned in thought, word and deed; that we are lost by reason of our guilt; that we are deserving of wrath and can live

94

only by the grace of forgiveness. What is confessed is not only individual sin but the sin of humanity and of the congregation in all its members. "Confession of sins evidences that the congregation is not a summation of individuals, but a body, a unit, in which all bear one another also in their sin." (205) Such a confession of sin will be possible only where there is a vital confession of faith. Faith is professed first in the very convening of the assembly around the Word and for the purpose of celebrating the Lord's Supper. To do this is a public testimony before the world.

The third component of the congregation's sacrificial service to God is glorification of the Triune God. Brunner has located the worship of those assembled in Jesus' name in the "already—not yet" tension between the kingdom initiated and the kingdom fulfilled. Thus when the congregation glorifies God and professes the dominion of Father, Son and Spirit, it does something that reaches far beyond this earthly time. "The congregation already participates, in its infirmity and stammering imperfection, in what will one day take place, and is already taking place, before the throne of God. This is a 'final' word that we are here trying to express on worship. The entire way of salvation, which God has traversed with man since creation, reaches its goal here. In the realm of the earthly creature, God again finds a mirror here which catches and reflects His glory." (207)

Brunner has distinguished the missionary Word to unbelievers from the anamnetic Word to the *ekklesia* primarily by speaking of the latter as a preservation of the saving apostolic Word. He has claimed that the reason worship remains an obligation after baptism is because God has commanded it, and because the baptized believer also needs to be preserved by God's nourishing and watering Word. Here he adds a third reason for worship in the *ekklesia*: it is participating proleptically in what is the *telos* of all creation. Not only the creatures and angels, but human beings especially were created in order to reflect back God's sacramental grace in sacrificial worship. When the mirror is dirtied by sin, human beings cling to God's ray of glory and treat it as their possession rather than reflecting it back through worship as glorification of the Triune God. Brunner portrays the entire plan-of-salvation as the means through which God restores humanity to its right relationship, therefore the purpose of all God's salvific acts throughout history is climaxed here. Worship as glorification of God takes the form of acclamation, hymn of praise, and *proskynesis*.

By acclamation Brunner means something different from an expression of an inward emotion. It is acknowledging Christ as Lord in the very presence of the Lord. He has in mind the liturgical expressions of the Gloria Patri, short exclamations (Glory to you, O Lord!), the Kyrie, and the Sanctus and Benedictus. By hymns of praise Brunner means that word of the Church about God which is a reflection of God's glory. The hymn of praise is a hymn of victory, the new song of the saints of God, the hymn in which the Church on earth harmonizes with the angels and archangels and all the company of heaven. He mentions the Laudamus, the Gloria in excelsis, the Sanctus and Benedictus, the Te Deum and related songs of praise. By *proskynesis* Brunner does not mean cultic groveling but rather summons the image in Revelations of the elders prostrating themselves, carrying out the *proskynesis*. Luther's translation as *Anbetung* (adoration) is part of the meaning, but the definite feature of falling down before God is connoted by the word. "Where the doxological acclamation is heard, there the physical part of its execution should not be missing . . . it behooves the congregation to drop to its knees even now before the King of kings and the Lord of lords . . . In *proskynesis* also man's body is drawn into his pneumatic response to the event of revelation."[3] The association between *proskynesis* and acclamation is therefore clear: both are done because the King is here and now present to the assembly.

Manifested in these distinct sacrificial actions of acclamation, hymning praise and *proskynesis* is the intertwining of sacrament and sacrifice toward which Brunner has been directing us all along.

"In the proclamation of the Gospel and in the Sacrament of the Altar Jesus Christ approaches us in order to serve us. . . . But

---

3. Brunner, 212. In the footnotes he quotes Luther: "Worship is not a function of the mouth but of the whole body. It is to bow the head, bend the body, fall on the knees, prostrate oneself, and so forth, and to do such things as a sign and acknowledgment of an authority and power. . . ." *Von Anbeten des Sakraments des heiligen Leichnam Christi* (WA 11, 443).

one day He will appear, no longer to serve us, but to receive the *proskynesis* of all creatures. This 'one day' already casts its rays into the worship of the church. . . . The glorification of the Triune God and the adoration of the *Kyrios* Jesus in the church's worship is the only point in the cosmos in which the voice of man unites even now in the indescribable hymn of praise of the angels and the hidden laudation of the nonhuman creatures.'' (212–13)

### DETERMINING WORSHIP'S *USUS*

To review, in part one Brunner has identified the place of worship in God's universal plan of salvation, and in part two he has distinguished two pillars of worship: God's sacramental gesture whereby the human race is reached by God's Word, and humanity's sacrificial gesture which is its response through prayer, confession and glorification. In this Brunner believes himself to have addressed the question of what should be taught in the Church of Jesus Christ relative to that assembly which we call *Gottesdienst:* the worship service. But the reader will remember that Brunner has assigned himself a further task. The answer to this doctrinal question will determine, he said, what the leaders of the Reformation termed the proper *usus* of worship. Without a correct doctrine of worship, he claims, we will never arrive at worship's proper *usus*. In part three of Brunner's study he therefore addresses quite pragmatic questions regarding (a) the dogmatic basis of the form of worship, and (b) the materialization of the form. If dogmatics serves the Church, then the upshot of this investigation of worship should yield guidelines for the conduct of worship. Not only can we find a doctrine of worship in the practice of worship, but the practice of worship must be determined by the guidelines of worship.

Like Vajta, whose work is cited in a footnote at this point, Brunner believes that ''the Reformation has demonstrated impressively that far-reaching dogmatic decisions are involved in the manner in which we appraise the form of worship and especially in the concrete form in which we conduct worship. Consequently, there must be a doctrine of the form of worship.'' (217) Since worshipers are corporeal creatures, worship is carried out by means of concrete acts which necessarily stipulate order and form. Brunner

proposes to advise about the way in which the Word is proclaimed and Holy Communion is distributed, even though "under
no circumstances may we conceive of the form of worship as a
legal-ritual regulation." (219) The outward framework can never
be treated as a condition for salvation. It is enough for the unity
of the Church to agree on the doctrine of the gospel and the administration of the sacraments; it is not necessary that human traditions (rites and ceremonies) be everywhere alike. There is a
required form, but beyond this there is eschatological liberty.

What constitutes the former and what the latter? Brunner lists
three elements of form which are required by reason of Christ's
institution: (a) the Word of God must be proclaimed—i.e., the witness of Christ as contained in Scripture must be publicized in the
proclaiming word; (b) Holy Communion must be celebrated by the
congregation in conformity with Christ's institution—i.e., Jesus
and his Meal commemorated in prayer and thanksgiving, and the
elements distributed and eaten and drunk; (c) these must be carried out in a gathering convened in the name of Jesus—i.e., the
assembly's intention is worship by invocation of the Triune God.
These three elements of form have been enacted by human communities in a variety of ways, and Brunner does not deny their
historical variety and development. "It would . . . reflect an utter
misunderstanding of the Word-bound nature of the form of worship if we were to subject this form to a liturgical Biblicism. Our
demand that the words [and signs] of worship correspond from
beginning to end with the testimony of prophets and apostles
does not imply that only Biblical words or the linguistic style of
the Bible be used in an order of worship. No, the Gospel and the
Holy Spirit do not insist on liturgical Biblicism." (224)

The assembly stands in the width between what is absolutely
commanded and what is absolutely forbidden, but, again, "No divisions in Christendom dare arise over the question of form of
worship within this wide area." (225) There are guidelines for the
pneumatic appropriateness of word and sign, but no commands
for uniformity. Brunner repeats his threefold guidelines thus: the
form of worship must be appropriate to the fact that this worship
is an assembly in the name of Jesus, that the Gospel's proclamation is being heard here, and that the command "Do this in
remembrance of me" is being obeyed. The actual form of worship

is a free, Spirit-wrought conjunction of these commanded elements. The connection between word/sign and what word/sign designates is neither logical nor arbitrary; it should be pneumatically appropriate. "That which is to be designated by the form of worship is certainly no eternal, immutable idea, but the unchangeable historical commission of Jesus Christ, the immutability of which reflects the uniqueness and the contingency of revelation." (228) This permits wide ecumenism. As Luther rejected both the legalism of Rome on the one hand, and the legalism of the Enthusiasts on the other, so Brunner insists that the Church must always approach with due respect and reverence all traditions within Christendom which do not conflict with the threefold criteria mentioned above. Formal traditionalism is a poor principle for liturgical forms, but standing in fear of tradition is not necessarily a sign of freedom. As love rules all charisms, so love rules the form of worship.

This dogmatic foundation of form and order in worship is materialized in a basic and ecumenically shared form. A doctrine of worship yields a form for worship, as follows. "If any form of worship may lay claim to ecumenical character, it is the one in which the following basic order is observed: After an introductory invocation, God's Word is presented to the congregation by the reading of Scripture and by the sermon; the congregation submits its petitions to God; it collects the thankofferings; and amid thanksgiving it celebrates the Lord's Supper." (234)

Brunner pauses to mention and critique a few means by which this basic form might be expressed in the assembly's worship. From what he has said it is understood that liturgical ministers are required. Each of those who assemble in the name of Jesus for *Gottesdienst* have a role (all need not do everything, neither is any one required to do everything), but if the assembly is to be liturgically confronted by God's Word, a bearer must proclaim it for hearers to hear. As this liturgical confrontation is manifold, so many play a role: lectors, choir, petitioners, assisting ministers, etc. The liturgy may be done in elementary simplicity or with elaborate richness by abridging or expanding certain parts in the basic order in accord with the Church year. And within the basic materialization of the form of worship there is also a tension between what is constant and what is changing. Brunner thinks the history of worship demonstrates that some traditions have employed great change, others little at all, and some have struck a well-balanced mean. He identifies the almost complete exclusion of all change with the Eastern Church, and the almost complete change of all parts with the Gallican form of the Mass. Rome's compromise of a constant Ordinary with a limited changing Proper is another option, and one which was retained by the Wittenberg Reformation. Offering an analysis of the situation of his Lutheran tradition Brunner writes,

"If we were asked where the greater danger lies, in too much emphasis on the constant or on the changing, the history of liturgy would reply—and experience to date confirms this—that the Germanic peoples are especially prone, by their predilection for change and for emphasis of the individual aspects of the salvation-event, to jeopardize an appropriate order of worship. Allied with this, we find the present-day inclination to compress all the texts of every worship service into unified themes." (241–42).

Brunner also devotes a number of pages to considering what role art plays in the materialization of this form of worship. "In the case of the time-bound play, the material for the form is the word of speech, the musically animated tone, and the gesture; in the case of space-bound ornamentation, it is composed of space outlined by construction of plastic form, of line and color." (261) An artistic contribution to the liturgy will serve worship so long as the artistic word and sign do not obtrude in worship. This is true of all the forms which art takes: rhetorical eloquence in the sermon, the text of prayer, poetry, the orderly liturgical word spoken by the congregation, the hymn which is elevated speech of the heart elevated once again to God by the Spirit, music, the manipulation of light and the visual impact of plastic arts and ornamentation, the architectural form of the house of worship, etc. In all these, the Gospel word must be perceived in, and not be clouded by, the symbol. Brunner sees liturgical art as capable of expressing the doctrine of worship once it has been explicated.

Brunner has thus offered the reader a few pragmatic suggestions of how the *usus* of worship can be achieved and enhanced. He has one more form to consider in worship, namely, the form of the administration of the sacrament. He has already affirmed that

Holy Communion should always be celebrated in connection with the Liturgy of the Word, never in isolation. But what words must be spoken in the administration of communion? Should the words recite the institution command or may they be in the form of prayer? Luther inherited a tradition which reckoned the words of institution essential for consecrating the elements. "With an unprecedented, but obviously intended, radicalism he [drew] the final liturgical conclusion for the organization of the rite of the sacrament" (292) when he advocated detaching the Mass, entirely and completely, from the prayers and gestures added by tradition. The words of institution may—nay, must—be excised from the Roman Canon in order to liberate what Christ instituted from the Roman Mass. "For Luther, the words of institution and the distribution of the elements constitute the Sacrament of the Altar. With regard to the emphasis on the power effective in the words of institution, Luther is the finisher of this Occidental doctrine, which dates back to Augustine, the doctrine of the exclusive power of the words of Christ in the administration of the sacrament." (292)

However, Brunner reminds us of the principle for judging the pneumatic appropriateness of liturgical words. Fidelity to the position of the Reformation, he says, requires that this principle be based not on liturgical biblicism but on evangelical organization. Even in Luther's *Deutsche Messe* one can discern anamnetic words, words of thanksgiving and praise, and prayer in preparation for receiving the sacrament. That is, "the words of institution and the distribution of elements are surrounded and accompanied by words which the church does not speak in the person of Christ, but in its own person." (294) Therefore the Church today is at liberty to ask itself whether its situation does not demand a different, a more highly developed arrangement of those elements which are also contained in Luther's order of the Mass, the elements of anamnesis, thanksgiving and praise. Brunner answers in the affirmative. He finds it not only permissible, but imperative that evangelical Churches return to an ecumenical type of the sacrament's celebration, namely to a Eucharistic prayer. Holy Communion is certainly a meal, but the meal at which Jesus presided and which he entrusts to the Church was one which offered to God a hallowing blessing: a *berakah* or *eulogia*. "If the church is intent on doing what Christ did in instituting the Meal, it will not neglect the *eulogia*. . . . [The elements become Holy Communion] by the blessing spoken over it, and this blessing is unquestionably prayer, glorifying, anamnetic prayer of thanksgiving." (296) To recite the words of institution within prayer form is not a betrayal of Reformation principles.

Brunner's theology of worship, which he has derived from worship practice, culminates then in an attempt to express how the Church should pray over bread and wine. He offers the following guidelines: in accord with Christ's example the Church should not only pronounce the words of institution but pray in words of grateful, anamnetic praise; the words of institution should project prominently in their special function; a consecratory prayer is possible and appropriate preceding Christ's words; it is appropriate to join the spoken anamnesis to the words of institution; petition for the salutary reception of the gifts should not be left to the priest as individual but expressed in the liturgical We; the congregation may pray for the perfection of the body of Christ; and this action of blessing begins with the preface and is best concluded with the Lord's Prayer. When the doctrine of worship, taking account of the texts and activities of worship, is thus clarified, worship can achieve its proper *usus*.

### b. *Geoffrey Wainwright*, Doxology

One receives a fuller indication of what Wainwright reckons himself to be doing from the subtitle of this work which reads, *Doxology. The Praise of God in Worship, Doctrine and Life: A Systematic Theology*.[4] This is, then, a systematic theology which tries to take doxology seriously as it is present in worship, doctrine and life. He describes it as a "liturgical way of doing theology" because in his opinion the thread of worship must be woven into the fabric of the Church's life and thought. The theme has long occupied Wainwright's attention, evidenced in many articles and especially in an earlier book entitled *Eucharist and Eschatology*. He described the aim of this earlier book as developing

4. Geoffrey Wainwright, *Doxology* (New York: Oxford University Press, 1980). We hope that our punctuation correctly communicates his intent; there is none on the title page.

"in a systematic way the more or less isolated insights into the eschatological character of the eucharist displayed by the liturgies and the earlier theologians.

. . . [T]he eucharist should figure among the interests of all the various disciplines of Christian theology: our understanding of the eucharist should be aided by all the theological disciplines as they apply themselves to its study from their own particular angle, *and (in the reverse direction)* the eucharistic phenomenon itself should help to shape the total outlook of the various theological disciplines."[5]

In much systematic theology the current flows in only one direction, that direction being from the various disciplines to the Eucharistic event; in *Eucharist* Wainwright was trying to also reverse that flow such that the Eucharist helps to shape the understanding and agenda of the various theological disciplines.

Nine years later, in *Doxology*, Wainwright repeats his claim, now in a broader and more explicit way. In this later work he says he is trying "on a broader canvas" the liturgical way of doing theology which he attempted in his earlier work and, what is of particular interest for us, the center of *Doxology* contains explicit reflection upon the interrelationship between theology (*lex credendi*) and worship (*lex orandi*). For this reason, we have chosen to deal here with his later work.

*Doxology* may be taken in two ways, Wainwright says. It is primarily intended as a systematic theology written from a liturgical perspective, but it can also be considered a theology of worship. Throughout the work Wainwright provides frequent apologetic for the need and fruitfulness of such an approach. This is clearly asserted in the preface. "My conviction is that the relations between doctrine and worship are deeper rooted and further reaching than many theologians and liturgists have appeared to recognize in their writings. In recent years there has indeed been a growing awareness of the links between worship and doctrine, but writers have still usually stopped short after a paragraph or two on the subject. Certainly I know of no complete systematic theology deliberately composed with these links in mind." (Pre-

5. Geoffrey Wainwright, *Eucharist and Eschatology* (London: Epworth Press, 1971). Underscoring mine.

face) He repeats this claim in a later footnote. First he reiterates that he "knows of no other complete systematic theology written from a liturgical perspective," (his note 12) and then he provides a bibliography of what he calls theologies of worship, citing works by J. J. von Allmen, *Worship in the Name of Jesus* by Peter Brunner, F. W. Dillistone, W. Hahn, J. A. Kay, E. J. Lengeling, *Introduction to Liturgical Theology* by Alexander Schmemann, E. Underhill, C. Vagaggini, P. Verghese, A. Verheul, N. Clark, J. D. Crichton, B. Häring, F. J. Leenhardt, O. C. Quick, and J. L. Segundo. (In this list he does not mention our other two authors, Vajta and Prenter, but does refer to them later as examples of treatments on Luther's theology of worship). In other words, he evidently understands his work to be a unique sample of what he calls a liturgical way of doing theology. What does Wainwright mean by a systematic theology written from a liturgical perspective, his own efforts being the sole representative of this class?

SYSTEMATIC THEOLOGY FROM A LITURGICAL PERSPECTIVE

Wainwright acknowledges that theology is an intellectual activity, yet he wants to point out that "the sources and resources of theology are richer than the human intellect. . . . In so far as the theologian is a believer, his thinking cannot be disengaged from his faith. His faith engages him as a total person, so that even his intellectual reflexion *upon* his faith is, dialectically and within the unity of his personality, still an activity *of* faith. . . . [The theologian's] intellect is at the service of his existential vision and commitment." (1) This is to say that a theologian's intellectual reflection, if it is in service to the Church, is conditioned not merely by rational constraints but also by the activity and belief structures of the faith community in which he or she stands. The specific task of the theologian lies in the realm of doctrine, defined as "a coherent intellectual expression of the Christian vision" (3), but this vision which the theologian tries to express in a coherent intellectual way derives from a larger source. It is true that the theologian will utilize logical argument in theological formulation, "but the total vision has other roots in life and experience. My own vision of faith is firmly shaped and strongly coloured by the Christian liturgy. It is this comprehensive vision which the present book seeks to express in the genre of a systematic theology." (1)

A liturgical way of doing theology is when doctrine is shaped and colored by Christian liturgy.

Theology will inevitably be individual expression because it is done by individuals, however it is not individualistic since the theologian is a member of a community that shares a common vision. And just where is this vision found with greatest force and clarity? In worship. "Worship is the place in which that vision comes to a sharp focus, a concentrated expression, and it is here that the vision has often been found to be at its most appealing. The theologian's thinking therefore properly draws on the worship of the Christian community and is in duty bound to contribute to it." (3) The point which Wainwright believes he uniquely accents is that the intelligent activity of theologians cannot be divorced from their experiential matrix. While this matrix includes both the larger human and the smaller Christian communities, and while the theologian may dialectically use language from both communities, the vision itself is focused and expressed in ritual worship and if one is struggling to make intelligible expression of the Christian vision, then that is where one must begin. Theology done in a liturgical way is theology which acknowledges its resourcement in the experience of worship.

We called Brunner's work a theology from worship because the doctrine of worship in the name of Jesus was obtained by looking at certain of its moments. We call Wainwright's work a theology from worship for this reason and also for an additional one. He considers this doctrine of worship to be liturgical because it is obtained from out of the existential experience of the Christian community in which the theologian, as believer, participates. This is not strictly contrary to Brunner, since he also advocated looking not only at texts but at the activity of worship, but the center of gravity has shifted. Wainwright's specific concern is to chart the intimate connection between a theologian's thought and experience, or between the systematic interpretation of the Christian vision and worship's place as the living experience of that vision. "Put simply, the claim is that a historical community, in this case the Christian church, can transmit a vision of reality which helps decisively in the interpretation of life and the world." (2)

Brunner and Wainwright agree, however, that the current flows in both directions: from worship to doctrine and also back again from doctrine to worship. Wainwright recognizes the focal position and function of worship as it provides the theologian with the subject matter to reflect upon, but he is not thereby denying theology's guardian role over worship. The theologian should examine the liturgy from the angle of doctrine "both in order to learn from it and in order to propose to the worshiping community any corrections or improvements which he judges neccessary." (3) As believer the theologian participates in the Christian community's application of its vision to interpret and change the world of humanity, but the theologian's intellectual task further obliges him or her "to measure up the vision and the application in order to propose to the Christian community the most effective ways of allowing its vision to illuminate and transform reality to the advantage of all humanity." (3–4)

To recap, doctrine is the coherent intellectual expression of the Christian vision. This expression is intellectual and reflexive, but the total vision has deeper roots as well, roots in life and experience. Worship is the "point of concentration at which the whole of the Christian life comes to ritual focus."[6] Therefore the systematic theology of the Christian vision which Wainwright here offers is one which has been firmly shaped and strongly coloured by the Christian liturgy: theology from worship.

This, then, gives the book its tripart structure. It first deals with substantial matters (a sketch of the Christian vision as Wainwright perceives it now within the historic Christian community), second with traditional means (a formal examination of the instruments of Christian tradition, or the means by which the vision is transmitted through time) and third with contextual questions (questions posed by the Christian and human context in which the vision is expressed). Our primary interest lies in part two, for here Wainwright gives his most explicit explanation of liturgy's influence on theology and theology's influence on liturgy. We will, however, review his work in part one, not only for the reason which stood

6. Wainwright, 8. Wainwright mentions that his use of the word "ritual" is not pejorative, as in "merely ritual." "On my sense of the word, even those communities which pride themselves on their freedom from 'ritual' will generally be found to use ritual; only they will not be aware of it, and so will be unable either to enjoy its pleasure to the full or to be properly vigilant about its dangers."

behind our look at Prenter, Vajta and Brunner, i.e., to observe what is the content of those works which are sometimes called a "liturgical theology"; we will review it for an additional reason as well. Wainwright claims that "Into the liturgy the people bring their entire existence so that it may be gathered up in praise. From the liturgy the people depart with a renewed vision of the value-patterns of God's kingdom, by the more effective practice of which they intend to glorify God in their whole life." (8) For the theologian, "one's whole life" also means one's thought. Wainwright will affirm that at its own level theology is doxological. This systematic theology will find worship, doctrine and life—all three—liturgical in the sense of rendering praise to God. In the case of the second in that triology, one can then say that theology is at its own level and in its own way doxological. (This is how he will interpret the eastern dictum that theology, properly understood, is prayer.) Part one of *Doxology* examines four substantial components of the Christian vision: creation, Christ, Spirit and Church. How will the Christian vision, ritually expressed in worship, shape and color these substantial doctrines? What do they, in turn, contribute to worship? We will be cursory in our review of the content in order to highlight the methodology.

### THE CHRISTIAN VISION OF CREATION

The Christian vision of creation essentially proposes that human beings are created in the image of God. In biblical exegesis there are three main strands to this: to be in the image of God is to be endowed with the possibility of communing with God (even if in sin humanity forfeits the actuality); the earthly task assigned to humanity is to use God's gift of natural creation properly, which is humanity's royal and priestly function; and to be capable of receiving and returning divine love implies human love for each other. The heart of social being is love, whether human or divine, so the image of God in humanity is the God-given capacity to love and implies the vocation of exercising brotherly and sisterly love. In sum, being in God's image and likeness entails a call to commune with God, the task to administer the earth on God's behalf, and a vocation to imitate the loving character of God. All three strands, Wainwright says, are woven into Christian worship.

Relationship of the human person to God, earth and neighbor is affirmed on the level of doctrine, and experienced on the level of worship. Being in the image of God means men and women are capable of rendering God glory by a kind of reflection. Communion with God, which worship is, is experienced as the enjoyment of God. "This communion with God, symbolically focused in liturgy, is the primary locus of religious language for the Christian. *Theological* language belongs to the second order: it is the language of reflexion upon the primary experience. The language of worship mediates the substance on which theologians reflect; without that substance, theological talk would have no referent." (21) What theologians speak about is the primary experience, it is the substance of theological speech, but worship is where this substance is experienced as primary. The substance itself, says Wainwright, is mediated through the language of worship in three ways: a shared universe of discourse which in this case is the Christian grammar kept before the community in worship; a language game wherein the assembly enters into conversation with the God who is creator and redeemer; and a logic of action (events and bodily gestures) since God calls into communion with himself an embodied humanity. Being in the image of God, humanity is endowed with the possibility of communing with God in speech and act. This is experienced in worship, mediated through the language of worship, and in turn spoken about in second-order theological language.

"Yet the 'architectonic' and 'critical' functions of theological reasoning, secondary though that reasoning is in relation to substantial communion with God, play a proper part in shaping and pruning the continuing primary experience. For *reflective* reason is part of God's endowment to humanity. . . . The second-order activity of theology is therefore, at its own level, properly doxological. . . . It is indeed a traditional dictum in Eastern Christianity that the true theologian is the person who prays." (21)

Theology is from worship, yet worship is shaped and pruned by theology.

Worship reveals to the theologian the character of God the Creator, which should therefore be expressed in doctrine in so far as it is the coherent, intellectual expression of the Christian vision.

Wainwright proposes that "the character of God, his intention for humanity, his action to achieve his purpose and the human response to God's vocation are all expressed, by words and gestures, in the various 'moods' of the Christian liturgy." (32) He lists eight of them: adoration, confession of sin, proclamation and thanksgiving, commitment, intercession, expectation, absence (in the sense of a perceived and expressed distance from God), and wrestling in prayer. Humanity's vocation to administer the world by ministering to the earth is experienced by the Sabbath character of worship and the employ of human artistic creativity in liturgy. Humanity's social obligation of love is experienced in baptism as entry into a new set of relationships; it is experienced as agape within the community both in the pre-Eucharistic sharing of the peace and in the communion; and it is expressed outside the community by distributing the thank offering to the needy.

### THE CHRISTIAN VISION OF CHRIST

By worship itself we are thus brought back to Jesus as the paradigm of worship. The doctrine of creation leads to Christology as the paradigmatic restoration of creation. Christology is the second substantial matter with which Wainwright deals.

In contemporary Christology the issue which seems to have commanded attention is a demand for coherence and economy, i.e., how can we explain Jesus' simultaneous divinity and humanity? And in what way is Jesus the Christ? Wainwright wishes to exercise his methodology at this point as well: ". . . coherence, perhaps, and economy certainly, are not the most obvious characteristics of worship, even Christian worship. It will therefore be interesting and important to relate the theological reflexion of these doctrinal critics to the first-order activity of worship. The subject of christology offers a vital example, both historically and systematically, of the interaction between worship, doctrine and theology." (45) Under Wainwright's scheme, to know the function of Jesus as mediator between God and humanity will require specifying how these questions come to expression in worship. Modern Christology's "neuralgic point," as he calls it, has been the issue of Christ's divinity; but the liturgical starting point for dealing with this problematic is to observe Christ as object of worship. To ask what is the central place of Jesus is to ask what is Jesus' central place in worship.

When the community worships, Christ is confessed, invoked, and prayed to as Lord. This cultic confession is Christology incipient. Wainwright digresses through a history of early Christology, noting that when popular piety addressed prayers to Christ there was an initial reaction to downplay Christ's divinity in order to protect monotheism. Thus the Christologies of modalism, dynamic monarchianism (Paul of Samosata), Origen and Arius. But with the Athanasian victory over Arianism and the spread of the Nicene category *homoousion*, the way was opened not only to address the Father through the Son but also to address the Son directly. "The frequency of collects addressed to the Son in surviving gallican and mozarabic texts indicates a keenness on the part of Catholics to score against the persistent arianism of the visigothic rulers in Gaul and Spain." (52–53) Throughout the Middle Ages, even though the canon of the Mass adhered to the classical pattern of addressing God the Father through Christ, in para-liturgical hymns and prayers and processions the Church continued worship of Christ as the divine Son.

However, alongside Christ's place as object of worship in liturgy, we can also discern in worship Christ's function as mediator. "It is not only as mediating human worship to God that Christ figures in the liturgy: he also figures as the mediator of divine blessings to humanity." (64) Is Christ the only mediator of God's blessings? This modern problem has also commanded volumes of attention. Wainwright proposes that we need not fence the activity of God solely within Christian boundaries with an "exclusive-inclusive" alternative or with a "culture-bound/imperialist" attitude. Wherever self-giving love is shown by human beings, wherever people are set free from self-regard and self-interest, God can be said to be present because there redemption is happening and salvation is being tasted. It might then be said that the mediatorial function of Christ in worship bears symbolic witness to God's Christ-pattern in the world, and Wainwright's theology from worship sheds some light on this problem, too. If we speak of Christ as "pattern for worship and therefore for life" our predominantly cultic definition of sacrament is also transformed. "The sacraments may . . . be seen as the ritual expression of a pattern which is set by Christ and whose intended scope is nothing less than the universal divine kingdom." (70) The Christ-pattern, which is God's way in the world, comes to expression in the principal rites of the Church, and Wainwright deals briefly with each of them in turn: baptism, confirmation, penance, unction of the sick, orders, marriage and Eucharist.

When one observes the pattern of God's activity in these ritual expressions, one finds a clue also to the riddle of interventionism. The mediatorial role of Christ in the sacraments of worship provides a clue to understanding God's intervention in the world: God works from within, not from outside, the creation; God does not quasi-magically interfere in creation but rather when God presents himself it is an interpersonal event; and one should conceive of God's actions less in spatial terms and more in terms of values. This is another example of Wainwright's thesis that theology done in a liturgical way has bearing on systematic theological questions, in this case, the relationship between grace and freedom. This would lead us to a doctrine of the Holy Spirit.

Before continuing on to pneumatology, however, we return to highlight an earlier affirmation by Wainwright that "in [the] Church's confession and cultus of Jesus as the exalted Lord and Christ, lay the essential elements of all later Christology."[7] Here Wainwright is proposing that the doctrine of Christ derives from worship of Christ. But we have seen all along that in his opinion the flow of current runs in both directions, and that theology should in turn guide and form worship. We are then not surprised when, at this juncture in his historical recount of Christological development, he inserts a systematic embolism to clarify the relationship between the language of worship and the language of theological reflection.[8]

7. The quote is from A. M. Hunter, *Paul and his Predecessors* (London: SCM, 1961) 82, but Wainwright affirms it sympathetically as his own position. Further, H. E. W. Turner is cited: "That Jesus was Lord and therefore to be worshipped is the 'given,' more fundamental than any doctrine, from which Christology starts, but in the long run it required a doctrine to explain and support it. . . . This is the starting point of Christology, not the goal which the theologian hopes to reach." *Jesus the Christ* (Oxford: Mowbray, 1976) 1.

8. Wainwright remarks, "There are hints here of how Wiles would apply the principles of 'doctrinal criticism' to worship both as a creative factor in the

His partner in dialogue here is Maurice Wiles who cautions,

"Undoubtedly the practice of prayer has had its effect on doctrine; undoubtedly the practice of prayer *should* have its effect on doctrine. But that is not to say that the effect which prayer has actually had is at every point precisely the effect which it should have had. . . . At the point where the worship of Christ was of decisive significance for the development of doctrine, it was a question of popular devotion rather than formal liturgical worship. Popular devotion is not without significance but it is no infallible guide."[9]

Doctrine, as the coherent and intellectual articulation of the Christian vision, must necessarily derive from where that Christian vision is experienced in sharpest focus, namely, worship. We saw that the language of worship mediates the substance on which theologians reflect; without that substance, theological talk would have no referent. But on the other hand, "from the outset, it must be granted that it is a legitimate and indeed salutary task to apply critical theological reason to the realm of Christian worship." (56) We find examples of this even within the New Testament (the altering of the Colossians Christ hymn, Hellenistic revisions of baptismal theology, eschatological qualification of mistaken antinomianism) and Wainwright points to Reformation theologians as examples of people whose doctrinal understanding applied a theological critique to the practice of worship as they knew it.

What we are faced with is the question of how language and belief inside the Christian liturgy are related to Christian language and belief outside the liturgy. In Wainwright's opinion, "There needs to be at least a consistency, if not an identity, between the belief expressed in worship and the belief expressed in the forms of reflective theology. This is necessary on two scores: first, because worship and theology are both 'intending' a single object, namely the truth of God; and second, because worship and the-

earlier formation of doctrine and as a continuing mode of maintaining and transmitting it. In the nature of the case, we need to begin with historical description. We can now pursue in more systematic terms our discussion of the relations between worship, doctrine and theology, taking Wiles as our principal partner in dialogue." (55)

9. Cited, 54; from Maurice Wiles, *The Making of Christian Doctrine* (Cambridge: University Press, 1967), 93.

ology are each occupations which engage the person of the one who practices both." (57) One acknowledges that liturgical language, compared with the language of theological reflection, is more typically and appropriately poetic, but what does one do when there is an incongruity between one's own belief and the belief that is expressed in the liturgy in which one participates? (As Wainwright pointedly notes, that liturgy is poetic language is hardly license for holding that one may be a Trinitarian within the charmed circle of the liturgy and a Unitarian in the academic study.)

"If [the theologian] is convinced of the truth of his own position, he may seek to alter the worship, and thereby the belief, of the community with which he is associated. . . . On the other hand, the individual may judge it wiser to let the inherited and continuing pattern of the community's worship and belief impress itself 'correctively' on his own tentative position. Whether in the one direction or the other, it is clear that integrity requires a movement towards congruity." (58)

Theology is from worship, but theology is architectonic to worship.


### THE CHRISTIAN VISION OF THE SPIRIT

The third substantial matter to be dealt with is pneumatology. After a brief look at the place accorded the Spirit in Scripture and early Church practice, Wainwright identifies three pneumatological patterns in worship. First, the Spirit acts transformingly. The possible communion between God and men and women created in God's image is actualized by the Holy Spirit when human character and conduct is shaped according to the divine model and purpose. This is reflected liturgically in confirmation prayers and in prayers at the ordination of presbyters, deacons and bishops. Second, the Spirit functions as enabler of worship. Worship takes place in the Holy Spirit, expressed liturgically in the pattern of prayer addressed to the Father, through Christ, in the Holy Spirit. But alongside this emphasis, a third pneumatological pattern may be discerned wherein prayer or worship is addressed to the Spirit, either with the other persons of the Trinity or separately, particularly in baptismal practice. Wainwright asks whether the full Trinitarian doctrine was a necessary development from the baptismal practice and concedes this might be overstating the case, yet "does not all this in the long run *imply* the position which Athanasius and Basil will make explicit? . . . [T]hey argued that Christ *needed* to be divine in order to reveal and to redeem, and that the Holy Spirit *needed* to be divine in order to sanctify and to divinize." (99) At stake is a soteriological concern which drives both Christology and pneumatology toward fuller Trinitarian doctrine. The question is to what extent God needs to be engaged with the world in order to bring humanity to the kind of salvation God intends. Athanasius' response was that Christ had to be divine to reveal and redeem, and the Spirit has to be divine to sanctify and divinize. "If the 'economy' is read and experienced in a trinitarian way, then there is so much grounding for 'immanent trinitarianism'. . . ."[10]

Wainwright has tried to historically establish a liturgical link between pneumatology and Trinitarian doctrine. He next considers the matter systematically by observing how the Spirit dimension in worship affects four matters in the area of soteriology, and three in the area of ecclesiology.

In the Church's worship there is a strong Christological coloring to pneumatology which comes to expression in liturgical epiclesis, particularly the invocation of the Spirit upon the waters in baptism and upon the elements in Holy Communion. In the Church's worship the gift of the Spirit is manifested in the self-giving love of the worshippers which is a response to God's self-giving love through the Spirit. The Spirit's presence in the worship of the Church confirms or seals that God's purpose is coming closer to achievement, and the place of the saints in the Church's worship is an acknowledgement that the Holy Spirit was at work in their lives and persons. It is due to a perceived pneumatological presence in their lives that they are venerated, addressed for help in

10. Wainwright, 100. He again cites Wiles sympathetically (98) when Wiles writes "when little theological interest was shown in the person of the Spirit, it was the continuing fact of baptismal practice which did most to keep alive the idea of the Spirit as a third alongside the Father and the Son." *The Making of Christian Doctrine*, 80.

prayer, function as examples for holy living, and the whole liturgy is considered to take place in communion with the saints already glorified in heaven. From all these worship activities—epiclesis, transformed lives, eschatological promise of the kingdom, and communion with the saints—a doctrine of the Holy Spirit is derived.

Furthermore, from the Spirit's place in worship are derived three ecclesiological tenets. In the liturgy it is the Spirit's presence which transforms the Mass as institution into the event of Christ's presence. Again, this is the significance of the epicletic moment and, as the Orthodox valuably point out, the waning of a pneumatological epiclesis in the Catholic rite is "symptomatic of a more general undervaluing of the Spirit in Western thought and experience." (113) This casts light upon two dialectics in ecclesiology, that between structure and liberty and that between unity and pluralism. With this observation Wainwright has effected his transition to the final substantial matter, a doctrine of the Church.

Before turning to it, however, we pause to clarify what Wainwright has tried to accomplish. His thesis was that substantial matters of systematic theology, coherently and intellectually expressed as Christian doctrine, derive from the larger Christian vision as brought to concentrated focus in worship. To make good on this claim, he had to both indicate historically and explain systematically the connections between worship and Christology, and between worship and pneumatology.

In other words (ours, not his), what the theologian as believer experiences in worship is what the believer as theologian expresses in doctrine. Regarding Christology, the theologian as believer experiences Christ as both object of and mediator in worship, and experiences the vision of the Christ-pattern in ritual worship with sharp focus, concentrated expression, and in a form often appealing. The believer as theologian unpacks this in a coherent and intellectual Christology. Regarding pneumatology, the theologian as believer experiences the Holy Spirit in the event of worship as the prerequisite for saving communion with God. This comes to ritual expression in a pneumatological epiclesis in varied circumstances: upon the water in baptism, upon penitents being reconciled to the Church, upon ministers being ordained, and upon the elements and assembly in the Eucharist. The believer as theologian unpacks this in a coherent and intellectual pneumatology. Theology is from worship.

THE CHRISTIAN VISION OF CHURCH

Doctrines of Creation, Christ, and Spirit lead with a certain inevitability, says Wainwright, to a fourth substantial subject, the Church, because the human vocation of communion bears a social character, and because Christ attracted disciples to be a community of his presence, and because the Spirit continues to transform and enable people to conform to the Christ-pattern for the achievement of the kingdom. Wainwright begins with an anthropology of signs, examines the four marks which Nicea says characterize the Church, and concludes with practical questions about the composition of the Church. All this is viewed "from the perspective of the liturgy."

From out of recent investigation of the phenomenology of ritual, Wainwright gives this functional definition: "A recurrent function of religious ritual is to put successive generations in dramatic touch with an archetypal story which accounts for the present order of the people or the world. Representation, by word and deed, of a primal event asserts the foundational value of that event and allows late-comers to participate in its benefits and commit themselves to the maintenance of the established order." (119) Most religions center ritual around rhythms of nature and culture and even dateless mythical events among the gods. Israel's ritual is distinctive in that although they derive from agricultural rhythms, the Old Testament has historicized the cultic observances so that now instead of permanent repetition there comes the expectation of a new deliverance. This deliverance will be historically novel, even though it is patterned after the first. It is into this context that Jesus came, and out of this context that early Christian ritual developed, for they saw in Jesus "the beginning of the end." Particularly at baptism and in the meal, the Church expressed ritually the fact that a new age had dawned. It continues to initiate catechumens into this reality and recapitulate this reality in the lives of communicants. Christian rituals are transformative in character because the Church is a pilgrim community on its way to becoming the people of God's final kingdom.

For this reason the liturgical creed confesses the Church as one, holy, catholic and apostolic—imperfectly enjoyed now, but communicated in the sacramental rituals with judgment and forgiveness. Disunity among Christians is a sinful absurdity, for the community is grounded in Christological and soteriological unity. The Church is holy on three counts: it is the people of God, it is the body of Christ, and it is indwelt by the Holy Spirit. The Church is catholic because the Christological and soteriological claims made by Christians are an implied vocation of catholicity. Christ will draw all men and women to himself when he is lifted up, both in suffering on the cross and in glory when the Father gives him the name above every name. As catholic, the Church is necessarily apostolic.

These, then, are the four substantial issues with which Wainwright deals in part one of his work: creation, Christology, pneumatology and ecclesiology. If as a historical community the Church transmits a vision of reality by which it interprets life, and if worship is the place where that vision comes to sharp focus and concentrated expression, and if in doctrine theologians present not versions of their individualistic vision but a coherent intellectual expression of the Christian vision, then one would expect to find doctrines of creation, Christ, the Holy Spirit and the Church ensconced in worship. Wainwright has tried in part one to make this clear, both by historical example and systematic elaboration. This book is proferred as a liturgical way of doing theology; it therefore looked at creation, Christology, pneumatology and ecclesiology through the lens of liturgy.

### CHRISTIAN TRADITION: SCRIPTURE

In part two of the book Wainwright turns his attention to the lens itself. He no longer looks through the lens at substantial systematic theology, he now looks at the lens itself. He supplies a formal examination of the instruments of Christian tradition, that is, an examination of the means by which the vision is transmitted through time. These means are Scripture, Creed and hymn, and *lex orandi*.

Scripture functions in the Church as sacred book. Its special character is acknowledged in the liturgy by the special ritual recognition it is accorded, even down to how it is handled and where it is placed. "Both in its resting position and even more in its liturgical use, the Bible as an actual book serves as some kind of sacrament of the Word of God."[11] While Scripture's place in worship is not undervalued, Wainwright takes an approach which seems designed to impress the reader with the methodology of theology from worship. He reverses the usual question about the presence of Scripture in liturgy to inquire about the presence of liturgy in the Scripture.

He first invokes biblical scholarship to remind systematic theologians of the ways in which worship contributed to the formulation and transmission of the material that came to be deposited in Scripture. As examples from the Old Testament, he points out that Von Rad detects an ancient liturgical confession in the hexateuch; post-Exilic Passover practice influenced the textual Passover account; scholars on the prophets have reevaluated the earlier assumption of antagonism between the cult and the prophet's cry, finding not a criticism of sacrificial worship as such but of cult which did not issue in social righteousness; and the liturgical origin of the psalms is an obvious case of liturgy in Scripture. As examples from the New Testament, form and redaction criticism have revolutionized modern reading of the text by making us always cognizant of the *sitz im leben*; form criticism particularly has identified various types of liturgical material in the text: confessions, hymns, prayers, and material deriving from various liturgical occasions; and of course the very formation of the canon was itself influenced by liturgical practice, as the Church struggled to establish a core of books to be read in Church, *legi in ecclesia*. Even after the actual canon was established, liturgical use continued to influence the effective canon since some books were drawn upon more than others in liturgical worship, and liturgical familiarity influenced theologians.

11. Wainwright, 149. Wainwright playfully borrows scholastic categories to describe the Bible's sacramental reality: "the printed and bound object is the *sacramentum tantum*, the external sign, like the bread and wine at the eucharist; the substantial or ideational content of the Bible is the *sacramentum et res*, the thing as signified, like the eucharistic body and blood of Christ; the *res sacramenti*, the purpose or fruit is in both cases the communion of the Church with the God who gives himself to us in Christ."

All this makes it clear that liturgy made a major contribution to the "content, composition, establishment, delimitation and doctrinal exploitation of the scriptures," which suggests to Wainwright that "the liturgy itself supplies an essential hermeneutical perspective for the biblical and doctrinal theologian." (165) As the primary and connatural context for the Church's understanding and use of the Scriptures, liturgy makes a fourfold contribution to the hermeneutical task.

First, it is within the liturgical context that Scripture may be treated as foundational. The foundational character of Scripture has hitherto hinged on the text's avowed historical and apostolic veracity, but modern scholarship has cast doubt on this assumption in the majority of texts, discrediting their apostolic authorship. The liturgical use of Scripture, says Wainwright, will maintain commitment to the quest of the historical Jesus, but also make frank commitment to the authoritative character of Scripture as an adequate foundational record of God's self-revelation in Jesus (its canonical function).

Second, a challenge arises from modern sensitivity to diversity and contradictory theologies/Christologies in those texts which call into question the unity of the Bible as a whole, and within the New Testament. "We shall find that liturgical practice gives a nuanced view of the matter, a view which can in fact help the biblical and systematic theologians in their own problematic." (169) The liturgical usage of Scripture binds all the writings by their witness to Christ, despite their variances. The distinction between gospel and epistle indicates that Christianity needs both the story of Jesus and a paradigm for proclamation and application of the message. The Church makes uneven use of the New Testament in its worship while nevertheless maintaining the whole of the canon. "Theologians would be wise to pay respectful attention to the Church's more or less instinctive usage in the matter of proportionate weightings when it comes to the evaluation of the New Testament writings and to the shaping of their own thought." (171). The liturgical use of the entire Scripture, Old Testament and New, reminds us of Christianity's roots in Israel, of the religious and cultural background of Jesus, and of the greater salvation history.

Third, Wainwright suggests that liturgy acts as a hermeneutical continuum for Scriptures. Scripture's use in liturgy has preserved and transmitted the text; it sets the proper atmosphere for exegete and interpreter, supplying them with thematic guidelines; it is the pre-eminent place in which the Church ponders and applies the Scriptures; and liturgy can assist in surmounting the historico-cultural gulf between the ancient writings and the present community. Overcoming this gap and applying the message is specifically the task of preaching, the fourth place of liturgy's contribution to the hermeneutical task.

There is not a simple equation between theology and preaching, admits Wainwright, and the practical task of proclamation should not hobble the more complex task of formulating doctrine. Yet, theology should serve the Church's proclamation. In the dialectical tension between dogmatic theology and preaching, liturgy's concern with the worshiping community grounds the latter pole, thereby contributing to the hermeneutical task of biblical and systematic theology.

It is no novelty to recognize biblical theology's influence upon Scripture interpretation and the liturgy, but Wainwright has also striven to point out the influence exerted upon biblical theology by the presence of liturgical elements in Scripture. In short, the current flows both ways. We can highlight a passage in which Wainwright makes explicit this bilateral relationship. In the middle of his concatenation of liturgical forms in the New Testament (confession, hymns, prayer, etc.) he pauses to note that in the epistles Paul quite definitely sets out corrective guidelines for liturgical practice. Wainwright has been giving examples of how narrative forms were influenced by liturgical practice, but now he also acknowledges that "worship requires certain practical, and ultimately doctrinal norms. This is already apparent in New Testament times, and it continues to be the case in the later worship of the Church." (161) Within the New Testament, such doctrinal adjustments have been incorporated into the texts themselves. In the one direction, the authors engage doctrine as architectonic and critical norms for worship; "in the other direction, it is equally important to notice that the New Testament writers find it valuable to draw upon the recognized liturgical practice of the community . . . when they are themselves establishing points of doctrine or giving ethical teaching." (161) He refers to doctrine and liturgy as "correlative norms" and promises to treat them thematically in later chapters, but at this point admits that "it might almost have been possible to entitle the whole book *Lex orandi, lex credendi.*" (161)

## CHRISTIAN TRADITION: CREED AND HYMN

Scripture was the first instrumental means of transmitting the Christian vision; the second is the creed, within which Wainwright includes hymns as a sung confession of faith. In worship, Christians have used creeds as an initiatory and recapitulatory confession of faith. Baptism is the primary setting of the early creeds whereby Church tradition was handed over to catechumens (*traditio symboli*) to be handed back at their baptism as their personal affirmation (*redditio symboli*). Within the liturgy this baptismal faith is recapitulated in the creed. The fundamental category is one of identity.

The creed's role in achieving and maintaining identity raises the question to what extent the Christian faith is tied to the specific language of the traditional creeds, and provides Wainwright with the occasion to remark on the character of creedal language. "Although it is impossible . . . to make a divorce between 'the basic faith' and rational theology, it is fair to state that the place of creeds is on the basic level of faith: their baptismal origin and their regular liturgical use suffice to demonstrate that. They are fundamentally 'first-order' language, expressing with a somewhat naive obviousness the heart of the religious belief."[12] The most useful example for understanding creedal language is poetry. The meaning of the poem may be interpreted and extrapolated in second-order language, but the poem itself is an expression in

12. Wainwright, 191. Here one notices a similarity to the problem which provoked Bultmann to propose his famous demythologization process. On the one hand, advocates of the process see the possibility of cutting through the linguistic shell to reach a meaningful kernel. Critics of the process, on the other hand, suggest "that the peeling of an onion offers a more appropriate model. . . . One peels away each layer until finally there is nothing left, though one has cried a lot on the way. The onion *was* the onion." Wainwright voices his opinion: "Probably, however, the relation between the faith and the ancient and traditional language of its expression is neither as extrinsic as Bultmann's understanding of demythologization seemed to imply nor yet as totally intrinsic as the onion model would suggest." (193)

first-order language. It has a substantive referent which can speak transhistorically, transculturally, and transpersonally from one age, one culture and one person to another. "Poetry critics may perform a useful function in sharpening the naive reader's appreciation of the poem; yet it is the poem itself which stands and lives on." (195) Creeds are like poems in this way. They are not so much secondary-language summaries of an idea, as they are first-order expressions of the faith itself. For this reason "the same creedal core can tolerate a certain range of theological explicitations; or, to put it the other way round, a certain variety of theological positions can all see in a single short creed their own condensation on the plane of faith." (191) In the first-order language of the creed "faith is saying as well as it can what it needs to say," and it is not required to enter into more second-order details "than are necessary to prevent grave misunderstanding." (191)

As a sung creed, hymns also share this characteristic of being first-order expression of religious faith. St. Augustine's three criteria for recognizing a hymn are mentioned. A combination of three characteristics is sought: a hymn is *praise*; it is praise *of God*; it is the *sung* praise of God. There is fair latitude allowed here. Praise may be diverse in form (confession of sin, self-offering, dedication, invocation for help) if praise is defined to include all moods or attitudes which are doxologically motivated. Praise will have God as its object, but the style of address may be second or third person, or quite oblique. And praise will be sung, but the variety of literary and musical forms may be tremendous.

To assist in evaluating hymn forms of praise Wainwright suggests three motifs: the hymn should be doctrinal in its interplay of words stemming from Scripture, tradition, reason and experience; it should be existential as the hymn assists the Christian in his or her growth in grace; and the hymn should be a fusion of poetry and piety. By merging these motifs excellently the hymn will be able to celebrate paradox. Theologies have difficulty holding paradox properly; creeds and hymns celebrate the paradox more richly.

### CHRISTIAN TRADITION: *LEX ORANDI*

This returns us to Wainwright's earlier admission that the divorce between 'the basic faith' and theology is rational and not real. "Faith and theology shade into one another; belief and reflexion each affect the coloration of the other." (191) But wondering to what extent and in what manner faith and theology shade into one another brings us to *lex orandi, lex credendi.* Each of these concepts receives its own chapter by Wainwright. He has already said that he could just as well have used this tag for the title of his book, so we may expect that these concepts hold the key to his understanding of a liturgical way of doing theology. "The Latin tag *lex orandi, lex credendi* may be construed in two ways. The more usual way makes the rule of prayer a norm for belief: what is prayed indicates what may and must be believed. But from the grammatical point of view it is equally possible to reverse subject and predicate and so take the tag as meaning that the rule of faith is the norm for prayer: what must be believed governs what may and should be prayed." (218) In systematic theology the current almost always flows from doctrine to worship; Wainwright's entire agenda (and one which he thinks he alone has worked out in preliminary systematic form) is to bring his readers to see that it is equally possible to reverse the flow since "worship influences doctrine, and doctrine worship." (218) The articulation of the Christian vision occurs in both loci, but the former interplay has been largely neglected by Protestants. "One of my purposes in writing has been to rescue the interplay of worship and doctrine . . . as an area of interest for Protestant theology." (219) To do so will be to recover a more explicit doxological dimension of systematic theology and to theologize from a liturgical perspective. In the chapter on *lex orandi* Wainwright proposes to examine the criteria according to which worship is allowed to influence doctrine; in the chapter on *lex credendi* he will treat the influence of doctrine on worship.

Roman Catholic interest in *lex orandi* has numerous historical roots. Wainwright mentions the renewed interest (as of the seventeenth century) in eastern rites, Gallican alterations to Roman liturgy, the Modernist controversy and the liturgical movement. Yet even in the Roman Catholic treatment, the two-way relation between worship and doctrine is acknowledged. Wainwright cites with approval the interpretation of Pope Pius XII in the encyclical *Mediator Dei.* Popes and councils have used the liturgy as a theological source of argument, the Pope writes, seeking light in traditional sacred rites. "[T]his is the origin of the well-known and time-honoured principle: 'Let the law of prayer establish the law of belief,' *legem credendi lex statuat supplicanti*. . . . [But] If we wanted to state quite clearly and absolutely the relation existing between the faith and the sacred liturgy we could rightly say that 'the law of our faith must establish the law of our prayer,' *lex credendi legem statuat supplicandi*."[13] What is the historical origin of the *lex orandi* principle, and what systematic questions does it raise?

The axiom derives, Wainwright explains, from Prosper of Aquitaine who pointed out that the apostolic injunction to pray for the whole human race obligates us to believe that all faith is from start to finish a work of grace. This was an anti-pelagian polemic, and to bolster his argument Prosper made use also of liturgical prayers: "In addition, let us look at the sacred testimony of priestly intercessions which have been transmitted from the apostles and which are uniformly celebrated throughout the world and in every catholic church; so that the law of prayer may establish a law for belief."[14] The focus of Prosper's argument from liturgy, in Wainwright's interpretation, is an appeal to features of the worship practice itself: that it is universal, is the same everywhere, is followed in the whole catholic Church, and is the practice of people who are holy. To make his point, Prosper is not required to demonstrate that the liturgy receives its authority from the papal magisterium, nor prove that the authority of the liturgy derives directly from apostolic injunction; "neither the papal teaching . . . nor the apostolic injunction . . . can, as relatively external factors, detract from the value which is ascribed by the argument to the worship practice *as such*." (226) Prosper's doctrinal appeal is made not only to the word-content of prayers but to the complex ritual act. "If this kind of appeal is considered proper, an important principle is thereby established: it is recognized that the liturgy which may serve as a doctrinal locus is the liturgy understood as total ritual event, not simply a liturgy reduced to its verbal components." (227)

13. *Mediator Dei*, English translation *Christian Worship* (London: Catholic Truth Society) 28.
14. Prosper, *contra Collatorem*, capitulum VIII.

Others in the history of the Church have utilized this argument, and Wainwright points out significant examples in a historical overview (on pages 227–234). Even before Prosper formulated the principle, Augustine "had already made ample use of the doctrinal proof from the liturgy," both in controversial matters and as liturgical examples or illustrations in his sermons; "the regular doctrinal value of the liturgy is also evidenced in the practice of mystagogical catechesis"; Jerome argues that "a universal practice of the Church can be equivalent to an express biblical command"; Optatus of Melevis alleges a contradistinction between Donatist belief and Donatist liturgical practice; Cyprian grounds his arguments about the sacraments upon the Church's baptismal practices; Tertullian "attaches great weight to the *regula fidei* as a summary statement of the Christian faith. . . ."; Irenaeus makes "doctrinal appeal . . . to the eucharist because in the eucharist the faith comes to focal expression"; and for Ignatius participation in the Eucharist is a confession of the resurrection-hope.

Wainwright argues that doctrinal appeal can be made to the liturgy in all these examples because in the liturgy faith comes to focal expression. This is how he interprets those cases in which *lex orandi* has established *lex credendi*. Not only the magisterium of the Church, but also the worship of the Church functions as resource for understanding the Christian faith. This seems to Wainwright fully established at the Council of Trent, a favorite example for later Roman Catholic writers of "the use of the liturgy as a dogmatic locus by the conciliar magisterium. The strength of a dual establishment of dogma, by both liturgy and magisterium, is stressed." (236)

### WAINWRIGHT ON *LEX ORANDI*

But must *lex orandi* be evaluated, and if so, by what criterion? This question effects a transition from historical to systematical questions concerning the authority of Church worship over doctrine. What if popular devotion takes "an aberrant turn?" In the face of liturgical and doctrinal differences, how do we decide which of the divergent groups has taken the right course? Four questions require deliberation in determining what type of doctrinal authority can be imputed to worship: from whence does it arise, what is its relation to other instances of doctrinal authority, are all cases equally authoritative or are there internal gradations, and what is its role in the development of doctrine?

First, then, what gives to the Church's worship any authority in matters of doctrine? Wainwright answers by claiming that worship "is a source of doctrine in so far as it is the place in which God makes himself known to humanity in a saving encounter. The human words and acts used in worship are a doctrinal locus in so far as either God makes them the vehicle of his self-communication or they are fitting responses to God's presence and action." (242–43) And how would one know whether the liturgical words and acts used in worship are such a vehicle? Wainwright recommends applying three interdependent tests. One test is that of origin which will give most weight to ideas and practices which go back to Jesus; another is the spread of the liturgical practice in time and space; the last is an ethical component. These three kinds of tests—origin, spread, and ethical correspondence—will help determine when worship can in fact be properly drawn on as a doctrinal source.

The second question asks what is the relation between the doctrinal authority carried by worship and other instances of doctrinal authority in the Church—specifically Scripture and the teaching office (magisterium). The bilateral relationship between liturgy and Scripture has already been pointed out above where it was indicated that liturgy influenced the formation of Scripture and Scripture influences the formation of liturgy. The worship of the Church then "constitutes the connatural hermeneutical context" for scriptural texts which themselves, in turn, supply a permanent norm for the liturgy and doctrine of the Church. There is a parallel bilateral relationship between liturgy and the magisterium: "The task of the magisterium is to identify the true faith. . . . The magisterium has a responsibility *for* the liturgy as a doxological expression of the faith. . . . The magisterium also has a responsibility *to* the liturgy: it should draw on the experience of Christian worship, so that the doxological intention may spill over into doctrinal pronouncements, and dogma may be shaped by prayer." (247)

The third question is whether the worship practice of the Church is equally authoritative throughout, or are there internal gradations in its value as a doctrinal locus. It is obvious from what Wainwright has said so far that there must be gradations such that one seeks to measure any particular feature of the liturgy by a number of different criteria, to wit, its origin (dominical, apostolic and scriptural), its universal extension, its ethical congruence, magisterial control and community consent, and re-evaluation or re-formulation through the passage of cultural time.

The fourth question asks what the role of worship is in relation to the development of doctrine. The whole point of Wainwright's historical review of substantial matters in part one was to indicate the contribution worship has made to the formation of doctrine: confession of Christ in the cultus-shaped Christology, the three-fold pattern of baptism shaped Trinitarian doctrine, etc. By way of more recent example, the Marian dogmas of the Roman Catholic Church had a base in popular devotion. "In all three cases, worship practice was in advance of doctrinal decision. Yet it is also clear . . . that magisterial influence has been brought to bear on the liturgy for the sake of establishing a developing or developed doctrine—sometimes before, sometimes after formal definition." (250) The bringing to bear of magisterial influence upon the liturgy is the role exercised by *lex credendi* upon *lex orandi,* the subject of his next chapter, as follows.

It is an artificial yet helpful caricature to say that "Roman Catholicism characteristically appeals to existing liturgical practice for proofs in matters of doctrine . . . [while] Protestantism characteristically emphasizes the primacy of doctrine over the liturgy." (251) The distinction is artificial because both Roman Catholicism and Protestantism also know a relationship which functions in the reverse of the one stereotypically drawn. The difference is not absolute; it is a question about where the center of gravity lies.

"Both Roman Catholicism and Protestantism consider that there is properly a complementary and harmonious relation between worship and doctrine, and that it is the business of worship and doctrine to express the Christian truth. They differ on the question of which of the two, doctrine or worship, should set the pace, and they differ profoundly on the question of whether either or both—the Church's worship or its doctrine—may fall into error." (252)

Wainwright offers numerous historical examples of doctrinal control over worship, first from Scripture and the early Church and then in Roman Catholicism. Even within the New Testament period we see doctrinal control over worship: e.g., Paul critiquing the worship practice of the Corinthian Church on doctrinal grounds. Beyond canonical boundaries, it is doctrine which controls both the shape and content of the Eucharistic prayer which the presiding bishop prayed "according to his own ability," to cite Justin Martyr.[15] The Church adapted its liturgies to exclude heretical positions and to promote orthodox doctrine, the profoundest example being the anti-Arian motifs which appeared in liturgical prayer, epiclesis, the co-ordinated form of doxology by St. Basil, and the installation of the Nicene Creed in worship. Within Catholicism such doctrinal control over liturgy, suggests Wainwright, takes either a passive form of assuring that nothing "untoward would ever have been allowed by the magisterium to develop" or it takes an active form of deliberately using the liturgy to promote a teaching. As examples of the latter Wainwright mentions Marian piety, the feast of Corpus Christi, or the feast of Christ the King; examples of the former include Tridentine condemnation of Wycliffites and Hussites and Protestants.

Nevertheless, it is within Protestant traditions that one sees the strongest and clearest examples of doctrinal control over worship. "The Protestant Reformers sought a root-and-branch cleansing of medieval western doctrine and its liturgical expression. . . . In the liturgy, they operated both at the level of ceremony, where the pruning was severe, and at the level of the ritual structures and texts, where they set about a drastic re-shaping and re-formulation." (263) The more conservative reformers did not prune ceremonial needlessly but only insofar as a practice was doctrinally judged erroneous. Exactly what was retained or eliminated contributed to the character which distinguished the various Protestant traditions. It was the Calvinists who most severely

15. On this issue, see Alan Bouley, *From Freedom to Formula* (Washington D.C.: Catholic University of America Press, 1981). Although one might conclude from his study that there was doctrinal concern in the formulation of Eucharistic prayers, one receives quite a different picture of how this took place than that presented by Wainwright.

reshaped ritual structures and texts, but the common principle in all the Protestant reforms of worship was the effort to return directly to Christ. In terms of the liturgy, this meant concentrating on apparently simple, dominically instituted rites. Wainwright notes in detail how this was worked out regarding the sacrificial character of the Mass. He identifies the practical liturgical consequences of Luther's doctrinal distinction between the Mass as sacrifice or testament in Luther's *Deutsche Messe*; we have seen this already in Brunner, Prenter and Vajta. And Wainwright expresses hope for ecumenical reconciliation on this point by the use of more nuanced categories being worked out by contemporary scholars. "A more irenic way of putting the sixteenth-century sacrificial controversy would be to regret that Catholic theologians had no adequate conceptual framework in which to explain their affirmation that the mass and Calvary are one and the same sacrifice." (272)

Although the Protestant tradition has generally followed this Reformation pattern in which *lex credendi* controls *lex orandi,* some modern Protestant writers are noted exceptions. Wainwright mentions Dietrich Bonhoeffer, for whom "worship becomes the starting point and criterion for the theologian's task of christological investigation and reflection"; Regin Prenter, for whom Christology has two sources, the written tradition of Scripture and the oral tradition of worship which "remains existentially prior to the written tradition in the Church"; John McIntyre, who argues that "the liturgical element will condition christological method"; and M. F. Wiles is mentioned again. He was quoted earlier, questioning whether the effect which prayer has had on doctrine has been at every point the effect which it should have had. Wainwright comments: "The 'should' both recognizes the propriety of *some* influence of prayer on doctrine and rightly claims that this influence is in turn properly subject to critical examination." (279; the review of authors occurs on 274–78)

This again raises the question of how liturgical poetry is related to doctrinal/theological prose, and it is not an exaggeration to say that this question underlies all the others. Wainwright invokes the ruminations of Edmund Schlink to describe the distinct language forms in which the faith of the Church is expressed, poetic worship and prosaic theology.

Schlink's catalyst was his experience that "at any ecumenical gathering it may be observed that members of divided Churches find it much easier to pray and witness together than to formulate common dogmatic statements." Why should this be? Does something happen "when one transfers the theological meaning of statements expressed in prayer and preaching into the category of dogmatic statements?"[16] He thinks so. There is a category shift. Schlink identifies five basic forms of theological statements (prayer, doxology, witness, doctrine and confession) on the basis of to whom the utterance is directed, the degree of involvement by the speaker, and the form of the address. For instance, prayer is addressed to God, the speaker figures prominently, and it is in a first person form of address; doctrine, on the other hand, is addressed to people, the person of the speaker recedes, and the form of address is fairly objective. After noting these five forms of theological statements, Schlink reflects (in a loosely historical form) upon the structural problems of dogmatic statements. The trend has been to press multiple theological forms into one unified form. The early Church expressed dogma in a confessional structure, but "this basic credal form has not been retained in the history of dogma. On the contrary, single structural elements contained in the creeds as initial acts of faith began to become autonomous and to be differentiated into various forms of dogma."[17] Structural changes affect the meaning.

Schlink calls this "objectification" and provides some examples of what he means. Statements that make perfectly good sense in their home structure may appear problematic when a different context is considered. In doctrine, the act of personal encounter is objectified with the result that the historical nature of this encounter is replaced by general statements. When theoretical and timeless doctrinal statements are extracted from kerygmatic assurance, apostolic exhortation, prayer and thanksgiving, creeds and hymns, then

"attention moves away from the experience of salvation . . . [and] raises the theoretical problem of weighing up the contributions of

16. Edmund Schlink, *The Coming Christ and the Coming Church* (Philadelphia: Fortress Press, 1968) 16.
17. Ibid., 35.

divine grace and the human will. . . . There is a difference between faith which is attained by wrestling and groaning and clinging to the Gospel, and faith which is taught as a series of facts, such as that the sinner is saved by the Gospel and by wrestling and clinging to it, etc. Again, it is one thing for the believer to confess that he has been saved by the Gospel alone but quite another to teach that God's grace operates irresistibly."[18]

Wainwright uses Schlink to remind us that a structural shift occurs when we move from doxology to doctrine, but if the believer making worship and the theologian making doctrine are cognizant of this category shift then one can reconcile the poetic language of liturgy and the prosaic language of theology. The emphasis throughout his work has been that both are necessary; neither is dispensable. Each may be treated (if properly treated) as a source for understanding the meaning of the Christian vision. Worship is, as he has said, the place where that vision comes to a sharp focus, as a concentrated expression, and where the vision has often been found to be at its most appealing. Simultaneously, it is theology's task to make coherent, intellectual expression of the Christian vision. The theologian should examine the liturgy from that angle, both in order to learn from it and in order to propose to the worshipping community any corrections or improvements judged necessary.

"[Dogma] is needed in the debates with philosophy and with heresy. It is needed if prayer is not to be dissolved into individualism; if redemptive history is not to be reduced to existentialism; if actualistic missionary proclamation is not to lose the identity of the message. Yet dogma's tendency towards general and theoretical statements must not rob the faith of its particular and concrete qualities, which are experienced ever afresh in the confession of worship and witness, and *from which* dogma itself takes its origin." (281)

CONCLUSION

Here we may close our review of Wainwright's *Doxology*. He has a third part in which he again looks through the lens of worship,

---

18. Ibid., 41.

this time at contextual questions: What would this liturgical way of doing theology have to say regarding the ecumenical question, contemporary revision of the liturgy, the indigenization of liturgy in a culture, and ethics? But we have sufficiently discerned the contours of Wainwright's argument for our purposes. Worship is the doxological experience from which dogma itself takes its origin. The entire systematic agenda could take a breath of fresh air were it done in a liturgical way. ". . . [T]here are rewards for theology and for the whole life of the Church in doing the theological task in a liturgical perspective: the substance of the Christian vision is clarified, an effective vehicle of its transmission is recognized, and the history of the Church and of humanity is consciously kept in relation to God's final purpose." (5) Theology itself could become, at its own level, doxological. Not only would theology think about worship, it would come from worship. Not only would theology include worship on its menu of thought projects, but theology would become worshipful (so the Eastern dictum that the theologian is he/she who prays). The current would flow both ways. The law of prayer would shape, color and stimulate the laws by which we formulate our belief. The law of belief would architectonically propose to the worshipping community any corrections or improvements judged necessary, thereby preserving the law of prayer.


### c. Observations

Brunner proposes a doctrine of worship in the name of Jesus, and Wainwright proposes a systematic theology written from a liturgical perspective. We have offered them as samples of what we are calling a theology from worship because they consider it useful to look at worship when formulating their theology. Brunner therefore includes an outline of what the congregation does when it assembles in Jesus' name to worship. As he said in the Introduction, he is trying to provide theological clarity about "what happens in those assemblies of Christians by virtue of divine institution . . . and what must, in consequence, be done in such assemblies by us today." Wainwright offers what he calls a liturgical way of doing theology. Christian doctrine is the coherent intellectual expression of the Christian vision, and worship is the

132

place in which that vision comes to a sharp focus, a concentrated expression. To this end, it was necessary for both men to examine the words and actions of the Christian assembly in more detail than did either Prenter or Vajta in their theology of worship. They exemplify theology from worship because of how they go about their dogmatic task: they quarry a doctrine of worship from the texts of the worship event. Having done so, they feel in the position to offer theological critique of the event.

So on the one hand, the *lex orandi* provides the subject matter for the *lex credendi*. The way in which we attain a doctrine of worship, says Brunner, is by looking at the activity of worship; Wainwright feels his agenda is unique among all the other theologies of worship because as a liturgical way of doing theology he recognizes the influence worship has had upon the imagination of theologians, and he has gone to historical and systematical lengths to indicate such. Both are concerned with theology as it can be articulated when its light is trained upon worship. By acknowledging the instantiation of dogma in the practice of worship, Brunner and Wainwright have nudged *lex orandi* and *lex credendi* closer together. In the terms of our running metaphor, it is not merely a theological look at the subject of worship (worship has a theology as "I have a body") but a look at the theology which derives from worship (theology is expressed in worship as "I am a body"). One can read theology from worship because worship is an expression of Christian dogma (Brunner) or the Christian vision (Wainwright). They suppose that one mode of expressing dogma or the Christian vision is doxology or liturgy or ritual, and a doctrine of worship can be mined from the practice of worship and made dogmatically explicit. This is one agenda of theology from worship. The agenda can be perverted if the academic reflection becomes ideological. Then doctrines are quarried from worship practices, and any stones which the theologian reckons unusable are discarded. The raw material is sculpted by theological chisels honed in the academy, and the blocks are returned to the assembly through its leaders in order to build an edifice of worship measured along an ideological plumb line.

On the other hand, the *lex credendi* which is produced is not only an enunciation of the *lex orandi*, it can also exercise a corrective influence upon the latter. For Brunner, doctrine should protect and preserve worship's proper *usus,* and for Wainwright (as also, indeed, for Pius XII) doctrinal control should be exercised over worship. This is the second agenda of theology from worship, and accounts for the supposition in both these authors that the current of influence flows in both directions. Brunner examines the worship event but affirms at the outset that the answer to the dogmatic question regarding what should be taught relative to the worship assembly will be determinant for the proper *usus* of worship. Wainwright argues that worship shapes and colors the theologian, but claims a critical and architectonic role for theology too. Theology from worship offers help and guidance to worship practice. Within this framework, the "chicken-or-the-egg-question" —which came first?—must be answered by affirming mutual influence. Does theology influence worship practice, or does worship practice influence theology? The answer by theology from worship is both. Insofar as worship is an expression of the Christian vision, it will influence the articulation of doctrine; in so far as theology is an expression of the Christian vision, it will influence details in worship's practice and expression. (Thus Wainwright can show historically how doctrine changed worship and how worship shaped doctrine, and he explains systematically why this is so.)

Brunner expresses this mutual influence as follows: "The formulary of the Agenda serves the implementation of the form of worship. The Agenda is the concretization of the dogma of worship. To be sure, the Agenda is more than a logical conclusion drawn from a presupposed dogmatic premise. The composition of the Agenda stems from a decision of the church. . . . But, on the other hand, dogma must be effective in the composition of the Agenda as the formative eidos, as the formative entelechy."[19]

Worship is theological. Therefore the liturgical formulary, as the concretization of the dogma of worship, can be translated (or transmuted) into analytical form and the outcome is a study such as Brunner's. Worship is one resource, among others, for a doctrine of worship. But, on the other hand, the dogma of worship must be a vital agent or force directing worship's growth and life (an entelechy). The answer to the doctrinal question of what

19. Brunner, 290.

should be taught relative to *Gottesdienst* will be determinant for the believer's proper worship. To be sure, the proper pneumatic application of worship depends on God's spirit rather than our insightfulness, still, "without a correct doctrine of worship we will never arrive at the proper *usus*, especially not in our present situation, which is so confused in many respects. If error relative to what is done in worship is taught and preached to the congregations and their servants, or if they, perhaps, are told nothing at all, how can they arrive at a proper pneumatic application?"[20]

Our question to Brunner is, can the assembly never arrive at worship's proper *usus* unless they are taught a correct secondary doctrine in analytical form? When we look at Fr. Schmemann's Orthodox perspective, we shall see that it is also his opinion that liturgical theology must be concerned with correct doctrine. Liturgical theology is theology, he says, not merely research about rubrics, esthetics, and ceremonial ritual. But is the only form for this theological work an academic form? Have liturgy and theology been so bifurcated that we believe the assembly to be bereft of theological guidance without the secondary analysis in books such as those by Brunner, Wainwright, Prenter and Vajta? If the community's adjustment to its liturgical encounter with God is truly a theological act, then the *lex credendi* comes from the community itself, from the community's *theologia prima*. The theologians are not only the academics; the liturgical assembly itself is a theological corporation.

Wainwright can devote one chapter to how *lex orandi* influences *lex credendi*, and another to the reverse doctrinal control over worship because the Christian vision for which he is trying to find a place seems to be a reality which precedes its expression. It precedes its expression as "I" precede my body, even as our unity is affirmed. The vision is then expressed either doctrinally or liturgically.

Really, Wainwright seems to have two lines of defense for his way of doing theology from worship. At first he rests his defense on the claim that the theologian's ratiocination has roots in the community. As historical community, the Christian Church transmits a vision of reality; individual theologians should recognize

20. Brunner, 25.

that they stand within a community and their thinking is shaped and colored by its experience. The book, Wainwright says several times, is written from faith to faith. As participant in the Christian community, the theologian's coherent and intellectual expression is informed by existential commitment. The problem we see in this line of defense is a reductionism which supposes that liturgy creates feelings which in turn influence the thinker. We will maintain that liturgy does more than (even if not less than) create feelings. What does it create? We will examine this further when we look at Fr. Schmemann, but for the moment let us invoke an essay by Jean Ladriere to distinguish between feeling and what he calls attitude.

LITURGY AS ILLOCUTIONARY ACT

Ladriere's essay, entitled "The Performativity of Liturgical Language,"[21] considers the ways in which linguistic analysis can help us understand the expression of faith in liturgy. He describes the question this way:

"The basic problem is to discover how liturgical language works. Clearly this kind of language cannot be analysed in terms proper to information theory: it does not consist in the reporting of events, the description of objects, the formulation of theoretical hypotheses, the statement of experimental findings, or the handing on of data. It is characterized in that it is a certain form of action; it puts something into practice: in short, it possesses an 'operativity.' It is not merely a verbal commentary on an action external to itself; in and of itself, it is action."[22]

Employing J. L. Austin's distinction, Ladriere notes that some types of linguistic utterances can be called "performative," meaning they perform a certain kind of action solely by virtue of their enunciation. Promises are like this. A person creates a new situ-

21. Jean Ladriere, "The Performativity of Liturgical Language," in *Concilium: Liturgical Experience of Faith* (New York: Herder & Herder, 1973) 50–61. See also Gerald V. Lardner, "Communication Theory and Liturgical Research," *Worship* 5 (1977) 299–306.
22. Ladriere, 51. Doesn't his description of what liturgical language is not, correspond exactly to what worship would do as expression of doctrine? It reports, states, describes, formulates, and hands on data.

ation which did not exist the moment before the promise was stated, and this new situation exists in no other way than by virtue of stating that promise. This has been further elaborated by John Searle where four kinds of "speech acts" are enumerated, one of them being illocutionary acts: the accomplishment of a specific linguistic operation (for example, affirmation, description, interrogation, thanking, promising, ordering, asking, approving, recommending, deciding, etc). This theory of illocutionary speech acts, suggests Ladriere, "enables us to reformulate our problem more precisely, as follows: What is the characteristic illocutionary power of sentences in liturgical language?"[23]

The answer is complex, not simple. There are multiple deployments of illocutionary speech acts in a liturgy. Liturgical language features sentences which are tantamount to exhortation, confession, interrogation, adulation, statements of beliefs, wishes, and imperatives, among others. But all these statements together make up one language which "definitively constitutes the totality of liturgical language." The unity of liturgical language lies in the fact that it is made up of all these language types together. Their unity belongs to a pragmatic type because it considers the relations between the language units and their users. We are not asking about syntactical structure or semantic order, but about what the people are doing (performing) with the language in its entirety. Ladriere thinks that liturgical language, conceived of as a whole, possesses a threefold performativity: it includes existential induction, institution, and presentification.

He defines existential induction as "an operation by means of which an expressive form awakens in the person using it a certain affective disposition which opens up existence to a specific field of reality."[24] The same utterance may be made by different persons, or at different times, or by different persons at different times, but each time it is uttered it places the speaker in relation to a specific field of reality and opens in the speaker a certain affective disposition. This is true whether spoken in the first person and affecting myself alone, or spoken collectively as if there were only one speaker.

23. Ibid., 54.
24. Ibid., 56.

"Liturgical language uses certain characteristic performative verbs, such as 'to ask,' 'to pray,' 'to give thanks.' . . . Such verbs express illocutionary acts presupposing certain attitudes: trust, veneration, gratitude, submission, contrition, and so on. These attitudes come into effect at the very moment when, by virtue of the enunciation of the sentence, the corresponding act takes place. The performative verb is not a description of the attitude which its enunciation presupposes; its function is not to indicate the existence of this attitude, but is, so to speak, the attitude itself: it makes it exist. . . ."[25]

These attitudes form a system (remember, liturgical language consists of a multiplicity of illocutionary acts but held together in a pragmatic unity). In its very functioning, says Ladriere, such liturgical language puts into effect certain specific acts which will, by their enacted utterance, have repercussion in the affectivity of the speakers. "The term 'affectivity' is used here in a very basic sense. It is not a question of emotion, nor really of feeling, but of that form of constitutive receptivity which makes us capable of adjusting to reality in its several manifestations: to the reality of salvation which comes to us from God by the mediation of Jesus Christ . . ."[26]

As the performative utterance awakens in the speaker this affective formation, it accomplishes the other two tasks of liturgical language. The second task of liturgical language is institution. Liturgical language institutes a community, it does not merely dispose souls to certain feelings. The community is initiated in this meeting as their speech acts create a common, objective space. "Language is not the expression of a community constituted before it and apart from it and is not the description of what such a community would be, but the location in which and the instrument by means of which the community is constituted."[27] The reality of what is done in illocutionary acts establishes the community: the mystery establishes the body of Christ. And third, liturgical language is presentification. The language makes present for the participants a reality whose efficacy they take into their own life. It

25. Ibid., 57.
26. Ibid., 58.
27. Ibid., 59.

makes it present not as a spectacle to be spoken about or expressed, but as a mystery which comes to pass.

We suppose that Wainwright would like to think himself in agreement with this analysis. We suppose that what he wants to call a "liturgical way of doing theology" is exactly a theology which is grounded in liturgical illocutionary speech. However, he remains hobbled by the description of worship as an "expression" of the Christian vision. It sounds as though the Christian vision precedes its expression and this is why the vision can also be expressed doctrinally in a way which will then control the *lex orandi*. As Ladriere reminds us, the liturgy is not the expression of a vision constituted before it and apart from it, rather the liturgy is the location in which and the instrument by means of which the community is created by the mystery. For Wainwright, it seems that the community which provides the theologian with the vision he or she will articulate coherently and intellectually is only one mode (an existential one) of two possible expressions, the other being doctrinal. This is indicated when he insists that the relationship between *lex orandi* and *lex credendi* to be bilateral instead of unilateral.

We said Wainwright rests his defense for a liturgical way of doing theology on two lines, and we have described the first as the existential impact of the community upon the individual. The second is the historically demonstrated fact, and the systematically explained condition, that in worship the faith of the Christian community comes to focused and concentrated expression. One can make doctrinal appeals from worship because in texts and practices and ceremonies the faith comes to focal expression. Because the law of prayer and the law of belief are two different types of expressions of the faith, the current can flow in both directions between them.

Wainwright seems to have a "canon within the canon" throughout most of his description. Liturgy will create an existential community climate which will influence the theologian's individual effort, but worship's expression of that Christian vision will have to be tested against a doctrinal canon. He thinks that because the Christian vision precedes its illocutionary act, the vision's expression in *lex credendi* can critique the vision's expression in *lex orandi*—indeed, this is its very function, as Maurice Wiles repeatedly reminds Wainwright. ". . . Wiles would apply the principles of 'doctrinal criticism' to worship both as a creative factor in the earlier formation of doctrine and as a continuing mode of maintaining and transmitting it."[28] Ladriere describes liturgical language on a more primary level than this. For him, liturgical illocutionary and symbolic acts create the community and create attitudes which come into effect when liturgical rite is transacted. The liturgy creates the attitudes (theological attitudes toward God, self and world), it does not merely give expression to them. Liturgical theology proper will have to do with the attitude coming into being through ritual structure, not with a structured expression of a reality or attitude which preexists its expression.

### LITURGICAL THEOLOGY AND CRITIQUE OF LITURGY

We do not propose that liturgical practice should be immune to theological critique. Such would be the position of those who suppose that liturgy has only to do with esthetic expression (in which case, the only basis one would have by which to judge liturgy is whether it "turns you on"). There must be room for theological critique of liturgy or else the divorce remains in place: liturgy has to do with esthetics (not theology) and theology has to do with doctrine (not liturgy). No, our quarrel is not with a theological critique of liturgical practice, it is with the source of that critique. Liturgical theology affirms that *lex credendi* is established in the community's *theologia prima*. The *lex orandi*, as it comes into being in the liturgical rite, is theological. This is the proper meaning of the Eastern Orthodox dictum (which Wainwright misinterpreted) that theology is prayer.

Theology from worship considers worship language to be only an expression of the Christian vision, and for most systematicians, a rather awkward one at that (Wainwright at least gives a positive estimate to what he perceives as the poetic expression of liturgy; many others would not go even this far). The consequence of this assumption is that the proper *usus* of worship (Brunner) and worship as a doctrinal locus (Wainwright) can be guaranteed only in so far as the law of belief holds the reins over the law of prayer. At the beginning of his chapter on *lex orandi* Wainwright wanted

28. Wainwright, 55.

to know "according to what criteria is worship allowed to influence doctrine and *vice versa?*" And the bulk of the chapter on *lex credendi* was "devoted to an examination of the reverse relationship: doctrinal control over worship." If worship and doctrine are each, in their own way, expressions of the Christian vision, then they stand in bilateral relationship. Theology exercises doctrinal control over worship, and worship provides the existential matrix for what the theologian expresses. The "chicken-or-the-egg-question" is answered by observing times when a shift in liturgical expression influenced theological expression, and observing other times when the theological expression influenced liturgical expression. Liturgy does not possess the sort of normativity that is expressed in Prosper of Aquitaine's formula as Fr. Kavanagh takes it: *ut legem credendi lex statuat supplicandi.*[29] Wainwright instead adopts a formulation of the principle in which "from the grammatical point of view it is equally possible to reverse subject and predicate and so take the tag as meaning that the rule of faith is the norm for prayer: what must be believed governs what may and should be prayed."[30] We have already seen his appeal to Pius XII to justify this formulation.

As Ladriere points out, in the performance of the liturgical rite (symbolic acts and speech acts) the reality comes to be, it does not merely come to expression. This is the ground for the unilateral relationship between *lex orandi* and *lex credendi*. The law of prayer establishes the law of belief not because, as Wainwright thinks, worship is the place where the vision comes to sharp focus, and is found appealing, but because here is where faith comes to be. Liturgical theology affirms the normative position of *lex orandi* from a different framework because there is a different understanding of what leitourgia means.

In theology of worship and theology from worship, liturgy is treated as a ritualized expression of the faith. Liturgy is defined merely as the order or structure of a worship event. We wish to

29. Kavanagh comments: "The statement . . . *ut legem credendi lex statuat supplicandi* of Prosper of Aquitaine is cited differently by various authors. This form is Migne, *Patrologia Latina* vol. 50: col. 555." Footnote 1, *On Liturgical Theology,* 181.
30. Wainwright, 218.

use the word in a deeper sense. In order to do so clearly, a distinction must be proposed between liturgy and leitourgia, leitourgia meaning rite which creates a theologizing community.

Leitourgia is where faith comes to existence, where it is done and enacted. When liturgy is treated as an expression of an idea, the current can flow from liturgy to theology or vice versa; but when leitourgia is treated as a rite which creates the faithful theologizing community, the current flows unilaterally from *lex orandi* to *lex credendi*. In this case, there is not a preexistent theology or vision which then is expressed in either doctrine or worship; there is not a preexistent ''I'' which then has a body or is a body. Rather, ''I am bodily.'' The community, which does primary theology, exists liturgically.

But propaedeutic to defining leitourgia in this sense will be an investigation of one of liturgical theology's foremost proponents, Alexander Schmemann.

## Chapter 4

## An Orthodox Perspective: Fr. Schmemann

We shall attempt in this chapter to grasp what Alexander Schmemann means by liturgical theology. By his own account there is an irreconcilable difference between two approaches to the issue, which he calls liturgical theology versus theology of liturgy. To discern this difference requires care when dissecting his writings so we shall here confine ourselves to his work, making interpretive but not evaluative comments.

Fr. Schmemann says, startlingly, of his own work: "In the approach which I advocate by every line I ever wrote, the question addressed by liturgical theology to liturgy and to the entire liturgical tradition is not about liturgy but about 'theology,' i.e. about the faith of the Church as expressed, communicated and preserved by the liturgy."[1] This is an enigmatic remark coming from a person whose work is famed in the field of liturgics, and it forces us to ask what he means by "theology." How can Fr. Schmemann maintain that the agenda of liturgical theology is not liturgical but theological? Is he not a liturgiologist whose purview is such non-theological subjects as the evolution of rite, ordo and rubrics, piety, cult, symbols in liturgy, and so forth? Isn't the task of liturgical theology to recover the essence of the liturgy and relegate the accessories to their place? This is how Fr. Schmemann's work has been frequently misunderstood.[2] He must have a special notion of theology in mind to assert that the question addressed by liturgical theology is not about liturgy but about theology. In-

1. Schmemann, "Liturgical Theology, Theology of Liturgy, and Liturgical Reform," *St. Vladimir's Quarterly* 13 (No. 4, 1969) 128.
2. W. J. Grisbrooke characterizes it in this way, and Fr. Schmemann explicitly denies it: "The fact, however, is that such is *not* my concept of liturgical theology. . . ." Ibid., 217.

deed he has. He understands liturgical theology to be the faith of the Church itself coming to be in leitourgia.

## a. An Organic Definition

It is tempting to suppose one could understand the complex term "liturgical theology" by summing the definition of each simple constituent part, resulting in a sort of connective definition. Under such a definition it would appear that there are two independent enterprises which some imaginations might relate, others might not. There would be the field of liturgiology which busies itself with uncovering historical liturgical data, and the additional task of theology which may (or may not) make use of this supplied data when considering a theology of worship. Under this connective definition, then, theology would involve itself with matters liturgical either when it turns its attention to liturgy as an object of study, or when it utilizes liturgy as a source of data, in the form of texts and practices. The two fields would thus be connected at the periphery, as when two circles touch at one point of their arcs.

Fr. Schmemann considers this solution to defining liturgical theology inadequate, albeit a common one. It is inadequate because it fails to integrate liturgy and theology into an organic definition. For him, the complex definition of liturgical theology determines the definition of its constituent part, theology. "[L]iturgical theology—and I cannot over-emphasize this—is *not* that part of theology, that 'discipline,' which deals with liturgy 'in itself,' has liturgy as its specific 'object,' but, first of all and above everything else, the attempt to grasp the 'theology' as revealed in and through liturgy. There is, I maintain, a radical and indeed irreducible difference between these two approaches to liturgical theology whose task then obviously depends on whether one opts for one or the other."[3] Fr. Schmemann's definition of liturgical theology is organic such that the word "liturgical" identifies the ontological condition for theology; the definition is not connective such that the word "liturgical" identifies the object of theological discourse or the source of theological data.

3. Ibid., 218.

Fr. Schmemann's organic understanding cannot be had cheaply, though. In his article "Theology and Liturgical Tradition" he sets the terms for his definition, with the result that both theology and liturgy are understood in harmony with the organic term liturgical theology.

"There is much confusion and ambiguity in the use of certain terms. One speaks, for example, of liturgical theology, of a liturgical 'resourcement' of theology. For some, this implies an almost radical rethinking of the very concept of theology, a complete change in its structure. The *leitourgia*—being the unique expression of the Church, of its faith and of its life—must become the basic *source* of theological thinking, a kind of *locus theologicus* par excellence. There are those, on the other hand, who, while admitting the importance of the liturgical experience for theology, would rather consider it as a necessary *object* of theology—an object requiring, first of all, a theological clarification of its nature and function."[4]

In other words, some see liturgy as a source for theological reflection, others see liturgy as the object of theological study—but note that both distinguish theology on the one hand from liturgy on the other. There is liturgy and there is theology, and somehow they must relate to one another, either as source or object, but they are discrete activities. As a distinct activity, theology might require data from liturgy or it might scrutinize liturgy, but this is quite different from saying that liturgy is theological.

Both of these views appeal to historical antecedents. They are each "based to some extent on a conscientious desire to recover positions that are supposed to have been held previously. And, indeed, one can discern in the history of the Church two main types or patterns of relationship between theology and the *leitourgia*."[5] The first pattern of relationship, liturgy as resource for theology, has of late been identified with the patristic tradition

4. Schmemann, "Theology and Liturgical Tradition," *Worship in Scripture and Tradition*, ed. Massey Shepherd (Oxford: Oxford University Press, 1963) 166.
5. Ibid., 167.

(however, Fr. Schmemann later makes clear that our modern perception fails to do justice to what the Fathers meant). Reference is made to the connection between liturgical experience and theological thought in the Fathers. For this first view, to say liturgy is the living source of all Christian thought is taken to mean that theological dogma is authenticated or authorized when it finds antecedence in liturgical expression. It takes the axiom *lex orandi est lex credendi* to mean "that the liturgical tradition, the liturgical life, is a natural milieu for theology, its self-evident term of reference."[6]

The other pattern of relationship Fr. Schmemann calls a scholastic pattern. By this he does not simply mean a historical school or period, but any structure in which theology has an independent status such that "The position of worship in relation to theology is reversed: from a *source* it becomes an *object*, which has to be defined and evaluated within the accepted categories. . . . Liturgy supplies theology with 'data,' but the method of dealing with these data is independent of any liturgical context."[7]

It would be a temptingly easy solution to identify the patristic tradition as liturgical theology and the scholastic tradition as theology of liturgy. In this case, proponents of the liturgical movement could be seen as advocating the patristic pattern and denouncing the scholastic pattern as a deviation. But to Fr. Schmemann's mind it is not this easy. Do we today understand *lex orandi est lex credendi* in the same way as the Fathers?

"It is at this point that the question must be asked: Can either of these two attitudes, in their pure expression, be acceptable to us today, and be the starting point of a reconsideration of the relationship between worship and theology? It seems to me that in the modern discussion of the liturgical problem, one essential fact is very often overlooked, or at least not given sufficient attention.

6. Ibid. This existential milieu seems precisely what Wainwright and Vajta recommend.

7. Ibid., 168. Throughout this section we will try to present Fr. Schmemann's criticism of Scholasticism without amelioration, but we would point out to the reader that we think Fr. Schmemann means by "Scholasticism" a certain approach or method. Therefore, whether his criticism applies to the historical period or authors traditionally called "scholastic" would be a matter for case by case consideration.

Yet it is this fact that makes the liturgical problem of our time much more complex than it may seem. I define it as the *metamorphosis of the liturgical conscience.*"[8]

The problem of defining liturgical theology cannot be solved as simply as repeating the slogans of the Fathers, because our understanding of both theology and liturgy has changed. Not only has theology come to be perceived through the lens of scholastic theology, but there also exists a liturgical crisis in which the understanding of leitourgia has shifted. In a moment we shall examine more fully what Fr. Schmemann means by a metamorphosis of the liturgical conscience, but in brief it can be described as the loss of the eschatological dimension of worship (which, in turn, he attributes to a form of modern reductionism which confuses symbol with representation).

Let us recapitulate. We were faced with two alternatives, the one being a theology of liturgy which considers liturgy to be one of many possible objects of theological discourse, and the other sounding like liturgical theology but in fact missing the mark, in Fr. Schmemann's opinion, because it continues to understand theology as an activity independent of and in addition to liturgy, although making much noise about utilizing liturgical sources in the form of texts and practices. Liturgical theology, as Fr. Schmemann understands it, is far more radical than either of these because it restores theological status to liturgical tradition itself. "Its fundamental presupposition is that the liturgy not only has a theological meaning and is declarative of faith, but that it is the living norm of theology."[9] The liturgy is not an object for theological discourse, or a data source of texts and phrases and practices for theology to mine, or a ritualistic, pietistic or existential milieu in which to do theology. Rather, liturgy is the condition for theology. Thus Fr. Kavanagh's remark: "What emerges most directly from an assembly's liturgical act is not a new species of theology among others. It is *theologia* itself."[10] Thus Fr. Schmemann's correction to our modern perception of the patristic pattern:

8. Ibid., 170.
9. Ibid., 169–170.
10. Aidan Kavanagh, *On Liturgical Theology,* 75.

"The formula *lex orandi est lex credendi* means nothing else than that theology is *possible* only within the Church. . . . The problem of the relationship between liturgy and theology is not for the Fathers a problem of priority or authority. Liturgical tradition is not an 'authority' or a *locus theologicus*; it is the ontological condition of theology, of the proper understanding of *kerygma*, of the Word of God. . . ."[11]

Expressed in our earlier terms, a connective definition of liturgical theology persists when theology treats liturgy as either source or object; an organic definition is not truly attained until it is understood that liturgy is theological. Both liturgy and theology suffer a distortion if they are severed one from another.

The task, then, for the liturgical theologian is not to insinuate liturgy into theology but to gainsay the presupposed dichotomy in so far as it exists at all. The task is not to make liturgy an object of study (Prenter and Vajta) or to make liturgy the source of theological study (Brunner and Wainwright), but to realize how liturgy is the ontological condition for theology. In the terms of one of our metaphors, we may say liturgical theology does not come from liturgy like a babe detaching itself from the womb: it arises in and as liturgy, and never leaves it.

CRISIS FOR THEOLOGY

What are the consequences to theology when it is detached from its liturgical womb—from its ontological condition? In many of his treatises Fr. Schmemann describes the crisis in theology which ensues. He thinks theology suffers an unhealthy pluralism[12] dis-

---

11. Schmemann, "Theology and Liturgical Tradition," 175. Fr. Schmemann does sometimes call liturgy a *locus theologicus* but can use the term two different ways, distinguishing between *locus* as a data source or as the ontological condition. We shall try to keep this distinction vivid.

12. There is such a thing as a healthy pluralism, e.g. "there certainly were substantial differences among the Fathers, but they did not break the basic unity of a common experience and vision." But today's theology suffers an unhealthy form. "Orthodox theologians do not seem to understand one another, so different are the respective 'keys' in which they approach the same problems, so opposed to one another their basic presuppositions and thought forms. This leads either to meaningless polemics . . . or to a kind of 'peaceful coexistence' of theological orientations mutually ignoring one another." "Lit-

abling the communication it should share with the Church. Such isolated theology

"seems deeply alienated from the Church, from her real life and needs. . . . Theology is no longer the conscience and the consciousness of the Church, her reflection on herself and on her problems. It has ceased to be *pastoral* in the sense of providing the Church with essential and saving norms; and it has also ceased to be *mystical* in the sense of communicating to the people of God the knowledge of God which is the very content of life eternal. A theology alienated from the Church, and a Church alienated from theology."[13]

Theology is in crisis when it is divorced from the life of Christians in the Church. Theology has been alienated from the Church, made into an exclusively intellectual activity, a subdiscipline of the academy.

"Theologians avoid discussing the trivial reality of the Church's life, and do not even dream about influencing it in any way. In turn, the Church, i.e. the bishops, priests and laity, are supremely indifferent to the writings of the theologians, even when they do not regard them with open suspicion. . . . No wonder, therefore . . . theology is guided in its inner life not by the experience, needs or problems of the church but by individual interests of individual theologians."[14]

Etymologically, the word theology of course means to talk about God, but this generic definition does not get us very far. To theologize is to talk about God for what purpose? For whom? The theology which Fr. Schmemann wishes to identify is one done for and by the Christian community. "Ideally theology is the conscience of the Church, her purifying self-criticism, her permanent reference to the ultimate goals of her existence"[15] in order to refer

urgy and Theology," *The Greek Orthodox Theological Review,* 17 (Spring, 1972) 86.

13. Ibid., 87.

14. Schmemann, "Theology and Eucharist," *St. Vladimir's Seminary Quarterly* 5:4 (1961) 11.

15. Ibid.

humanity and the cosmos constantly to God. When theology is liturgical, then it remembers its reason for speaking.

Theology suffers a crisis when its logic no longer comes from the liturgy which is God's action in the community of faith, for then *lex credendi* no longer flows out of *lex orandi*. This is the crisis that Fr. Schmemann characterizes as scholastic theology, school theology. "The basic defect of school theology consists in that, in its treatment of the sacraments, it proceeds not from the living experience of the Church, not from the concrete liturgical tradition that has been preserved by the Church, but from its own *a priori* and abstract categories and definitions, which hardly conform to the reality of church life."[16] In scholastic theology *lex credendi* is ruptured from *lex orandi* and theology decides *a priori* what is important or secondary. If theology is "above all the search for words appropriate to the nature of God,"[17] and if worship and theology should be organically related such that the former is the ontological condition for the latter, then their severance results in a distortion. "If today both theology and liturgy have ceased, at least to a substantial degree, to perform within the Church the function which is theirs thus provoking a deep crisis, it is because at first they have been divorced from one another; because the *lex credendi* has been alienated from the *lex orandi*."[18]

A theology which is liturgical is not one which has theology as its object, as if the spotlight of theological discourse momentarily shines upon worship. If, then, Fr. Schmemann can say that the question addressed by liturgical theology to liturgy is not about liturgy but about theology, it is because he sees his work as an effort to clarify the Church's *lex orandi* which, by his organic definition of liturgical theology, simultaneously clarifies its *lex credendi*. Research into the Church's liturgical Ordo is research into the Church's theology; to study the Church's faith in its liturgical form is to encounter the Church's faith theologically as well.

"What I tried to say in my book, and also in some other writings,

16. Schmemann, *The Eucharist* (New York: St. Vladimir's Seminary Press, 1987) 13.
17. Schmemann, *Introduction to Liturgical Theology* (New York: St. Vladimir's Seminary Press, 1966) 14. (Hereafter, *Introduction*).
18. Schmemann, "Liturgy and Theology," 89.

150

is that the 'essence' of the liturgy or *'lex orandi'* is ultimately nothing else but the Church's faith itself or, better to say, the manifestation, communication and fulfillment of that faith."[19] A theology of liturgy sees liturgy as an expression of the faith, while Fr. Schmemann's method of liturgical theology sees liturgy as an epiphany of the faith. They begin from different frameworks.

Thus Fr. Schmemann's essential definition: "As its name indicates, liturgical theology is the elucidation of the meaning of worship."[20] But what is elucidated? Wherein does the meaning of worship lie? Not in superficial and arbitrary symbolism, not in rules and rubrics, not in "how to" manuals. Although this is what the study of liturgy has sometimes disappointingly contented itself with, Fr. Schmemann insists that it is not what he perceives to be the point of liturgical theology. Having noted the affect which the rupture of liturgical theology has had upon theology, he also notes the affect it has had upon the deterioration of liturgics. "What is called liturgics in the religious schools was usually a more or less detailed practical study of ecclesiastical rites, combined with certain symbolical explanations of ceremonies and ornaments. Liturgical study of this kind, known in the West as the study of 'rubrics,' answers the question how: how worship is to be carried out according to the rules, i.e. in accordance with the prescriptions of the rubrics and canons."[21] Liturgical theology's ultimate concern is not with texts as resources, but with the Church's living faith itself. Questions about liturgical Ordo are penultimate to the ultimate theological issue. Since the meaning of worship is God's act upon God's people, its interpretation is nothing less than the elucidation of the mystery of divinely bestowed new life, i.e. theology. As the explanation of worship, liturgical theology

"ought to be the elucidation of its theological meaning. Theology is above all explanation, 'the search for words appropriate to the nature of God,' i.e. for a system of concepts corresponding as much as possible to the faith and experience of the Church.

19. Schmemann, "Liturgical Theology, Theology of Liturgy, and Liturgical Reform," 217.
20. Schmemann, *Introduction*, 14.
21. Ibid., 9.

Therefore the task of liturgical theology consists in giving a theological basis to the explanation of worship and the whole liturgical tradition of the Church. . . .

If liturgical theology stems from an understanding of worship as the public act of the Church, then its final goal will be to clarify and explain the connection between this act and the Church, i.e. to explain how the Church expresses and fulfils herself in this act."[22]

## b. The Underlying Ecclesiology

Liturgical theology is thus distinguished from both theology of liturgy and from the traditionally conceived boundaries of liturgics. Say it this way: theology is a "logos"—a talking about. What does a theology of liturgy talk about? The liturgy. The liturgy is the subject of talk. But surely this is not the goal of theology, whose proper subject matter is God! Therefore, what is talked about in liturgical theology is not ritual but God, God liturgically present. Liturgy is the presence of that about which we speak, viz. the reign of God, the kingdom at hand, the eschaton present, Christ among us, redeemed life, eschatological existence. Theology is talk about God in self-revealing action, and liturgical theology can be considered genuine theology because God acts in the liturgy. Liturgical theology unpacks the faith of the Church because in the liturgy the Church experiences itself as the handiwork of God. There God's creative *kerygma* is manifested and faith is actualized. Liturgy, then, is not just a source for theology, but its root. And liturgical theology may be said to be Eucharistic, not in the sense that the Eucharist is an object of theological contemplation and analysis, but in the sense "that in the moment of the Church the Eucharist is the *moment of truth* which makes it possible to see the real 'objects' of theology: God, man and the world, in the *true light*, which, in other words, reveals both the *objects* of theology as they really are and gives the necessary *light* for their understanding. . . . Theology, like any other Christian service or *'leitourgia'* is a *charisma*, a gift of the Holy Spirit. This gift is given *in the Church*. . . ."[23]

22. Ibid., 14.
23. Schmemann, "Theology and Eucharist," 22.

The task ascribed by Fr. Schmemann to liturgical theology is rooted in liturgy's eschatological dimension, but eschatology is not so much a doctrine in his view as it is a dimension of both faith and theology. "It permeates and inspires from inside the whole thought and life of the Church . . . If [the Kingdom] is to have a consistent orientation and this means precisely a theology, this theology must be rooted, first of all, in the recovered Christian eschatology."[24]

Christian eschatology requires recovery, Fr. Schmemann thinks, because this dimension of liturgy is missing, and its loss is what he meant by the metamorphosis of the liturgical conscience. What the patristic period knew naturally and existentially, today's liturgical conscience has forgotten. "It is not Christian worship that changed, but it is comprehension by the believers, by the Christian community. In a simplified form one can say that, in the conscience of the community, the *leitourgia* became once again a cult. . . ."[25] Leitourgia as rite was reduced to form, order, sequence: liturgy as ritual form. We must therefore inquire about what Fr. Schmemann means when he says that liturgy is not cult although liturgy can only be expressed by cult!

Fr. Schmemann does not deny that Christian liturgy exists in cultic form, nor that its antecedents are in Jewish cultic traditions, but he insists that in the Christian context these cultic categories are understood in a wholly transformed way. "[T]his transformation consists in *the abolishment of cult as such,* or at least in the complete destruction of the old philosophy of cult."[26] Cult is required where something or someone or some action needs to be

24. Schmemann, "Prayer, Liturgy and Renewal," *The Greek Orthodox Theological Review,* 16:1 (1969) 12.

25. Schmemann, "Theology and Liturgical Tradition," 176.

26. Ibid., 172. Fr. Schmemann's double, antinomical use of the word may be confusing. Fr. Kavanagh seems to make the same point, using the term 'rite' instead of 'cult' and his remark may help to clarify. "Rite involves creeds and prayers and worship, but it is not any one of these things, nor all of these things together, and it orchestrates more than these things. Rite can be called a whole style of Christian living. . . . Rite in this Christian sense is generated and sustained in this regular meeting of faithful people in whose presence and through whose deeds the vertiginous Source of the cosmos itself is pleased to settle down freely and abide as among friends. A liturgy of

sanctified or made sacred because it is otherwise unholy or profane. Cult therefore presupposes a radical distinction between the
sacred realm and the profane realm, as if God dwells within the
tabernacle, the *fanis*, and the people stand outside this area in the
*pro-fanis*. Untransformed cult is "a sacred action, or rite, performed in order to establish 'contact' between the community and
God. . . . A 'cult' by its very essence presupposes a radical distinction between the 'sacred' and the 'profane,' and, being a
means of reaching or expressing the 'sacred,' it posits all the non-
sacred as 'profane.' "[27]

Christian liturgy is not a cult in this sense because within the ecclesia, which is a royal priesthood, the distinction between the
sacred and the profane has been abolished. Yet this seems to be
precisely what has been forgotten in our modern, metamorpho-
sized conscience. "In the popular approach—and 'popular' by no
means excludes the great majority of the clergy—the Church is,
above all, a 'cultic' or liturgical institution, and all her activities
are, implicitly or explicitly, directed at her liturgical needs. . . .
The Church is essentially an institution existing for the fulfillment
of the 'religious needs' of her members. . . ."[28] Originally the
Greek word "leitourgia" had no cultic connotations, and it is not
accidental that the New Testament writers chose this word to
speak about the Church's activity even in its cultic form. "The fact
that the Church adopted [the term leitourgia] finally for her cult,
and especially for the Eucharist, indicates her special understanding of worship which is indeed a revolutionary one."[29] Leitourgia
means to put on Christ; the Church is itself the presence of the
eschaton, the actuality of restored life which is ours in Christ. The
liturgy is therefore not a cultic means of grace, it is all those
ministries and offices in which the Church manifests and fulfills
her nature and vocation. The unique function of the divine liturgy
is to " 'make the Church what she is'—witness and participant of
the saving *event* of Christ, of the new life in the Holy Spirit, of the

Christians is thus nothing less than the way a redeemed world is, so to
speak, done." Aidan Kavanagh, *On Liturgical Theology*, 100.
27. Schmemann, "Theology and Liturgical Tradition," 172.
28. Schmemann, "Theology and Eucharist," 13.
29. Ibid., 17.

presence in 'this world' of the Kingdom to come."[30] Theology's subject matter is this saving event, and thus theology is liturgical in the sense that theology's ultimate term of reference is the faith of the Church, a faith created not by propositions but by the real experience of this saving event. This experience of the Church is primarily the experience given and received in the Church's leitourgia—in her *lex orandi*.

The term leitourgia originally meant "an action by which a group of people become something corporately which they had not been as a mere collection of individuals—a whole greater than the sum of its parts. It meant also a function of 'ministry' of a man or of a group on behalf of and in the interest of the whole community."[31] If liturgy is the work of a corporate few for the many, then who does liturgy for whom? Not the priest for the Church, but the Church for the world. It is not the case that the priest does a liturgy for the Church, rather the Church does its liturgy for the world. The former is cult, the latter is leitourgia in the Christian sense. The former perceives the Church as an institution which dispenses grace to individuals through various means; the latter perceives the Church as a renewed and sanctified people. "The Church itself is a *leitourgia*, a ministry, a calling to act in this world after the fashion of Christ, to bear testimony to Him and His kingdom."[32] The former perceives Eucharist as one means of grace among others, but the latter perceives Eucharist as the very epiphany of the ecclesia's eschatological identity. Confusion about this is the source of our confused orientation today. "[T]he experience of worship has long ago ceased to be that of a corporate liturgical act. It is an aggregation of individuals coming to church, attending worship in order to satisfy individually their individual religious needs, not in order to *constitute* and to *fulfill* the Church."[33]

The loss of this eschatological corporate identity is what Fr. Schmemann means by a liturgical crisis. It is not that worship—its

30. Schmemann, "Liturgy and Theology," 91.
31. Schmemann, *For the Life of the World* (New York: St. Vladimir's Seminary Press, 1973) 25.
32. Ibid.
33. Schmemann, "Theology and Eucharist," 13.

structure, form and content—has changed, but a discrepancy has appeared between the basic purpose of worship and the way it is understood. Things have been reversed.

"The fact is that worship has ceased to be understood as a function of the Church. On the contrary, the Church herself has come to be understood as a function of worship. . . . [T]he Church cannot be equated or merged with 'cult'; it is not the Church which exists for the 'cult,' but the cult for the Church, for her welfare, for her growth into the full measure of the 'stature of Christ' (Eph. 4:13). Christ did not establish a society for the observance of worship, a 'cultic society,' but rather the Church as the way of salvation, as the new life of re-created mankind."[34]

A function is the purpose for which something is designed or exists. Worship should be the function of the Church because it is the purpose for which the Church exists; what the Church does as the Body of Christ is worship. Instead the Church has become the purpose for which worship exists; worship is taken as a means of individual salvation. And with this secularized view of liturgy, "there has occurred a very significant shift in the understanding of the sacraments. They have become private services for individual Christians, aimed at their personal sanctification, not at the edification of the Church."[35] Leitourgia should exist to enact eschatological existence, but instead liturgy has become a resource for solipsistic religious therapy, usually expressed didactically.

Leitourgia is the sacramental presence of God in an eschatological community, whose kingdom identity is manifested and comes to being in the celebration of the Divine Liturgy in order to be a light to those in darkness so they might witness the joy which the cosmic redemption has restored to humanity. The Church embodies in its Eucharistic worship its participation in God's kingdom—

34. Schmemann, *Introduction*, 23.

35. Schmemann, "Theology and Eucharist," 18. See also "Problems of Orthodoxy in America: III. The Spiritual Problem," *St. Vladimir's Seminary Quarterly*, 9:4 (1965) where he writes, ". . . no word is used more often by secularism in its dealing with religion than the word *help*. 'It helps' to belong to a religious group, to be identified with a religious tradition, to be active in the Church, to pray; 'it helps,' in short, to 'have religion'."

its "eighth day" existence. The eighth day is both on the chronos calendar (as Sunday, the day after the Sabbath, the day Jesus rose) and it is not (it is kairos time, an eschatological day). This octagon concept had widespread influence in the early Church and Fr. Schmemann makes frequent use of it. "For the early Church the Lord's Day was not a substitute for the sabbath; . . . The appearance of [the day introduced by the Church] is rooted in the expectation of salvation . . . It was precisely in connection with or as a result of this eschatology that there arose the idea of the Lord's Day, the day of Messianic fulfillment, as the Eighth Day, 'overcoming' the week and leading outside of its boundaries."[36]

### A NEW CREATION

What is the kingdom of God? Where and how does one experience it so it may become the root of the Church's theological word to creation? "To this question the early Church, at least, had an answer: to her the Kingdom of God was revealed and made 'known' every time she gathered on the eighth day—the day of the Kyrios—'to eat and drink at Christ's table in His Kingdom' (Luke 22:29-30), to proclaim His death and confess His Resurrection, to immerse herself in the 'new eon' of the Spirit."[37] Worship is the purpose of the Church by which it witnesses to God's redemptive act in Christ which restores relationship between God and the world. The Church fulfills its nature and manifests itself most fully at the Eucharistic table when estrangement between God and the world is overcome (the sacred-profane distinction is obliterated) and the giver is acknowledged with thankfulness. The Church is the sacramental anticipation of the world still to come, the first fruits of the messianic banquet, so the liturgy is precisely the passage from this world into heaven. It is frolicking in the new relationship which has been restored to us by God in Christ.

---

36. Schmemann, *Introduction*, 61. See also Jean Danielou, *The Bible and the Liturgy* (Notre Dame: University of Notre Dame Press, 1956), chapter 5; baptismal fonts were frequently octagonal to indicate that one is baptized into an eighth-day existence, cf. J. G. Davies, *The Architectural Setting of Baptism* (London: Barrie & Rockliff, 1962).
37. Schmemann, "Prayer, Liturgy and Renewal," 11.

When the Church is said to be a new creation, therefore, it is not in the sense of being a novel cultic relationship, but in the sense of being the manifestation of our restored relationship with God, a relationship for which humanity was created but which humanity forfeited in sin. According to the Christian story, human beings are distinguished from other creatures by their capacity to be *homo adorans*. "All rational, spiritual and other qualities of man, distinguishing him from other creatures, have their focus and ultimate fulfillment in this capacity to bless God, to know, so to speak, the meaning of the thirst and hunger [for God] that constitutes his life. '*Homo sapiens*,' '*homo faber*' . . . yes, but, first of all, '*homo adorans*.' The first, the basic definition of man is that he is *the priest*."[38] The original sin of humankind is not that religious duties were neglected, but that the priestly vocation was abandoned making religion into a duty at all. Sin made men and women think of God only in terms of religion, supposing a profane world which in its autonomy did not include God. "In our perspective . . . the 'original' sin is not primarily that man has 'disobeyed' God; the sin is that he ceased to be hungry for Him and for Him alone, ceased to see his whole life depending on the whole world as a sacrament of communion with God."[39] The real fall of humanity is non-Eucharistic life in a non-Eucharistic world. In this context Christianity is the end of all religion and leitourgia is the end of cult by its transformation. Religion is required where there is a wall of separation between God and the human, but precisely this wall has been dismantled by Christ. In fact, the lack of religious, cultic trappings led pagans in the first centuries to accuse Christians of atheism. The Christians had no sacred places and no cult that could be recognized as such by the pagan population. In Christ the whole world was redeemed, not just sacred pockets of it; the Church's liturgy witnesses to this cosmic redemption. In Christ "eucharistic life was restored to man. For He Himself was the perfect Eucharist; He offered Himself in total obedience, love and thanksgiving to God. God was His very life. And he gave this perfect and eucharistic life to us. In Him God became our life . . . [This Eucharist] is the movement that Adam

38. Schmemann, *For the Life of the World*, 15.
39. Ibid., 18.

failed to perform, and that in Christ has become the very life of man. . . ."[40] In Christ life was returned to us because life was given again as sacrament and communion. The Church's entire life is a ministry, a leitourgia, because it bears witness by being what it is: redeemed, restored and joyful. "The Eucharist is the entrance of the Church into the joy of its Lord. And to enter into that joy, so as to be a witness to it in the world, is indeed the very calling of the Church, its essential leitourgia, the sacrament by which it 'becomes what it is.' "[41]

The Church is a new creation, the Scriptures say, but what is this new creation? Not a new substance, a hypostatic organism which has never existed before—not some kind of ontological novelty cultically present. It is not a novel creation, it is the new creation of the one world. The Church exists as an institution in order to reveal in this world the world to come.

"She [the Church] is the passage of the 'old' into the 'new'—yet what is being redeemed, renewed and transfigured through her is not the 'Church,' but the old life itself, the old Adam and the whole of creation. And she is this 'passage' precisely because as institution she is 'bone of the bones and flesh of the flesh' of this world. . . . She is indeed instituted for the world and not as a separate 'religious' institution existing for the specifically religious needs of men. . . . The Church is thus the restoration by God and the acceptance by man of the original and eternal destiny of creation itself . . . As institution the Church is in this world the sacrament of the Body of Christ, of the Kingdom of God and the world to come."[42]

This is precisely what Fr. Schmemann means by the eschatological dimension of the Church. Leitourgia is God's act, it is the sanctification of the world by the divine act which restores. As first fruits of this cosmic drama, the Church is more than the sum of its members; it is the passage of the old world into new life. The Church is the presence in this world of the world to come (which is what the world was meant to be in the first place). The

40. Ibid., 34–35.
41. Ibid., 26.
42. Schmemann, "Theology and Eucharist," 15.

Church's identity is properly understood only within this eschatological dimension. The Church is a new creation because it is the enactment or epiphany or manifestation of transformed relationship with God, a relationship which is not our own doing but is God's gift in Christ. As Fr. Kavanagh puts it, the Church in liturgy does the world the way the world was meant to be done.

If the Church is not an institution which is guardian of certain divinely revealed doctrines, then liturgy is not *locus theologicus* in the sense of a resource for dogma. When Fr. Schmemann calls liturgy a locus for theology he does not mean it in this way. Rather, he means that liturgy is the very ontological condition for the Church's word to the world (theology). Liturgy is the accomplishment of the good news which theology speaks to the world. It is in this sense that theology is rooted in liturgical experience. The Church at prayer is not merely an expression of a vision, it is the very epiphany of God's transforming work upon the world. Theology's task is to "bear witness to this truth, and there is no end to this task. Each theologian will see it only partially and partially reflect it, and each one will remain free, indeed, to reflect it according to his own particular charisma and vocation, but just as all charismata have one and the same source, all vocations ultimately contribute to the edification of one catholic theology of the Church."[43] The varying theological contributions relative to each *sitz im leben* bear witness to the ongoing cosmic and eschatological redemptive act. The Church's faith is not detachable from its ritual enactment, so theology is nothing else but the description of that experience in human words and concepts. Faith is not assent to doctrine but a "living relationship to certain events: the Life, Death, Resurrection and Glorification of Jesus Christ, His Ascension to heaven, the descent of the Holy Spirit . . . a relationship which makes [the Church] a constant 'witness' and 'participant' of these events. . . ."[44] The Church theologizes because in faith it is witness to and participant in these events as present experience. This is why theology, as reasonable discourse about this experience, "is 'description' more than 'definition' for it is, above all, a search for words and concepts adequate to and expressive of

43. Ibid., 23.
44. Schmemann, "Liturgy and Theology," 90.

the living experience of the Church; for a reality and not 'propositions.' . . . [The Church is] the very epiphany of these events themselves. And she can teach about them because, first of all, she knows them; because she is the experience of their reality. . . . Her *lex credendi* is revealed in her life."[45]

Regretably, cult is today deprived of this liturgical function, so liturgy is reduced to cultic categories alone, accompanied by the return of the sacred and profane division. "The *leitourgia* became once again a cult, i.e. a system of sacred actions and rites, performed in the Church, for the Church and by the Church, yet in order not to make the Church 'what it is,' but to 'sanctify' individual members of the Church, to bring them in contact with God."[46] Why? What were the causes for this pseudomorphosis of the liturgical conscience? Why did a corporate and cosmic act become individualized therapeutic help? How did the Church come to be seen as a sacred enclave in a profane environment where troubled individuals could go for help with their religious needs? A reduction has occurred here, one in which the ecclesiological meaning of the Eucharist and the eucharistic dimension of ecclesiology have been forgotten. It is, Fr. Schmemann charges, a reduction typical of scholastic theology and has infected both the East and West. Liturgy is now isolated from Eucharist as the sacrament of the kingdom, the Eucharist is now separated from the Church's eschatological existence, and *lex credendi* is now divorced from *lex orandi* and wed to school theology. What is the source of this liturgical crisis which so dramatically affected liturgical theology?

### SYMBOL AND REALITY

Fr. Schmemann answers by pointing to the skewed perception of liturgy and Church which results when symbol is reduced to representation or illustration. Instead of the Church's Divine Liturgy being, *in actu*, the sacramental presence of God, it is taken to represent a certain event of the past to its participants. The liturgy is thus treated as mere illustrative symbolism of a different reality,

45. Ibid.
46. Schmemann, "Theology and Liturgical Tradition," 176.

as though the liturgical symbol should direct our attention to the real thing. "The reasons for this lie in the fact that 'symbol' here designates something not only *distinct* from reality but in essence even *contrary* to it."[47] When symbol is taken to represent or illustrate the reality which stands behind (beyond?) it, when symbol ceases to designate something real, then two consequences followed: "where [someone] is concerned with 'reality' there is no need for a symbol, and, conversely, where there is a symbol there is no reality. This led to the understanding of the liturgical symbol as an 'illustration,' necessary only to the extent that what is represented is not 'real.' "[48] The reductionism against which Fr. Schmemann pits himself treats symbol as antithetical to reality, instead of a disclosure and conveyance of reality. And then what is left to symbolism in liturgy? So reduced, it recalls to us the significance of an event by serving as a particularly vivid audio-visual aid (a *souvenir* in the original meaning of the French) so that the participant can get in touch with the reality that stands behind the symbol. Rites are reduced to didactic dramatization. When this reductionism invades ecclesiology it produces a view of liturgy which is illustrative (of theological doctrine) rather than epiphanous (of new eighth-day life). The basic difference between liturgical theology and theology of liturgy comes down to different ecclesiologies. If the Church's liturgical life is illustrative then it can be arbitrarily quarried to authorize a pre-determined theological doctrine; but if the Church's liturgy is epiphanous, then it is normative for theology's expression of the reality which leitourgia manifests.

One example of the contraposition between symbol and reality offered by Fr. Schmemann is the difference between the scholastic definition of sacrament and an eschatological, symbolic treatment of the Eucharist. This is particularly evident, he thinks, in the critical role which scholastic theology assigns to the consecratory formula of the Eucharistic prayer.

"In the study of the Eucharist, theological attention was focused exclusively upon the question: what happens to the elements, and

47. Schmemann, *The Eucharist*, 30.
48. Ibid.

162

how and when exactly does it happen? For the early church the real question was: what happens to the *Church* in the Eucharist? The difference is radical; it shows perfectly clearly the nature of the change, from the eschatological to the ecclesiological 'dimension' of the sacraments. Theology shifted to a purely 'cultual' inquiry, which is centered always on the question of the validity and modality of a rite."[49]

Questions of this sort about the efficacy of the consecration are motivated by the need to be certain of Christ's real presence in the Lord's Supper. But to Fr. Schmemann's mind, even feeling the necessity of insuring certainty is evidence of a fear that Christ's presence has been degraded to the category of mere symbol; and this could happen only when symbol is seen as the antithesis of reality instead of the revelation of reality. When symbol is understood as the opposite of what is real, then sacrament is understood as an exception to nature. When symbol is estranged from reality, then the sacrament must be a special sort of symbol, a reality *sui generis*.[50] From this perspective, sacrament is not revelation about the world, sacrament is an exception within it, distinct unto itself. Sacraments then constitute a special reality:

49. Schmemann, "Theology and Liturgical Tradition," 177. We reiterate an earlier comment, that we take Fr. Schmemann to be describing an approach when he speaks of "scholastic theology." To determine whether the persons and historical eras traditionally labeled "scholastic" do in fact exhibit this approach would be another project. For example, it may have come to pass that scholastic theology defended transubstantiation only to answer what happened to the elements, but the source of this line of thought, Paschasius Radbertus, seems to have had more than merely this in mind. Cf. Gary Macy, *The Theologies of the Eucharist in the Early Scholastic Period* (Oxford: The Clarendon Press, 1989) wherein he argues that early Scholasticism in fact displays three approaches to the mystery of communion with Christ in the Lord's Supper: the Paschasian, the Mystical and the Ecclesial.

50. Fr. Schmemann takes as his foil Dom Anscar Vonier who so labels the sacrament. "The world of the sacraments is a new world, created by God entirely apart from the natural and even from the spiritual world. . . . [The sacraments] have their own form of existence, their own psychology, their own grace. . . . We must understand that the idea of the sacraments is something entirely *sui generis*." The passage is from *A Key to the Doctrine of the Eucharist* (Maryland: The Newman Press, 1948) 41 ff., and quoted by Schmemann in *The Eucharist*, 32.

"special in their being established directly by Christ himself, special in their essence as 'visible signs of invisible grace,' special in their 'efficacy' and, finally, special as the 'causes of grace' (causae gratiae)."[51] In this scholastic antithesis between symbol and reality it is therefore necessary for the consecratory formula to make the symbolic presence into a real presence. Since the symbol cannot be real, the symbolic elements must be transubstantiated into the reality itself.

This is not, Fr. Schmemann insists, the Orthodox understanding of the Real Presence. Since it is the Holy Spirit who is the sign of the new age, coming after the completion of Christ's work and bringing the new time, Orthodoxy stresses that it is the Holy Spirit who transforms bread and wine into spiritual food—not, however, to make symbolic food into real food, as if the representational elements must in fact be made real presence.

"[The transformation] happens not because of some strange and miraculous power left by Christ with some people (priests) who therefore can perform this miracle by virtue of their power, but because we—the Church—are in Christ, i.e. in His Sacrifice, Love, Ascension, in the whole of His movement of deification, or transforming His Humanity by His Divinity; because, in other words, we are in His Eucharist and offer Him as our Eucharist to God. . . . The mystery of the Eucharistic transformation is thus the mystery of the Church herself, of her belonging to the new age and to the new life—in the Holy Spirit. For 'this world' for which the Kingdom of God is yet to come . . . the Bread remains bread and the Wine remains wine. But in the wonderful and transfigured reality of the Kingdom, revealed and manifested in the Church, they are verily and totally the very Body and the very Blood of Christ."[52]

The mystery of the Eucharistic transformation is the mystery of the Church liturgically being what she is for the sake of the world.

51. Schmemann, The Eucharist, 32.
52. Schmemann, Liturgy and Life: Christian Development Through Liturgical Experience (New York: Department of Religious Education, Orthodox Church in America, 1974) 60.

The entire Church and the entire liturgy is the sacramental presence of God, not just the transubstantiated elements.[53]

Because symbol is treated as antithetical to reality, school theology deals with the sacraments independently of the liturgy, and liturgy becomes a nonessential, symbolical framework for the action and words necessary for validity. Fr. Schmemann, on the contrary, would have us see the whole liturgy as one sacramental, transforming act. Sacramentology must be rooted in liturgy as *lex credendi* is rooted in *lex orandi*. This is only another instance of the difference between the approach of liturgical theology and theology of liturgy. In the latter, "something is lacking because the theologian thinks of the sacrament and forgets the liturgy. As a good scientist he first isolates the object of his study, reduces it to one moment, to one 'phenomenon'—and then, proceeding from the general to the particular, from the known to the unknown, he gives a definition, which in fact raises more questions than it answers."[54]

COSMIC AND ESCHATOLOGICAL

A sacrament is both cosmic and eschatological. It is cosmic because all of creation is embraced and returned to God as God's own; it is eschatological because it is oriented toward the kingdom which is to come. Since the Church is sacramental, it is likewise both cosmic and eschatological. "She is a sacrament in the cosmic sense because she manifests in 'this world' the genuine world of God, as he first created it. . . . She is a sacrament in the eschatological dimension because the original world of God's creation, revealed by the Church, has already been saved by Christ. . . . Being a sacrament in the most profound and comprehensive sense of the term, the Church creates, manifests and fulfils herself in

53. It is Fr. Schmemann who identifies this interpretation as Orthodox contra Western. It is of course true that the evolution of the Eucharistic Prayer's theological treatment has found the West focusing upon the words of institution and the East focusing upon the epiclesis, but this should not be taken to mean that western scholars are not also critical of this narrowed scope. For an excellent overview of how the Eucharist transformed from 'holy meal' to 'sacred food' see Nathan Mitchell, OSB, *Cult and Controversy: The Worship of the Eucharist Outside the Mass* (New York: Pueblo Publishing Co., 1982).

54. Schmemann, *For the Life of the World*, 42.

and through the sacraments."[55] This is the ecclesiological meaning of the Eucharist, and the Eucharistic dimension of ecclesiology. The liturgical crisis, the metamorphosis of liturgical conscience mentioned above, is exactly the fact that both the cosmic and eschatological facet of ecclesial identity have been lost. Then symbol hides reality instead of disclosing it, and the Church's liturgy is symbolic illustration of a reality which exists not in the actuality of the Church but somewhere else, as something else. Symbol is understood as the sign of an absent reality.

Faith is required for the symbol to function the way it should. Faith is not empirical knowledge, yet it is knowledge which can be communicated. It is communicated through the symbolic presence of the reality (by "symbolic presence" is meant real presence, not a one-step-removed presence). "Faith certainly is contact and a thirst for contact, embodiment and a thirst for embodiment: it is the manifestation, the presence, the operation of one reality within the other. All of this *is* the symbol (from *sumballo*, 'unite,' 'hold together')."[56] The relationship is not logical (this stands for that), nor analogical (this illustrates that), nor causal (this generates that). The relationship is epiphanous: this communicates the other. Faith sees Christ on the table, at the altar, in the elements, with the Church, through the priest, within his Body the Church. There is not one object which represents Christ, but many objects and actions and people which symbolize Christ, i.e. make Christ known to faith. The Church's ritual liturgy is the epiphany of eighth-day existence which is eschatological life in the kingdom. This is what Fr. Schmemann means when he says the liturgy is the passage from earth to heaven.

The Church is sacramental not because it dispenses hypostasized grace, or because it is the warden of divine revelations, or because by the cultic power of its priests it can transubstantiate the symbol into the reality. On all these levels, the cultual acts still do not reach their fulfillment as leitourgia. The liturgy does exist as cult, yes, but it is "a cult which eternally transcends itself, because it is the cult of a community which eternally realizes itself, as the Body of Christ, as the Church of the Holy Spirit, as ultimately, the new

55. Schmemann, *The Eucharist*, 35–36.
56. Ibid., 39.

*aeon* of the kingdom. It is a tradition of forms and structures, but these forms and structures are no longer those of a 'cult,' but those of the Church itself, of its life 'in Christ.' "[57] The Church is sacramental because in its cultic (i.e. ritual, i.e. liturgical) act it fulfills the cosmic reality to which it eschatologically points. The reality is still to come, yet already present, making the liturgical tradition of the Church fundamentally antinomical in its nature.

So long as this antinomy persists—and it will persist until Christ's second coming—the kingdom must be celebrated in symbolic cult (which is not at all to say the kingdom is confined to cult). "In this world, the *eschaton*—the holy, the sacred, the 'otherness'—can be expressed and manifested only as 'cult.' "[58] In the liturgical rite, wherein the gathered Church becomes something corporately which it had not been as a mere collection of individuals, the kingdom is expressed—in the sense of "pressed out": conveyed, manifested, epiphanized, made known to those with eyes of faith to see it. The kingdom of Christ is known by faith and is hidden within us. For those who believe it and accept it, the kingdom is already here and now, but it is not known in external and empirical signs. "The Lord's glorification does not have the compelling, objective evidence of His humiliation and cross. His glorification is known only through the mysterious death in the baptismal font, through the anointing of the Holy Spirit. It is known only in the fullness of the Church, as she gathers to meet the Lord and to share in His risen life."[59] Because the Church is in this world but not of it, because the cosmos has been redeemed by Christ but this redemption is not yet fulfilled (the world is not yet filled full of Christ), because life in Christ is eighth-day kairos existence and not yet the whole chronos of the world, the eschaton is expressed and manifested as cult. "Not only in relation to the world, but in relation to itself as dwelling in the world, the Church must use the forms and language of the cult, in order eternally to transcend the cult, to 'become what it is.' "[60] This is why the journey to the kingdom begins with leav-

57. Schmemann, "Theology and Liturgical Tradition," 175.
58. Ibid., 174.
59. Schmemann, *For the Life of the World*, 28.
60. Schmemann, "Theology and Liturgical Tradition," 174.

ing. Entrance into Christ in the cultual acts of the liturgy is "an entrance into a fourth dimension which allows us to see the ultimate reality of life. It is not an escape from the world, rather it is the arrival at a vantage point from which we can see more deeply into the reality of the world."[61] The first liturgical act of the eighth day takes place when Christians leave their beds and homes and gather at the assembly (the term by which the Church's worship was identified in the New Testament: synaxis). This is already a sacramental act taking place, for Christians " 'come together in one place,' to bring their lives, their very 'world' with them and to be more than what they were: a *new* community with a new life," not in order to add a religious dimension to the natural world but "to *fulfill the Church,* and that means to make present the One in whom all things are at their *end,* for all things are at their *beginning.*"[62]

### c. Where to Find Liturgical Theology: Method

Now we are at last in position to see the true task of liturgical theology. Apart from this ecclesiology, liturgical theology will always be underestimated. The ekklesia does not assemble so that individuals can discretely participate in private means of grace, but in order to constitute the Church. If only the former happens then a cultic act has occurred but it has not been transcended to become liturgical cult. Leitourgia is an action by which a group of people become something corporately which they had not been as a mere collection of individuals, in order to perform a ministry on behalf of and in the interest of the whole community. "Thus the Church itself is a *leitourgia,* a ministry, a calling to act in this

---

61. Schmemann, *For the Life of the World,* 27. This occurs weekly, and it is also the image under which the entire season of Lent must be discussed: "When a man leaves on a journey, he must know where he is going. Thus with Lent. Above all, Lent is a spiritual journey and its destination is Easter. . . . [T]he liturgical traditions of the church, all its cycles and service, exist, first of all, in order to help us recover the vision and the taste of that *new life.* . . . [The worship of the Church] was from the very beginning and still is our entrance into, our communion with, the *new life of the King-dom.* . . ." *Great Lent: Journey to Pascha* (New York: St. Vladimir's Seminary Press, 1974), 11, 13.

62. Ibid.

world after the fashion of Christ, to bear testimony to Him and His kingdom."[63] The Eucharistic liturgy must not be understood in cultic terms alone; as Christianity is the end of religion, so the liturgy in general and the Eucharist in particular is the end of cult. Again, the liturgy exists in order to constitute Church, which is the epiphany of the kingdom.

### LITURGICAL THEOLOGY IN MOTION

If this is true—and it is critical for grasping Fr. Schmemann's agenda of liturgical theology to understand leitourgia and ecclesiology thus intertwined—then the liturgical theology which he seeks is found nowhere else but in the liturgical tradition of the Church. "If liturgical theology stems from an understanding of worship as the public act of the Church, then its final goal will be to clarify and explain the connection between this act and the Church, i.e. to explain how the Church expresses and fulfills herself in this act."[64] The *lex credendi* is found in the Church's worship itself, which is to say in its Ordo or structure or concrete historical shape. Thus "the first principle of liturgical theology is that, in explaining the liturgical tradition of the Church, one must proceed not from abstract, purely intellectual schemata cast randomly over the services, but from the services themselves—and this means, first of all, from their *ordo.*"[65]

Access to the subject matter of liturgical theology will be denied those who will not look at real liturgies in detail (we are here opposing real liturgies to ideas of worship). This ecclesiology understands the assembly to somehow enact the mystery, not merely reflect it, and therefore those who strive to bespeak this mystery will only find their subject matter in these concrete enactments, not in ideation about the phenomenon of worship in general. As Fr. Taft puts it, "One of the great contemporary illusions is that one can construct a liturgical theology without a profound knowledge of the liturgical tradition."[66] And again, the purpose of this

---

63. Schmemann, *The Eucharist*, 25.
64. Schmemann, *Introduction*, 14.
65. Schmemann, *The Eucharist*, 14.
66. Robert Taft, "The Liturgical Year: Studies, Prospects, Reflections," *Worship* 55 (1981) 2.

careful historical research "is not to recover the past (which is impossible), much less to imitate it (which would be fatuous), but to *understand liturgy* which, because it has a history, can only be understood in motion, just as the only way to understand a top is to spin it."[67] It is a mistake (even if a long-practiced one) to first invent a theory of worship and then look for liturgical texts or practices to support the *a priori* theory. Because liturgy does not exist in general, the task propaedeutic to liturgical theology is historical analysis of liturgical structure and evolution. There are no shortcuts here. The structure of liturgy is not our invention, and it will not be charted by the creative work of theological theorists but by the careful work of liturgiologists.

Furthermore, since liturgy is the faith of the Church in motion, the *lex orandi* which establishes *lex credendi* is not located on the pages of prayer books but in the dynamic action of the liturgy. After all, rite is more than the text.

"Worship simply cannot be equated either with texts or with forms of worship. It is a whole, within which everything, the words of prayer, lections, chanting, ceremonies, the relationship of all these things in a 'sequence' or 'order' and, finally, what can be defined as the 'liturgical coefficient' of each of these elements (i.e. that significance which, apart from its own immediate content, each acquires as a result of its place in the general sequence or order of worship), only all this together defines the meaning of the whole and is therefore the proper subject of study and theological evaluation."[68]

What is needed, then, is not historical research performed upon the books, or ideation about the phenomenon of worship (liturgical or otherwise), but rather historical analysis of the structure of

67. Robert Taft, "The Structural Analysis of Liturgical Units: An Essay in Methodology," *Worship* 52:4 (July 1978) 318. Fr. Aidan Kavanagh eloquently utilizes this image in his work. "This means that the liturgy of a church is nothing other than that church's faith in motion on certain definite and crucial levels. . . . Thus a church's worship does not merely reflect or express its repertoire of faith. It transacts the church's faith in God under the condition of God's real presence in both church and world." Aidan Kavanagh, *On Liturgical Theology*, 8.
68. Schmemann, *Introduction*, 15–16.

concrete liturgies, which is why this study must have its own distinctive method. Liturgical theology will occupy a special, independent place in the general system of theological disciplines. "Liturgical theology is therefore an independent theological discipline, with its own special subject—the liturgical tradition of the Church, and requiring its own corresponding and special method, distinct from the methods of other theological disciplines. Without liturgical theology our understanding of the Church's faith and doctrine is bound to be incomplete."[69] The attempt to reach meaning apart from structural analysis is a mistake. As Fr. Kavanagh puts it, "Here the student of liturgy may be of some modest service in aiding the secondary theologian to read the primary body of perceived data in a living tradition of Christian worship. What needs to be read is rite."[70] This is a profound and arduous task, but its forfeit risks arbitrariness in the theological use of liturgical material.

### LITURGY'S CRITIQUE OF THEOLOGY

Liturgical theology must therefore begin with the historical study of worship—begin with it, but not end with it. Liturgical theology sets its sights on more than smells and bells in the chapel (the "how to" approach to liturgics which is prevalent in seminary catalogues). While Fr. Schmemann insists that liturgical theology begin with historical study, he also wishes to prevent liturgical theology's premature conclusion. Yes, one must acquaint students with the Ordo (that collection of rules and prescriptions which regulate the Church's worship, set forth in Orthodoxy in the *Typicon* and other books of rites; western "rubrics"). If liturgical theology is not to be pulled out of the air, like a magician's rabbit, it will be necessary to look with the liturgiologist's eye at the prayers and rites and actions with which Christians through the ages have interacted with the living presence they discern in liturgical assembly. There must be an investigation of specific rites, canonical injunctions, symbols, concepts, stories, and cultual actions—and this means discerning their functional meaning in the deep structure, not merely a surface reading of the text, for these

---

69. Ibid.
70. Kavanagh, *On Liturgical Theology*, 147.

basic structures "fix the 'liturgical coefficient' of each element and point to its significance in the whole, giving to worship a consistent theological interpretation and freeing it from arbitrary symbolic interpretations."[71]

Such is the task of liturgiology. But as noted, it is only half of liturgical theology's complete task. "Historical liturgics establishes the structures and their development, liturgical theology discovers their meaning: such is the general methodological principle of the task."[72] Although Fr. Schmemann is concerned to ground faith in liturgy (lest it suffer the unhealthy pluralism of splintered specialization and arbitrariness), he protests that he is not trying to reduce the former to the latter. That the law of prayer establishes the law of belief does not imply a reduction of faith to liturgy; it does not imply a confusion between faith and liturgy such that one is made indifferent to doctrinal content; it does not imply the separation of faith and liturgy into two essences. And this, again, is why Fr. Schmemann can claim that what concerns him is theology, and why he can make the surprising assertion that *lex orandi lex est credendi* "implies, as its first condition, a double task: a liturgical critique of theology and a theological critique of the liturgy."[73] After all this talk about theology being grounded in and springing from the liturgy, after this defense of liturgy as the ontological condition for theology and its norm, after arguing for a special methodology for liturgical theology which begins with historical structural analysis, Fr. Schmemann is able to say—with a straight face, apparently—that there also needs to be a theological critique of the liturgy!

71. Schmemann, *Introduction*, 18. Robert Taft also advocates a methodology which begins with structural study. "My own approach is structural and historical, that is, I try to identify and isolate individual liturgical structures or units, then trace their history as such, rather than attempt to study the entire rite as a unity in each historical period. For it has been my constant observation that liturgies do not grow evenly, like living organisms. Rather, their individual structures possess a life of their own. More like cancer than native cells, they can appear like aggressors, showing riotous growth at a time when all else lies dormant." "How Liturgies Grow: The Evolution of the Byzantine 'Divine Liturgy,'" *Orientalia Christiana Periodica* 43 (1977), 360.

72. Schmemann, *Introduction*, 18.

73. Schmemann, "Liturgy and Theology," 95.

Surely it is manifestly evident that by theological critique of liturgy Fr. Schmemann envisions something quite different from that proposed by Prenter, Vajta, Brunner or Wainwright. He does not mean finding a doctrinal key to the liturgical rite, a theological plumb line for liturgical reform. He is not lapsing back to a liturgical resourcement of *a priori* doctrinal propositions. This is what theology of liturgy has often done, yes: searched for a consistent theology of worship with which liturgy must comply once it is formulated. But the theological task is to find the meaning of the Ordo exactly in its structures. For liturgical theology, liturgy is not the illustrative representation of some consistent theological principle, it is "the 'locus theologicus' *par excellence* because it is its very function, its *'leitourgia'* in the original meaning of that word, to manifest and to fulfill the Church's faith and to manifest it not partially, not 'discursively' but as living totality and catholic experience."[74] Because epiphanous of the Church's faith, liturgy is the ground for the theological enterprise.

Because in the liturgy the Church becomes what it is, one must look to liturgical structures to discern the Church's *lex credendi.* This implies "an organic and essential interdependence in which one element, the faith, although source and cause of the other, the liturgy, essentially needs the other as its own self-understanding and self-fulfillment. It is, to be sure, faith that gives birth to, and 'shapes,' liturgy, but it is liturgy, that by fulfilling and expressing faith, 'bears testimony' to faith and becomes thus its true and adequate expression and norm: 'lex orandi lex est credendi.' "[75] It is therefore erroneous to think that every theological doctrine must be supported by a liturgical rubric (and the older, the better). One does not justify doctrines by grounding them in rubrical footnotes. This does injustice both to liturgy, which is not meant to be a historical source book but a living rite, and to theology, which has its own integrity and is not merely exegesis of liturgy. But liturgical theology does insist that since the liturgy is the corporate

---

74. Schmemann, "Liturgical Theology, Theology of Liturgy, and Liturgical Reform," 219. Here the term *locus theologicus* obviously means something different from a source of theological data.
75. Ibid., 218.

epiphany of faith (the ritual locus of *lex orandi*), it is normative for *lex credendi*.

If liturgical theology is prehending the theology of the Church epiphanized in and through liturgy, then methodologically the first step is to look at the deep structures of the liturgy. Liturgiology should establish the structure and development of liturgies and lead to liturgical theology. Unfortunately, this methodology has fallen apart. The deep tragedy which Fr. Schmemann denounces is the three-way rupture between liturgy, theology and piety. Liturgy is no longer the expression and norm of either reasonable faith (theology) or affective faith (piety). As a result of the metamorphosis of our liturgical conscience, both theology and piety run autonomous courses. He demonstrates what he means in the following example which, lying on the fault line as it does, creates many smaller tremors when it suffers this disruption.

In the early Church there was a self-evident connection and interdependence between the Lord's Day, the Eucharist and the Ecclesia (the coming together of the faithful as "church"). There was a unity and interdependence between the cosmological, eschatological and ecclesiological dimensions of faith. The Lord's Day was an eighth day in the cosmos in which our eschatological status was manifested in the Eucharist by the gathering together of a new people, the Church. Although this connection still exists liturgically (since Christians do assemble on the Lord's day to receive communion) it is clear that it is neither understood nor experienced in the way it was understood and experienced by the early Church.

"Why?. . . . The connection itself remained a part of the 'lex orandi' but it ceased to be related in any way to the 'lex credendi,' was no longer regarded as a theological datum and no theologian has even bothered to mention it as having any theological significance, as revealing anything about the Church's 'experience' of herself, the World and the Kingdom of God. Thus the Lord's Day became simply the Christian form of the Sabbath, the Eucharist one 'means of grace' among many, and the Church—an institution with sacraments but no longer sacramental in her very nature and 'constitution'."[76]

76. Ibid., 220.

174

The Lord's Day, the Lord's Supper, and the Lord's Body (by which we mean the Church, not the consecrated elements) should be mutually illuminating. The cosmic, eschatological and ecclesiological dimensions should cast light one upon the other. Like they interpenetrate in the historic structure of the liturgy, they must interpenetrate in our theological consciousness. These three do not accidentally coincide in liturgical structure, they epiphanize the redemptive theology of the Church whereby a new humanity has fellowship with God on the basis of Christ's symbolical sacrificial presence, and an eschatological theology whereby a foretaste of the feast to come is offered. If *lex orandi* establishes *lex credendi* then (a) the assembly is to be understood in its context of the eighth day and at Eucharist, (b) the Eucharist is to be understood as being for the assembly and on the eighth day, and (c) the eighth day is to be understood as already presenting a foretaste of the messianic banquet in order to create a new humanity which is Christ's body, the Church. Without this theological matrix, born in the womb of the liturgical structure, how can one discourse about redemption, God's kingdom, Christology, sacraments, God's self-revelation, forgiveness, atonement, eschatology, ecclesiology, etc.? This triunity of assembly, Eucharist and Church is so important that Fr. Schmemann can say "the fundamental task of liturgical theology consists therefore in uncovering the meaning and essence of this unity."[77] To do so would be to uncover the Church's *lex credendi* in the Church's *lex orandi*.

It has become popular to speak of "Eucharistic ecclesiology" but this phrase itself must be understood under the methodology of liturgical theology. Eucharist is "the *moment of truth* which makes it possible to see the real 'objects' of theology: God, man and the world, in the *true light*, which, in other words, reveals both the *objects* of theology as they really are and gives the necessary *light* for their understanding."[78] The theological task is to see God, humanity and world in their true light. Theology needs a liturgical critique because God, humanity and the world are seen in truth where the epiphany of the kingdom occurs, viz. in the eighth-day banquet of the new humanity redeemed by Christ. The light

77. Schmemann, *The Eucharist*, 11–12.
78. Schmemann, "Theology and Eucharist," 22.

175

makes possible understanding, and this understanding is incumbent to theology. But by saying that theology needs a liturgical critique, Fr. Schmemann is not trying to conflate theology and liturgy. To suggest this is already a sign of their mutual alienation. That all theology ought to be liturgical does not mean that theology should have liturgy as its sole object of study, or that theology should be sprinkled with liturgical phrases, or that doctrine should be authenticated with footnotes from rubrics. It does mean that theology has its "ultimate term of reference in the faith of the Church, as manifested and communicated in the liturgy."[79] This would require a conversion not so much of theology's structures and methods but of the theologian. "He has mastered to perfection the necessary ascetism of intellectual discipline and integrity, the humility proper to all genuine rational effort. He now has to learn how to immerse himself into the joy of the Church. . . . He has to rediscover the oldest of all languages of the Church: that of her rites, the rhythm and the *ordo* of her *leitourgia* . . . He has to become again not only the student of the Church's faith but, above all, its *witness*."[80] Theology performs this service for the Church and world when it is rooted in the liturgical epiphany of the kingdom.

### THEOLOGY'S CRITIQUE OF LITURGY (TRADITION)

So theology needs liturgy's critique. To say, on the flip side, that liturgy also needs theology's critique is to recognize that the faith ritually expressed can be lost to arbitrariness. The intent in *lex credendi* would be to discern the Church's catholic faith and not impose private concerns. This, it seems clear, is the role of Tradition in the Church. The liturgy is where the Tradition is normatively maintained and the theological critique to be applied to liturgy is simply assuring its concordance with Tradition. During the long centuries of liturgy's divorce from theology, says Fr. Schmemann, the Tradition's theological critique of liturgical rite has been "obscured by several strata of pseudo theological and pseudo pious explanations and interpretations, by a superficial pseudo symbolism, by individualism and legalism. And it is not

79. Schmemann, "Liturgy and Theology," 95.
80. Ibid., 98.

easy today . . . to rediscover and to communicate the real 'key' of the Orthodox liturgical tradition, to connect it again to the *lex credendi*."[81] Liturgical study fails to be theology if it becomes so transfixed by the rules of the Ordo that it fails to consider the theological structure of the Ordo. This has occurred in some recent liturgiology which fixates on historical development of rite without any ultimate theological interest and attention, i.e., without revealing the Tradition. "Absolutely indispensable as it is, this historical aspect not only can never be an end in itself, but, in the last analysis, it is only from a theological perspective that it can receive its most important and proper questions. Very good and knowledgeable historians, because of their theological ignorance, have nevertheless produced monuments of nonsense comparable to those produced by the theologians of liturgy ignorant of its history."[82] Tradition critiques theology to make sure it is catholic; Tradition critiques liturgy to make sure it is not idiosyncratic, cultural, and arbitrary. Liturgical theology discovers, does not invent, the Tradition in the Ordo.

The task of interpreting the Ordo is more than knowing its content and rubrics. The Ordo is not the list of rules, but the principle which animates those rules; it is not the regulations alone, but is the grammar which the rubrics are attempting to embody. This is the "problem of the Ordo" as he calls it.

"To find the Ordo behind the 'rubrics,' regulations and rules—to find the unchanging principle, the living norm or 'logos' of worship as a whole, within what is accidental and temporary: this is the primary task which faces those who would regard liturgical theology not as the collecting of accidental and arbitrary explanations of services but as the systematic study of the *lex orandi* of the Church. This is nothing but the search for or identification of that element of the Typicon which is presupposed by its whole content, rather than contained by it, in short, its general 'philosophy.' It is the elucidation of those principles and premises upon which all the regulations contained within it are founded."[83]

81. Ibid.
82. Ibid., 99–100.
83. Schmemann, *Introduction*, 32–33.

The claim which was our beginning point no longer looks so amazing: the question addressed by liturgical theology to liturgy and to the entire liturgical tradition is not about liturgy but about theology. The essence of the liturgy is ultimately nothing else but the Church's faith itself. The objective is to grasp the theology as revealed in and through the liturgy. This is an interpretive task. This general element is not found written within the Typicon itself because "the written Ordo arose after worship, and arose not as the elucidation of its theory, or as the outline of a liturgical rite for given conditions, or even as an aid for deciding disputed questions of liturgical practice."[84] Fr. Schmemann compares the relationship of the written rubrics to worship with the relationship of the canons to the structure of the Church. The canons did not create the Church, they arose for the defence, clarification and definition of that structure which already existed. Likewise the written Ordo does not determine the law of worship, it presupposes this *lex orandi*. The law of worship is operative in the evolution of ritual structure and can there be read by those trained to read the rites of the Church. "The written Ordo does not so much determine the law of worship as it adapts this law to this or that need. And this means that it presupposes the existence of this law or 'general element.' The search for, elucidation and explanation of, this basic principle constitutes the problem of the Ordo."[85] We should expect nothing else from worship which is led by the living Spirit and not by dead rules.

Methodologically, the problem of the Ordo falls under three headings. First, the question is raised regarding the basic structure of worship presupposed, revealed and established by present rubrics, but such structure is found only in historical liturgies, the living Tradition of worship. The second question is the origin and development of this structure, addressed when the liturgiologist investigates the history of the Ordo. The third question to be answered concerns the meaning of the Ordo, its theological content as the *lex orandi* of the Church. In sum, "The liturgy has to be explained once again as the *leitourgia of the Church*—and this is the task of the theologian. But for this task, the real liturgical tradition

84. Ibid.
85. Ibid.

178

must be rediscovered—and this is the task of the liturgiologist. If it is for theology to purify the liturgy, it is for the liturgy to give back to theology that eschatological fullness, which the liturgy alone can 'actualize'—the participation in the life of the Kingdom which is still to come.''[86] The task for liturgical theology is not, as it was for theologies of/from worship, to give expression to the doctrine which lies buried in liturgical form, but to give voice to the *lex orandi* of the leitourgia. To do so will be to simultaneously hear the Church's *lex credendi*, for it lies here and nowhere else.

This was the agenda in Fr. Schmemann's book *Introduction to Liturgical Theology*. This book is his treatment of liturgical theology's twofold method of historical analysis and theological meaning regarding the problem of the Ordo. We shall not, however, follow him down this path. We shall instead offer a topography of liturgical theology in the next chapter, and follow it with a look at two samples to see how they fulfill Fr. Schmemann's definition.

86. Schmemann, ''Theology and Liturgical Tradition,'' 178.

## Chapter 5

## Liturgical Theology: A Topography

Theology seems to abhor a vacuum as much as nature does. If the meaning is no longer evident in the structure of the rite (liturgical theology) then theological meaning will be assigned to it (theology of/from liturgy). The telos of theology is understanding or meaning. Our claim has been that only when the meaning is read off the structure of the rite itself may the effort properly be called liturgical theology. Thus the two affirmations about what we call our third approach, liturgical theology: (a) it is real theology, although *theologia prima* and not *theologia secunda,* and (b) this theology is manifested in the Church's *lex orandi* because it is worked out under ritual logistics. The topic of liturgical theology is the faith of the Church coming to existence, epiphanized and preserved in liturgical rite. We have not refused to apply the name "theology" to other strikes at meaning, we have mainly wished to establish that the meaning epiphanized in the ritual structure can also be appropriately called theology.

We hope it is clear, then, that attention to liturgy involves more than fussing with smells and bells in the chapel. Liturgical theology has to do with the "what," not merely the "how." We understand this to be the reason why Fr. Schmemann can say that in the approach he advocates, by every line he ever wrote, the questions addressed to liturgy are not about liturgy but about theology. It is the reason why Fr. Taft patently says "Liturgy, therefore, is theology. It is not history or cultural anthropology or archeology or literary criticism or esthetics or philology or pastoral care. . . . Like every other respectable branch of theology, it of course uses these and various other disciplines and methodologies for what I take to be the first and self-justifying end of all study:

*understanding.*"[1] Liturgy is not just feelings, and not just a condescendingly esthetic expression of doctrines which are too sophisticated for simple believers to understand. Liturgy is the Church's "sustained summons home to God in Christ," as Fr. Kavanagh defines it, which requires a considerably more robust vision of liturgy than it usually receives when it is associated mainly with robes, banners and stoles. "The relationship of embroidery to the driving of a diesel locomotive seems easier to demonstrate than the connection between stoles and proclaiming the Gospel. Something here seems to have been enthusiastically trivialized."[2] If concern for liturgy degenerates into caring about nothing more than protocol and rubric for their own sake, then by liturgy's own criterion something has gone vastly wrong with the enterprise.

We do not dispute that something has gone vastly wrong with the enterprise. For many, liturgy means exactly no more than protocol, order, pastoral care, or esthetics, which is why what sometimes passes for liturgical theology is nothing more than neatening up the "how." Thus liturgy comes to be the province of quirky seminarians who get a thrill out of rubrical tidiness. We suppose that what drives Prenter, Vajta, Brunner and Wainwright is a desire to restore some theological verve to the project. For this, we applaud them. We have tried to indicate how each of these authors desired to nudge liturgy and theology closer together. Unfortunately, insinuating some theology into this vision of liturgy will not do the trick. As laudable the effort, and as helpful as it is for some purposes, it should not pass for liturgical theology. An organic, not merely connective definition is required. If the operating definition of liturgy is inadequate, the resultant vision of liturgy's influence on theology is faulty.

## a. Liturgy and Leitourgia

If the Church does suffer the reductionism which Fr. Schmemann diagnosed—if symbol has degenerated to sign, icon to picture, performative speech to didactic explanation, and sacrament to

1. Taft, "Liturgy as Theology," *Worship,* 56:2 (March 1982) 115.
2. Kavanagh, *Elements of Rite* (New York: Pueblo Publishing Co., 1982) 47.

souvenir—if this reductionism has gripped the liturgy, it has correspondingly gripped liturgical theology. To the degree that liturgy is treated as doxological expression of theological principles, to that same degree what passes as liturgical theology will only utilize liturgy, either as an object of study or as a resource from which to quarry data supportive of doctrinal presuppositions already in place. But to the degree that liturgy is the ontological condition for theology, liturgical theology gives voice to the theology epiphanized in the faithful's leitourgia. It is not a matter of expressing *theologia secunda* doxologically, but of giving voice to the assembly's *lex orandi*. Wainwright had Eastern Christianity's dictum backwards ("the true theologian is a person who prays") when he supposed it meant we should put an existential spin upon doctrine; it means the opposite, as Fr. Kavanagh notes. "The dictum, so far from endowing a doxological quality upon the second-order activity of theology, in fact confers a theological quality upon the first-order activity of people at worship. . . . The 'theologian' in this Eastern view is a contemplative whose life is suffused with the *leitourgia* of a cosmos restored to communion with its trinitarian Source."[3]

We are trying to point out the peculiarity of this starting definition by conceiving four approaches, thus permitting distinctions among the body of literature indiscriminately called liturgical theology. Only one of them should be called liturgical theology because of how its vision of liturgy differs from the first two (and the fourth approach is simply the effort of pointing this out). In this we are thinking of the ekklesia's activity as rite, as faith in motion, as adjustment to encounter with the Holy. Let us say it this way for the moment: liturgical theology has less to do with liturgy than leitourgia.

By this distinction we mean to tag two tacitly different understandings of the ekklesia's eighth-day activity. In the first understanding, liturgy refers to the "how," the order and style, the sequence and protocol of worship. It is that which can be written in the front pages of the prayer book because it is about whether or not the clergy chants, how decoratively symbolic are the vest-

3. Kavanagh, *On Liturgical Theology*, 124.

ments, how to implement more meaningful liturgical phrases, where one stands and how one moves in the chancel, and so forth. Now, if the ekklesia does no more than liturgy in this sense (a frilly, if somber, expression of faith and doctrine) then a theology is additionally required in order to provide theological kick to this very untheological activity. Such a product would allegedly be liturgical theology, and any and all theological projects which use liturgy as source for rumination about God, or which make the patterned worship of the community an object of study, could indiscriminately qualify. Someone has to organize this inchoate raw data and the liturgical theologian volunteers. The task would be to make theological sense of the non-theological brute experience of faith. In the liturgy the faithful reflect this doctrine or that, but they are rather unclear and clumsy about it, so *theologia secunda* offers to clarify the doctrine and in turn critique the expression. We saw three of our earlier authors make the claim at some point that doctrine or dogma "is called upon to bring about a correction" (Vajta), is necessary to establish the correct *usus* (Brunner), and should exercise doctrinal control over *lex orandi* (Wainwright).[4] This is not liturgical theology proper because it does not research the liturgical act itself but instead treats, on a secondary level, a doctrine extracted (abstracted) from the action.

To speak of liturgical theology as springing from within rather than being imposed from without requires, it would seem, an understanding of liturgy pitched in a different key and one which is

4. On this point we feel that Prenter's work is friendlier to liturgical theology; the point at which he is vulnerable will be remarked on later. He said, it will be remembered, "Academic theology is not a different theology than the theology of the liturgy. They are substantially the same. Academic theology, however, is a reflective unfolding of the content of the theology of the liturgy apart from the worship of the Church, whereas the theology of the liturgy is the unreflected, living manifestation in the worship of the Church of that truth analyzed by academic theology." "Liturgy and Theology," *Theologie und Gottesdienst: Gesammelte Aufsatze, op. cit.,* 147. Although he distinguishes two theological homes for academic theology and theology of the liturgy, he speaks positively of liturgy having a theology, and not merely being a reflection of one. The dogmatic task is essential, but not necessary. It can be said to contribute to understanding, but one would still have theology—and not just the rudiments of theology—without dogmatics.

perhaps less familiar to our ears today. To believe liturgy is the community's *theologia prima* will require us to understand liturgy as more than mood or style or expression; liturgy must be treated as rite, not merely as protocol. We will distinguish this second understanding with the tag leitourgia. Liturgy deals with rubrics; leitourgia deals with what gives rubrics their reason and value.[5] Liturgy deals with the content in the Typicon; leitourgia deals with that element of the Typicon which is presupposed by its whole content, rather than contained by it.[6]

## WORSHIP OR LITURGY?

A difficulty presents itself right away. The distinction between liturgy and leitourgia which we propose might imply that while nearly all worship services have some sort of liturgy, i.e., function according to a more or less loosely defined protocol, not all worship services could be characterized as leitourgia. We do not deny the implication. Perhaps not all worship can be characterized as leitourgia, not all assemblies as liturgical, not all Sundays as an eighth day. Need they be? The Church has historically appeared to say so, yet more recently leitourgia's absence seems to be not greatly missed. Fr. Kavanagh traces the loss of rite to developments culminating by the sixteenth century, developments which continue to leave their mark upon the modern world.

"A sense of rite and symbol in the West was breaking down and under siege. And since it now appears that those who sought to repair the breakdown were its products rather than its masters, they may be said with greater accuracy to have substituted some-

5. We have taken liberties with a line from Fr. Kavanagh's book, *Elements of Rite*. He uses the phrase there to describe the book, saying, "[it] is not about rubrics. It is about what gives rubrics their reason and value. If it cannot avoid occasionally calling attention to them, this is because adequacy of liturgical celebration rests upon them as adequacy of language rests upon rules of grammar" (3). Later he writes that though the book is about liturgical laws and rubrics, he is endeavoring to put them into proper perspective. "Taken together, rubrics and laws constitute a checklist of the factors to be considered in the art of putting a liturgy together and celebrating it" (8).

6. "The problem of the Ordo" which Fr. Schmemann defines in ch. 1 of *Introduction*. The reference alludes to 32–33.

thing in its place that was new and, to them, more relevant to the times. It was a new system of worship which would increasingly do without rite, one in which printed texts would increasingly bear the burden formerly borne by richly ambiguous corporate actions done with water, oil, food, and the touch of human hands. . . . *Liturgy had begun to become 'worship'.* . . . And the primary theological act which the liturgical act had once been now began to be controlled increasingly by practitioners of secondary theology whose concerns lay with correct doctrine in a highly polemical climate.''[7]

Why has the substitution of liturgy for leitourgia scarcely been noticed? Because of the reductionism of which Schmemann spoke? Because rite has receded, as Kavanagh charges?[8] Yes, to both.

The most troublesome result of this diminished sense of leitourgia has been the apparent loss of sensitivity to ecclesial identity and to the deep structure of liturgy. Worship is looked upon as a means to an end rather than an end in itself. Liturgy thus becomes one means among many to edify, instruct, stimulate or exhort the congregation about God rather than being an encounter with God which sends liturgical shock waves into both the believer's life and the believers' rite. R. Taylor Scott has aptly named this modern confusion an instrumental error. ''As I see it, the chief misunderstanding of liturgy today is *the instrumental error.* This error has it that all these words, vestments, songs, sermons, movements, and so on, which, taken together, constitute the liturgy, exist for one's own spiritual enrichment and nurture. In short, the liturgy becomes an instrument for one's own personal enrichment. There is absolutely nothing problematic to pri-

---

7. Kavanagh, *On Liturgical Theology,* 108–109; underscoring mine.

8. ''Once rite receded, so did the need for that kind of assembly whose common burden was the enactment of rite rather than attendance upon didactic exposition of set texts. . . . Liturgical hypertrophy and the invention of printing by movable type were not, of course, the only factors involved in the reform movements of Catholics and Protestants during the sixteenth century and after. But when one tries to account for the fate of rite and symbol in Reformation and Counter-Reformation churches, the combined effects of liturgical hypertrophy and printing technology cannot be ignored safely.'' Ibid., 104–105.

vate devotion, but that is not what constitutes liturgy. . . ."[9] To paraphrase in our present jargon, there is nothing problematic to private devotion, but that is not what constitutes leitourgia. And furthermore, there is nothing problematic to public devotion (liturgy as protocol) but that is not what constitutes leitourgia either.

It would be an unacceptable case of overkill to try to defend the importance of liturgical rite by implying that if an assembly's worship lacked leitourgia then it lacked God's presence and was devoid of praise, grace, gospel, prayer, faith, etc. Although we are indeed charging that a non-leitourgia assembly is oxymoronic to Christian tradition, this should not commit us to accuse such worshipers' faith of being inadequate and imperfect. Such stone-throwing between Christian houses would not be in the Spirit of things. The fire before Moses at the burning bush is not confined to the wick of a votive candle, for this Spirit blows where it will. It would be excessive to suggest that only worship done with ritual precision can conjure up God; more than excessive, to suggest such ritualistic control of God would be blasphemous. But this is not the point of ritual, and to suppose so reveals exactly where our modern understanding has gone astray. Cult need not only mean "cultivating" the gods,[10] it can also mean creating a "culture." Leitourgia creates the Church. That is the sense in which Fr. Kavanagh defines cult. "The functions of conceiving and enacting the values of the group . . . are what I understand to be cult. The conceiving aspect I take to be myth, and the enactment aspect I take to be

9. R. Taylor Scott, "The Likelihood of Liturgy: Reflections Upon Prayer Book Revision and Its Liturgical Implications," *Anglican Theological Review*, 57:2 (April 1980) 106.

10. "Nothing bespeaks the novelty of Christian worship so plainly as the terminology employed for its concepts . . . Cultic terminology is consciously avoided for Christian worship." Ferdinand Hahn, *The Worship of the Early Church* (Philadelphia: Fortress Press, 1973) 35–6. See also chapter one of John Burkhart, *Worship* (Philadelphia: Westminster Press, 1982); Robert Daly, S.J., *The Origins of the Christian Doctrine of Sacrifice* (Philadelphia: Westminster Press, 1978); Joseph Jungmann writes, "Among the pagans . . . the [ierus] was someone who himself, in his own name or at the command of the community, acted as mediator with the deity. Such a possibility does not exist in the New Covenant." *The Early Liturgy to the Time of Gregory the Great* (Notre Dame: University of Notre Dame Press, 1959) 18.

ritual. Both myth and ritual thus appear to me as strictly correlative and inseparable functions: their reciprocal union is what I mean by cult. The outcome of cult, so understood, is what I understand as culture . . ."[11] Leitourgia creates a people, a people called ekklesia. The Church might develop liturgy, but leitourgia creates Church. It is true that over time the assembly will develop stylistic accouterments, expressions, symbols and gestures, but leitourgia as encounter with God is the source for the ekklesia's life and thus the ontological condition for any such development. And not only stylistic development, but since the ekklesia is birthed and sustained by encounter with the Holy One, leitourgia is also theological adjustment to the Word heard from the Living One.

It could be said playfully in this manner. It is not as if traditions which ignore leitourgia have no *orandi*, but it does seem as though the *lex* is missing! Is this any loss? Yes. It trifurcates liturgy, theology and piety. If liturgy becomes worship understood as essentially individual expression of a personal commitment, then it is ludicrous to claim liturgy is theology because the most liturgy could be passed off as is the opinion of an individual or committee. Its grammar has no binding force upon theology. Or if liturgy becomes worship understood as private pious exercise then it is ludicrous to claim that liturgy should form one's piety because the most liturgy could be passed off as is one of several formats which might or might not be helpful.

The divorce between liturgy, theology and piety has been made evident to this author during the past couple years teaching in a college of the Church. All manner of opinion about baptism has been heard from first-year religion students, none of it ecclesial and little of it sacramental. Commiseration about the dismal state of baptismal theology usually takes the form of complaining that these young people have never done sustained reflection, that theology is different than religion, that television has sabotaged academic pedagogy, or that pastors in the area have offered too few classes on baptism. This is not the point. These young people

11. Kavanagh, "The Role of Ritual in Personal Development" in *The Roots of Ritual*, ed. James D. Shaughnessy, (Grand Rapids: William Eerdmans Publishing) 148–49.

aren't expected to be practiced in academic theology. The way they express their baptismal theology isn't the problem, it's that they have none at all. Why not? They haven't seen one. Apparently, baptismal realities have been so poorly expressed in the lives of believers communally and individually, and so poorly performed in the rite of initiation that liturgy, theology and piety are separate. Despite having sat through scores, perhaps hundreds of baptisms, these folks have not seen baptismal theology epiphanized.

Usually worship is thought of as the larger, general category, and liturgy as a smaller category within it. To make our point, we shall try to reverse this mental picture. It is popularly thought that one of the many ways of worshiping is in liturgical format, but one may take it or leave it according to need and disposition. Some people enjoy team sports like bowling and so join a league, while others do not and prefer to recreate in solitude; likewise, some people like liturgical flourish and so come to church, while others do not and prefer to worship in solitude. Rubrical pomp and protocol might aid some people's worship and faith, but really one's prayer, praise, doxology, service or thanksgiving might equally be private and personal and spontaneous. By this understanding, theologians with an interest in liturgy wrongly accede to the misperceived obligation of apologizing for how liturgical doxology is more inspiring than private doxology, or how liturgical prayer can be as meaningful as extemporaneous prayer, or how liturgical pomp might make worship more exhilarating. This frequently seems to be the line at which defense of "liturgical" versus "non-liturgical" worship is drawn.

All this may be true if liturgy is merely a form of worshiping, but as we are defining rite, the categories are reversed. Leitourgia is the larger category and worship is only one of many other activities that takes place within it. "Christians do not worship because they believe. They believe because the One in whose gift faith lies is regularly met in the act of communal worship—not because the assembly conjures up God, but because the initiative lies with the God who has promised to be there always."[12] Leitourgia includes worship, yes, but much more as well. One petitions for

12. Kavanagh, *On Liturgical Theology*, 91.

salvation, intercedes in prayer, offers up one's self and the world to the Creator, makes anamnesis and eucharistia and epiclesis, fortifies one's identity in *koinonia* for servanthood in the world, and so forth. Fr. Kavanagh's list is better: liturgical place is not a quiet, private place, it is

"a vigorous arena for conducting public business in which petitions are heard, contracts entered into, relationships witnessed, orations declaimed, initiations consummated, vows taken, authority exercised, laws promulgatd, images venerated, values affirmed, banquets attended, votes cast, the dead waked, the Word deliberated, and parades cheered. . . . It is not a carpeted bedroom where faith may recline privately with the Sunday papers. . . . [The place of the ekklesia] is the Italian piazza, the Roman forum, the Yankee town green, Red Square moved under roof and used for the business of faith."[13]

One does more than merely worship in leitourgia. One does the world as it was meant to be done (Fr. Kavanagh), it is eschatological and cosmological (Fr. Schmemann).

Fr. Robert Hovda obliquely corroborates this theme in an address critiquing our contemporary view of Sunday. He maintains that contrary to longstanding opinion, the early Church did not suppose the Christian Sunday to have replaced Israel's Sabbath. "[I]t is clear that the sabbath remained the sabbath . . . Among the followers of the way of Jesus, there was a great feeling of fulfillment, a conviction that a new age had dawned. . . . There could not be a 'sacred-profane' dichotomy, or even distinction, in this new creation . . . All places, all days, and all work belong to God in a quite new sense. The preparation for all this was over, the eschaton had dawned, the realization was here."[14] The Lord's

13. Kavanagh, *The Elements of Rite* (New York: Pueblo Publishing Co., 1982) 16–17. So his sixth rule of liturgical usage which states "The church building is both shelter and setting for the liturgical assembly. Nothing more, but nothing less" (14).

14. Robert Hovda, "Sunday Assembly in the Tradition," in *Sunday Morning: A Time for Worship*, ed. Mark Searle (Collegeville: The Liturgical Press, 1982) 35. On the theological point, see Schmemann, *Introduction to Liturgical Theology*, 55–67 and *Great Lent*, 67–76; on the development of Sunday see Willy Rordorf, *Sunday* (London: SCM Press, 1968), Part One: The Day of Rest;

way had been prepared and while sacred time/space were part of that preparation, for those living in the light of the irruption of God's eschatological rule there was no interest in carving out from the profane week a sacred time, Sunday. Thus the Christian's conscious avoidance of cultic terminology for the place, the time, the officiant, the action, even for naming the action, which is therefore simply called "the assembly." But at some point, Fr. Hovda observes, this eschatological sense was surrendered to an institutional sense: Sunday became a Sabbath, a sacred day, and the assembly became a people saved from the world rather than being Christ's body for the world. The sacred-profane distinction was restored. As a result, we tend to think that "God, Christ, our oneness as the body of Christ and as agents of the new age—these are absent everywhere else. I have to 'go to church' to find them."[15] This is not correct. The people do not assemble on Sunday to worship because God is confined to a sacred place on a sacred day. They do not assemble to do Church, they assemble to do redeemed world. The arena of the life of faith is not some kind of sacred precinct, it is the world. Then what is the purpose of assembling on Sunday? Not because God is here and not there, but so that the assembly, in their individual mundane vocations, can transform what is there by what was ritualized here.

Sunday is for ecclesial leitourgia, not private worship—even if in "liturgical" form. Fr. Taft's remark may be taken as prescriptive: "The purpose of all Christian liturgy is to express in a ritual moment that which should be the basic stance of every moment of our lives."[16] If leitourgia also stimulates and nourishes one's private doxology, that is nevertheless not its first purpose. "What is really important is that the Christian community celebrate its origin, existence and destiny and thereby build itself up. In other words, it is not primarily the individual Christian's fulfillment of a personal responsibility to worship God that is at stake in regard to

Thomas J. Talley, *The Origins of the Liturgical Year* (New York: Pueblo Press, 1986) and the essay preceding Hovda's in the same book by Eugene Laverdiere, "The Origins of Sunday in the New Testament."

15. Hovda, 39.

16. Taft, "Sunday in the Eastern Tradition," *Beyond East and West: Problems in Liturgical Understanding* (Washington, D.C.: The Pastoral Press, 1984) 32.

Sunday worship, but the responsibility of the Christian community to grow.''[17]

In a different context Fr. Schmemann inadvertently calls attention to what leitourgia involves by describing what its absence would feel like. He describes the Orthodox Lenten observance of the Liturgy of the Presanctified Gifts. A normal Eucharistic celebration expresses the fact that the Church is already at home with Christ, but during Lent the other fact of Christian existence is expressed, namely that Christians are still in sojourn. So during Lent, the Divine Liturgy is under no circumstances celebrated Monday through Friday. However, on Wednesday and Friday a special evening service of communion is prescribed, the Liturgy of Presanctified Gifts. Communion is received by bread which was consecrated at an earlier service, i.e., presanctified. (In the West this occurs on Good Friday of Holy Week when the assembly communes Friday on bread blessed Thursday.) Fr. Schmemann describes the transfer of the presanctified bread to the Holy Table.

"Externally this entrance is similar to the Great Entrance of the Eucharist but its liturgical and spiritual meaning is of course totally different. In the full Eucharistic service, we have here the Offertory procession: the Church brings herself, her life, the life of her members, and indeed that of the entire creation as sacrifice to God, as re-enactment of the one full and perfect sacrifice of Christ. Remembering Christ, she remembers all those whose life He assumed for their redemption and salvation. At the Presanctified Liturgy, there is no offering, no sacrifice, no Eucharist, no Consecration, but the mystery of Christ's presence in the Church is being revealed and manifested!''[18]

The absence of leitourgia makes Holy Communion into a perpetual Liturgy of Presanctified Gifts. Christ's once-for-all sacrifice is understood to preclude any sacrifice at the Mass, and so ministers in such services may be said to be distributing Christ's two-thousand-year-old presanctified gift without offering, sacrifice, Eucharist, or consecration.

17. Christopher Kiesling, The Future of the Christian Sunday (New York: Sheed and Ward, 1970) 33.
18. Schmemann, Great Lent, 58.

We aren't suggesting that Christ is present exclusively in leitourgia, as if God's grace is not available in worship which treats liturgy only as protocol. But what does appear to be absent is the work of the Church as leitourgia through which it offers, sacrifices, gives thanks for and consecrates to God the whole cosmos in its liturgical rite and its liturgical life. As public, corporate event, leitourgia involves more than (though never less than) one's private doxology. Is leitourgia's absence not felt because modern Christianity has contented itself with privatized religion?

### b. Liturgical Theology, Fundamental and Derived

Since the Church's response to encounter with God is preserved in the rite's structure, we have said leitourgia can be called theological. The body of Christ gathers to be shaped by the Holy One; the liturgical transaction creates the Church. Leitourgia stands to theology as violin stands to melody. Therefore liturgical theology is defined in a fundamental sense as the ekklesia's corporate search for meaning after it has been accosted by the word of God. The ekklesia preserves its theology in the community's ritual structures. The structure does not merely provide data for theological meaning, it is itself a theological effort. The meaning preserved and manifested in the structure of the rites is as truly theological as what is contained in the books of the community's dogmaticians, academics and pastors.

"Liturgy is an object of theological investigation because it is just as much an expression of belief as are the verbal monuments of tradition (patristic writings, theological treatises, conciliar decrees, even the Bible). To think that a homily of John Chrysostom or John Calvin, or a book by Karl Rahner or Karl Barth, is worthy of the theologian's attention, and fail to understand how the ways and the prayers by which these same gentlemen . . . have worshiped God is worthy of the same, is the prejudice of those so locked into a narrow concept of expression as to think that only words communicate anything theological."[19]

But there is more. Sometimes it happens that someone gives voice to what transpires in the leitourgia, either by speaking about

19. Taft, "Liturgy as Theology," *Worship* 56:2 (March 1982) 114.

192

it or writing it down. Someone tries to enunciate what is expressed, communicated and preserved by the structure. Such a person is neither formulating a theology of worship, nor expressing a theology from worship; he or she is giving voice to the theology which transpired in the community's leitourgia. This task is a derivative definition of liturgical theology. Within what we have identified as a third approach, there are two uses of the term liturgical theology. Its fundamental definition is the rite itself (in action, so to speak) and its derivative definition is the giving voice to the people's *theologia prima*. We propose that the venerable tradition of liturgical commentary in Eastern Christianity would fit this derivative definition.[20] A book is not rite. Rites are events, books are paper and ink. But a written commentary is liturgical theology in a derivative sense as it directs one's attention to the theology transacted by generations of faithful Christians who assemble, encounter God, are theologically exercised, and preserve their liturgical theology in ritual structure.

We are merely reiterating a distinction alluded to in the introduction. Liturgical theology means fundamentally the community's transaction with the Almighty, it means derivatively giving voice to the liturgists' activity. (The term "liturgist" is used to refer to the people; we have tried to put this in a surprising form. The liturgy is so often thought of as the clergy's work alone that the

20. For an overview of the liturgical commentaries of Maximus, Germanus, Nicholas and Theodore of Andida, Symeon and Cabasilas, see Hans-Joachim Schulz, *The Byzantine Liturgy, Symbolic Structure and Faith Expression* (New York: Pueblo Publishing Co., 1986). Though it does not fit our tight definition of liturgical commentary, a reader from the western tradition might find interesting the eastern interweaving of liturgy and catechesis in *The Living God: A Catechism for the Christian Faith* (New York: St. Vladimir's Press, 1989). A group effort by persons within the Orthodox Fraternity of Western Europe, this catechism illustrates God's saving covenants by using "certain elements within the life of the Church—hymns, icons, sacraments—which express them, render them present, and enable us to participate in them." Scripture or theology "studied apart from the life of the Church is nothing more than a history of past events rather than the New Covenant, the encounter between man and the living God. The aim of this book is to help our readers in achieving that very encounter." (xvi) This catechism is not liturgical commentary illuminating the structure of the rite, but it surely is a long way from the theology of liturgy which Brunner or Prenter exemplified.

term is usually taken to designate the one in the vestments, up front. But if liturgy is the work of the entire assembly, body and head, then the people may be called liturgists and the priest called presider.) This is not to be confused with what we have called yet a fourth approach which seeks to analyze, defend and explain liturgical theology. This book, for example, is neither fundamental nor derivative liturgical theology; it is about liturgical theology. But St. Germanus' *Ecclesiastical History* or Fr. Schmemann's *The Eucharist* gives voice to the community's theological activity in its leitourgia.

### BEGIN WITH THE RITE

We are at last in position to clarify the necessity of beginning with leitourgia itself instead of with a simple idea about liturgy. This is not due to a case of elitist historicism or idealistic repristination. God is encountered in the assembly's eighth-day leitourgia but this is not the community's accomplishment. That the infinite makes himself finitely present is the very definition of grace. It is the Almighty's iterant presence which calls this community into being and shapes its identity. Confrontation with the holy results in a "deep change in the lives of those who participate in the liturgical act. And deep change will affect their next liturgical act, however slightly. To detect that change in the subsequent liturgical act will be to discover where theology has passed. . . ."[21] Insofar as this is true, we can call the liturgical act itself theological. Insofar as this is true, Fr. Schmemann can say liturgical theology has to do with the theology manifested in the deep structures of the rite, not just with surface rubrics. "To find the Ordo behind the 'rubrics,' regulations and rules—to find the unchanging principle, the living norm or 'logos' of worship as a whole, within what is accidental and temporary: this is the primary task which faces those who regard liturgical theology not as the collecting of accidental and arbitrary explanations of services but as the systematic study of the *lex orandi* of the Church."[22]

Thus our first assertion about liturgical theology: it is genuine theology. Liturgical theology is different from theology of worship

21. Kavanagh, *On Liturgical Theology*, 74.
22. Schmemann, *Introduction*, 32.

simply because leitourgia is different from worship. This is why one must begin with the leitourgia itself in order to do liturgical theology, which was our second assertion: liturgical theology is *lex orandi* in motion. Liturgical theology is not what issues when a theologian prays as he or she thinks, or focuses attention upon some doxological expression of Christian dogma, or examines theological and anthropological dimensions of the liturgy, or leafs through rubrics to quarry support for a controlling thesis. Fundamentally, liturgical theology is the assembly's adjustment to the sustained summons home to God in Christ; derivatively, liturgical theology is giving voice to the meaning epiphanized in the structure of the leitourgia itself.

This is why *lex orandi* establishes *lex credendi* and not vice-versa. This is not affirmed merely because it can be demonstrated that in most cases a doctrine's formulation was influenced by some antecedent liturgical practice. No, the claim means that the ekklesia's *lex credendi* is fundamentally worked out in the ritual logistics of leitourgia which brings the Church and its faith into being. Therefore we reject the very set-up of what we have been calling the chicken-or-the-egg question. The historical question of which influence came first, liturgical practice or doctrinal teaching, is irrelevant. That the law of prayer establishes the law of faith does not hang on the question of temporal priority. Leitourgia is not an expression of an idea (I have a body or I am a body), it is epiphanous (I am bodily).

Fr. Kavanagh puts it frankly.

"[An] aliturgical Christian church is as much a contradiction in terms as a human society without language. By this I mean something harder and more definite than the general assertion that Christians worship. I mean that *ecclesia* and *leitourgia* are coterminous in origin and very nearly convertible as terms. The community in which my faith is worked out is Christian because the cult it practices is Christian throughout. . . . In this sense a human community does not merely use a language; it *is* the language it speaks. Similarly, a Christian church does not merely use a liturgy; it *is* the liturgy by which it worships."[23]

23. Kavanagh, *On Liturgical Theology*, 97. Anthony Ugolnik seeks to make

Liturgical theology is fundamentally the ritual enactment of *lex supplicandi* and derivatively the giving voice to that eighth-day reality.

CAN PRIMARY AND SECONDARY THEOLOGIANS DIALOGUE?

To be comfortable with the unfamiliar ground of *theologia prima* required a different definition of liturgy, and to keep our wits about us we tagged one "liturgy" and the other "leitourgia." But this is not easily maintained. Why not? Fr. Schmemann says because of a metamorphosis of liturgical conscience; Fr. Taft ascribes it to a contrary shift in the history of liturgical explanation from structure to symbolic interpretation; Fr. Kavanagh points to our atrophied sense of rite and the academy's uneasiness with *theologia prima*. At any rate, the understanding of leitourgia as eighth-day rite is at root so different from the understanding of liturgy as style and protocol that dialogists from each camp can scarcely engage each other. One player has set his or her presuppositions on red squares, the other on black squares, and although theologians and liturgists scurry around the board on their respective disciplinary squares, they can't jump each other. On the black squares, leitourgia does not function as a significant source of theological thinking (what Fr. Schmemann meant by liturgy as "*locus theologicus*") and liturgical studies remains in the practical section of the seminary curriculum explaining how to cover the ciborium. On the red squares, it is Fr. Schmemann's diagnosis that theologians avoid discussing the trivial reality of the Church's life and do not even dream about influencing it. Their theology ceases to be pastoral and mystical.

To overcome this will require a profounder definition of *lex orandi* and a more sensitive definition of *theologia prima*. It is why we described Schmemann's understanding of liturgical theology as organic, not merely connective. An organic liturgical theology

the same point when he writes, "Theology, like language, is a communal act. The theologian cannot work in a white lab coat, nor can he or she make a scientific treatise of the gospel. A theologian who does not speak from or for a community has forgotten the reason for speaking." *The Illuminating Icon*, 141. We wonder about changing one word in this passage: Theology, *because* it is language (logos), is a communal act.

would require an effort more critical than the innoculation of liturgy with some ideology of God, and more arduous than uncovering liturgical precedence for theological doctrine. Yet not much more than this seems to be happening. Theologians with liturgical interests, and liturgists with a theological avocation search for evidence of liturgy's influence upon doctrine. Presumably these data are adduced by the liturgically minded in order to argue that liturgy should be an important resource for Church doctrine and not overlooked in the seminary curriculum or book indices of systematic theologies. The approach is seductive because it appears as if it will apologize to the theological community at large for the value of liturgical studies.

If we were simply looking for examples of how changes in liturgical style reverberated through doctrine and piety we need not have looked further than Gregory Dix. His *Shape of the Liturgy* abounds with examples.[24] Ecclesiology was affected when the priest began to face the altar with his back to the people though the change in position "appears to have begun, almost accidentally . . . due to certain architectural and devotional changes of fashion" (30, 591); "considerable structural variations between Eastern and Western rites" developed out of a "trifling original difference in the treatment of the people's offerings" (123); innovative phrases in the liturgy preceded the doctrine of transubstantiation, they did not follow it (199); "a 'high' doctrine of the sacrament has always been accompanied by an aroused conscience as to the condition of the poor" (251); Cyril's "theology is based upon his prayer" and the inclusion of such an invocation has "clear and novel doctrinal implications in prayers" (280); Theodore elaborated his scheme of the Eucharistic elements as Christ's dead body in order to accommodate the elaborate procession of elements from the sacristy which began as a convenience (290). One could go on to see Dix's views on how the faith of the Church was impacted by liturgical calendars, vestments, the passivity of the laity at Eucharist and ocular communion, but enough.

Of course liturgical practice has exerted influence upon the formation of Christian doctrine, and of course Christian doctrine has

24. Gregory Dix, *The Shape of the Liturgy.*

influenced liturgical practice. But the whole question is altered by a profounder definition of liturgy. Then the verb in Prosper of Aquitaine's formula identifies unequivocally what is foundational.

"That verb was *statuat*, as in *lex supplicandi legem statuat credendi:* The law of worshiping founds the law of believing. So long, I think, as the verb stays in the sentence it is not possible to reverse subject and predicate any more than one can reverse the members of the statement: the foundation supports the house. Having said that, one cannot really say that the house supports the foundation. One must say something different, such as the house puts great stress upon its foundation, or the house influences its foundation in ways different from those by which the foundation influences the house resting upon it. . . . The old maxim means what it says. One thing it does not, however, say or mean is that the *lex credendi* exerts no influence upon the *lex supplicandi:* only that it does not constitute or found the *lex supplicandi.* That is all. But it is a precious, because fundamental, insight. . . ."[25]

The community *is* the leitourgia by which it worships—as my body is not an expression of another hypostatic identity, it is the way I am in the world. The Christian Church does not use a liturgy, the liturgy establishes the Church as theological community, as a human community does not merely use a language, language is the way in which it is society. The theology ushering from this activity, preserved in ritual structure and given voice in spoken or written form, is liturgical theology fundamental and derivative.

A LOOK-ALIKE VARIANT OF LITURGICAL THEOLOGY

At this point we are compelled to point out a look-alike variant of this thesis. The biggest stumbling block in the position we are advancing is this affirmation that the law of prayer establishes (*statuat*) what is believed. What if one could sidestep this stumbling block by proposing that rite does not establish theology, neither does theology establish rite, rather the Church establishes both rite and theology? In other words, the faith of the Church could issue in two formats, one liturgical and the other dogmatic.

25. Kavanagh, "Response: Primary Theology and Liturgical Act," *Worship* 57:4 (July 1983) 323-24.

The faith of the Church, this approach would say, could be expressed both academically and devotionally. This move would have the advantage of avoiding the *statuat* question by proposing a meta-foundation. The *statuat* conundrum could be calmed by positing the Church as source for both faith and theology, devotion and doctrine, liturgy and dogma. If this sounds familiar to Wainwright's agenda it is not by accident; we have only entered theology from liturgy by the back door. And phrased in this way it sounds a bit more familiar to Prenter too. He said that the dogma (singular) of the Church is reflected in two forms, liturgical and doctrinal. The faith of the Church which is ensconced in existential, devotional form could be translated by some well-meaning theologian to aid the theological task and, conversely, the faith of the Church rationally outlined in doctrinal contours could be translated by some well-meaning liturgist to aid the liturgical task. And liturgical theology would be adducing evidence that the practice of prayer has influenced what a community believes and that the law of belief has influenced how a community worships.

So far, so good. But now arises the question which distinguishes liturgical theology from this "devotional theology." Where is this Church? The Church whose faith will be expressed both devotionally and rationally, where is it? The Church does not exist hypostatically apart from the assembly of laos, clergy, Christ and Spirit for the celebration of empty tomb and coming parousia. To speak of some thing called "Church" as antecedent to both liturgical expression and doctrinal expression such that it can issue in both is like speaking of an "I" antecedent to my body. The attempt to prescind from the *statuat* problem by invoking Church as antecedent to both liturgy and doctrine fails because the assembly becomes Church in its leitourgia. The ekklesia which theologizes is birthed in its liturgical assembly. The first liturgical act is assembling. Leitourgia meant "an action by which a group of people become something corporately which they had not been as a mere collection of individuals—a whole greater than the sum of its parts. It also meant a function of 'ministry' of a man or of a group on behalf of and in the interest of the whole community."[26]

26. Schmemann, *For the Life of the World*, 25.

This perception of the unity between Eucharist and ecclesiology was self-evident to the patristic understanding of liturgy. Liturgical theology is not simply theology done prayerfully or doxologically or in an existentially committed way. The Eucharist was not one means of grace among others, rather its celebration both revealed and fulfilled the body of Christ. This body struggles under the theological urgency to speak to God and of God, not merely about God. This is Tradition coming to be. "The very purpose both of the Church and of her worship [is] above all precisely a *liturgy*, an action (ergon), in which the essence of what is taking place is simultaneously revealed and fulfilled."[27] If the ekklesia struggles to do theology by addressing God and addressing the world about God, then *lex supplicandi legem statuat credendi* because liturgy brings theologians into being.

## c. The Capacity for Liturgical Theology

Of course, this theology is different than the formulation of propositions. It is not as if the leader bespeaks a proposition and the congregation antiphonally echoes catechisms; it is not as though the people are listening for propositions at all. Liturgical theology forms a subject, a self. In the liturgy the laos do the *ergon* of believing, hoping, grieving, rejoicing, repenting, making glad noises, etc. The Word is proclaimed, and the people do the Word; it grips them, and they exercise it. The mouth can speak "theos-logos" because the heart is filled with Christ, the logos of God. Leitourgia doesn't just make the thinker think doxologically or theologize prayerfully, it forms a believer whose life is theological. The person who prays may be called a theologian. Theology occurs because the community has been beckoned to be conformed to the image of Christ, who is the icon of the Father. Leitourgia establishes theology in the way community establishes individual, Tradition establishes icon, gospel establishes homily. It is not mainly a chronological relationship, but a normative one. *Lex orandi* establishes *lex credendi*.

As much significance as all this gives to the liturgical rite, so much necessity does it give to extending the liturgy's parameters

27. Schmemann, *The Eucharist*, 165.

beyond the rite (and, therefore, beyond the section of the seminary catalogue having to do with merely practical skills of the trade). The liturgy exists not to stimulate worshippers, but to make them over into new sons and daughters of God. Paul Holmer insists on the point.

"It would be odd to say that Christian worship and liturgy are only stimulating or expressive. For worship requires not that one like the liturgy but that one come to abide in God himself. To worship God requires that one really worship him and not get engrossed in the liturgy. The liturgy gets its legitimacy and point from the fact that God requires an offering, enjoins contrition and repentance, promises a pardon, and proffers redemption. But this makes sense only because there is a God whose will is our law, whose pardon is our renewed life, and whose mercy reads our very hearts. . . .

Liturgy is not an expression of how people see things; rather it proposes, instead, how God sees all people."[28]

Perhaps this is the distinction between liturgy and leitourgia for which we are groping. Treating liturgy like self-expressive estheticism makes it a statement of how this age or that culture understands the Christian vision. It is true that as a work of theology, liturgical form will reflect the community's struggle for meaning, but this always in the context of Tradition. Leitourgia is ontological (not just esthetic) because leitourgia reveals how God sees the world. It shapes and changes us to fit God's vision of what a human being is, it is not a series of snap-on liturgical formats which express the theological ideals of one generation or another, one culture or another. Leitourgia is revelation-in-motion: the picture as icon, the Bible as Scripture, speech as proclamation, bath and meal as sacrament. To come into the presence of this God is to be deeply changed, to stand in judgment, and being thus changed, to practice theology upon the world by speaking God's word—both holiness and mercy—to it.

There is nothing deadlier than didactic liturgy, but there is nothing more antithetical to leitourgia than one that does not form. For

28. Paul Holmer, "About Liturgy and Its Logic," *Worship* 50:1 (January 1976) 21, 23.

this reason, a significant portion of the literature dealing with liturgical matters addresses the subject of liturgy's influence upon the worshiper. Points of connection are drawn between liturgy and the formation of faith and theology. Let us glance at a few samples.

### LITURGY'S INFLUENCE UPON THE WORSHIPER

Don Saliers suggests that a "crisis of liturgical language" has occurred. He is not referring to a linguistic problem which could be solved by developing a new vocabulary or a new set of symbols for our time, he means that many people do not seem to understand the language of faith. "[M]any people do not understand it, not because they lack the definitions of the words, but because they fail to see the point of speaking that way. . . . To see the point of the language does not mean that we can always comment upon it or theorize about it. No, to see its point is to take it to heart, to act upon it, and to let it shape our life."[29] To speak the language of faith requires formation in the Christian life, he suggests, which could be called liturgical formation. The *lex orandi* of the Church at prayer provides a language of faith which can shape us even if we cannot theorize about it. Considered from this perspective, one's ability to think theologically requires more than just clear-headedness or logic learned from other disciplines. Primary theology, by this analysis, aims to do more than provide a lexicon of terms, it aims to allow the thinker to hang concepts together by the logic of theological grammar.

This is a theme which Saliers sounds elsewhere as well. "Worship is something done, not something merely said or merely experienced. It is the work of the people of God, training themselves in the language of faith and using the language to address God. If understood fully, it is linked with doing God's work in the world. We may, if you like, call worship the rule-keeping activity of the language of faith."[30] Elsewhere he expresses the same theme by arguing that prayer and worship are not so much

29. Don Saliers, "On the 'Crisis' of Liturgical Language," *Worship* 44:7 (August–September, 1970) 405.
30. Saliers, "Prayer and Emotion" in *Christians at Prayer*, ed. John Gallen, S.J. (Notre Dame: University of Notre Dame Press, 1977) 58.

derived from as generative of a doctrine of God. Although this does not mean "a simple 'reading off' of a doctrine of God from the surface diction of . . . prayer," nevertheless the logic suggests that prayer is not so much a consequence of first having believed as it is constitutive of believing in God in particular ways. If there is an intrinsic relation between theology as language about God and prayer as language addressed to God, then Christian prayer is generative of the doctrine of God in crucial respects. "Christian prayer is a cognitive encounter with God which governs central features of how God is to be conceived and expressed in language. . . . The eucharistic prayers may be said to be 'grammatical' in that they provide rules governing the formulation of doctrines."[31] And in the fifth chapter of *The Soul in Paraphrase* he relates prayer to theology again. "What has praying *to* God to do with thinking *about* God?" In the context of this book on religious affections he proposes that "the central and decisive Christian affections require concepts, judgments, and thoughts which yield insight into the nature of God."[32] (The line of connection which Saliers makes between liturgy and doctrine as grammar, on the one hand, and liturgy and the religious affections on the other, we find to be helpful and significant, but caution that sufficient specificity must be given to liturgical rite or the approach can become a variant of Wainwright's seesaw by which it could be argued that the affections influence liturgy as truly as vice-versa.)

David Power also asserts a formative connection between liturgy and theology. A common definition of theology, he notes, is faith seeking understanding. On this ground alone "we would have to assert the role of cult in the life and thought of the theologian." As the primary language of faith, liturgy "is a kind of theology, because it is already an attempt to express the movement of the heart towards God in Christ. . . . It is primary, because ritual and symbolic language is the core language of religious reality and faith."[33] He continues by considering what implications this has

31. "Prayer and the Doctrine of God in Contemporary Theology," *Interpretation* 30 (1980) 265–278.

32. Saliers, *The Soul in Paraphrase: Prayer and the Religious Affections* (New York: Seabury, 1980) 77.

33. David N. Power, "Cult to Culture: The Liturgical Foundation of Theology," *Worship* 54:6 (Nov. 1980) 482.

for transcendental method, i.e., for a secondary theology whose role is to interpret the language of the imagination and analogy, but the point is that this secondary task finds its point of reference in liturgy. If theology's role can be described as mediating cult to culture, then "liturgy is not just another discipline in religious studies. It is in its way foundational to theology. . . . [R]ite and sacrament provide a basis for such disciplines as christology, ecclesiology and God-talk."[34]

Elsewhere Power speaks of two expressions of faith, the symbolic and the theoretical (he identifies them as *theologia prima* and *theologia secunda*) but insists that these are complementary and not competitive or alternative. "To put it very simply: there must be modes of devotional expression which makes it possible for the Christian person to enter fully and personally into the faith-experience of communion with God, but there must also be modes of theological enterprise which guide the devotional and make intelligent inquiry possible without the hazards of self-interest and sentiment."[35] These two expressions of faith must not interfere with each other, but neither may one or the other be sacrificed without peril. It appears to have been the case that the "living experience of spiritual brotherhood . . . [was] not absorbed into the church's institutions or liturgy," the consequences being that as devotional expression waned in the West the official Church had nothing of the devotional whereby to attract its people or to inspire the theologian to fresh questions. Besides a language of objective study, the Christian community needs "a language which can incite it to respond intersubjectively to God's call and to dispose of itself to God. It is this latter which ought to be the language of liturgy."[36] The liturgical transmits the Christian experience, deeply felt and demanding, in which God makes his claims upon us. This will form and influence the alternate expression of faith, theology.

Peter Fink emphasizes the formative influence of the liturgical community by defining liturgical theology as an interaction be-

34. Ibid., 494.
35. David N. Power, "Two Expressions of Faith: Worship and Theology," *Concilium: Liturgical Experience of Faith* (New York: Herder & Herder, 1973) 99.
36. Ibid., 101.

tween three parties: theologians, liturgists and the praying Church. "The problematic to which a liturgical theology must address itself is the all too observable discrepancy between actual liturgical celebrations in the church and the claims which theological reflection makes for those celebrations."[37] Theologians can establish interpretation, liturgists can establish one or another past practice, but it is in ritual celebration that the praying Church will answer the question about the credibility of this interpretation or practice. Therefore it is the liturgist's task "to structure a worship service that will render what the church promises perceptible to the senses. At the same time it is important for the theologian to remember that the ultimate test of his theological model is not its theological correctness, but the ability of the praying church to recognize in its prayer the richness which the model promises."[38]

David Newman challenges the widespread assumption that "if we get our principles right then our liturgy will naturally follow in good order." When he says that liturgical theology is rooted and grounded in the liturgy itself, he means that theology must follow the liturgy. "What does it mean to follow the liturgy?" he asks. "We have been thinking of it in the sense of succeeding rather than preceding. But I want also to think of it as a dynamic category that presupposes liturgy as an action or movement to be followed." Rely less on the metaphor of worship as a shape, and think of it more as a body that has life and movement. "Liturgical theology that follows the liturgy can be described as a hermeneutic of word, symbol and action. Paul Ricoeur has said that 'the symbol gives rise to thought.' This could be a motto for liturgical theology."[39] Insofar as liturgy is an active, dynamic body and not a static shape, theological expressions will be affected when they are played out in practice in liturgy.

Michael Aune also utilizes the concept of hermeneutic. His piece is addressed to a Lutheran audience, asking for a rationale for the why and wherefore of liturgical reform in the Lutheran Church in

37. Peter Fink, "Towards a Liturgical Theology," *Worship* 47:10 (Dec. 1973) 602.
38. Ibid., 603.
39. David R. Newman, "Observations on Method in Liturgical Theology," *Worship* 57:4 (July 1983) 379.

the United States. Is there any hermeneutic for interpreting liturgy from a Lutheran perspective? He answers yes by arguing that Luther came to see words in a new way. Western tradition saw words as signaling or pointing to things out there; Luther, based on his biblical studies, saw words as God's own performative utterances. Words incarnate the Word: in hearing "you are forgiven," you are forgiven. That means, suggests Aune, that for Luther the rite no less than the Word communicates the full reality of Christ. "What is remarkable about such a liturgical perspective is the recognition that the truth which theology examines and seeks to understand, namely 'Word' as God's visible and verbal communication, happens *somewhere* and looks and sounds like *something*."[40] Although in the centuries following the Reformation this perspective was generally lost, the Lutheran liturgy could be reformed according to a liturgical hermeneutic contained in its own confessions.

In their neglect of matters ritual Lutherans have bifurcated word and rite (or, meaning and communication) and then wonder why word and rite have not moved the hearer to believe! "Usual Lutheran approaches to the interpretation of worship have restricted meaning to theological intent or content—e.g., forgiveness of sins, grace, righteousness—and have left issues of communication to repristinators of (pick-your-century) ceremonial styles."[41] Aune only wants the salvific efficacy of the Word which Lutheran hermeneutics has recognized for biblical words and preached words to be also recognized for ritual words. "Luther's unique notion of the nature of language as performing a certain kind of action moves us from an understanding of liturgical activity and expression as a representation of historical and doctrinal truths to its purpose as an accomplishment or performance of the promise of the Gospel. . . . Such a promise is not an idea to be taught but a reality to be experienced."[42] This is what the Bible and the Reformation call faith, and it is what the liturgy does: "nothing less

40. Michael B. Aune, " 'To Move the Heart': Word and Rite in Contemporary American Lutheranism," *Currents in Theology and Mission*, 10:4 (August 1983) 212.
41. Ibid., 217.
42. Ibid., 221.

than the heart moved and hence transformed." Liturgy forms faith; liturgy forms the faithful theologian.

## CAPACITY AND GRAMMAR

All these authors have, in their various ways, argued the case that liturgy has impact on a theologian. We shall borrow a concept from Paul Holmer by which to loosely summarize the point they make about liturgy's influence. We shall say that liturgy capacitates a person.[43] Capacities differ from a skill or activity in that they are formed and developed over a long period of time and practiced consistently. They usually are not done by the hour but by the lifetime. A skill or activity has a beginning and an end ("I will read or study from noon until two") but it sounds odd to affix temporal parentheses to a capacity ("I will understand from noon until two"—the capacity to understand is different than the skill of reading or the act of studying). Capacities serve to shape a life; they are not so much the doing of something as the way in which something is done. So it is with capacities such as love, faithfulness or hope; kindness, tastefulness or the capacity to understand; gratitude, a sense of obligation, being joyful.

Along this line one could say that liturgy capacitates a person. More than an activity, skill, or mood, worship can be thought of as capacitating the participant in all manner of doxological life (the allusion to Wainwright is intentional as well as the equivocation between "liturgy" and "worship"). We do not disagree with this. One's faith is shaped when in worship one learns to pray (Saliers), or one's heart is moved (Aune), or one gives vent to the devotional expression of the faith (Power). The concern in these efforts,

---

43. We do not mean the Augustinian sense of capacity: *sensus mentis*. We do not mean to argue that western question of grace and nature at all, but for an Orthodox critique of it see John Meyendorff, "The Significance of the Reformation," *Catholicity and the Church* (Crestwood: St. Vladimir's Seminary Press, 1987) 66 ff. Holmer employs the concept "capacity" to wed Wittgenstein's remarks about grammar and Kierkegaard's studies on existential passion. For example, he believes the liberal arts education should capacitate a student, but alas, "Becoming wise would be almost as surprising and as embarrassing—certainly as unexpected—an outcome of the academic study of philosophy as becoming a believer would be out of the academic study of theology." *The Grammar of Faith* (New York: Harper & Row, 1978) 4.

we take it, is to ground theology in liturgical experience. One must be capacitated to theologize. In Holmer's words, one must learn "the grammar of faith."

What is meant by grammar? When we acquire mastery of a language, "we do not speak the grammar itself but we say everything else in accord with the rules we have already learned. The more skilled we become in writing or speaking, the more does our knowledge of grammar inform everything we say and write."[44] Theology is a grammar.[45] To call theology a grammar and to suggest that one must be capacitated to this grammar implies the existence of at least one theological language game in which more than second-order skill in analysis and background information is required (academic theology is one species in the genus theology). "If theology is like a grammar, and certainly it is, then it follows that learning theology is not an end in itself. . . . [Theology] is the declaration of the essence of Christianity . . . [its] aim is not that we repeat the words. Theology must also be absorbed, and when it is, the hearer is supposed to become Godly."[46] In this sense, liturgy capacitates one to theologize, prayer is the basis of reflection upon God, and if one's heart is moved one's brain might also be nudged. This is a customary means of arguing for liturgy's theological significance, and to repeat ourselves, we have no essential quarrel with doxologically motivated theology.

But we wish to view the matter from yet another angle, in addition to that outlined above. Theology is grammatical in another way, Holmer says. The grammar of a language (like logic) is not a personal invention. Grammar precedes the individual. If theology is imagined to function like a grammar, this would suggest that theology is not personal invention either; that it, too, precedes the individual. "Theology answers the question—what is Christianity?

---

44. Ibid., 17.

45. Wittgenstein casually remarked it, and Holmer is trying to explain it. The remark in Wittgenstein is from *Philosophical Investigations*, pars. 371–373: "*Essence* is expressed by grammar. . . . Grammar tells what kind of object anything is (Theology as grammar)." For Wittgenstein's reflections about God and theology, see especially *Culture and Value* (Chicago: University of Chicago Press, 1980) and *On Certainty* (New York: Harper & Row, 1969).

46. Paul Holmer, *The Grammar of Faith*, 19.

But it tells us the answer by giving us the order and priorities, the structure and morphology, of the Christian faith. It does this by placing the big words, like *man, God, Jesus, world,* in such a sequence and context that their use becomes ruled for us. And if we begin to use those words like that, with the appropriate zest and pathos, then we, too, become Godly as those earlier believers were."[47] We think Holmer is correct that a theological grammar precedes the individual. We think it exists in the liturgy's *lex orandi,* which is why the law of prayer not only influences theology, it establishes the law of belief. Liturgy is theological. Regardless of how important one thinks it is for theologians to believe while they think, this is not the main thrust of liturgical theology; the latter refers primarily to the prior and foundational ritual theologizing of the assembly. In their transaction with God the assembly (as theological corporation) speak the big words according to the grammar of faith. Although practitioners of such theology may not be able to analytically rear back and explain the grammar, they do possess the capacity to employ it. That they don't use the furniture of academic theology does not mean the adjustment they make to their encounter with the Holy One is non-theological, it only means it is non-academic.

Liturgical theology is not simply *theologia secunda* done devotionally. Liturgical theology is the product of the assembly's ritualized grammar wherein the liturgists (once more, we mean the laos) celebrate not their own ideas but what has been revealed. The assembly's product—*lex orandi*—is ordered, structured, disciplined and formed; this makes liturgy theology. If one knew this *lex orandi,* one could make "god-talk." It is not the encounter with the Holy One which is theological but the adjustment to that encounter, epiphanized and preserved in the community's leitourgia where the community struggles to understand the big words.

Allow a momentary detour in order to pick up a couple helpful concepts from Friedrich Waismann (a student of Wittgenstein) who made the following distinction between natural and formalized languages. He is discussing the notion of a language being open-ended, or as he calls it, incomplete. "[Incompleteness] is the

47. Ibid., 20.

criterion by which we can distinguish perfectly *formalized* languages constructed by logicians from *natural* languages as used in describing reality. In a formalized system the use of each symbol is governed by a definite number of rules, and further, all the rules of inference and procedure can be stated completely."[48] Liturgical language, we might say, is a natural language, open-ended and not tightly screwed down; second-order theological language is created for a particular purpose and is therefore a bit tighter. It is formalized language. Its functions vary—to combat heresy, to more finely tune a definition, to exclude one idea or include another, to interface with a philosophical tenet or illumine faith for a culture—but whatever its function, this formalized language is governed by a definite number of rules, rules which can be taught to initiates and which can be stated more or less completely. (Thus the numerous courses in theological method!) However, one would be hard pressed to state completely and formally the grammar by which leitourgia works. It might be fairly easy to chart the surface rubrics, but the depth grammar is open-ended.

Wittgenstein evokes an allegorical picture of the difference between natural and formalized language when he writes, "Our language can be seen as an ancient city: a maze of little streets and squares, of old and new houses, and of houses with additions from various periods; and this surrounded by a multitude of new boroughs with straight regular streets and uniform houses."[49] Liturgical language spoken naturally by believers according to the grammar of faith consists of affirmations which wind, maze-like, through their lives, while second-order theology is laid out according to straight regular rules of inference, cast in vocabulary that struggles to be uniform. Both neighborhoods use ruled speech, but different kinds. Talk of God made by the worshiper can be just as ruled and disciplined as talk about God made by the systematician. Theology is a grammar, and liturgy is theology in ritual grammar. Liturgical theology fundamentally conceived is the community's adjustment to God's grammar, preserved and passed on in the structure of the assembly's rite; liturgical theology

48. Friedrich Waismann, "Verifiability," in *Essays on Logic and Language* ed. Antony Flew (Oxford: Basil Blackwell, 1955) 129.
49. Ludwig Wittenstein, *Philosophical Investigations*, par. 18.

derivatively conceived is when someone enunciates this grammar, by having examined the historical rites.

ECCLESIA AS THEOLOGICAL CORPORATION

To recap, we first reviewed a perspective in which worship or prayer was treated as a formative influence upon the theologian as believer. Who can deny that? Who would want to? Points of connection are therefore urgently drawn between liturgy and theological formation in order to affirm the importance of liturgy. We do not dispute these existential connecting points, but they do not sufficiently reveal the character of the "law of prayer—law of belief" relationship. They establish a connective definition, but do not yet reach an organic definition. In order to make the distinctiveness of liturgical theology clear it was necessary to change the focus of this popular argument for liturgy's value. Theology is influenced by liturgy, yes; but leitourgia establishes theology because the grammar of *lex orandi* precedes (normatively) the *lex credendi* of the community and individual.

The definition of liturgical theology which we are exploring not only acknowledges the theologian as believer, but asserts the believer as theologian.

As we are struggling to define it, liturgical theology is much more than putting devotional spin on *theologia secunda*; it is recognizing the innate *theologia prima* worked out by the assembly, manifested and preserved in leitourgia. The organic definition points out that there exists a theology which liturgists in assembly do in a primary way, under ritual logistics.

Theology, defined as adjustment to encounter with God, is worked out here "not in the modes and terms of secondary theology as practiced in academe, but in the modes and terms of prayer, of life, and of concrete practical reflection."[50] Yes, liturgy capacitates theologians, but this means primary theologians too, collectively named "Mrs. Murphy" by Fr. Kavanagh.

"The language of the primary theologian . . . more often consists in symbolic, metaphorical, sacramental words and actions which throw flashes of light upon chasms of rich ambiguity. As such,

50. Kavanagh, "Response: Primary Theology and Liturgical Act," 322.

Mrs. Murphy's language illuminates the chaotic landscape through which I must pick my professional way with the narrow laser-like beam of precise words and concepts—which is why what she does is primary and what I do is secondary; which is why, also, what she does is so much harder to do than what I do. My admiration for her and her colleagues is profound, and it deepens daily."[51]

If with Fr. Schmemann we call theology the search for words appropriate to God, then the Sunday morning worshiper who searches for the right words, and who struggles to use these words rightly in order to praise God, pray to God and glorify God finds himself or herself under a discipline of theology equally as rigorous as that imposed upon the second-order theologian, only it is not analytical. It is not formalized language, being natural, but it is ruled nonetheless. Theology is a discipline because one cannot think any way one pleases. Mrs. Murphy's theology is disciplined, even if the complete set of inferences cannot be worked out by academic convention. This is what eastern Christianity has called Tradition, or what western Christianity means by canon.[52] It will be remembered that our first affirmation about liturgical theology was that it is genuine theology.


THE TWO-TIERED MODEL

Peter Brown proposes an explanation of why Mrs. Murphy's theology has been ignored and even denigrated. The context of his remarks is a study on the origin of the cult of saints in Latin Christianity. Brown suggests that this subject and others like it have been treated suspiciously at best and contemptuously at worst because of an attitude held during the last three centuries, an attitude which pits enlightened religion against superstitious popular religion.

---

51. Ibid, 323.
52. Fr. Kavanagh identifies four canonical sources which govern liturgy and thereby discipline our thought: canon of Scripture, canon of baptismal faith (summed up in the creeds), canon of Eucharistic faith "carried in the assembly's repertoire of eucharistic prayers" (canons of the Mass), and the body of canonical laws regulating daily living and public processes of the community. *On Liturgical Theology*, 140–41.

"In modern scholarship, these attitudes take the form of a 'two-tiered' model. The views of the potentially enlightened few are thought of as being subject to continuous upward pressure from habitual ways of thinking current among 'the vulgar'. . . . When applied to the nature of religious change in late antiquity, the 'two-tiered' model encourages the historian to assume that a change in the piety of late-antique men, of the kind associated with the rise of the cult of saints, must have been the result of the capitulation by the enlightened elites of the Christian church to modes of thought previously current only among the 'vulgar'."[53]

In other words, modern scholarship has assumed an upper tier for the few, consisting of enlightened, spiritual religion, and a lower tier for the many, consisting of quasi-superstitious popular religion.

From whence arose this two-tiered model? Brown suggests that the religious history of late antiquity and the early middle ages "still owes more than we realize to attitudes summed up so persuasively, in the 1750s, by David Hume, in his essay *The Natural History of Religion*."[54] Hume's argument, against his religious contemporaries, was that human beings were not natural monotheists and never had been. But the unnaturalness of monotheism was caused less by sin than by the intellectual limitations of the average human mind. Monotheism was rare because it depended upon social and cultural preconditions and upon a coherent, rational view of the universe which was not easily attained by the vulgar mind. In Hume's own words: "The vulgar, that is, indeed, all mankind a few excepted, being ignorant and uninstructed, never elevate their contemplation to the heavens . . . so far as to discern a supreme mind or original providence."[55]

53. Peter Brown, *The Cult of the Saints: Its Rise and Function in Latin Christianity* (Chicago: University of Chicago Press, 1981) 17.

54. Hume drew on evidence in classical authors and "placed this evidence together with such deftness and good sense that the *Natural History of Religion* seems to carry the irresistible weight of a clear and judicious statement of the obvious" making it virtually "impossible to challenge . . . the accuracy of his portrayal of the nature and causes of superstition in the ancient world. . . ." Ibid., 13.

55. Ibid., 14.

In this description of the vulgar, Hume exemplified the then prevailing attitude. Progress in religion was thought to be the story of the top tier suppressing superstitious popular religion, and regress in religion was the story of vulgar practices corrupting enlightened religion. "The religious history of mankind, for Hume, is not a simple history of decline from an original monotheism; it is marked by a constant tension between theistic and polytheistic ways of thinking."[56] Brown suggests this attitude was mainstreamed into modern scholarship by Gibbon, who expanded on the theme when he described the early Christian cult of the saints as if the vulgar merely pasted a Christian facade over pagan practices,[57] and by nineteenth-century religious revival which "hardened the outlines of Hume's model and made a variant of it part of many modern interpretations of early medieval Christianity."[58] In the words of John Cardinal Newman, "the religion of the multitude is ever vulgar and abnormal; it will ever be tinctured with fanaticism and superstition, while men are what they are."[59]

Feeling a repristination urge stirring in our hearts, we might be moved to defend popular religion. In the face of this overwhelming denigration of the lower tier, one might respond by lionizing whatever originates in the vulgar. In our opinion, one can observe an increase in this line of defense of popular religion. Certain pieties, theologies, or practices are portrayed as invulnerable to criticism by virtue of the fact that they originate among and belong to the populus. We would not want the reader to gain the impres-

56. Ibid.
57. "The imagination . . . eagerly embraced such inferior objects of adoration as were more proportioned to its gross conceptions and imperfect faculties. The sublime and simple theology of the primitive Christians was gradually corrupted. . . ." From ch. 28 of Gibbon's *Decline and Fall*, quoted by Brown, 15.
58. Brown, 15. He cites Dean Milman's *History of Latin Christianity* which contains the observation, "As Christianity worked downwards into the lower classes of society, as it received the crude and ignorant barbarians within its pale, the general effect could not but be that the age would drag down the religion to its level, rather than the religion elevate the age to its own lofty standards."
59. Ibid., 16.

sion that we have fallen victim to this pendulum extreme. Mrs. Murphy's theology is not out of range of criticism simply because it belongs to Mrs. Murphy. This would be a reactive, romanticised account of popular religion, as though because modern scholarship has for three centuries assumed that vulgar expressions of religion can contain nothing good, we should now assume it can contain nothing wrong. Were this liturgical theology's conclusion, it would be as guilty as Hume of blind prejudice regarding the lower tier, only this time pro instead of con. Scholarship needs to rectify its neglect of popular religion, but in so doing it should not lose critical faculties. We are adopting a middle ground here. Not (a) there can be no theological critique of popular religion, nor (b) only *theologia secunda* can critique popular religion; rather (c) it is possible for *theologia prima* to critique popular religion.

Brown seems to advocate this as well, when he points out a problem in the two-tiered model. He does not offer a romantic defense of popular religion of the sort described in the paragraph above, but he does claim that this two-tiered model has a weakness because it overlooks a crucial fact. "The basic weakness of the two-tiered model is that it is rarely if ever, concerned to explain religious change other than among the elite. The religion of 'the vulgar' is assumed to be uniform. It is timeless and faceless. It can cause changes by imposing its modes of thought on the elite; but in itself it does not change."[60] This perception of popular religion is not true, Brown concludes, at least from his research into the cult of saints. But it is tenacious. The prejudice of modern scholarship is that vulgar religious expression is a monotonous continuity and distinctions can only be made between the upper and lower tier, never within the lower tier itself. Practices regarded as superstitious are an embarrassment to modern scholarship and it assumes that the uneducated (read: "non-theological") Christian laity mimicked pagan practices without distinction or transformation.

In this two-tiered model, liturgical cult is reckoned atheological. "Up to the present, it is still normal to assume that the average *homo religiosus* of the Mediterranean, and more especially, the average woman, is, like Winnie the Pooh, 'a bear of very little

---

60. Ibid., 18.

brain.' ''[61] Mrs. Murphy, as a resident of the lower tier, is assumed to be a bear of very little theological brain. Because her
theological language is not formalized, it is assumed to be non-
theological. Because her theological language is natural, it is assumed to be unruled opinion. These assumptions are wrong. In
point of fact, Mrs. Murphy's liturgical theology (both linguistic
and symbolic) is stringently theological, even if the rule formation
comes from inside the assembly and not from above it.

Liturgical theology is the elucidation of the meaning of worship,
Fr. Schmemann said. We have called what is transacted under
leitourgia's ritual logistics fundamental liturgical theology, and its
elucidation derivative liturgical theology. Now we must insist that
Mrs. Murphy can do both (though the latter not necessarily in
propositional form). After going all this way, it would vitiate
everything to say she can do the former but not the latter. All
would be lost were we at this point interpreted as saying that
Mrs. Murphy participates in the fundamental theological activity of
the assembly but she cannot understand or tell about it at all.
Were that the case, then she really would be engaged in mindless
activity, and the difference between liturgical religion and superstition would truly be indistinguishable. It would be mindless (i.e.,
irrational) ritualism indeed if the people did the liturgical act without knowing why. Our third approach, called liturgical theology,
insists that the people do understand and can elucidate the meaning of leitourgia, though of course in a manner quite different
than the manner of secondary theology.

''This means that *lex credendi* is at root not merely something
which is done exclusively by secondary theologians in their
studies, as opposed to *lex supplicandi* done by nontheologians in-
dulging in religious worship elsewhere. On the contrary, *lex
credendi* is constantly being worked out, sustained, and established
as the faithful in assembly are constantly working out, sustaining,
and establishing their *lex supplicandi* from one festive, ordered, aes-

---

61. Ibid., 20. The feminist reference is an acknowledgment that in this two-
tiered model the vulgar was a class ''to which all women were treated as
automatically belonging, as members of 'that timorous and pious sex.' ''
Brown, 28, the interior quote belonging to Hume.

216

thetic, canonical, and eschatological liturgical act to the next under grace."[62]

Brown finds that within the so-called lower tier itself tremendously imaginative changes were effected, changes which transformed pagan reverence of the dead into a Christian cult of saints.[63] He concludes that while certainly some possessed the ability to articulate theology in more abstract terms, there is no evidence to suggest they felt elitist. Christianity was committed to complex beliefs, and understanding all the ramifications

"assumed a level of culture which the majority of the members of the Christian congregations were known not to share with their leaders. Yet it is remarkable that men who were acutely aware of elaborating *dogmas,* such as the nature of the Trinity, whose contents were difficult of access to the 'unlettered,' felt themselves so little isolated for so much of the time from these same 'unlettered' when it came to the shared religious practices of their community and to the assumptions about the relation of man to supernatural beings which these practices condensed."[64]

One must not take this in the context of the modern bifurcation between theology and faith. The point of the above quote does not mean that the lettered person lived most of the time above the masses in the rational world of clear thought, but occasionally forsook theology and condescended to the irrational world of atheological religious practice. No, not this opposition between theology and faith (or theologians and believers). There was indeed an expression of beliefs in a tightly formalized linguistic style, with all the rules of inferences accounted for, whose full understanding and accurate formulation assumed then and still do today a level

62. Kavanagh, *On Liturgical Theology,* 150.
63. ". . . the rise of the cult of saints was sensed by contemporaries, in no uncertain manner, to have broken most of the imaginative boundaries which ancient men had placed between heaven and earth, the divine and the human, the living and the dead, the town and its antithesis. I wonder whether it is any longer possible to treat the explicit breaking of barriers associated with the rise and the public articulation of the cult of saints as no more than foam on the surface of the lazy ocean of 'popular belief.' " Brown, 21.
64. Ibid., 19.

of culture which the majority of congregations do not share since they are not called to a vocation of scholarship. Yet what these lettered men and women elaborated in the secondary order is what all Christians celebrated in the primary. In fact, Brown writes, differences of class and education played no significant role in the area of life covered by religious practice. He cites the words of another scholar, Arnaldo Momigliano, to express his own conclusion. "Thus my inquest into popular beliefs in the Late Roman historians ends in reporting that there were no such beliefs. In the fourth and fifth centuries there were of course plenty of beliefs which we historians of the twentieth century would glady call popular, but the historians of the fourth and fifth centuries never treated any belief as characteristic of the masses and consequently discredited among the elite."[65]

Gregory Dix commented upon the matter nicely forty-five years ago: "The people have a certain right to be vulgar; and the liturgy, even while it must teach them, has never a right to be academic, because it is their prayer."[66]

### LITURGICAL THEOLOGY AND PRAXIS

This is difficult for us to comprehend, so deep now is the rift between theologian and believer. As Fr. Schmemann charged, today the laity is scarcely interested in the theological curriculum of the university or seminary (indeed they grumble when a young pastor, newly hatched and knowing no better, tries to present theology from the pulpit) and many theologians avoid discussing the Church's life and do not even dream about influencing it. But it

65. Ibid., quoting A. D. Momigliano, "Popular Religious Beliefs and Late Roman Historians," *Studies in Church History*, vol. 8 (Cambridge: At the University Press, 1971).

66. Dix, *The Shape of the Liturgy*, 586. At a point too late to integrate into this work, I have discovered Romano Guardini's passionate concern that liturgy not become aristocratic. For example: "The liturgy is essentially not the religion of the cultured, but the religion of the people. If the people are rightly instructed, and the liturgy properly carried out, they display a simple and profound understanding of it. For the people do not analyze concepts, but contemplate." *The Church and the Catholic and The Spirit of the Liturgy* (New York: Sheed & Ward, 1953) 29.

was not always so. For example, the Byzantine Church, claims Timothy Ware, was at one time characterized by a theological passion shared by both speakers of natural liturgical language and formalized dogmatic language, even though "today, in an untheological age, it is all but impossible to realize how burning an interest was felt in religious questions by every part of society, by laity as well as clergy, by the poor and uneducated as well as the Court and the scholars."[67] Theological questions were not isolated from the people behind a door which required an academic degree to unlock. Gregory of Nyssa describes the unending theological arguments in Constantinople at the time of the second Council. "The whole city is full of it, the squares, the market places, the cross-roads, the alleyways; old-clothes men, money changers, food sellers: they are all busy arguing. If you ask someone to give you change, he philosophizes about the Begotten and the Unbegotten; if you inquire about the price of a loaf, you are told by way of reply that the Father is greater and the Son inferior; if you ask 'Is my bath ready?' the attendant answers that the Son was made out of nothing."[68] Gregory's words only bring a smile to our lips, for we can hardly take them as anything but hyperbole. Why should the old-clothes men, the money changers and Mrs. Murphy care a whit about Arianism or subordinationism? Why, indeed, unless Christology is not as much about Jesus' metaphysical make up as how we might become by grace what he is by nature? Why, indeed, unless the doctrine of the Trinity is not philosophical speculation about the interior of the deity, but has to do with the way of salvation revealed? Why, indeed, unless Eucharistic doctrine is not concerned with the transformation of bread-substance, but with our becoming the living body of Christ?

Today it requires a stretch to imagine doctrines having existential impact (inside or outside the divinity school) because they generally belong to an abstract world of their own. *Homoousion* is not only elite jargon, but to the lay person a foreign language, foreign because the language doesn't communicate meaning. It is about a supernatural event long ago rather than the divine-human

67. Timothy Ware, *The Orthodox Church* (New York: Penguin Books, 1964) 43.
68. *On the Deity of the Son* by Gregory Nyssa, quoted in Ware, 43–44.

reconciliation which even now restores to humanity the likeness of God. Trinity seems to have something to do with a mystery before the Big Bang or beyond the galaxy rather than God's intimate person-to-person and infinite-to-finite disclosure. Doctrines should be windows of glass to see through, but instead our attention has been diverted to the pane of glass itself in which we see our own reflection, as in a mirror.

If doctrines are chapters in the story, liturgical theology includes them all because in the Divine Liturgy the entire story is celebrated. The liturgical theologian can know it in open-ended liturgical language because he or she knows the entire story, even if that person cannot break it down into formalized language. Liturgical theology involves ecclesiology, for this identifies the assembly which celebrates; ecclesiology involves Christology, for this confesses whose body the Church is; Christology involves soteriology because this reveals the (functional) identity of the incarnate one into whose Paschal mystery we are grafted; and why do soteriology without a doctrine of sin? and how can one understand what sin is without a doctrine of creation which reveals what humanity was meant to be? These doctrines are not stories in themselves, they are chapters in the single story, facets on the single diamond, which the Church puts into song and sings in its Divine Liturgy in anaphora and incense, speech and symbol, kerygma and icon. Theology is enacted and proclaimed at each liturgical celebration, symbolically and completely. Although this theology is quite distinct from that of journals and classrooms, we are arguing in favor of calling it theology because it is an effort to understand what God's love in Christ entails. Those whose lives are hid in Christ know this paschal grammar.

If liturgical theology is the elucidation of the meaning of worship, how do the laos demonstrate their understanding of it? Probably not by articulating propositions; perhaps not in linguistic form at all, and if so, not by speaking about the grammar but by speaking with it. Most likely the understanding of liturgy's theology will be demonstrated when the structure of one's life is put in concord with the deep structure of the liturgy. In Fr. Taft's words, the purpose of all Christian liturgy is to express in a ritual moment that which should be the basic stance of every moment of our lives. The meaning of baptism will be elucidated when one lives a regenerate life, of Eucharist when one becomes a *eucharistos* (thankful one),[69] and of liturgy when the rite becomes a joyful summons home to God. The theology which Mrs. Murphy is capacitated to do is liturgical theology.

The fact to be rued is that so few speak this primary grammar any longer because in matters liturgical so many have been tongue-tied. At some point, leitourgia was replaced by "a new system of worship which would increasingly do without rite"[70] and leitourgia became liturgy. The texts (with instruction) are pre-printed and handed down from the upper tier because practitioners of *theologia secunda* do not trust the vulgar to create liturgically. *Theologia prima* is not flexed by the lower tier because they are accustomed to receiving pre-packaged liturgies mailed out from Rome or Philadelphia, and are told that theology is not their business or concern.

Fr. Schmemann spoke of the metamorphosis of liturgical consciousness such that something besides leitourgia now occupies the assembly in its gathering. Symptomatic of this metamorphosis is the reduction of leitourgia to one of two anemic forms.

"Our approach to worship is either rational or sentimental. The rational approach consists of reducing the liturgical celebration to ideas. [For such an approach] liturgy is at best a raw material for neat intellectual definitions and propositions. . . . As to the sentimental approach, it is the result of an individualistic and self-centered piety. . . . For that kind of piety worship is above everything else a useful framework for personal prayer, an inspiring background whose aim is to 'warm up' our heart and direct it toward God. The content and meaning of services, liturgical texts,

---

69. "Clearly, the one idea predominating from the end of the first century is that what the Lord established at the Last Supper and what the Church has since been celebrating is an *eucharistia*. The word was suggested already by the *eucharistesas* of the New Testament accounts. In the linguistic usage of that time it means to consider and conduct oneself as *eucharistos*, that is, as one richly overwhelmed with gifts and graces—an attitude that found expression in words but did not exclude expression in the form of a gift." Joseph Jungmann, *The Mass* (Collegeville: The Liturgical Press, 1974) 33.

70. Kavanagh, *On Liturgical Theology*, 108.

rites, and actions is here of secondary importance; they are useful and adequate as long as they make me pray."[71]

Consider an example in which one can see either reduction at work: fasting. The purpose of Lent is to recover our Christian sense that sin is alien, so that we are not content in this fallen state but are roused to begin the spiritual journey toward Easter. For this purpose, people fast during Lent. There is no Lent without fasting. Fasting is how one means Lent, like people mean themselves bodily, or words are how one means. The meaning of Lent is to fast. But with the loss of liturgical consciousness, this theological meaning is attenuated to either side. On the one hand, one fasts for half a day and then stops, concluding, "Now I get it! I see the point!" On the other hand, one makes a symbolic fast in order to create a sentiment in the heart rather than a hunger in the stomach. When Mrs. Murphy does primary theology, she truly fasts and knows the reason why. Liturgical theology elucidates the fundamental meaning of worship. The point is not to elucidate the idea of Lent, and once the academic "gets it" the fasting is no longer necessary; nor is it to elucidate the symbolism of Lent, and once the esthete "gets it" a symbolic fasting will do. Practitioners of lower tier popular religion have theologized about the meaning of Lent by fasting. They did not have a thought about it, they did not have a feeling about it, they did theology-in-action (*lex supplicandi*). They struggled for, expressed, preserved and experienced the meaning of Lent by fasting, and their theology can be observed in the liturgical rubrics and canon law regarding the Lenten fast. Theology which is liturgical consists of the myriad ways in which the people address God and address the world about God. Their acts are ruled and meaningful and so theological, even if not propositional.

LITURGICAL CELEBRATIONS ARE GRAMMATICAL

Leitourgia is ordered, logical, grammatical, canonical, meaningful, deeply structured, and functions according to Tradition. As

71. Schmemann, *Great Lent*, 80. It was my idea to use the example of fasting as an illustration of primary theology in action; Schmemann is quoted because his categories of "rational" and "sentimental" inspired it.

such, it is itself theological. "What emerges most directly from an assembly's liturgical act is not a new species of theology among others. It is *theologia* itself."[72] The shop keeper of whom Gregory of Nyssa wrote may not have understood the "lettered" form of the doctrine, but he would have recognized the doctrine from the Divine Liturgy because there he would have witnessed it in word and symbol, in ritual and icon. Liturgical theology and secondary theology are not in competition, they are two different tasks for two different callings, and both are theological. Leitourgia is not a substitute for secondary theology; how could it be a substitute for analyzation when it is not analytic? In leitourgia the content of *lex credendi* is beheld by the people week after week in their *lex orandi*. Speaking of liturgy in the Orthodox rhythm, Fr. Taft writes,

"Worshiping in this atmosphere of profuse symbolism through which the supernatural splendor of the inaccessible divine majesty is approached, Eastern Christians witness the exaltation and sanctification of creation, the majestic appearance of God who enters us, sanctifies us, divinizes us through the transfiguring light of his heavenly grace. It is not only a matter of receiving the sacraments, but also one of living habitually within a liturgical atmosphere which stirs us in body and soul in order to transform us before a vision of spiritual beauty and joy."[73]

Fr. Taft is describing liturgy as divine epiphany. Were it not so—if the Spirit inspired an idea but the successive liturgical form as well as the successive liturgical theology were human creation alone—then liturgy would be the assembly's corporate opinion! In which case, why should liturgical theology have any more weight or authority than a solitary opinion? Why should the opinion of prayer (not law of prayer) establish the law of belief? If liturgy were the assembly's consensus, not God's epiphany, then liturgy could be either a rational or sentimental act, but it could not be a religiously ontological one. Something is witnessed in liturgy because a reality is celebrated, and that reality may in turn echo in human faculties of reason, piety or ritual.

72. Kavanagh, *On Liturgical Theology*, 75.
73. Taft, "Sunday in the Eastern Tradition" 69.

To "celebrate" means to accomplish or repeat. The pervading reality is focused and consciously remembered, as when birthdays or anniversaries celebrate the life or relationship which extends throughout one's existence. The celebration does not create the reality within its borders, as if someone were only really alive on his or her birthday, or really married on the anniversary day; rather the celebration enables one to express in specific moments what is constantly real. Liturgy celebrates a reality by bringing to ritual moment what is steadfastly and pervasively true. This is the point at which liturgy is so often confused with cult. Cult seeks to effect the reality itself and can only do so within supernatural borders, but liturgy does not suppose God is conjured into this world by cultic snatches of transcendence. God is in the world already; humans need ritual moments to celebrate this in reality. Resurrection is the appearance in this world (not in some other world) of life that shall have no end, says Fr. Schmemann. In a world dominated by death, "there appeared one morning someone who is beyond death and yet *in* our time. . . . Christianity is first of all the proclamation in this world of Christ's Resurrection."[74] The Divine Liturgy is a celebration of Christ's ongoing heavenly liturgy. The resurrecting power of God is celebrated, accomplished, made present in a moment, realized, displayed and epiphanized. Jean Corbon reminds us that this is the purpose and necessity of the Christian liturgical celebration.

"A celebration can now be seen as a 'moment' in which the Lord comes with power and his coming becomes the sole concern of those who answer to his call.

"That concern should pervade every other concern of Christian life. Every celebration of the liturgy is geared to that lived liturgy in which each instant of life should become a 'moment' of grace. The liturgy cannot be lived at each moment, however, unless it is celebrated at certain moments. Furthermore, the celebration contains an irreducible newness which is an argument for its necessity; for it is in the celebration that the event of Christ becomes the event of the Church assembled here and now. The celebrating

74. Schmemann, *Liturgy and Life: Christian Development through Liturgical Experience*, 76.

Church welcomes the heavenly liturgy and takes part in it. The Church is thereby shown to be the body of Christ and becomes that body more fully. . . ."[75]

Church celebrations are moments when we are taken up into Christ's eternal, heavenly liturgy to the Father. Our whole life is to become a liturgy to the Father, but we cannot live this each moment if we do not do it some moments. That is the point of ritual: it epiphanizes states of affairs. For human beings, some realities are ritually as I am bodily. The celebration of family rituals like Thanksgiving, suppertime, a birthday, and a bedtime backrub are the ways a family is family. The Church is Church by ritually celebrating leitourgia.

Those who are of the Lord (kyriakos—Christian) participate in his heavenly liturgy when at the Eucharist Christ's liturgy before the Father is celebrated and accomplished on the eighth day, the Lord's day (he kyriake hemera—Sunday).[76] The Church assembles to celebrate "a triunity of the assembly, the eucharist and the Church. . . . The fundamental task of liturgical theology consists therefore in uncovering the meaning and essence of this unity."[77] This unity, we suggest, is displayed at each celebration and can be witnessed by Mrs. Murphy and the shop keeper of whom Gregory of Nyssa spoke. If it is not understood meaningfully, more theologians are called for at the assembly, but by now it should be obvious that we don't mean more professors, pastors and graduate students. The liturgical renewal will not accomplish anything if it only expands the ranges of "how" and does not revivify the "what." The renewal must be a theological renewal, not just a stylistic one, but this must occur within the lower tier, it cannot just trickle down from the upper, secondary tier.

75. Jean Corbon, The Wellspring of Worship (New York: Paulist Press, 1988), 79.

76. See Eugene Laverdiere, "Origins of Sunday in New Testament" Sunday Morning: A Time for Worship, 17 ff. The simple designation he kyriake ("the Lord's") even without the noun hemera ("day") was understood by early Christians to mean Sunday, the eighth day, the day on which resurrection is encountered. Thus Ignatius refers to "the Lord's of the Lord" (kata kyriaken de kyriou) an expression which appears tautological but refers both to the day and to the people: the Lord's [day] of the Lord.

77. Schmemann, The Eucharist, 11-12.

Men and women were created for Eucharistic life. We are *homo adorans*. The Eucharist is humanity fully alive (which is God's glory, according to Origen). When in Christ Eucharistic life was restored to humanity, God was only completing what had been undertaken from the beginning. "After the Fall, human history is a long shipwreck awaiting rescue: but the port of salvation is not the goal; it is the possibility for the shipwrecked to resume his journey whose sole goal is union with God."[78] The Divine Liturgy is a cosmological event because what humanity was meant to be comes to fruition in the Eucharistic act and the cosmos is finally completed. Cult must be transformed, or else communion with God and *diakonia* to neighbor will be spasmodic, confined to some places and absent from others. Christianity is the end of cult since Christ has collapsed the wall separating sacred and profane; on the other hand, eighth-day reality can only be lived because it is celebrated. "Only when the life that burst from the tomb had become liturgy could the liturgy finally be *celebrated*—only when the river returned to its fountainhead, the Father. The liturgy begins in this movement of return."[79]

And because it is celebrated, it can be thought about. The economy of salvation is witnessed in the liturgy. The Divine Liturgy is the current epiphany of God's kingdom, brought to perfection in Christ even though it is hidden except to faith. Because the mystery is seen here it can be proclaimed there. Because the mystery is celebrated here it can be lived there and they will know we are his disciples by our love. Christian liturgy is the end of old cult because God's kingdom has come and preparation for the kingdom is complete, yet transformed cult is liturgy's mode in this world.

78. Vladimir Lossky, *Orthodoxy Theology, An Introduction* (New York: St. Vladimir's Seminary Press, 1978) 84. Or in Kavanagh's words, "a Church is the central workshop of the human City, a City which under grace has already begun to mutate by fits and starts into the City-of-God-in-the-making. . . . This is because it is not fundamentally the Church which has been redeemed in Christ but the World itself." Kavanagh, *On Liturgical Theology*, 43.

79. Corbon, *Wellspring of Worship*, 39.

"In this world, the eschaton—the holy, the sacred, the 'otherness'—can be expressed and manifested only as 'cult.' Not only in relation to the world, but in relation to itself as dwelling in the world, the Church must use the forms and language of the cult, in order eternally to transcend the cult, to 'become what it is.' And it is this 'transition' of the cult—the cult which itself fulfills the *reality* to which it can only point, which it can announce, but which is the consummation of its function as cult—that we call sacrament. . . .

"Theology is *possible* only within the Church, i.e. as a fruit of this new life in Christ, granted in the sacramental *leitourgia*, as a witness to the eschatological fullness of the Church."[80]

Liturgy is the celebration of a sacramental reality, the fruit of which is theology. Liturgical theology is fundamentally the paschal mystery ritually displayed, and derivatively the elucidation of what is celebrated in the Divine Liturgy. This law of prayer, epiphanized and elucidated, establishes the law of belief because *lex credendi* is describing what the ekklesia witnesses in *lex orandi*.

We turn then to two examples of liturgical theology (derivatively defined), commentaries on the Eucharist by Germanus and Schmemann. Having described liturgical theology abstractly, we should be able to recognize what these authors are doing; and if we recognize what they are doing, we will reaffirm what we have described.

---

80. Schmemann, "Theology and Liturgical Tradition," 174–75.

## Chapter 6

## Two Examples of Liturgical Theology

Liturgical theology is different from theology of worship because *leitourgia* is more than a format for worship. Theologians ruminating about worship can consider many topics: the logic of doxology, why humanity should praise, the basis of prayer, the covenantal structure of worship as response, or the influence of faith community upon theological formation—but this is not liturgical theology. Liturgical theology is fundamentally the rule in motion; derivatively it is the rule enunciated; the rule extrapolated on various problematic fronts is *theologia secunda*. If one wished to witness the rule in motion, visit a liturgy; to witness second-order theology, follow the rule into the storm fronts of theological conundrums; but we shall now witness the rule elucidated by looking at two liturgical theologies which give voice to the rite's *lex orandi*.

We turn to two derivative liturgical theologies, one ancient and one contemporary, one sounding more foreign to our ear and the other more familiar, but both are offered as examples of liturgical theology. The contemporary example is *The Eucharist* by Fr. Alexander Schmemann. The ancient example is *Ecclesiastical History and Mystical Contemplation* by St. Germanus of Constantinople.

### a. Ecclesiastical History, *by St. Germanus*[1]

Liturgical commentary has its origin in fourth-century mystagogical catecheses. These originally oral instructions were intended to explain the Christian mysteries, particularly baptism and Eucharist, to the surging number of people joining the Church in the fourth

1. Translation, introduction and commentary by Paul Meyendorff (New York: St. Vladimir's Press, 1984).

century. The mystagogies were recorded and expanded, and continued to be useful in written form. As Paul Meyendorff describes it, "The goal of the commentary was to make its recipients understand the meaning of what they were supposed to experience in the liturgy, as well as to inspire in them a feeling of awe and fear."[2]

Two ancient strands of tradition can be identified in liturgical commentary, one from Antioch and one from Alexandria. These two traditions are sometimes complementary but often divergent, as is familiar from their contribution to the Christological debates.[3] The Alexandrine tradition follows Origen in its talent for anagogical allegory, and receives systematization by Dionysius who in the third chapter of his *Ecclesiastical Hierarchy* gives an interpretation of the liturgy which becomes a primary model for later Byzantine commentators, notably Maximus the Confessor and Symeon of Thessalonia. On the other hand, the Antiochene approach, first seen in the writings of Isidore of Pelusa and John Chrysostom, is synthesized by Theodore of Mopsuestia in a different direction and is continued in the liturgical commentaries of Germanus, Nicholas and Theodore of Andida, and Nicholas Cabasilas. Later

2. Ibid., 24. On mystagogy in general see Hugh M. Riley, *Christian Initiation* (Washington: Catholic University Press, 1974). He distinguishes theology and mystagogy by claiming the former offers a meaning of the event while the latter offers a meaning of a given liturgical ceremony (215). His thesis in the rough is that mystagogy must include three factors: the liturgy itself, the world of consciousness of the candidate, and materials employed to give exposition (220). Thus his is a study of what *materials* were adopted to explain to *these neophytes* what had happened in *these rites*.

3. E.g., Alloys Grillmeier, S.J. *Christ in Christian Tradition* vol. 1, (Atlanta: John Knox Press, 1975) comparing 133 ff. with 421 ff.; P. Smulders, S.J. *The Fathers on Christology* (DePere, WI: St. Norbert Abbey Press, 1968); or note studies on the development of Christian doctrine such as J.N.D. Kelly, *Early Christian Doctrines* (New York: Harper & Row, 1960) or Jaroslav Pelikan, *The Christian Tradition*, vol 1: The Emergence of the Catholic Tradition (100–600) (Chicago: University of Chicago Press, 1971) ch. 5. On specific exegetical differences between Alexandria and Antioch see James Wood, *The Interpretation of the Bible* (London: The Camelot Press, 1958) ch. 5 "Alexandria and Antioch." And a summary of their respective spiritualities is contained in Louis Bouyer, *The Spirituality of the New Testament and the Fathers* (New York: Seabury Press, 1960).

Byzantine theology will balance and integrate these two traditions, even though they are fundamentally opposed in orientation.[4] Dionysius' focus is exclusively eschatological; he scarcely mentions Christ's earthly ministry, death and resurrection (the main focus is the incarnation as source of our union with God); the liturgy is perceived as an ascent from the material to the spiritual. The Antiochene tradition emphasizes a typological approach which, when applied to liturgy, stresses connection of the rites with the historical Jesus; "the focus is on Christ's earthly ministry and the historical events of his life which are reenacted and made present in the rites, *as well as* the high priesthood which Christ now exercises in heaven."[5]

## ALEXANDRIA AND ANTIOCH

To understand what is unique about Germanus' commentary one must first understand the Antiochene tradition. We will do this by comparing it to its Alexandrine counterpart. Second, one must come to terms with the roots and purpose of allegorical interpretation in general.

Dionysius can serve as representative of the Alexandrine school. He places his explanation of the liturgy after a meditation on two hierarchies, heavenly and ecclesiastical. "According to Dionysius, the function of both the heavenly and the earthly hierarchies is to mediate the divine illumination that radiates from the Most Holy Trinity, the source of all hierarchies, and descends through the ranks of the angelic world and the ordained priesthood to the believing people, and by means of this communication to lead the people to the knowledge of God."[6] The illumination which is communicated in a spiritual manner in the angelic sphere, Dionysius writes, "is repeated in the Church in symbols, sacraments and images, that is, in half-spiritual, half-visible forms which at

4. "Dionysius" explanation of the liturgy is thus opposed diametrically to that of Theodore of Mopsuestia. The later Byzantine explanation of the liturgy will strike a balance between these two basic possibilities." Hans-Joachim Schulz, The Byzantine Liturgy (New York: Pueblo Publishing Co., 1986) 28.

5. The terms of the comparison are from Meyendorff, 26–33; the quote is from 29 (underscoring mine).

6. Schulz, 25.

once copy and conceal the spiritual process occurring in the higher sphere."[7] The liturgy presents the concurrent heavenly liturgy in symbolic forms to enable the participant to ascend from material to spiritual realities. Typical is Dionysius' interpretation of the opening action in the synaxis, in which he compares the incensation of the church by the bishop with a divine action. "[He] walks from the altar to the farthest reaches of the church with the fragrance rising from the censer and, having completed his round, returns again to the altar. Inspired by his own goodness, the blessed God who is supreme above all beings, comes forth from himself to enter into communion with those who share in his holy gifts; and yet he does not abandon his essential and immutable repose and immobility."[8] What God enacts in the mystery of heaven is unfolded in a varied fullness of symbolic ceremonies; the liturgical symbols are the figurative representation of the divinity as the liturgy mediates the supratemporal saving action of God.

The great church in Constantinople, the Hagia Sophia, will witness to this view paradigmatically. "The star of Dionysius will be in the ascendent in the now beginning age of Justinian, whose most brilliant creation, Hagia Sophia, bears witness to the same view of the world."[9] Under the influence of this Alexandrine perspective, both Byzantine liturgy and architecture reflect a hierarchical view of spirit and matter, the angelic and the human. The Temple, as place of worship, is a world controlled by heaven, an earthly place filled with heavenly reality. The church structure itself, as well as the use of images within it, manifests the celestial vision of Dionysius (and that of his disciple, Maximus).[10] "By rea-

7. Ibid.

8. Ibid., 26.

9. Ibid., 28. Another sign of its potency is that while Theodore's Antiochene tradition eventually takes firm root also, "it was possible for the ideas of Theodore to enter the Byzantine liturgy of the sixth century only through the transposing medium . . . of the Dionysian vision of the world" (36).

10. The *Mystagogy* by Maximus begins with a meditation on the church and relates it symbolically to the heavenly-earthly bipolarity. "The holy church of God presents itself as an image and likeness of the entire cosmos, which encompasses visible and invisible beings. . . ." (Schulz, 43–49 on Maximus). Thomas Mathews points out that Maximus' divisions are not structural but

son of the images that adorn it the church itself henceforth becomes a liturgy, as it were, because it depicts the liturgico-sacramental presence of Christ, the angels, and the saints, and by depicting it shares in bringing it about. The iconography of the church also shows it to be the place in which the mysteries of the life of Christ are made present."[11] For Dionysius, the great mystery of redemption is revealed in all the liturgical realities: the church structure, icons, the priest, sacraments, rites and symbols. "The liturgy is an allegory of the soul's progress from the divisiveness of sin to the divine communion, through a process of purification, illumination, perfection imaged forth in the rites."[12] We will see that this allegorical interpretation is quite different from the Antiochene tradition which Germanus inherits.

ALLEGORY

First, however, the other task necessary in order to appreciate Germanus' commentary. Both Alexandrine and Antiochene traditions employ allegorization. What is its origin and purpose? It does not mean for Dionysius, or Theodore and Germanus, what it seems to mean today. In modern usage, allegory connotes an interpreter fixing arbitrarily to the object of interpretation any meaning the interpreter wishes (like fitting a square peg in a round hole). It feels like free-floating pedagogy by which any allegorical meaning which roughly fits can be applied if it suits the interpreter's needs. Schulz explicitly denies that this describes Dionysius' procedure. The explanation of the ceremonies is not arbitrary, "on the contrary, in his system every 'allegoresis' (relating of one thing to 'another') is kept within bounds because in

functional, i.e., liturgical. "The division is made to carry a variety of symbolic interpretations: it represents the whole created universe divided into the invisible angelic world and the corporeal world of men, or the visible world divided into heaven and earth, or man himself in his two-fold nature of soul and body, or the soul of man in its division between higher and lower faculties." *The Early Churches of Constantinople: Architecture and Liturgy* (University Park: Pennsylvania State University Press, 1971) 121.

11. Schulz, 51.

12. Taft, "The Liturgy of the Great Church," *Dumbarton Oaks Papers*, Numbers 34 and 35 (1980–81), 61.

every case the meaning of the rite emerges from a 'higher' and never from 'another' irrelevant reality.''[13]

Such an argument will sound like liturgical legerdemain, both here and when we read Germanus, unless it is taken within the context from which it arose: early Christian scriptural exegesis. So Fr. Taft devotes some effort to explaining the purpose of liturgical allegorization. It simply applies to the liturgy an interpretive process that had already been applied to Scripture. "All healthy liturgical interpretation depends on a ritual symbolism determined not arbitrarily, but by the testimony of tradition rooted in the Bible. Like the scriptures, the rites of the Church await an exegesis and a hermeneutic and a homiletic to expound, interpret, and apply their multiple levels of meaning in each age. Mystagogy is to liturgy what exegesis is to scripture. It is no wonder, then, that the commentators on the liturgy used a method inherited from the older tradition of biblical exegesis.''[14] Sacred Scripture presents more than history, holy or otherwise. In addition to its literal (historical) meaning, Scripture is also reckoned to contain a higher meaning, variously labeled as ''spiritual'' or ''mystical'' or ''allegorical.'' Whatever it is called, this higher meaning has traditionally been divided into three classifications. Scripture's allegorical meaning (dogmatic aspect) refers to the mystery of Christ and the Church, its tropological meaning (moral aspect) relates the text to an individual's life, and its anagogical meaning (eschatological aspect) directs us to the kingdom to come.[15] In other words, when the historical event is contemplated in faith it is ''perceived as containing a higher truth . . . as well as a practical application for here and now, and a sign that points to what is to come.''[16]

13. Schulz, 27.
14. Taft, ''The Liturgy of the Great Church,'' 59.
15. A medieval ditty was created in the West as a memory tool:
''The Letter shows us what God and our fathers did; the allegory shows us where our faith is hid; the moral meaning gives us rules of daily life; the anagogy shows us where we end our strife.'' Steven Ozment, *The Age of Reform* (New Haven: Yale University Press, 1980) 66 ff.
16. Taft, ''The Liturgy of the Great Church,'' 59. Scripture is read within the realms of history, faith, charity and hope (60). For a positive estimate of this allegorical reading of Scripture see also Louis Bouyer, *The Meaning of the Monastic Life* (London: Burns & Oates, 1955) Part Two, ch. 5, ''Lectio Divina.''

This threefold spiritual meaning of Scripture is its mystical or its allegorical meaning. In classical rhetoric, allegory is an extended metaphor. Allegorization is a helpful and necessary tool for understanding; what is condemned is arbitrary application of allegory.

"Christian exegetes borrowed this figure of *speech* and applied it not to *language*, but to event, as when the passage of the Red Sea is seen as a figure of Christ's baptism. . . . It is not a question of the hidden sense of the text, or of the relation between visible and invisible realities, but of the relation between two historical events of different epochs in salvation history, such as the passover of the Jews and that of Jesus. But in addition to this *allegoria facti* there was also the *allegoria dicti*, which sought hidden meanings, often contrived, in the biblical text. As we have seen it is the application of this arbitrarily extended metaphorical interpretation to liturgical rites in the Middle Ages that contemporary liturgists generally refer to pejoratively, as allegory."[17]

When this method was applied to the phenomenon of liturgical worship in the fourth century, the genre of Christian mystagogy was born. It was entirely natural for the composers of the mystagogies to apply the method of Scripture interpretation to interpret liturgy, since "They understood the liturgy, like scripture, to be a channel leading to God, a means of experiencing divine life here and now. . . . This exegetical method was thus a most appropriate tool to present all these different levels and to keep them in dynamic tension."[18] At stake was the ability to understand and integrate the historical unfolding of the mystery of salvation. What the Old Testament foreshadowed by prophetic type was fulfilled in Christ, therefore the Divine Liturgy can be perceived as already the banquet of the anticipated kingdom. We have seen which allegorical meaning was emphasized in the Alexandrine tradition where in the person of Dionysius anagogy predominates. But Theodore of Mopsuestia (three centuries before Germanus) takes it in quite a different direction.

17. Ibid., 60, footnote 72.
18. Meyendorff, introduction, 24. Taft: "It is part of a much larger problem manifested in all areas of patristic theology, not just in liturgy" ("Historicism Revisited," 106).

Schulz describes Theodore as "the most typically Antiochene representative of the new, anti-Arian emphasis on the high priesthood of Christ. He sees Christ as the heavenly high priest. . . . Therefore this priestly activity must also be imaged forth in the liturgy. Just as the priest is an image (eikon) of Christ, so too must the liturgical actions become images of the historical work of redemption and in particular of the resurrection."[19] For Theodore, the liturgy not only images an individual's internal spiritual journey, as suggested by the Alexandrines, it also images forth Christ's priestly activity. And where does Christ function as priest? In heaven, to be sure, and so "we are taught to perform in this world the symbols and signs of the blessings to come;"[20] but the economy of salvation was accomplished by the High Priest as a human being. Therefore the liturgy not only images Christ's priestly activity in heaven, in it we can also see Christ as he is led away to his passion, as he is stretched out on the altar to be immolated for us. Theodore explains that this is why some of the deacons spread cloths on the altar, to remind us of burial sheets, while others stand on either side and fan the air above the sacred body. Theodore focuses dually upon the high priesthood which Christ exercises in heaven, and the historical events of his life, which are reenacted and made present. In this type of allegorical mystagogy, specific rites and objects naturally begin to take on specific meanings. Theodore synchronizes individual rites of the liturgy with stages in the life of Christ, that is to say, phases in the work of redemption. For example, the offering procession images Christ being led to his passion; the deacons standing round the bishop image the angels; the linen spread on the altar represents the liturgical service of Joseph of Arimathea; and the epiclesis and subsequent liturgical actions correspond to the resurrection. Even though Theodore was no longer a direct authority for the Church after the year 533, "by then his approach to the liturgy had become so much a part of ecclesiastical tradition that his

19. Schulz, 17.
20. Theodore, Homily 15, cited in Meyendorff, 30. See otherwise Edward Yarnold's translation in *The Awe Inspiring Rites of Initiation* (England: St. Paul Publications, 1971).

interpretative motifs are interwoven inextricably with the later Byzantine explanation of the liturgy."[21]

In exegesis of Scripture, observes Fr. Taft, Antioch was more prone than its Alexandrine counterpart to interpret the Old Testament in terms of typology; "this same bias is manifest in their mystagogy, with its strong emphasis on the relation between the liturgical rites and the saving acts of Christ's life."[22] What was prefigured in the Old Testament and fulfilled in Christ has passed into the sacrament in expectation of its eschatological fulfillment. These four phases of salvation—Old Testament foreshadow, fulfillment in Christ, ecclesial celebration, and eschatological parousia—are to be integrated. To be sure, Theodore does not ignore the heavenly, mystical element of the liturgy. Indeed, he put into words the expectation which typifies every Orthodox liturgy ("Every time, then, there is performed the liturgy of this awesome sacrifice, which is the clear image of the heavenly realities, we should imagine that we are in heaven . . ."[23]) but what is new in Theodore, says Fr. Taft, is his systematic interpretation of the liturgy as a dramatic reenactment of the passion of Christ. As noted, the actions of priest and deacon, the vestments and table linens, the altar and bread represent to us the economy of salvation by dramatic reenactment of the passion of Christ.


THE ANTIOCHENE PERSPECTIVE

To summarize, a systematic Christian liturgical theology appeared in fourth-century catechetical homilies, and was worked out from two perspectives. Both observed the eschatological dimension of liturgy, but each in its own way. "Among the Antiochenes the emphasis shifts rather to a cultic, 'realised eschatology' of the presence of the Risen One among His own as proleptic experience of the Pasch of the final days. Among the Alexandrines a moral, individual eschatology is stressed: the true Christian does not wait for the Pasch of the parousia, but is 'passing continuously from the things of this life to God, hastening towards His

21. Schulz, 20.
22. Taft, "The Liturgy of the Great Church," 62.
23. Para. 20 of Baptismal Homily IV, quoted in Taft, 63; also Yarnold, 224.

city.' ''[24] From whence arose this Antiochene perspective? Fr. Taft suggests at least a couple influences: Arianism and Jerusalem.

The struggle against Arianism ''shifted attention from Christ's second coming at the parousia to His first coming in the incarnation''[25] and emphasized Christ's pre-existent divinity and equality with the Father. If the Son is equal to the Father, then the Son is mediator (read: subordinate) only as human being, not as Son. This is intended to directly contradict the Arian agenda of scripturally proof-texting Christ's heavenly subordination, as Joseph Jungmann explains in his classic study. ''In order to support their heresy, the Arians zealously collected all texts in which a 'humbling' was attributed to Christ, especially a subordination to the Father. They particularly favoured the texts of scripture in which there was a mention of the praying of Jesus. On the tacit assumption that the Logos took the place of the human soul, they concluded triumphantly: therefore the Son himself is subordinate to the Father; consequently, he is only a creature.''[26] Limiting subordinational phrases to the earthly Jesus, and relating them solely to his humanity, was the Church's anti-Arian reaction. Therefore Christ's role as mediator of our prayers and sacrifices was decreasingly described in the present, even as his priestly activity was increasingly described in the past as a historical work of redemption. There was increased stress upon the general anamnetic character of the Eucharistic celebration. ''In Alexandrine theology, this resulted in a weakening of Christ's mediatorship. Among the Antiochenes it provoked greater stress on Christ's high priesthood as pertaining to His humanity. . . . What happened is that the middle fell out . . . and we are left with the two, unbridged poles of the dilemma: God and the historical Jesus.''[27]

The second influence upon the Antiochene tradition came from Palestine. It was there, in Jerusalem, that we first hear of ''the topographical system of church symbolism'' in which various parts of the building are interpreted to symbolically represent places hal-

24. Taft, ''Historicism Revisited,'' 102.
25. Ibid.
26. Joseph Jungmann, *The Place of Christ in Liturgical Prayer* (London: Geoffrey Chapman, 1965) 172.
27. Taft, ''Historicism Revisited,'' 102.

lowed during Holy Week, and also there that the city's liturgy revolved around its sacred topography.[28] In Fr. Taft's opinion, "What was spread across the map of Jerusalem's holy history came to be written small in the humbler churches of eastern Christendom. . . . Thus the sanctuary apse becomes the cave of the sepulcher, and the altar the tomb from which salvation comes forth to the world. . . . Its application to the eucharist was so congruous as to be inevitable. The next step, or perhaps a concomitant one . . . was the burial cortege symbolism at the transfer and deposition of the gifts."[29]

The rise of a sense of historicism in the fourth century is more complicated than the impression given by Gregory Dix when he suggested that Jerusalem's new historical consciousness transformed or even displaced the more primitive, original eschatological outlook. Thomas Talley argues that Jerusalem was in fact conservative in such matters, and it is more likely that it was the expectations of pilgrims coming to Jerusalem which led to the association of liturgical celebrations and historical events, nurturing the rise of historicism. "Jerusalem was much more conservative and resisted such partition of the paschal season into the fifth century. We shall be concerned to argue later that many fourth-century observances that have been considered innovations at Jerusalem are better accounted for as responses to the expectations of pilgrims who had learned in their home churches to associate certain events in the life of Christ with particular days in the liturgical year."[30] According to Talley, the situation seems to be more complicated than smaller churches simply copying Jerusalem; the expectations held by visiting pilgrims was conditioning the Jerusalem liturgy too. However, it is true "that the recovery of the tomb of Christ following the Council of Nicea and the Constantinian

28. Such as described by Egeria's Diary. Cf. *Egeria: Diary of a Pilgrimage,* trans. George Gingras (New York: Newman Press, 1970).

29. Taft, "The Liturgy of the Great Church," 66.

30. Thomas Talley, *The Origins of the Liturgical Year* (New York: Pueblo Publishing Co., 1986) 39–40. Thus his judgment: "If at the end of the fourth century in much of the Church the individual moments of that redemptive *transitus* were celebrated as distinct festivals, it would be wrong to suppose that this was because they were looked upon only as events in a departed past, to be recalled in our now distant present" (70).

building program in Jerusalem and environs did much to the way in which liturgical events were celebrated."[31] The symbol-system which sees tomb and resurrection reenacted in the liturgy was given a substantial boost by Jerusalem's historical concreteness, but it depended also upon Antiochene typological exegesis. And this exegesis, applied by Theodore in the early fourth century, inaugurated a tradition of interpretation that eventually spread throughout the whole of Christendom appearing simultaneously in the west in Venerable Bede and in the east in Germanus, contemporaries at the turn into the eighth century.

All of this—Antiochene exegesis of Scripture, its application by Theodore to liturgy, Arianism and the vividness of Palestine geography—feeds the anamnetic quality found within the New Testament itself. Christ did say, "Do this as my memorial." What was memorialized was simply expanded in two directions. First, the content of the memorial was expanded to include his entire human economy of salvation as well as the Passion[32] and second, the synchrony between the liturgy and the historical Jesus was worked out not only in the anaphora but throughout the entire rite. Therefore it would be misleading to suggest the fourth-century Fathers of the Antiochene school invented salvation-history symbolism; it is more accurate to say they chose to emphasize and synthesize it. It was Theodore's accomplishment to systematize this, but in Fr. Taft's opinion, "he was developing a trend present in eucharistic thought from the start."[33]

GERMANUS

It is in this context, then, that we meet Germanus. Born probably in the early 640's, he was Patriarch of Constantinople from 715 until 730. He thus overlaps by several years the first iconoclastic attack (726–780) begun by Leo III. He was deposed for resisting this threat and died three years later in 733. He was anathema-

---

31. Ibid.

32. Schulz notes that the anaphora of Hippolytus simply says "Mindful of his death and resurrection we offer. . . ." but in the Byzantine anaphora texts the object of remembrance becomes the passion, cross, burial, resurrection, ascent into heaven, session at the right hand of the Father, and second coming in glory (11).

33. Taft, "The Liturgy of the Great Church," 67-8.

tized by the iconoclastic Council of 754, but after the later restoration of icons (what came to be called the triumph of Orthodoxy) he was eventually canonized in 787. Through him, Theodore's Antiochene interpretation from the early fifth century enters the Byzantine tradition in the eighth. The two leitmotifs in Theodore, the historical self-offering of Christ and the heavenly liturgy, become a permanent basis of the later Byzantine synthesis through the popular influence of Germanus' commentary. Fr. Taft acknowledges that Maximus Confessor is a more significant author and that his is the first extant Byzantine commentary, and that Nicholas Cabasilas represents the final synthesis of liturgical symbolism, but Germanus' patriarchate from 715–730 overlooks the beginning of a watershed period in Byzantine tradition. His work is therefore "our earliest witness to the new synthesis in popular liturgical piety;" it is thus not to be judged as fanciful allegory "but a viable, consistent eucharistic theology, suited to the mentality of his times and in continuity with the patristic tradition to which he was heir."[34]

Germanus writes this liturgical commentary at a period when piety was changing profoundly on two fronts: first, there was developing a larger rank of Christians who attended Eucharist but did not commune, and second, a new estimate of the liturgy was required in the face of iconoclasm. Germanus' synthesis of the "new" historical emphasis with the anagogical emphasis which had hitherto marked Byzantine identity and tradition can be considered a new liturgical theology, one which remained faithful to tradition and yet spoke to a new *sitz im leben*. For this reason Fr. Taft defends him as being "what every theologian must be: a man of tradition and a man of his times," and suggests that we ask of Germanus no more than what we would ask of theology today, "that his 'model' of the eucharist present a valid expression of the common tradition so as to make it alive for the genius of his age. For it is at that intersection of tradition and contemporary culture that the theological craft is exercised, and in Byzantine liturgical explanation at the start of the eighth century this crossroad was occupied by Germanus."[35]

34. Ibid., 46.
35. Ibid., 72 and 47.

A new liturgical piety had developed, in the first place, as a result of an increased number of people who attended the Eucharist but did not commune. Due to a number of factors (including the massive influx of new members, returning apostates undergoing an extended period of penitence, and catechumens who postponed their own baptism indefinitely) the community was fractured "into a communicating minority and a majority who were in church only as observers. . . . In the same century came the development of a spirituality of fear and awe with regard to the eucharist, and this only encouraged the flight from the eucharistic banquet."[36]

It was as if the community was rearranging into concentric circles of degrees of participation. In the Hagia Sophia, for example, new and old social divisions in the church (clergy, laity, catechumens, the faithful, men and women, the common folk and the imperial court) were coordinated with symbolic reflection upon the physical divisions in the church building (atrium, narthex, nave, aisles and galleries). One account of the social and physical ranks is found in a letter by Gregory Thaumaturgus who distinguishes five degrees of participation in the liturgy,

"based on the individual's standing in the community: 'weeping,' which was done outside the door where one asked the prayers of the faithful who entered; 'listening,' which was done in the narthex where one heard the scripture and preaching, but left before the prayers and before the catechumens had gone out; 'falling down,' which was done within the doors of the church before one left with the catechumens; 'standing by,' which meant remaining with the faithful throughout the liturgy but abstaining from Communion; and finally 'communicating.' "[37]

A new approach to the liturgy arose which took into account these new divisions. Communion was decreasingly a common sharing of gifts which instantiated koinonia, and increasingly an act of personal devotion. "Under such conditions the eucharist could no longer sustain its former ideology as a rite of koinonia,

36. Meyendorff, 40.
37. Mathews, 126.

and Antiochene liturgical explanation begins to elaborate a symbolism of the presence of the saving work of Christ in the ritual itself, even apart from participation in the communion of the gifts."[38]

In the second place, liturgical piety was rocked by a challenge that had just begun to arise during Germanus' patriarchate, one which would rend the eastern Church for the next century, viz. iconoclasm. This also presented a new circumstance, one for which "the traditional Byzantine approach was no longer fully adequate: more attention had to be paid to the historical man, Jesus. The danger no longer came from the Arians, who had denied Christ's divinity, but from the iconoclasts, who now challenged the dogma of Christ's full humanity, and who in consequence saw the eucharist only as a symbol. . . . This shift is clearly reflected in Germanus' commentary."[39] Patriarch Germanus was deposed because of his public defense of images. In 726 Emperor Leo III openly took a position against the veneration of icons and insisted that the Patriarch of Constantinople sign a decree to this effect.[40] Germanus categorically refused. He was the first to see that this threatened the incarnation, and the first leader of the Orthodox opposition to the iconoclasts. He writes a letter on the matter in which he already states the same argument that John of Damascus or Theodore the Studite will use. "We make no icon or representation of the invisible divinity. . . . But since the only Son himself, Who is in the bosom of the Father, deigned to become man . . . we draw the image of His human aspect according to the flesh. . . ."[41]

38. Taft, "The Liturgy of the Great Church," 69.

39. Meyendorff, 51.

40. For the history of iconoclasm, see Leonid Ouspensky, *Theology of the Icon* (New York: St. Vladimir's Press, 1978); George Ostrogorsky, *History of the Byzantine State* (New Jersey: Rutgers University Press, 1969); John Meyendorff, *Christ in Eastern Christian Thought* (New York: St. Vladimir's Press, 1975); or A. A. Vasiliev, *History of the Byzantine Empire*, vol. 1 (Madison: University of Wisconsin Press, 1952).

41. Germanus' letter to John of Synades, quoted Meyendorff, 49. Compare with Theodore's argument: "In so far as [Christ] proceeded from a Father who could not be represented, Christ, not being representable, cannot have an image made by art. . . . But from the moment Christ was born of a

In consideration of the iconoclast challenge, the emphasis in Dionysius or Maximus had to be recast. By no means is the anagogical emphasis eliminated; in fact, Germanus builds upon the commentary by Maximus, adding representational references to salvation's historical economy. Although the foundation of Byzantine liturgy was laid in the age of Justinian, this representational perspective exercised no less lasting an influence on its development. An adjustment in meaning was made to fit the new circumstances of decreased table participation and iconoclasm. We suggest this was a theological adjustment, one which was not only worked out in dogmatic treatises but also worked out iconographically and liturgically.

## THE CHALLENGE OF ICONOCLASM

It is therefore possible to chart a parallel change in the iconography of this period. It becomes representational too. Both the choice of images and their arrangement within the church space were influenced by this shift. As regards the choice of images, the iconophiles moved to greater realism, invoking the Trullan Synod of 692 where it was argued that although the Church "lovingly accepts the ancient shadows and images that have been handed down to the Church as symbols and hints of the truth," it gives preference to grace and truth themselves. Therefore the Church prescribes "that from now on, in place of the lamb of old, Christ our God, the Lamb who takes away the sins of the world, is to be portrayed in human form in the icons, so that in his state of abasement the majesty of God the Word may be seen and we may be reminded of his life in the body, his suffering, his saving death and the redemption of the world which his death accomplished."[42] The focus in iconography shifts to a more realistic representation of Christ, particularly to the details of his earthly life. Icons depict

representable Mother, he clearly has representation. If he had no image made by art, it would mean that he was not born of a representable mother." Ouspensky & Lossky, *The Meaning of Icons* (New York: St. Vladimir's Press, 1983) 31.

42. Schulz, 57. For a discussion of early iconography in its evocative and not representative stage, see Andre Grabar, *Christian Iconography: A Study of Its Origins* (New Jersey: Princeton University Press, 1968).

Christ, angels, saints, prophets and not scenes, because historical facts have little place in this kind of iconography. The same principle is at work as regards the arrangement of the icons within the Church. "It is no longer the historical course of Christ's life but the salvific importance and continuing efficacy of what is represented that primarily determines the rank of images."[43]

As iconography became more representational in opposition to iconoclasts, so also the liturgy was treated representationally. Liturgical symbols were conceived after the manner of sacred images, and correspondingly, as many new symbolic elements as possible were introduced into the liturgy (although Schulz notes that given the traditional and sacrosanct organization of the liturgy the introduction of new symbols had limited possibility and as a result occurred primarily at the prothesis—the preparation of the elements which occurred at the beginning of the liturgy and was freer for elaboration). Antiochene scriptural exegesis lay at hand as a model of *allegoria facti* by which two historical events of different epochs in salvation history could be related. "The command that the commemoration of redemption be proclaimed in a perspicuously visible way was applied not only in iconography but also and especially in the development of the liturgy."[44]

Germanus knows the eschatological tradition inscribed by Maximus and embodied in the Hagia Sophia, but like a Richter scale his commentary registers a shift in the Byzantine perception of the Eucharist, a shift which took place in order to deal with a swelling number of Christians who attended the Divine Liturgy but for various reasons did not commune, and to refute the growing iconoclastic movement. The shift is indicated in the very title of the work which registers it: *Ecclesiastical History and Mystical Contemplation.* "In Maximus and in Dionysius before him, the focus had been on *theoria*, that is, on the understanding of the realities which lie *behind* or *over* that which is visible. Contemplation thus becomes an ascent from the image to its archetype. . . . In con-

43. Ibid., 55. He goes on to make this intriguing comparison: "The images of this period seem comparable in function, therefore, to the liturgical *proclamation* of the gospels according to the liturgical cycle rather than to the *account* as found continuously in the gospels themselves."
44. Ibid., 64.

trast to *theoria*, but not opposed to it, is *historia*: this too is contemplation, but a contemplation which seeks to clarify the spiritual dimension of an event, of a rite. Here, the outer forms are taken very seriously and are not secondary."[45] *Theoria* leads the spiritual seeker to the reality which is God, while *historia* focuses on God's self-revealing incarnation; the former struggles to ascend from image to archetype while the latter takes the outer form more seriously; in the former, contemplation means to understand realities which are behind the visible, while in the latter it means to discern the spiritual dimension of the visible rite. Still, *historia* is not arbitrary or imposed. Its purpose is to draw the observer into salvation history, to make the observer a participant in it, by anamnetically portraying the unified salvation event.

Schulz concludes, and we agree, that iconoclasm provoked a change in iconography ("Symbolic representation is replaced by portraitlike image in which the higher reality becomes accessible to direct vision") which was paralleled in the liturgy. However, Schulz renders a negative judgment on this process, and this we question. He thinks that liturgical explanations which transform symbols into images (as he thinks Germanus has done) risk losing sight of the real human community doing the activity of praying, offering, sacrificing or thanking. "This community can hardly be given its due place in a liturgy that is interpreted in a purely pictorial way, whereas this is not difficult when the liturgy is understood as symbolic."[46]

Fr. Taft, on the other hand, characterizes the struggle with iconoclasm which Germanus registers as "the victory of a more literalist popular and monastic piety, precisely in favor of a less abstractly symbolic and more representational, figurative religious art."[47] He agrees that symbolism was replaced by representational portrayal—both in art, where Orthodoxy defended the portrayal of

45. Meyendorff, 48.
46. Schulz, 69–70. At the end of his book Schulz therefore gives a brief pitch for a methodology which he finds more palatable, that of Nicholas Cabasilas. He affirms that Cabasilas stands in the Antiochene tradition with Germanus and the Andidans, but thinks the former turns the mind to the event without reducing the rite to a sequence of pictorially represented historical details (190).
47. Taft, "The Liturgy of the Great Church," 72.

a human Christ over a merely symbolical portrayal as a lamb, and in liturgy, where a rite which symbolized the soul's spiritual ascension into heaven was recast to also representatively portray the earthly economy which makes such an ascent possible. The abuses of iconoclasm forced a rethinking of the spiritualized symbolism contained in Maximus and for both icon and liturgy, the line was redrawn between symbol and pictorial image or pictorial rite. As art became less abstractly symbolic and more representational, so liturgy became less abstractly spiritual and more anamnetically connected to historical event. "Now symbolism and portrayal are not at all the same thing either in art or in liturgy, and the effect of this popular mentality on liturgical theology can be observed in the condemnation of the iconoclastic view that the eucharist is the only valid symbol of Christ. Orthodoxy responded that the eucharist is not a symbol of Christ, but indeed Christ Himself."[48] Leonid Ouspensky characterizes the argument as one of classic equivocation: the two parties differed in their definition of icon. Iconoclasts called the Eucharistic bread and wine the only true icons, while the Orthodox responded that only icons are icons, and the Eucharist is Christ himself.

Iconoclasts believed that a true icon must be of the same nature as the person it represents (consubstantial with its model). Therefore they could only accept an image when this image was identical to that which it represented. Under this definition, a painted image simply cannot be an icon of Christ. If the painted image was called an icon, one of two blasphemies would be committed. Either the icon represented both the human and divine nature of Christ, in which case the natures are confused (the Monophysite heresy), or the icon represented only the human nature of Christ, in which case the natures are separated (the Nestorian heresy). The iconoclasts wished to overcome the essential difference between the image and its prototype, because they understood iconic image to be of the same nature as the person it represents. "Basing themselves on this principle, the iconoclasts came to the inevitable conclusion that the only icon of Christ is the Eucharist."[49]

48. Ibid.
49. Ouspensky, *Theology of the Icon* (New York: St. Vladimir's Press, 1978) 149.

Christ chose bread as the image of his incarnation because bread has no human likeness and thus idolatry can be avoided.

This understanding was completely different from the Orthodox understanding. The iconoclasts defined an icon as that which is consubstantial with its model; the Orthodox defined an icon as that which represents not the nature, but the person. For the Orthodox, "the Holy Gifts are *not* an icon precisely because they are identical to their prototype."[50] For the iconoclasts, because the Eucharist is consubstantial with Christ it is the only icon; for the Orthodox, because the Eucharist is consubstantial with Christ it cannot be an icon. There must be an essential difference between the image and its prototype, argued John of Damascus. The iconoclasts felt something could not be icon if the portrayal does not share the nature of the prototype; the Orthodox, fully aware of the distinction between nature and person, maintained that the icon does not represent the nature, but the person. "When we represent our Lord, we do not represent His divinity or His humanity, but His Person which inconceivably unites in itself these two natures without confusion and without division, as the Chalcedonian dogma defines it."[51] The icon is an image not of Christ's divine nature or human nature but of the divine person (incarnate).

If there is no difference between the image and its prototype, as

50. G. Ostogorsky, cited in Ouspensky, 149. Underscoring mine. This might prompt a question from the closing chapter of Nathan Mitchell's *Cult and Controversy* (New York: Pueblo Publishing Co., 1982). He argues that the relation between action and object in the Eucharist should come full circle. The action of Eucharistic liturgy produces an object (Eucharistic bread and wine) which should return to an action, viz. eating and drinking. He finds Eucharistic devotion permissible so long as it is only a delay in the circle, not a disruption of the circle which comes to revere the elements in themselves. Next, in an apologetic for popular piety's sense of Christ's presence even in the reserved host, he considers the relation between visual perception and ritual symbols, and he invokes icons as an example of "visual symbolism." (376 ff.) Question: can one use the category of "icon" to describe the bread? If the reserved host is in some sense iconic because even as object people see Christ's presence and hence adore it, would it be as defined by the iconoclasts (the reserved host is consubstantial with its symbol) or as defined by the Orthodox (there is an essential difference between the image and its prototype, as John of Damascus insisted)?

51. Ouspensky, 152.

the iconoclasts said, then the only way something earthly can symbolize the divine is if the earthly thing is transformed. But such an idea exactly contradicts the incarnation, and here is what was at stake in the controversy. Icons are not only permissible, they are necessary because icons safeguard a full and proper doctrine of the incarnation. The fault of iconoclasm, says Timothy Ware, is a kind of dualism. Regarding matter as a defilement, they want a religion freed from contact with what is material. To be spiritual is to be non-material. But the doctrine of incarnation is precisely the affirmation that matter can and has also been redeemed. The body as well as the soul is to be transfigured. "The Incarnation has made a representational religious art possible: God can be depicted because He became man and took flesh."[52]

REPRESENTATIONAL LITURGY

The incarnation has also made possible representational liturgy.

"In its perception of the liturgy, the Antiochene approach of Theodore of Mopsuestia, with its greater attention to the historical Jesus and to his humanity, was clearly more suited to this new, more realistic approach of the Orthodox. It supported the Orthodox polemic against the iconoclasts far better than the older, more spiritualizing approach of the Alexandrians. . . . In fact, the iconoclastic position was heavily dependent precisely upon [this] Origenistic approach. . . . It was probably from Dionysius that the iconoclasts derived their notion of the eucharist as the only valid 'image' and 'symbol' of Christ, because only here is the image consubstantial with its prototype. . . ."[53]

Liturgical outer forms are not secondary, existing only to be transcended as the soul makes its ascent; they are taken seriously. This is *historia*. God enfleshed is dramatically represented in the liturgical rite. This is a new liturgical theology at work.

Though dealing with a liturgy which was essentially unchanged, each author of liturgical commentary reflects a different element

52. Timothy Ware, *The Orthodox Church*, 41.
53. Meyendorff, 50–51.

which is being worked out by the community's differing social conditions and theological reactions. Dionysius allegorized the liturgy anagogically, highlighting deification through ethical imitation of the incarnate Logos; Theodore reflected a reenactment typology, influenced by anti-Arian themes and Palestinian topographical symbolism; St. Maximus the Confessor wished to show the importance of the liturgy for monastic life, thereby correcting a trend which had little use for Eucharistic piety; in Nicholas and Theodore of Andida, says Schulz, the comparison between present liturgy and the historical Jesus was worked out superlatively while in Nicholas Cabasilas the same sacramental actualization was reflected without requiring an unbroken sequence of rites representing historical details. Each commentator provides a different emphasis, but a theological emphasis made by the assembly in leitourgia—a liturgical theology. "Underlying all these commentaries, therefore, is a sense that the liturgy is itself a source of theology. Just like Scripture, the liturgy is a revelation, which implies a multiplicity of meanings, and indeed offers the possibility for participation in divine life."[54] For his part, Germanus writes for a day in which the situation involved a decline of koinonia participation at the Communion table and a changed sense of symbolism which threatened iconography's affirmation of incarnation. Germanus is not only doing theology upon the liturgy, he is giving voice to a fundamental liturgical theology worked out by a community in a new setting. His commentary develops by pastoral necessity. This theology was worked out liturgically. By applying the representational symbolism of Antioch, Germanus' commentary presents a liturgy absorbed into "mystical contemporaneity" with events in the life of Jesus, yet without dissecting the mystery. In addition to the liturgy's anagogical character, a typological character of the rite is emphasized without splintering the unified mystery. It is a single mystery which is celebrated, even if this is worked out through distinguishable historical events represented in discrete liturgical acts.

54. Ibid., 41. So Taft writes about Germanus: "A theology is not *the* theology; *his* times are not *all* times. But studies in the history of theology always show the fatuousness of seeking anything more." "The Liturgy of the Great Church," 46.

Germanus' synthetic flexibility is promptly demonstrated in the first ten chapters of his work. In chapter one he describes the church as "the temple of God, a holy place, . . . an earthly heaven in which the supercelestial God dwells and walks about," and immediately, in the next sentence, adds "It represents the crucifixion, burial, and resurrection of Christ. . . ." In the next nine chapters he gives allegorical interpretation of the physical details of the church. The simandron represents the trumpets of the angels (ch. 2); the apse corresponds to the cave in Bethlehem and the tomb (ch. 3); the holy table corresponds to the spot in the tomb where Christ was placed (ch. 4); the ciborium represents here the place where Christ was crucified (ch. 5); the altar corresponds to the holy tomb of Christ (ch. 6); the ambo manifests the shape of the stone at the Holy Sepulchre (ch. 10).

Germanus continues in this way throughout 43 chapters of the commentary, ending with an interpretation of the anaphora (Eucharistic prayer) which in length is approximately one quarter of the commentary. Chapters 1–10 allegorize the structure and furnishings of the church; chapters 11–13 explain prayer action (facing east and why one doesn't kneel); chapters 14–19 allegorize vestments worn by the priest (stole, embroidery on the sleeves, why the phelonia is unbelted, the representation of presbyters and deacons); chapters 20–22 deal with the sacramental elements (the bread's symbolism, the lancing of the bread, and wine mixed with water); chapters 23–33 allegorize mainly the Liturgy of the Word (antiphons, Little Entrance, Trisagion, ascent of bishop to throne, prokeimenon, alleluia, censor, gospel and people's blessing) and chapters 34–41 allegorize the Liturgy of the Eucharist (eiliton cloth on altar, catechumens' departure, proskomede, Great Entrance, the discos and chalice and veil).

What is to be observed, however, and what is badly represented by a list such as in the paragraph above, is that the same object or action can receive layered, i.e. multiple, interpretation. This is especially striking as Germanus, within the same chapter, allegorically refers an act or object to both Jerusalem and Heaven. Allow four examples. In chapter four the holy table "corresponds to the spot in the tomb where Christ was placed," and it "is also the throne of God, on which, borne by the Cherubim, He rested in the body;" furthermore, it is the table at which Christ sat among his disciples, and that prefigured by the table of the Old Law upon which the manna was placed in the tabernacle (the bread descended from heaven is obviously Christ). In chapter six "the altar corresponds to the holy tomb of Christ," and "the altar is and is called the heavenly and spiritual altar." In chapter thirty "the censer demonstrates the humanity of Christ, and the fire, His divinity" (even more graphically, the interior of the censer is the womb of the Theotokos who bore the divine coal, Christ) and also the sweet-smelling smoke reveals the fragrance of the Holy Spirit. Immediately following this the censor is compared to the font of holy baptism which issues forth sweetness through the operation of the Holy Spirit. And chapter thirty-eight we quote in full: "The discos represents the hands of Joseph and Nicodemus, who buried Christ. The discos on which Christ is carried is also interpreted as the sphere of heaven, manifesting to us in miniature the spiritual sun, Christ, and containing Him visibly in the bread."

In most cases Germanus makes connection with the historical Jesus; sometimes he only makes connection with Christ Pantocrator (the presbyters are compared in chapter sixteen to seraphic powers "covered, as if by wings, with stoles," and the deacons as images of the angelic powers, "go around the thin wings of linen oraria as ministering spirits sent out for service"); and sometimes the allegory includes not only Jerusalem and Heaven, but the Temple of Israel too.

Such an allowance of multiple meanings is frequently looked upon as a sign of ancient carelessness. It is taken to be a sign of imprecision or thoughtlessness to ascribe multiple allegorical meanings to the same object, or at least it confirms the suspicion that one can impose any interpretation one likes, and as many. Fr. Taft responds:

"This misses the point, I think, because it fails to grasp Germanus' methodology, the whole basis of his symbol-system. For the problem of later medieval liturgical allegory consists not in the multiplicity of systematically layered symbols, such as we find here and in patristic exegesis. The later one-symbol-per-object correspondence results not from the tidying up of an earlier incoher-

251

ent primitiveness, but from the decomposition of the earlier patristic mystery-theology into a historicizing system of dramatic narrative allegory."[55]

As just witnessed, Germanus allows the multiple meanings of a symbol to stand, issuing in multiple allegorizations. He seemed not to feel the same urge toward unequivocal coherency as did those who assign singular allegorizations. Because symbol can in fact entertain several layers of meaning simultaneously, allegory theologizes several layers of the liturgy simultaneously.

In Waismann's terms, the allegory invoked by Germanus is natural and not formalized. A formalized system of allegory would be one in which the use of each symbol is governed by a definite set of rules, and further, all the rules of inference and procedure could be stated completely. Mathematics, logic, or second-order theology are formalized systems in this respect. Equivocation should be suppressed as far as necessary to communicate without misunderstanding. "It means this, not that." But only specialists speak formalized language, and they do so only for certain tasks, not all the time. Germanus' allegorization is not an attempt at formalization, as though the table symbolizes where Jesus was laid and not the throne of God, or the discos means the hands of Joseph and not the sphere of heaven. The natural grammar at work in liturgical theology can issue in multiple allegories because the liturgy, like Scripture, is a revelation, which implies a multiplicity of meanings. "It is not the multiplicity of meanings but the attempt to parcel them out that can lead to an artificial literalism destructive of symbol and metaphor, and this is precisely what Germanus refuses to do. . . . He rejects the later temptation of the historicizing decomposition of the unitary mystery into the component parts of its actual historical enactment."[56]

The Antiochene tradition gave pictorial representation to a particular facet of the mystery, or to a particular phase in Jesus' life. Once this happened, could it again become integral to the mystery? If a facet has been lifted out, allegorically, by a liturgical commentary for theological appreciation, must that ritual action be

55. Taft, "The Liturgy of the Great Church," 73.
56. Ibid., 74.

forever delimited by that allegorical meaning? "Even though many interpreters of the liturgy in fact succumbed to this danger, the developing liturgy itself did not yield to it in an excessive degree. Theodore of Mopsuestia did not pave the way for this kind of deterioration. . . . [And Orthodox] life and piety is accustomed even today to looking upon its faith as articulated less in doctrinal definitions than in its liturgical tradition, which is indeed respectful of the old and yet possessed of ever new vitality."[57] Germanus did not succumb to this danger, either. The liturgy is the source for his theology (a *locus theologicus*) because his commentary exegetes the natural language of liturgical theology; it does not seek actions upon which to fix *a priori* principles and ideas by means of allegory (cramming a square allegory in a round liturgical hole). The reader—better, the worshipper—is simultaneously directed to Sinai, Bethlehem, Jerusalem and heaven. "All levels—Old Testament preparation, Last Supper, accomplishment on Calvary, eternal heavenly offering, present liturgical event—must be held in dynamic unity by any interpretation of the eucharist. To separate these levels, then parcel out the elements bit by bit according to some chronologically consecutive narrative sequence, is to turn ritual into drama, symbol into allegory, mystery into history."[58]

After chapter forty-one, when Germanus treats the anaphora, it is Schulz's opinion[59] that the synthesis of the new Antiochene tradition with the established Alexandrine tradition diminishes, but at least in the opening lines their interweaving still seems evident.

"Thus Christ is crucified, life is buried, the tomb is secured, the stone is sealed. In the company of the angelic powers, the priest approaches, standing no longer as on earth, but attending at the heavenly altar, before the altar of the throne of God, and he contemplates the great, ineffable, and unsearchable mystery of God. He gives thanks, proclaims the resurrection, and confirms the faith

---

57. Schulz, 157-8.
58. Taft, "The Liturgy of the Great Church," 73.
59. He remarks that in the earlier part of the commentary "the symbolism based on the life of Christ was to some extent combined harmoniously with a symbolism based on the heavenly liturgy. . . . From this point on, however, the symbolism of the heavenly liturgy takes over completely" (74).

in the Holy Trinity. The angel wearing white approaches the stone of the tomb and rolls it away with his hand, pointing with his garment and exclaiming with an awed voice through the deacon, who proclaims the resurrection on the third day, raising the veil and saying: 'Let us stand aright'—behold, the first day!—'Let us stand in fear'—behold, the second day!—'Let us offer in peace'— behold, the third day! The people proclaim thanks for the resurrection of Christ. . . .''[60]

The earthly economy of salvation has been completed, the stone is sealed, and we await the resurrection. The angel exclaims it, with awed voice, through the deacon. Where is this resurrected Christ? At Jerusalem? at table with the disciples behind locked doors? at table with the faithful behind the open-doored iconostasis? at the right hand of the Father? Yes. He was, and is, and shall be.

Germanus lets the symbol play according to multiple grammars, in multiple language games. In doing this, he is faithful to the type of Christian liturgical signification which is rooted in biblical typology, not in medieval allegorization. The allegorization which the patristic period applied to the Old Testament was based upon a typology which, by pneumatic revelation, discerned in Jesus of Nazareth the inauguration of a new phase of salvation history yet connected with God's first covenant: Old Testament prototype, historical Jesus, and coming parousia. The liturgical theology of Germanus understands the present sacramental, ecclesial reality as also a temporal phase by which God's eternal salvific mystery is manifested. Liturgy epiphanizes in sacramental form the same mystery which was prefigured in the Old Testament, accomplished historically in the earthly life of Christ, lived mystically in souls, accomplished socially in the Church and will be consummated eschatologically in the heavenly kingdom.[61] We argued that insofar as liturgy epiphanizes this, and insofar as theology is reflection in either primary or secondary form upon the mystery revealed, liturgy is the ontological condition for theology.

---

60. Germanus ch. 41, page 89 in Meyendorff.
61. The list is Jean Daniélou's, "Le symbolisme des rites baptismaux," *Dieu Vivant*, found in Robert Taft, "The Liturgical Year: Studies, Prospects, Reflections," *Worship* 55 (1981) 23.

The liturgical theology which Germanus offers is not a formalized language seeking to impose an allegorical system, but a natural language seeking to express the tradition in a new way needed by his day. It thus avoids two misunderstandings of contemporary allegory.

"Christian liturgical signification is rooted in biblical typology . . . but it is the whole sacramental rite, not its individual details, that bears this signification. 'Allegory' violates these presuppositions either by overstepping the bounds of objective biblical typology, seeing in the rites meanings that are personal to the allegorist and have no warrant in the biblical interpretation of salvation history; or by fragmenting the integrity of symbol and signified, assigning to individual details of a sacramental action separate aspects of the signified reality. In both cases, symbol is stretched to the breaking point. . . . This is not, however, the traditional sense of 'allegory' in Christian tradition."[62]

Germanus thus manifests the first mark by which we identified liturgical theology. In his commentary he gives voice to a meaning of the liturgy which his community was forging and to which they apparently resonated. "The proof of the success of Germanus' synthesis is its viability: for over six hundred years it reigned with undisputed primacy over the field of Byzantine liturgical explanation."[63] In the face of new social circumstances and a challenge to the incarnation theology of icons, the divine word worked synergistically in the Byzantine Church a novel adjustment, a liturgical theology which grasped the Tradition in new ways. Germanus manifests our second mark as well, viz., liturgical theology is displayed by the rite, not imposed from without. This means first that liturgical theology is communal and not personal to the commentator (or theologian); second that the meaning must be read off the rite in its entirety, and not off pieces which in their splintered isolation do not reveal the liturgical theological grammar (*lex orandi*).

62. Taft, "The Liturgy of the Great Church," 55, footnote 62. Regarding the influence this typological method had upon western sacramentology, see Enrico Mazza, *Mystagogy* (New York: Pueblo, 1989).
63. Ibid., 74.

*b.* The Eucharist, *by Fr. Schmemann*[64]

In the introduction and in a few places within this work we have tried to disentangle a third approach which properly bears the name liturgical theology from a fourth approach which is simply the effort to point this out. This fourth approach might be called a study of liturgical theology, for the target upon which attention is trained is not liturgy but liturgical theology. It is one step removed. It makes methodological observations about liturgical theology, not theological observations about liturgy. For instance, we suggested Fr. Schmemann's work *Introduction to Liturgical Theology* is an example of the fourth approach, and *The Eucharist* an example of the third. It should be noted that this is our distinction, not Fr. Schmemann's, and so he is not bound by it. The latter work, which we are looking at, is predominately what we mean by the third approach (derivative) but there are numerous pockets within it where Fr. Schmemann turns his attention from the liturgy to the methods of liturgical theology. We hope to stay clear about this as we unfold this second example of liturgical theology by observing Fr. Schmemann's approach.

WHERE TO BEGIN?

The work consists of twelve chapters, already striking the academic eye as more familiar than was Germanus. Still, there is an oddity to the chapter titles. They all begin "The Sacrament of. . . ." The Sacrament of the Assembly, the Kingdom, Entrance, the Word, the Faithful, Offering, Unity, Anaphora, Thanksgiving, Remembrance, the Holy Spirit, and Communion. His reason for doing this is not explained until much later (160 pages later) in the chapter on the anaphora where, Fr. Schmemann says, the chief part of the liturgy is begun. However, he quickly stresses that the correlate to "chief" is "nonchief;" he believes Scholasticism to err when it supposes the correlate to "chief" is "unessential."

"I categorically reject this meaning. . . . Therefore it was not to sound more solemn but perfectly consciously and responsibly that

64. Fr. Alexander Schmemann, *The Eucharist* (New York: St. Vladimir's Seminary Press, 1987).

256

I have entitled each of the chapters . . . with the word *sacrament*. For I see the entire task at hand in demonstrating as fully as possible that the divine liturgy is a single, though also 'multifaceted,' sacred rite, a single sacrament, in which all its 'parts,' their entire sequence and structure, their coordination with each other, the necessity of each for all and all for each, manifests to us the inexhaustible, eternal, universal and truly divine meaning of what has been and what is being accomplished." (161)

One must not isolate an understanding of Eucharist from the entire liturgical act; liturgical theology must not become sacramentology. This is crucial in Fr. Schmemann's personal understanding of the Eucharist, and it will be crucial to our understanding of him.

Therefore this theology of the Eucharist does not begin with historical overviews, theories of real presence, comparative religion studies, or philosophical symbol theory; it begins by discussing the sacrament of the assembly. A liturgical theology of the Eucharist must begin with the first liturgical act, assembling. The fundamental task of liturgical theology, Fr. Schmemann writes, is to uncover the meaning and essence of the triunity of assembly, Eucharist and the Church. Scholastic dogmatics, that method which isolates sacrament from the Divine Liturgy to be a separate topic of investigation, "is simply unaware of the ecclesiological meaning of the Eucharist, and at the same time it has forgotten the eucharistic dimension of ecclesiology, i.e., the doctrine of the Church." (12) The gathering is Eucharistic and the Eucharist is constitutive of the assembly as Church. The Eucharist is not one of seven sacraments, one means of grace among others. It is the premiere sacrament because it is where and how the Church exists. Therefore, the liturgical theology contained in Fr. Schmemann's book will not be the dissection of a static rite, for the Eucharist is not static and the mystery is indivisible. One will not rummage through a list of meanings or pick from a pile of interpretations to accomplish theological explanation. "The first principle of liturgical theology is that, in explaining the liturgical tradition of the Church, one must proceed not from abstract, purely intellectual schemata cast randomly over the services, but from the services themselves—and this means, first of all, from their ordo." (14)

Who gathers at this assembly? The Church, which consists of

clergy and laity. The clergy alone is not Church, with lay spectators, and the laity alone is not Church which hires ordained leaders. The apostolic priesthood and the universal priesthood together make up Church in mutual dependence. This principle of correlation is expressed in various ways in the Ordo[65] and to greater or lesser degrees in each individual rite (antiphons, preaching, gift offering, the kiss of peace, etc). The celebrant and the people work in true synergy. They act in concert, collaboratively. The word "concelebration" does not apply to clergy alone, as if they together do something the laity do not; the word equally describes the relationship between laity and priest in the Divine Liturgy.

For what reason does the Church assemble? To experience and perceive the Temple as sobor, which is "the gathering together of heaven and earth and all creation in Christ—which constitutes the essence and purpose of the Church." (19) Sobornicity is epiphanized liturgically and iconographically, in the ritual and in the visible quality of the Temple. The dialogic structure of the liturgy (priest—people) is reflected in physical structure of the Temple. "The nave is directed toward the altar, in which we find its end and purpose; but the 'altar' necessarily entails the nave and exists only in relation to it." (20) Such dialogic unity was also the original purpose of the iconostasis. The icon is a witness to, or better still, a consequence of the unification of the divine and the human, of heaven and earth, standing as interface between sanctuary and nave.

The Eucharist is a Sacrament of the Kingdom, Fr. Schmemann next says. The purpose of the liturgy is to symbolize the divine kingdom, only how shall we understand this word "symbolize"? In the ancient understanding, a symbol meant the epiphany of reality, like a rose manifests love. The symbol communicated the reality it symbolized because it participated in it. In the modern understanding, however, a symbol seems to mean the absence of reality, like there is not real water in the chemical symbol for water. Symbols are taken to illustrate an absent reality by some-

65. "Every prayer is 'sealed' by the gathering with one of the key words of Christian worship, 'amen,' thus binding the celebrant and the people of God at whose head he stands into one organic whole" (Ibid., 17).

258

how resembling it slightly. That is why symbol has been identified with representation or illustration. When one now speaks of the Little Entrance "symbolizing" the Savior's coming to preach the gospel, it often seems to mean the Entrance represents or illustrates a past event. Symbol is treated not only as distinct from reality but even contrary to it.[66]

When one says that the Eucharist symbolizes the kingdom, it is crucial to remember Fr. Schmemann's use of the word. The kingdom is symbolized in the ancient sense of being manifested or made present and given to us in this sacrament. At the Eucharistic table, the Church symbolizes the kingdom—'symbol' is here used as a verb! The Church does not represent or illustrate the kingdom, as in the sense of calling it to mind for edification; rather the Church epiphanizes the kingdom, as a handshake epiphanizes friendship or a kiss manifests love. The kingdom is symbolized by the Church at Eucharist, because the kingdom is where the Father's reign is mediated through the Son in the Spirit. That this reign of God has already come was the central message of Jesus. The kingdom is unity with God, reconciliation between a world in rebellion and its loving creator. Christ's atonement reestablished fellowship with the Father, and for those who have believed in it and accepted it, the kingdom is already here and now.

"Returning now to what we said above about the symbolism of Christian worship, we can now affirm that the Church's worship was born and, in its external structure, 'took shape' primarily as a *symbol of the kingdom*, of the Church's ascent to it and, in this ascent, of her fulfilment as the body of Christ and the temple of the Holy Spirit. The whole newness, the uniqueness of the Christian *leitourgia* was in its eschatological nature as the presence here and now of the future *parousia*, as the epiphany of that which is to come. . . ." (43)

To forget this and change eschatology into a "then" would pro-

---

66. When symbol is thus estranged from reality, the sacrament is taken to be a special, supernatural symbol! That is, the sacrament is treated as *sui generis* reality, having its own form of existence, its own psychology, its own grace. These latter are the very words of Anscar Vonier, whom Fr. Schmemann here takes to task.

foundly change liturgy. From this fully realized symbol, the whole of the Christian *lex orandi* was born and developed.[67]

The third chapter commences the discussion of parts of the liturgical rite *per se*, beginning with the Sacrament of Entrance. Originally, the first act of the liturgy after the assembly of the faithful was the entrance of the celebrant. A pre-entry rite has since grown up consisting of the Great Litany, three antiphons and three prayers. Fr. Schmemann provides a brief liturgiological background to the growth of these pre-entry rites[68] but admits this would be of mere historical and archeological interest if it did not emphasize that the beginning of Eucharist is the dynamic ceremony of entering. The Eucharist is movement. In the Eucharist, the Church moves from fallen world toward the kingdom of God. This is the evangelical service of the body of Christ.

"If 'assembling as the Church' presupposes separation from the world . . . this exodus from the world is accomplished *in the name of the world,* for the sake of its salvation. For we are flesh of the flesh and blood of the blood of this world. We are a part of it, and only by us and through us does it ascend to its Creator, Savior and Lord, to its goal and fulfilment. We separate ourselves from the world in order to bring it, in order to lift it up to the kingdom, to make it once again the way to God and participation in his eternal kingdom. . . . For this [the Church] was left in the world, as part of it, as a symbol of its salvation. And this symbol we fulfil, we 'make real' in the eucharist." (53)

67. If liturgical symbolism is illustrative and representative, then liturgy can be no more than comic-book theology: illustrative catechism. There is nothing special enough about "worship in liturgical format" to deserve the *statuat* claim. Only if liturgical symbol is epiphany can liturgical Ordo be *lex orandi*. Revelatory symbol is not the same as illustrative symbol.

68. The antiphons originally constituted a separate service, which took place before the Eucharist and outside the church building, but "following that logic of liturgical development in which a kind of law functions according to which the 'peculiarities' become the 'general rule' this antiphon became part of the liturgy—an entrance before the Little Entrance." Schmemann, 52.

This is clear in the Great Litany which comprises the first act of these pre-entry rites. The Church detaches itself from the world in order to know what to pray for on the world's behalf; it ascends from the dusty whirlwind in order to see more clearly. The prayers of the Church are not simply those of an individual or a group of people, the Church prays the prayer of Christ himself. Christ's prayer for the world is entrusted to the liturgical assembly. So in the Great Litany the Church makes intercession and mediation for peace and the salvation of souls, for the peace of the whole world, for the holy churches of God, for the union of all, for a particular holy house and those there entered, for the hierarchy, for world and nature and humankind, and finally the Church commends itself with the saints and the Theotokos to Christ. We return our life to God.

The expression "Little Entrance" originally meant the entrance of clergy and people into the church nave. By and by, the entrance came to be understood as the priest's entrance through the inconostasis into the holy place, the altar. Fr. Schmemann calls this an application of "illustrative symbolism." The pseudo-entrances were performed at the altar and could then be rigged with historicized or allegorized interpretation (e.g., the entrance with the gospel book was a sacred dramatization of Christ's going out to preach). This development "certainly weakened the perception and experience of the 'assembly as the Church' itself as the entrance and ascent of the Church, the people of God, to the heavenly sanctuary." (59)

When the Church has assembled and stands before the Holy One the Sacrament of the Word is celebrated. As we have already noted, Fr. Schmemann insists that just because some part of the rite is not the chief part does not mean that it is unessential. He pauses a moment to register the consequences that have accrued from ignoring the Sacrament of the Word. In the first place, Scripture and Church have become two competing authorities, two sources of the faith, creating the bogus question of which interprets which. In the second place, Scripture and sacrament have been ruptured. The sacrament ceases to be biblical and so evangelical, and Scripture remains locked in history and functions as resource for theology. "In separation from the word the sacrament is in danger of being perceived as magic, and without the sacrament the word is in danger of being 'reduced' to 'doctrine.' " (68)

Scripture and homily were originally read and preached from a raised platform called a bema in the midst of the nave. Approach to the altar was restricted exclusively to the liturgy of the faithful, i.e., the offering and consecration of the holy gifts. The entire liturgy thus originally consisted of three entrances or processions: the entire Church into the Temple, the ascent of the celebrant to the bema for the Liturgy of the Word, and ascent into the sanctuary for the offering and consecration. This trifold pattern was disrupted by the disappearance of the first entrance and correlative development of pre-entry rites, by the gradual disappearance of the bema, and by keeping the gospel book on the altar. The Little Entrance should be the transport of the gospel book through the iconostasis, culminating in the proclamation of Scripture. "[T]he gospel book is a verbal icon of Christ's manifestation to and presence among us. Above all, it is an icon of his resurrection."[69] As such it is accompanied by alleluia verses, censing, and an epicletic prayer.

Organically connected to the reading of Scripture, not extraneous to it, is the homily which should not be a sermon about the gospel, but a preaching of the gospel itself. In other words, it should not be an explanation of what was read, nor the preacher transmitting theological knowledge, nor a meditation on the gospel theme, because all this depends on the preacher's own gifts and talents. What feeds the congregation is not the preacher's rhetorical or theological or devotional skills, but the gospel itself. "Here we see why all church theology, all *tradition*, grows precisely out of the 'assembly as the Church,' out of this sacrament of proclamation of the good news. . . . Tradition is the interpretation of the word of God as the source of life itself, and not of any 'constructions' or 'deductions.' " (78) This makes incumbent upon the laity a sort of participatory activity during the homily. If preaching were theological elaboration on a text, then only the elaborator would be active during the homily. But the gospel has been entrusted to the whole people of the Church, so

69. Ibid., 71. If the gospel book is a verbal icon of Christ's presence, then the Little Entrance cannot be a sacred dramatization of Christ going out to preach; it must be a real liturgical act.

they are active too. The ministry of the celebrant is preaching and teaching, and the ministry of the people is in accepting this teaching. One can neither proclaim nor accept the truth without the gift of the Holy Spirit, and this gift is given to the entire assembly, not just the preacher. Only the entire Church, lay and clergy, manifested and actualized in assembly, has the mind of Christ.

## LITURGY OF THE EUCHARIST

At this juncture the liturgy begins to change from its outward, kerygmatic, intercessory mode to its inner, Eucharistic, personal mode. The first half of the Divine Liturgy consisted of assembly as Church, the entrance and the sacrament of the Word; it is now completed in the Sacrament of the Faithful, considered in chapter five. The identity of the Church has two poles: on the one hand, the Church is directed to the whole world, to the cosmos, to all humanity; on the other hand, Christ's love is directed to each unique and unrepeatable individual. Religious thought must not polarize these truths in liturgy, piety or theology. Do not construe Christianity as only a cosmic and universal calling on the one hand, or, on the other, as a religion of personal salvation above all. The two poles must be held in tension. Christ sacrificed himself for all, and because the Church is his body, it too is directed to the world and will lay down its life for it. But Christ also turned to each human being uniquely and distinctly. "From here stems the antinomy that lies at the foundation of Christian life. The Christian is called to deny himself, to 'lay down his life for his friends'; and the same Christian is summoned to 'despise the flesh, for it passes away, but to care instead for the soul, for it is immortal.' In order to save 'one of the least of these' the shepherd left the ninety-nine, but the same Church—for the sake of her purity and fulness—cuts off sinners from herself." (82)

The Eucharist is a closed assembly of the Church. After this point only the faithful may remain. In this assembly all are ordained and all serve in the one liturgical action of the Church. The Church which does this liturgical action is constituted and made manifest in all fulness by everyone together.

Fr. Schmemann believes that one can understand what it means to be a royal priesthood only when one contrasts Church and world (the whole Church, laity too, are to serve a priestly vocation in the world); a false dilemma between clericalism and pseudo-democracy results if one contrasts clergy and laity. "A false dilemma arises: either the laity are a 'passive' element and all activity in the Church belongs to the clergy, or else some share of the clergy's functions can, and therefore must, be transferred to the laity."[70] All the faithful at the Eucharistic liturgy—whether priest by ordination or laos by baptism—are Church. Because everything was done by Christ and no one needs to add anything to his work, the Church is not a religious society in which God rules through priests. The Church is the body of Christ, which means "no one submits to another, but all together submit to each other in the unity of the divine-human life. In the Church the authority of the hierarchy is indeed 'absolute'—but not because this authority is granted to them by Christ. Rather, it is because it is the authority of Christ himself, just as the obedience of the laity is itself the obedience of Christ. For Christ is not *outside* the Church, he is not *above* the Church, but he is in her and she is in him, as his body." (91) The entire assembly constitutes a single body, realizing the priesthood of Christ. The Church's first service to the world is to proclaim the death of Christ, to confess his resurrection, and to await his coming. Everyone who was joined with Christ in baptism is ordained to this ministry. "We are ordained so that, together constituting the Church, we may offer his sacrifice for the sins of the world, and in offering it, witness to salvation."[71]

70. Ibid., 89. One sees the misplaced goal of the democratic agenda in this light. If one objects to excessive hierarchy, then of what advance is it to give a few hieratic duties to the laity? The discriminating structure remains. But Fr. Schmemann does not think that the clergy and lay distinction is discriminatory.

71. Ibid., 92. Besides intracongregational unity, Fr. Schmemann goes on to discuss intercongregational unity. "Both Protestant congregationalism, which simply identifies any parish with the Church, and Roman centralism, which identifies the Church only with the 'whole,' with the sum of all 'parishes,' are equally foreign to Orthodoxy. In the Orthodox understanding, the Church exists so that each of her parts can live in fulness and be an incarnation of the fulness of the Church—so that, in other words, each part can live *by the whole* and *wholly*. The parish is, on the one hand, only a *part* of the Church, and only in the bishop and through the bishop is it linked with the fulness of the Church. . . ." (98).

The catechumens have been dismissed, the doors have been closed, and the first act which it does is the Sacrament of Offering. Fr. Schmemann devotes some time to this subject in chapter six (the lengthiest in the book) because the issue of sacrifice has been so confused and confusing. It has become so because theologians normally treat the issue exclusive of liturgical action and liturgists usually make rubrical, not theological, explanation of the proskomide (the preparation of the bread and wine which will be taken to the holy table).[72] The inadequacy of either approach is evidenced by the lack of understanding about the sacrament of offering. Is it a preliminary sacrifice, or does it already constitute the essence of the Eucharist? "These questions are of tremendous importance for an understanding of the liturgy, and yet they are simply ignored by our school theology. And as far as liturgists are concerned, their answers consist entirely of references to that 'symbolism,' as though it were inherent to our worship, that explains precisely nothing." (106) Each approach propagates the fallacy that symbol and reality are contraposed.

Before one can understand the symbolism of the proskomide *per se*, a theological context of sacrifice is necessary. In bringing bread and wine the Church performs "that most ancient, primordial rite that from the first day of human history constituted the core of every religion: we offer a sacrifice to God." (101) From whatever angle this is explained—theological, historical, sociological, psychological—it remains indubitable that whenever human beings turn to God they sense the need to offer God the most precious thing they have as gift and sacrifice.

"From the time of Cain and Abel, the blood of sacrifices has daily covered the earth and the smoke of burnt offerings has unceasingly risen to heaven.

---

72. The term means the carrying or conveying of something to a certain place. Originally the deacons did this just before the anaphora, but the rite has long since been performed in much more elaborate detail by the ministers alone, before the people assemble and the Liturgy of the Word begins. A portion of bread is lanced out from the loaf and placed in symbolic order upon the plate.

265

"Our 'refined' sensibilities are horrified by these blood sacrifices. . . . In our horror, however, do we not forget and lose something very basic, very primary, without which in essence there is no religion? For in its ultimate depths religion is nothing other than *thirst for God* . . . and often 'primitive' people know this thirst better, they sense it more deeply . . . than contemporary man does, with all his 'spiritualized' religion, abstract 'moralism' and dried-up intellectualism."[73]

To thirst for God is to want and love God with one's whole heart and being. Ultimately, says Fr. Schmemann, there is only one sin, and that is to not want God and to be separated from God. Where one yearns for God, one makes sacrifice because therein one gives oneself over to God.

Sacrifices, however, were impotent to effect their purpose. They could not accomplish unity with God because they were powerless to destroy sin and restore that fellowship with the deity which humanity forfeited. All human sacrifice remains under the law of sin, and sin is "above all the rupture from God of life itself. That is why this fallen life . . . does not, and cannot, have the power to heal and revive itself, to fill itself with life again, to make itself sanctified once more . . . just as one who is falling into an abyss cannot turn back upward, one who is buried alive cannot dig himself up, a dead man cannot raise himself . . . Only [God] can fulfil that concerning which all sacrifices remain an impotent plea." (103) What sacrifice meant to do, it could not, because it flowed from an egocentric heart and remained under the law of sin.

In Christ the law of sin was broken, and as mediator between God and humanity his sacrifice resounds both in heaven and on earth. In heaven, the Lamb's sacrifice reconciles us to the Father, bringing forgiveness of all sins and fullness of sanctification. For that reason new sacrifices are both unnecessary and impossible— unnecessary because in Christ we have access to the Father, and impossible because through the sacrifice on the cross our very life was restored and regenerated as offering and sacrifice. And on earth, sacrifice is restored to those who in Christ's spirit offer

---

73. Schmemann, 102. The similarity to Peter Brown's category of the vulgar should not go unnoticed.

themselves to God. "In [Christ's] sacrifice everything is fulfilled and accomplished. In it, above all, sacrifice is cleansed, restored and manifested in all its essence and fullness, in its preeternal meaning as perfect love and thus perfect life, consisting of perfect self-sacrifice: in Christ 'God so loved the world that he gave his only Son,' and in Christ man so loved God that he gave himself totally. . . ." (104) What sacrifice was meant to accomplish but could not was thereby brought to pass. If sacrifice means perfect love and total self-giving, then Christ in his unswerving love for the Father was the perfect sacrifice, and our life in Christ, indeed the whole life of the Church, is offering and sacrifice. We offer ourselves and each other and the whole world "in a sacrifice of love and unity, praise and thanksgiving, forgiveness and healing, communion and unity."[74]

The Eucharist proper begins with a solemn rite called the Great Entrance. This name was applied, however, only when the meaning inherent in bringing the sacrifice to the table had become obscured, and so the offering became interpreted as Christ's entrance into Jerusalem. The Eucharistic offering was not intended as a symbolical illustration of the Lord's entrance into Jerusalem or his burial by Joseph, nevertheless this developed due to the gradual detachment of the preparation of the Eucharistic gifts from

74. Ibid., 104. Can a parallel be drawn between Luther's treatment of the Law and Fr. Schmemann's treatment of sacrifice? Luther capitalized on Paul's claim that the Law itself was not unholy, it was the affect which it had upon sinful nature which rendered the Law incapable of working salvation. The Law is holy and righteous (the Law's first use as expression of God's eternal will to love), but in the sinful heart it produces an opposite affect for it increases sin (the Law's second use). This Luther knew well from personal experience. Christ sets free from Law, and then the Law can again accomplish its true purpose (the third use of the Law). Could it be a Lutheran contribution to the discussion of sacrifice in the Mass to apply precisely this paradigm to sacrifice? Sacrifice in itself could be understood as an ordinance of creation wherein human beings turned to God in love and gratitude. But the sinful heart uses sacrifice to an opposite end: sacrifice is an attempt at self-justification. Luther's single concern against the teaching of the sacrifice of the Mass was that it not become an instance of works righteousness. Christ, however, has cleansed sacrifice, just as he has perfected the Law, and so long as we are in Christ it works its proper purpose. What objection, then, to calling the Mass a sacrifice?

the liturgy itself, and its isolation into a separate rite eventually called the proskomide. Is there a logic (or theo-logic) to the proskomide? Its symbolism in the liturgical Ordo must be uncovered.

To discover this requires at least a little knowledge of the historical development of the offering.

"In the consciousness, in the experience and in the practice of the early Church, the eucharistic sacrifice was offered not only on behalf of all and for all, but *by all*, and therefore the real offering by each of his own gift, his own sacrifice, was a basic condition of it. Each person who came into the gathering of the Church brought with him everything that . . . he could spare for the needs of the Church, and this meant for the sustenance of the clergy, widows and orphans, for helping the poor, for all the 'good works' in which the Church realizes herself as the love of Christ. . . ." (107)

The Eucharistic offering, then, is rooted precisely in a sacrifice of love. The origin of the offering is an expression of love. The elements brought by each Christian were received by the deacons, whose task it was to sort out the gifts they received and prepare a portion of these love-offerings to constitute the Eucharistic sacrifice. As agents for the Church's exercise of love, deacons in the Church were charged with a ministry of charity and to them fell the ritual preparation of gifts even into the fourteenth century.

Individual offerings of charity became more complicated to administer with the conversion of the empire. Now that most of the populace was Christian, the means of the Church's "philanthropy" was modified. "Not only was she recognized by the government, but with all 'charitable' activity being gradually concentrated in her hands, the Church could not but have been transformed into a complex organization, overcome by an 'apparatus'." (108) Other, more efficient means of gathering the Church's resources and administering them along with the State's resources were developed, yet the ancient connection between the Eucharist and the Church's self-sacrifice to the world through material gifts was not forgotten. The preparation of the gifts remained as a rite—even though it was strictly no longer required, since the deacon no longer sorted the Eucharistic offering from the charitable gifts intended for the poor. Fr. Schmemann sees this as an "example of that law of liturgical 'development' according to which changes in outward *form* are frequently determined by the necessity of preserving inner *content*. . . ." (109) The development of an organized charitable apparatus uncoupled the offering of love from the Eucharistic sacrifice, but to witness to this original inner link, a liturgical rite arose. No longer a functional necessity, the preparation of the gifts remained nonetheless as rite.

Even in its present position before the Divine Liturgy begins, before the people assemble, the proskomide possesses a theological meaning, Fr. Schmemann argues. There are not two offerings, bread in the proskomide and Christ at the altar (as though the former is a preliminary set-up for the latter). If at the proskomide bread and wine which has not yet been blessed is referred to as offering or sacrifice or Body of Christ, it is because this bread—like everything else in the world!—has been sanctified by the incarnation. Christ restored to creation its potential of being sacrifice to God and restored to humanity its vocation as *homo adorans* to offer it. By Christ the whole world has become sacrament and sacrifice, for in the whole world (not only in sacred places and sacred times) God's grace is encountered and humanity sings its song of offering and self-giving love. "Precisely because the sacrifice of Christ, which includes all things in itself and was offered *once*, occurred *before* all our offerings . . . likewise the proskomide, the preparation of the gifts, takes place *before* the liturgy. For the essence of this preparation lies in referring the bread and wine, i.e., our very selves and our whole life, to the sacrifice of Christ, their conversion precisely into *gift* and *offering*. Here is precisely the reality of the proskomide—the identification of the bread and wine as the sacrifice of Christ. . . ." (110)

The proskomide commemorates to Christ the whole Church, living and dead, saints, martyrs, and ourselves. In this act, the baptized offer and return themselves and the world to God. The connection remains between the Eucharistic sacrifice and the self-offering of the Church in charity, albeit now ritualized and less functional. At the Great Entrance, the elements are brought out from the room in which they were earlier prepared and placed upon the altar. In order to reveal that the entire Church is making an offering, Fr. Schmemann recommends "regenerating in every way possible" each member's inclusion in this act of offering, which in a day of monetary donations could mean joining the people's collection basket with the offering.

The act is accompanied by words, the commemoration. To commemorate is the verbal fulfillment of offering in which we give ourselves and each other to God. This is not yet the Eucharist, but the commemoration does refer everything to the memory of God by praying that God would remember. In Scripture, divine memory means the attentiveness of God to creation. To live is to abide in the memory of God, and to die is to fall out of God's memory. Human beings have the gift of memory, which is unequaled in any other creature. Out of all the ways of being, only human being can remember God and through this remembrance, truly live. Fr. Schmemann summarizes sacrament and sacrifice when he writes that God's remembrance of humanity is the gift of life, and humanity's remembrance of God is the reception of life. Conversely we might suggest that God's amnesia is wrath and human amnesia is sin. "Man forgot God because he turned his love, and consequently his memory and his very life, to something else, and above all to himself. . . . He forgot God, and God ceased to exist for him." (126)

But though humanity may have forgotten God, humanity has not been forgotten by God. The salvation history of Israel is "the gradually disclosed recognition of Christ, the 'creation' of this memory before his coming in time;" and Christ as divine is the incarnation of God's remembrance, Christ as human is the regeneration of our remembrance. "Faith is Christ's memory realized in us through our memory of Christ." (128) Faith does not mean having Jesus as an object of historical memory, nor doctrine as an object of rational understanding. Faith is possessing Christ's memory, love, obedience and confidence in the Father. Faith means having by grace the relationship with the Father which Christ had by nature. The sacramental memorial of Christ imparts this to faith. To believe in Christ means to remember him, to keep him always in mind. This kind of remembrance is the essence of leitourgia, not in order to recollect Jesus but so that through our memory of him, his memory of the Father may be realized in us. Since Christ is the incarnate icon of the Father, when Christ's image is imprinted upon the believer in baptism the Christian is anointed with God's own Holy Spirit. To realize divinization and unity with God is the telos of faith. The new life for which the baptized are destined is celebrated, actualized, received, accomplished—symbolized!—in leitourgia.

It is precisely Christ's love which is symbolized in the Sacrament of Unity, discussed in chapter seven. Love is the sign by which the body of Christ will be known, for love is the essence of the Church's holiness (the Holy Spirit is its source), unity (the community is built up in love) and its apostolicity and catholicity (for the Church everywhere is joined with the yoke of love). The Church is commanded to be a union of love. But doesn't this sound queer? How can love be commanded? "Christianity is not only the commandment but also the *revelation* and the *gift* of love. . . . In this is the staggering *newness* of Christian love—that in the New Testament man is called to love with the divine love, which has become the divine-human love, the love of Christ. The newness of Christianity lies not in the commandment to love, but in the fact that it has become possible to fulfill the commandment." (136) The kiss of peace shared by the Church at this liturgical point is then neither a personal gesture of good will, nor a pining for post-parousia love. It is the love of Christ made manifest (as all parts of the liturgy manifest Christ in his kingdom) and so the kiss of peace can be called "a sacred rite of love," a sacramental gift of love. This liturgical symbol vests each member of the body of Christ with the love of Christ which transforms the stranger into a brother or sister. This love is the fundamental reality of the liturgy. Love is what should be manifested liturgically, i.e., the reality to be symbolized.

The Eucharist is the sacrament of unity because at it we are united to one another by being united with Christ in one bread and cup. It was for loving unity that man and woman were created, and this cannot be eradicated. "The devil could turn man, and in him, the world away from God, he could poison and enfeeble life through sin, permeate it with mortality and death. One thing he could not and cannot do: change the very essence of life as unity." (152) We are made for unity, but in sin the instinct for unity becomes devilish (i.e., against God). Unity becomes an occasion or excuse for division. The cosmos is divided up into "us and them" and love for one's own revolves around enmity toward the foreign.[75] Unity is corrupted if the Church makes this kind of division between itself and the world. This must not happen. If the Church separates itself from the world, it does so in order to expose the devilish lies, but Christians must not confuse salvation of the world with salvation from the world. The Church remains and sojourns on earth to beckon a world wracked with divisions and hostilities back to a love for which it was created but which it has forfeited. The kingdom of God is manifest when the Church assembles in a unity of love which only the Holy Spirit can inspire. This is the Church's leitourgia and the task of each baptized initiate therein. The community's ritual leitourgia and the individual's lived leitourgia are oriented to enacting love.

After the brothers and sisters of Christ have symbolized this eschatological love (for truly, it is of heaven and not earth) they are summoned to a new act. "Let us stand aright! Let us stand with fear! Let us attend, that we may offer the Holy Oblation in peace." Fr. Schmemann suggests that this summons clearly indicates that something has been completed and a new thing is beginning, the Sacrament of Anaphora. This is the "chief part" of the Divine Liturgy, but we have already seen that other parts are not therefore denigrated. The other parts reach their climax here, and here the true character of other liturgical moments can be seen. In the Anaphora is discovered the answer to the question, What is accomplished in the Eucharist?[76]

### ANAPHORA AND THANKSGIVING

Fr. Schmemann discusses the Sacrament of Anaphora here in chapter eight but has yet a ninth chapter entitled the Sacrament of

75. The work of the devil is diabolical: literally, to "throw in two," from *dia* (two) and *baleo* (to throw). The unity of the Church in Christ, by redemptive contrast, is symbolical.

76. But remember—that question can be answered only by looking at the liturgy as a whole (liturgical theology), not by narrowing to one moment of it. What should be an indissoluble link of the sacrament with the liturgy, school theology destroys "through its arbitrary isolation of one 'moment' (act, formula) in the liturgy and the identification of it alone with that sacrament. . . ." (Schmemann, 161).

Thanksgiving. This tips off the reader that he means something more specific by "anaphora" than simply a title for the Thanksgiving Prayer. The deacon summons us to "stand aright," to "stand straight" or even to "be good." What would it mean for humanity to stand aright? or for the creation to be declared good and said to stand straight? In our corruption, we do not know. To really understand what this means, and what is therefore being manifested here at the beginning of the Eucharistic prayer, one must see in double vision: first in the light of creation where God saw that what had been created corresponded to God's own conception and was therefore right and good, and second in the light of the redemptive creation where the disciples saw the Lord transfigured and declared, "Lord, it is good that we are here." The Church shares a vision of what is good and this vision constitutes the Church and defines it. Such a reception of the divine good is humanity's calling. "The divine liturgy—the continual ascent, the lifting up of the Church to *heaven,* to the throne of glory, to the unfading light and joy of the kingdom of God—is the focus of this experience, simultaneously its source and presence, gift and fulfillment. . . . [A liturgy is] an action (ergon) in which the essence of what is taking place is simultaneously revealed and fulfilled." (165) When we are beckoned to "lift up our hearts" we are not being urged toward lofty disposition or mystical inclination. The Eucharist that the Church is about to do can only be done in heaven, and if it can be done here it is because Christ has unified heaven and earth. The state of being which God called "good" at the brink of history and again on Mount Tabor is now revealed and fulfilled again. This, not because we leave earth and ascend to heaven, but because heaven has transfigured earth, and earth has accepted heaven as the ultimate truth about itself.

"Salvation is complete. After the darkness of sin, the fall and death, a man once again offers to God the pure, sinless, free and perfect thanksgiving. A man is returned to that place that God had prepared for him when he created the world. He stands at the heights, before the throne of God; he stands in heaven, before the face of God himself, and freely, in the fulness of love and knowledge, uniting in himself the whole world, all creation, he offers thanksgiving, and in him the whole world affirms and acknowledges this thanksgiving to be 'meet and right.' This man is Christ." (170)

Because Christ returns the world to God, the Church offers thanksgiving of Christ in its sacrificial prayer.

The unity of this prayer, then, is thanksgiving.[77] But more than a grateful nod, this thanksgiving is the experience of paradise! It is an experience of the divine "good" which God affirmed. Fr. Schmemann speaks of paradise as our state before the fall (before our "banishment from paradise") and our state upon salvation by Christ. Paradise is the beginning and the end to which the entire life of man and woman as *homo adorans*, and through them all creation, is directed. The content of eternal life is revealed as the triunity of knowledge, freedom, and thanksgiving. When these concepts are investigated, we find that the first two are fulfilled in the last.

First of all, knowledge of God—not knowledge about God, but knowledge of God—was forfeited in our rebellion. "Adam did not cease to 'know about God' . . . but he ceased to *know God*, and his life ceased to be that meeting with God, that communion with him. . . ." (175) Eucharistic thanksgiving is the joy and fullness of knowing God. Second, freedom was forfeited; men and women were banished from paradise. With this loss of freedom, God appeared the enemy and was henceforth defined in categories of power, authority, necessity and law, which makes men and women slaves, and for the sake of freedom they find it necessary that God not exist. That God is in fact love, and human life is in fact freedom, was forgotten until Christ broke sin's categories. The Church meets its freedom in its thanksgiving.

77. Because the ones who lift up this Eucharist are the people, they should, in Fr. Schmemann's opinion, know the prayer. "The laity . . . have simply not heard and thus do not know this veritable prayer of prayers. . . . If we add to this the fact that in many Orthodox churches these prayers, being 'secret,' are moreover read behind closed royal doors, and sometimes even behind a drawn altar curtain, then it would be no exaggeration to say that the prayer of thanksgiving has for all practical purposes been dropped from the church service. I repeat, the laymen simply do not know it, theologians are not interested in it, and the priest, who is forced to glance over it while the choir is singing . . . is hardly capable of perceiving it in its fulness, unity and integrity" (Schmemann, 172).

Sin is thus revealed. In the highest moment of the liturgy we receive new knowledge of sin because one knows the depths only from the heights, the depravity only from the straight. ("Let us stand aright.") Christianity is not anthropological minimalism, says Fr. Schmemann, but anthropological maximalism. The former normalizes sin and death, and in turn supposes salvation to be supernatural; the latter recognizes the tremendous potential of humankind and understands deification as our natural end. The fall was not due to imperfection, deficiency and weakness, it was due to completion, overabundance of gifts, and power. Pride is the root of this sin, and pride is opposed to thanksgiving. Not giving thanks is the root and driving force of pride. To make Eucharistic thanksgiving both reveals and fulfills salvation (and this, it will be remembered, is how Fr. Schmemann earlier defined liturgy: an action which both reveals and fulfills). Christ's thanksgiving, knowledge and filial freedom has eternally become ours.

"Because it is of Christ and *from above*, this thanksgiving raises us up to paradise, as anticipation of it, and partaking while still on earth of the kingdom which is to come. And thus, each time it is raised up the *salvation of the world is complete*. . . . Man again stands where God placed him, restored to his vocation: to offer to God a 'reasonable service,' to know God, to thank and to worship him 'in spirit and in truth,' and through this knowledge and thanksgiving to transform the world itself into communion in the life that 'was in the beginning with God,' with God the Father, and was manifested to us." (181)

REMEMBRANCE

At this height the Church remembers one event: the Last Supper of Christ with his disciples. This is the Sacrament of Remembrance.

Fr. Schmemann rues that the Eucharistic prayer has suffered disjunction from the liturgy as a whole, and dismemberment within. Each portion of the prayer has been studied in isolation, therefore without attention to its connection with the whole. As a result, the anamnesis (remembrance) has suffered two reductions, the first theological and the second historical.

The scholastic, theological reduction has narrowed the understanding and definition of remembrance to "a 'consecratory' *reference* to Christ's establishment, at the last supper, of the sacrament of the eucharist. . . . The remembrance is the 'cause' of the actuality of the sacrament, just as the *institution* of the eucharist at the last supper is the cause of the actuality of the commemoration itself." (193) In other words, Christ's action is remembered in order to effect consecration, not enact liturgy. The Words of Institution are made the high point in order to accomplish a doctrinal theology of the Eucharist.

This scholastic focus upon the institution narrative appears in the three Christian traditions, Fr. Schmemann thinks. It exists (a) in pure form in Latin transubstantiation wherein the words of the narrative are defined as consecratory; (b) although Orthodoxy affirms consecration at the epiclesis and not at the narrative, nevertheless a special isolation of the narrative has occurred in the East as well, observed when the celebrant points his hand to the bread and says the narrative aloud even though the rest of the prayer is read in secret ("to himself"); and (c) although Protestant theology has dismissed any objective change of the gifts, they nevertheless isolate these words as a theological formulation of the proposition in which one is supposed to have personal faith. By the narrow emphasis upon the institutionary character of the narrative, the Golgotha sacrifice is variously reenacted in the Mass (Latin), described verbally for the opportunity of subjective commitment (Protestant), or given symbolic representation (Orthodox). Even though these three approaches are quite different otherwise, Fr. Schmemann calls them together a reduction because they have substituted a chief question with a derivative one. They ask "how" (how the institution of the Last Supper operates in the Eucharist?) instead of "what" (what did Christ accomplish through this last act of his earthly ministry before his death?). This has led to almost total rupture between Eucharist as sacrifice, and sacrament as partaking of Communion.

There is a second reduction at work, a historical one. Certainly Fr. Schmemann is not against historical scholarship, he is only pointing out that liturgiology is not liturgical theology. Our knowledge about the likely form of Christ's Last Supper has been greatly advanced by historical research, of course. "This knowledge itself, however, no matter how useful and necessary, cannot give us the *complete* answer to the question we posed at the beginning of this chapter: of the meaning of the *commemoration* of the last supper. . . ."[78]

The Eucharistic remembrance must not be reduced to either a scholastic question about what happens to the consecrated elements, nor to a history of worship services. These approaches may be valuable for their specialized problematics, but the method that lies at the basis of Fr. Schmemann's entire investigation and which corresponds to the goal of liturgical theology does not follow this path. "We must seek the complete answer to the question of the meaning of this commemoration, of the meaning of the liturgy as the *sacrament of remembrance,* in the eucharist itself—and this means in the continuity, in the identity of that *experience,* not personal, not subjective, but precisely *ecclesial,* which is incarnated in the eucharistic celebration and is fulfilled each time the eucharist is celebrated." (187) The method of liturgical theology which Fr. Schmemann advocates, we might say, seeks to answer the question "What does the Church do?" For to discuss the Ordo of the liturgy is to discuss what the assembly does as Church. He explained on the first page of the first chapter that "the fundamental task of liturgical theology is uncovering the meaning and essence of the unity between assembly, eucharist and Church." The meaning of the liturgy as the sacrament of remembrance must be answered within the liturgy itself, and this means in continuity with a liturgical, ecclesial experience of the heavenly Christ. The whole liturgy is a sacrament of Christ's presence, and the sacrament of remembrance (i.e., the consecrating power of the Words of Institution) can only be understood in this context. Being part of the thanksgiving, the remembrance is part of the faithful's ascension into heaven. Remembrance is the reality of the kingdom present in our midst. As the earthly Jesus mani-

---

78. Ibid., 197. In stronger words, "Therefore, unreservedly acknowledging the full indisputable use and, moreover, absolute necessity of historical research into liturgical theology, which I wrote of with—I hope—sufficient clarity in my *Introduction to Liturgical Theology,* I consider the lowering of the liturgy to a *history* of the worship services, which replaced the earlier imprisonment of theological scholasticism, to be wrong and harmful."

fested the kingdom to his disciples at the Last Supper, so the heavenly Christ is present in love to manifest the kingdom to his body at the Eucharistic supper.

Herein lies the connection between Eucharist-sacrifice and Eucharist-communion, the connection which was so badly ruptured in the two reductions. The sacrament of remembrance is not the power to convert elements, it is the kingdom in our midst; at the Last Supper, Christ did not institute an authority, he founded the Church. The Eucharist is not a means to distribute the benefits of the kingdom, it is the kingdom itself manifest. The whole meaning of this commemoration is precisely that it remembers the Last Supper not as a 'means' but as a manifestation. Jesus said to do something for the remembrance of him. Do what? A transubstantiation? A dramatic reenactment of the supper to assist faith? A mystical representation? No. ''The essence of the liturgy and its multifaceted nature consists in the fact that it is all, from beginning to end, a *remembrance*, manifestation, 'epiphany,' the salvation of the world accomplished by Christ.'' (221)

School theology has onesidedly and thereby falsely linked sacrifice with sin instead of love. To say that the Eucharist is sacrifice is only to say that the Eucharist is love, for sacrifice is the selfgiving of love. There is no love without sacrifice, love being the giving of one's self to another, but if sacrifice is now linked with suffering, it is a consequence of a fallen world. It was indeed a fallen world into which Christ came and his sacrifice meant a cross; it is still a fallen world in which the Church works and the Christian's sacrifice means carrying a Cross. Discipleship means being baptized into Christ, his sacrifice and victory handed over and granted to us. ''The sacrament of the assembly, the sacrament of offering, the sacrament of anaphora and thanksgiving and, finally, remembrance, are a single sacrament of the kingdom of God, of a single sacrifice of Christ's love, and therefore they are the sacrament of the manifestation, the gift to us of our life as sacrifice. For Christ took our life in himself and gave it to God.'' (210) To follow Christ is to be crucified to this world. It is a sacrifice love is willing to make.

That a liturgy served on earth could be accomplished in heaven requires God's own spirit. How else could it happen? So the liturgy is also the Sacrament of the Holy Spirit.

A simplified rendition of the difference between western and eastern Christians would have it that the squabble between them is over timing, the former supposing that consecration occurs at the institution narrative, the latter supposing it happens at the epiclesis. In that case, it would appear that nothing of consequence is debated; since both eastern Orthodox and western Catholic confesses the reality of the gift in the Eucharist, may we not say that the debate between consecration formula versus epiclesis is merely a debate about "when?" No. Fr. Schmemann challenges this simple construal in chapter eleven. For Orthodox theology to accept the argument on these terms already indicates that it has succumbed to school theology. A new understanding has crept in, one which he accuses of corrupting the Eucharist. "In all probability, this explains why, in contrast to the passions and emotions attendant to the great dogmatic disputes of the patristic era, the question of the epiklesis, of the transformation of the holy gifts, and of the theology of the sacraments in general did not arouse particular interest in the East." (214) It transforms the Eucharist from a sacrament of unity into one of the means for sanctifying the faithful. Instead of an act of the communal ekklesia, the sacrament becomes a personal act of piety. This new understanding is not then merely a matter of emphasis or opinion, it is a distortion of the liturgical tradition of the Church, of her *lex orandi*.

Fr. Schmemann's perspective (liturgical theology) finds elements of the liturgy to be multifaceted. To review,

"The liturgy, as a sacrament, begins with the preparation of the holy gifts and the *assembly as the Church*. After the gathering follows the *entrance* and the proclamation of the word of God, and after that the *offering*, the placing of the eucharistic gifts on the altar. After the *kiss of peace* and the confession of faith we begin the *anaphora*; the lifting up of the gifts in the prayer of thanksgiving and remembrance. The anaphora concludes with the *epiklesis*, i.e., the prayer that God will manifest the Holy Spirit, will show the bread and wine of our offering to be the body and blood of Christ and make us worthy to partake of it.'' (216)

Fr. Schmemann is struggling to indicate the interdependence of liturgy's elements, of all its rites. The entire Divine Liturgy is a single act, a common task. The sacraments should never be isolated as a separate object of study and definition. To do so is the defining mark of what he means by school theology, in either the east or west. Originally the word "sacrament" was not restricted to the list of seven, it referred instead to the entire mystery of salvation. The liturgy celebrates (accomplishes, symbolizes) one mystery, sacramentally. Again, this is why he begins each chapter title with the words "Sacrament of. . . ." The assembly is not one act, the offering another, the kiss of peace a socialization which warms one up for the lofty anaphora and now (at the end of the checklist of activities) comes the epiclesis. Rather, a single, unified sacred reality is realized in various symbols. He uses a favorite illustration: "The liturgy can be likened to a man going through a building—which, though familiar and beautiful, is hid in darkness—with a flashlight, part by part, and in these parts identifying the entire building in its wholeness, unity and beauty. So it is with our liturgy, which, while being accomplished on earth is accomplished in heaven.'' (221-22)

The liturgy does not build the building—this would be cult!—it confesses and experiences and celebrates what Christ has already accomplished. Liturgy remembers. The epicletic act is part of a prayer which is Eucharistic and anamnetic. This does not mean liturgy repeats or represents or effects the mystery, it means the Church in its liturgy ascends into the mystery of salvation which has already been accomplished. And this is why the epiclesis must not be understood as the moment of the gifts' supernatural change, because then it will seem that a sacred thing is created which was not before. To suggest that the reality becomes present "hocus pocus" in the epiclesis is to imply that the other liturgical moments are unessential preliminaries existing mainly for this transformation.[79] Then one winds up with cult which demarcates

79. We use this phrase with conscious reference to its origin. Medieval Christians attending Mass could not understand the Eucharistic prayer in

sacred things, sacred times, sacred places, sacred actions and sacred people from profane world, time, place, acts and folks. Christianity is not cult, because cult is the (temporary) replacement of profane with sacred, an exit from one world into a different creation. The liturgy's epicletic character certainly does reveal the Church as a "new creation" but this means precisely that creation is made new; not, another creation is made. The early Christians' consciousness of this explains the otherwise puzzling charge against them of being atheists. They lacked a sacred place. "Not a temple made by hands, but the opening of the heavens, the world transfigured into a temple, all life into the liturgy—such is the foundation of the Christian *lex orandi.*" (200) Christians call their space "church" (ecclesia, to gather) because in the assembly's Eucharist heaven is experienced on earth.

It is of this experience that liturgical theology should speak. For theology to be what it should be, it must refer us to the single mystery manifest in the liturgy, not to parts of the liturgy in isolation. Earlier, in chapter six, Fr. Schmemann defined the essence of theology as "the search for 'words appropriate to God' [*theoprepeis logoi*]," and suggested that such words are only spoken by the power of God. Theology fulfills its mission "not through 'words about words,' but by referring words to that reality . . . that is more primary than the word itself. . . ." We claim that liturgy establishes theology because "in Christianity, faith, as experience of an encounter and a gift received in this encounter, precedes words." (149) Liturgical symbol is the subject of liturgical theology because liturgical theology does not refer us to words about words, or to isolated moments, or to rubrics, it refers us to the reality itself. This theology is faith language because to perceive the reality in the symbol requires faith. "It is impossible to explain and define the symbol. It is realized or 'actualized' in its *own*

Latin, so instead of praying the canon they prayed during it. But their attention was lifted from private devotions when the priest uttered the transubstantiating words, "hoc est corpus meum" ("this is my body . . ."). Unlettered in Latin, the people understood the phrase as "hocus pocus." What Fr. Schmemann charges is that casting the difference between East and West as a question of timing (narrative or epiclesis) will turn the Orthodox emphasis on the epiclesis turned into an Eastern version of the hocus pocus.

reality through its transformation into that to which it points and witnesses, of which it is a *symbol*. But this conversion remains invisible, for it is accomplished by the Holy Spirit, in the new time, and is certified only by *faith.''* (222) The person who prays can be called a theologian. Theology is pneumatic speech first of all, whether or not it is also academic.

So the matter of Eastern epiclesis versus Western consecratory narrative is not just an insignificant matter of clocking the appearance of the gift, in Fr. Schmemann's opinion. Epiclesis is not hocus pocus which misfires late, after the words of institution.[80] The conversion of bread and wine into Christ's Body and Blood is accomplished invisibly for faith. The function of epiclesis is the organic connection of the anaphora prayer with the remembrance. The epiclesis constitutes the conclusion of the remembrance, for the latter is nothing else than confession of the knowledge of this mystery. The invocation of the Holy Spirit is not a separate act worked upon the bread and wine, it is woven interdependently into the complex of liturgical rites which manifests symbolically the reality already accomplished. While the liturgy is served on earth, it is accomplished in heaven. Thus, ''the *progression* here is not in the accomplishment but in the manifestation. For what is manifested is not something *new*, that did not exist before the manifestation. No—in Christ all is already *accomplished*, all is *real*, all is *granted.''* (225)

80. ''If it occurred 'palpably,' then Christianity would be a magical cult and not a religion of faith, hope and love. Thus, any attempt to *explain* the conversion, to locate it in formulas and causes, is not only unnecessary but truly harmful'' (Schmemann, 222). There is an ironic reversal in the flow of logic in transubstantiation. It begins with the premise that a substance is that which constitutes a thing and an accident is a quality belonging to the substance which can be perceived by the senses. A substance may exist by itself (*ens per se*) but an accident exists only by inhering in something else (*ens in alio*). Transubstantiation affirms a change in substance even though the accidents continue to exist as before, i.e., the substance is changed into body but the accidental qualities of bread (color, taste, shape, size) continue miraculously to be perceptible to the senses. The doctrine seems to be going the wrong direction, accounting primarily for the miracle of how bread can still taste like bread—how *ens in alio* can continue without sub-stantia.

This accomplished reality, manifested to faith in earthly symbol, is received by the communicant in the Sacrament of Communion. Unfortunately, "the contemporary faithful, churchly person sees no necessity of approaching communion at every liturgy." (230) Of all the changes the liturgy underwent over the centuries, none are judged more significant by Fr. Schmemann than those which distorted Communion into an individualistic perception. How did this happen? In the last chapter Fr. Schmemann suggests two causes for the disappearance of Communion as participation in the fulfillment of the Church.

A first factor is the regular reference to the need to be worthy in order to approach the cup frequently. In a vicious circle, more force is added to the feeling of unworthiness by one of its own consequences, the clericalization of the liturgy. With this, Fr. Schmemann writes, the whole "atmosphere" of the Church changed.[81] A second factor has been the emphasis upon private preparation for Communion. While there may be differences in people's spiritual journeys, and while there are the different categories of catechumen and baptized, nowhere in the liturgy of the faithful "do we find a single reference to the roles of two 'categories' of worshippers: the communicants of the holy mysteries and the noncommunicants." (233) The anaphora is organically linked with reception in Communion; to hang back from the table until one is subjectively satisfied with one's preparation is inconsistent with the Ordo. World, Church and kingdom come together at the table at this holy moment. No one is worthy to stand at such a juncture, therefore the preparation cannot be a calculation of one's preparedness or unpreparedness, it is the answer of love to love.

81. The changed atmosphere can be marked by the surprise the following words from John Chrysostom would register. Most understand the difference between priest and people to be most sharply drawn at the table. Chrysostom contradicts. "But there are cases where the priest does *not* differ from those under him, for instance, *when he must partake of the Holy Mysteries.* We are all equally honored with them, not as in the Old Testament when one food was for the priests and another for the people and when it was not permitted to the people to partake of that which was for the priests. Now it is not so, for the same body and the same cup is offered to all . . ." (Schmemann, 232).

The Church gracefully receives God's invitation to participate already in the Banquet of the Lamb.

OBSERVATIONS

In *Introduction to Liturgical Theology* Fr. Schmemann complained that what we call liturgics is usually a more or less detailed practical study of ecclesiastical rites—the study of rubrics—which answers the question how (how worship is to be carried out according to the rules) but does not answer the question what (what is done in worship). He therefore distinguishes liturgical theology from liturgics, because the approach he advocates addresses questions to the liturgy which are about theology, not liturgics. In the terms of this distinction, it is clear that *The Eucharist* is liturgical theology, not liturgics. In this book he has worked out in concrete example his definition of liturgical theology. Its task, he has written, is to elucidate the meaning of worship, to give theological basis to the explanation of worship, to explain how the Church expresses and fulfills herself in the liturgical act (all one-line definitions from *Introduction*). This study on the Eucharist fulfills these definitions, and in so doing exemplifies the first mark of our definition of liturgical theology. It is truly theology.

It exhibits the second mark of our definition as well. The meaning of the Eucharist which liturgical theology bespeaks must derive from the liturgical rite. If liturgical theology is fundamentally the community's adjustment to its existential encounter with God, then the only way for someone to write it down is to examine the rite in motion, just as the only way to understand a top is to spin it. This agenda Fr. Schmemann also assigned twenty years earlier in *Introduction* when he wrote,

"Worship simply cannot be equated either with texts or with forms of worship. It is a whole, within which everything, the words of prayer, lections, chanting, ceremonies, the relationship of all these things in a 'sequence' or 'order' and, finally, what can be defined as the 'liturgical coefficient' of each of these elements (i.e. that significance which, apart from its own immediate content, each acquires as a result of its place in the general sequence or order of worship), only all this together defines the meaning of the whole and is therefore the proper subject of study and theological evaluation." (15–16)

Fr. Schmemann has not only done this, but has with some delight frequently reminded his readers about it. Each chapter title was intended to demonstrate that although the liturgy is multifacted, it is a single sacrament in which all parts manifest the divine meaning of what is accomplished by their sequence and structure and coordination with each other. Regularly he complains about the defect in what he calls school theology which isolates one part of worship from its liturgical context. If one wants to know what happens in the Eucharist, one must look at the liturgy and the assembly as well, not merely at scholastic questions about how and when the bread is consecrated. Scholastic dogmatics, he complains, is unaware of the ecclesiological meaning of the Eucharist and the eucharistic dimension of ecclesiology. It is precisely the task of liturgical theology to uncover the meaning and essence of the unity between assembly, Church and Eucharist. The "liturgical coefficient" of the entrance, for example, or the offering or the epiclesis must be kept before the theologian as he or she tries to understand the individual rite. The *lex orandi* of the Church is a single diamond with multiple facets, not a series of beads on a string which can be removed and studied in isolation. This is the subject of liturgical theology, and to that extent, Fr. Schmemann remarks, liturgical theology is an independent theological discipline with its own special subject, viz. the liturgical tradition of the Church. Here will be found, in language which is primary and symbolic, *theologia* in its womb.

Fr. Schmemann's language is more amenable to the conventions of the academy and more familiar to our mode of publication than was Germanus' style, but each speaks to his own day. If Germanus' *sitz im leben* was the rise of iconoclasm and the pastoral challenge of witnessing salvation to new converts, Fr. Schmemann's is the reduction of symbol to mere symbolism and the continued distinction between sacred and profane. The theological craft is exercised at the intersection of tradition and contemporary culture, said Fr. Taft; then these two liturgical commentaries are surely an exercise of the craft. What they do, each in its own style, is not a history of worship services, or subjective devotions, or disjuncted allegorizations, it is theology. The subject matter is the liturgical coefficient of ritual acts which when enacted together symbolize the reign of God into the very midst of a people sent to proclaim this kingdom. This is the reality which both Germanus and Schmemann are describing. They can describe it theologically because it is enacted and witnessed liturgically.

## Chapter 7

## Consequences

If our gait has seemed somewhat ungainly throughout this
work, it is because we have had one foot in each of two worlds.
One marched through methodological observations about theology
while the other sought clarity about liturgy. The topics of liturgy
and theology have been as estranged in the systems of secondary
theology as they have been in the lives of believers. We have tried
to reconcile this estrangement, not by insinuating into secondary
theology such "liturgical" matters as devotion, a community identity, doxology, prayer, and so forth, but rather by recognizing the
theological character of leitourgia itself. The definition which alone
should receive the title liturgical theology is one which organically
connects these two (a Chalcedonian, not a Nestorian definition!)
and to clarify this we have had to migrate back and forth between
methodological comment and liturgical definition.

If by "liturgy" one means protocol and not leitourgia, then
there can be no liturgical theology. We have inherited a nonliturgical prejudice which considers liturgical ritual a fairly inconsequen-
tial part of the Christian life, and therefore treats liturgy simply as
an illustrative source for theology. Leitourgia has been replaced
with other prejudices—puritanism, biblicism, pietism and
rationalism—but so long as these movements occur within a non-
liturgical perception of the Eucharist, Eucharistic theology, piety
and practice will not be significantly impacted.

Not all worship is liturgical, but there is liturgical worship. Not
all assemblies are liturgical, but there is one which is, it is called
Church. Not all doxology or prayer is liturgical, but there is liturgical doxology and liturgical prayer. And, we have claimed, not all
theology is liturgical, but there is liturgical theology.

What does this adjective "liturgical" mean? This question has
not been answered completely, we acknowledge, for to under-

stand liturgy (and not just define it) would be a complete case of liturgical theology itself, and ours has been the fourth approach, not the third. Yet we hope that leitourgia's definition has been sufficiently established to make clear that the adjective "liturgical" means more than decorative or devotional. Worship, assembly, doxology or prayer are liturgical not by virtue of some pontificating style, but insofar as they are an instance of rite, a transaction in Christ between God and his people. Recognizing the difference between liturgy and leitourgia dramatically changes what is meant when one accuses a worship of being nonliturgical. And it dramatically changes the objective of liturgical reform: it does not mean shuffling the sanctuary furniture, redecorating the nave, permitting the laos some hieratic duties, or repristinating the liturgical style of a given era deemed golden, but rather the objective of liturgical reform is to make the assembly liturgical. Leitourgia means an action by which a group of people become something corporately which they had not been as a mere collection of individuals. In this case, believers become Christ's body.

This sense of leitourgia has frayed at the edges, if not unraveled right up the middle. Liturgical worship is not treated as constitutive of Christian identity, but more optionally, like a buffet line which one might opt to frequent instead of a family dinner where one's presence symbolizes family and one's absence diminishes the assembly. When the assembly is not liturgical then Eucharist and ekklesia are ruptured; people happen to coinhabit the same space at the same time but they make their worship solipsistically. Where liturgy is understood as a more or less elaborate format for worshipping (Orthodox more, Protestant less, Roman Catholic in the middle), it is rarely felt to be the telos and fructification of that new life begun in the waters of baptism.[1] However, if a pro-

---

1. Fr. Kavanagh says that "baptism and all it presupposes is the way the eucharist begins, and . . . the eucharist and all it causes is the way baptism is sustained," in "Christian Initiation: Tactics and Strategy," *Made, Not Born*, (Notre Dame: University of Notre Dame Press, 1976), 4. And G. W. H. Lampe retells the remark, not his own, that had St. Paul heard the phrase "the Blessed Sacrament" he would have thought it meant baptism. Lampe then goes on to describe baptism as "the initiation of which the subsequent course of the convert's entire life in the Church was a fulfillment and working

founder definition of liturgy can be appreciated then it will become clear that liturgical theology is distinct from a method which treats liturgy as either subject or resource. The method we have described discerns liturgy's theology—the theology worked out, preserved and manifested in ritual acts of that assembly called Church. To agree that liturgy is theological, one must admit that liturgical rite is ruled, shaped, traditional.

## THE GRAMMAR OF MRS. MURPHY

The upper tier may find it difficult to make such an admission. The tier that looks upon multisensate ritual as vulgar and therefore nontheological finds it difficult to suppose that Mrs. Murphy can speak her faith by a grammar which, even though not formalized, merits the name theology. That is why one consequence of our definition of liturgy as leitourgia was the widening of the usual perimeters of what is called theological activity. Truly, the theology worked out and preserved in ritual logistics is not the same in form as academic theology, but this only means it is not academic, not that it is not theological. What the assembly does in its liturgy does not have to be transmogrified to be real theology.

Let us say simplistically that theology is an answer to the question "What happened?" Theology is rooted in Scripture because Scripture witnesses to what happened, and theology is established by *lex orandi* (without competition to Scripture) because here it happens again. When God engages a human being in a self-disclosive Word, faith obeys and theology wonders at what happened. To do the latter without the former is empty; but the former unavoidably includes the latter since human beings are created with a restless need for meaningfulness, and faith is stirred to make a strike at meaning. This primary theological strike will not take the form of abstract discourse, but should not thereby be denigrated as though popular religion lacks meaning.

We have called frequent attention to Fr. Schmemann's claim that liturgy is the ontological condition of theology, of the proper understanding of the *kerygma*. But why does he say this? "Because it

out." "The Eucharist in the Thought of the Early Church," *Eucharistic Theology Then and Now*, Theological Collections 9 (London: SPCK, 1968).

is in the Church, of which the *leitourgia* is the expression and the life, that the sources of theology are functioning precisely as sources."[2] What happened is present again to beckon faith and provoke the theological struggle for meaning. The kingdom's coming was prepared by patriarchs, prophets, psalmists and priests, and when the time had fully come God sent forth his Son who in words and deeds proclaimed that the kingdom was at hand. Liturgy was born when the reign of God and the restoration of humanity was unleashed at the resurrection, and every eighth day, when the assembly is confronted by God, they ask themselves, What happened? As a result of the paschal mystery, what happened to us? to the world? to God? Liturgy is the ontological condition for theology because the kingdom is rendered present in the Divine Liturgy (it is "symbolized" in Fr. Schmemann's sense of a verb). Liturgy is foundational to theology because in liturgy's sacramental axis, what happened by Jesus happens to us.

There are reasons to describe this in formalized language, with the rules of inference clearly articulated to purge ambiguity and equivocation, but this is not the only language by which one might explain what happened, and frequently such language will fail to wonder at what happened. Mrs. Murphy knows a natural language which, it is true, is less tidy, but no less disciplined. She does not rear back and reflect upon the language (second-order theology) or the rite (liturgiology) but, then, that is the obligation of academicians anyway. Her theological understanding of the intersection of world and kingdom is accomplished and preserved as liturgical rite.

It was Wittgenstein's conviction that so many philosophical problems arose because language had "gone on holiday." His aim, he said, was to bring words back from their metaphysical to their everyday use. One example is the conundrum of certainty. Tongue in cheek, he describes the puzzlement of a philosopher's companion who is eluded by the deep brooding over the problem of certainty. "I am sitting with a philosopher in the garden; he says again and again, 'I know that that's a tree,' pointing to a tree that is near us. Someone else arrives and hears this, and I tell

2. Schmemann, "Theology and Liturgical Tradition," 175.

him: 'This fellow isn't insane. We are only doing philosophy.' "[3] Fr. Schmemann accused school theology of extracting sacramentology from liturgy when questions were asked of the Eucharistic species outside the liturgical event. The species were no longer considered within the context of their use; language gone on holiday. The theologian says again and again, "I know that that is transubstantiated." Someone else arrives and hears this and we tell him "We are only doing theology."

There are reasons for doctrinal precision. It can ask more questions than Mrs. Murphy can, but not questions more fundamental. If theological discourse about worship is not to become language on holiday, it must take the rite into account, the "liturgical coefficient" as Fr. Schmemann called it. A theology of prayer is not the same as a prayer's liturgical theology because the former does not take into consideration where that prayer lies in the rite, by whom it is prayed, and for what purpose. One can make some general remarks about prayer, as one can make some general remarks about games, but the difference between the Great Litany and the anaphora is as different as the rules between the games of chess and football. Take another example: incense. Why use it? Carolingian allegory said it is a symbol of our prayer rising to God, mimicking Old Testament themes. Prior to that time, the incense also had an honorific use (it preceded the bishop's entrance as it did the Emperor) and for a while a sacrificial meaning, one which precluded it from Christian use until that pagan connection wore out. So which is it—honorific, sacrificial or symbolic of prayer rising? The incense does not possess a naked theological meaning; its meaning is discovered by its liturgical coefficient. Its significance is acquired as a result of its use in the worship. Burning incense before the altar feels different than censing the congregation, or leading in the bishop. Knowing when, where, how, before whom, and why something is censed will disclose meaning. Precisely such a range of questions occupies liturgical theology, distinguishing it from theology of worship, on the one hand, and from liturgiology, on the other, despite the latter's usefulness in uncovering a rite's historical origin and trajectory.

3. Wittgenstein, *On Certainty* (New York: Harper Torchbooks, 1969) 61, par. 467.

In his study on the origins of confirmation Fr. Kavanagh provides a more detailed example of the need to consider the liturgical coefficient. His thesis, roughly, is that confirmation originated in a dismissal rite which "completed" the preceding rite only in the sense of formally concluding it. Such dismissal prayers did not at the outset take the form of an epiclesis of the Holy Spirit. "The purpose of the *missa* rite was to conclude and formally 'seal' a unit of public worship or instruction by dismissing the assembly either in whole or part with prayer and by physical contact between the dismissed and its chief minister—bishop, catechist, abbot or, by concession, ordained monastic."[4] But when the rite's liturgical structure was obscured and its blessing and dismissing role was forgotten, then theologians filled in a new meaning. Theology can't stand a vacuum, and when for various reasons the meaning of a rite was no longer connected to the rite's performance or visible in the structure of the rite, another meaning was provided to answer the question, What happened? In this case it was no longer evident that what happened was a *missa* (dismissal) and so in a letter written near 416 Pope Innocent I could interpret the rite in terms of the eighth chapter of Acts where the Holy Spirit is bestowed by laying on hands, concluding that "it belongs solely to the episcopal office that bishops consign and give the Paraclete Spirit." Fr. Kavanagh's examination of the evidence suggests that the original dismissal prayer had already been altered to include an epiclesis of the Holy Spirit, giving Innocent the opportunity to interpret the customary episcopal *missa* as an episcopal confirmation of the Spirit through handlaying. "Given all this in its historical setting, one must conclude that Innocent's letter . . . is propaganda rather than a serene and objective articulation of doctrine—well meaning, understandable in the circumstances, and for high motives, but propaganda nonetheless. Based on a selective biblical appeal, it seeks to justify a new understanding of an old post-chrismational structure in Roman baptismal procedure."[5]

---

4. Fr. Aidan Kavanagh, *Confirmation: Origins and Reform* (New York: Pueblo Publishing Co., 1987) 39.

5. Ibid., 58. Fr. Kavanagh conjectures about conditions which might have urged such a change: heightened pneumatological debate, plus the association

If by confirmation one means an epiclesis of the Holy Spirit then the early dismissal prayers had no confirmation rite. There is an episcopal *missa* of neophytes from their baptism into their first Eucharist, but "this is something that will be reiterated each time they commune sacramentally for the rest of their lives in the *ecclesia,* where the Spirit flourishes."[6] To appeal to this time period in an attempt to ground a later understanding of confirmation as episcopal epicletic handlaying is pure anachronism. More, it is a case of liturgy being bent to serve theology and pastoral needs. "Innocent is not doing mystagogy here. He is theologically enhancing one element in the old *missa,* the episcopal signation *in frontem,* in such a way that it eventually will alter people's perception of the structure as a whole and even alter the structure itself."[7]

We say, then, that when a rite's structure or Ordo loses force, then its liturgical purpose becomes invisible and its theological meaning as well. The theological meaning of the action escapes the laos if they can observe the rite but not know what happened. The subject matter of liturgical theology is precisely this theological meaning. Not that some theologian must invent it and reveal it to unthinking, ritualistic automatons; the whole community should be able to discern what happens. The questions which liturgical theology put to liturgy are about theology, not liturgics, says Fr. Schmemann, because they ask: What happens? Some historical knowledge may shed light on what this action or that symbol does, but liturgical theology is primarily theology, not history. It is not a history of worship services. The liturgy symbolizes the kingdom, but if liturgy's symbolic intelligibility is lost then liturgy has no theological muscle and it is replaced by flabby sentimentalism or rationalism. The service becomes a mystical, other-worldly, symbolism; or hieratic pageantry which might not even require a congregation's presence much less their participation; or audio-visual technique to set the mood for the speech.

of the Holy Spirit with handlaying, plus episcopal jealousy over presbyteral consignation, plus a dismissal rite with hand laying at the close of the baptismal rite equalled a shift from a *missa* prayer to an epicletic prayer. See 60 ff.

  6. Ibid., 70.
  7. Ibid., 63.

Lay people assume theology is beyond their ken because Sunday after Sunday they sit through liturgies so anemic that no one is provoked to furrow their brows and wonder what has happened. If nothing happens, one cannot ask the theological question of the rite. If liturgy does not make the kingdom symbolic, like a kiss makes one's love symbolic, then its *lex orandi* cannot establish the *lex credendi*. One consequence of liturgical theology would be to create more theologians, a true empowerment of the laity.

With the definition of liturgy as leitourgia, the boundaries of theology are therefore expanded to include a larger genus than the academic species. Theology should color every enterprise in which a Christian engages and not be a mere speciality, a separate language reserved for the initiated. To be Christian includes the capacity to theologize, to speak of God and to God, even if one's occupation isn't talking about God. What is made symbolic in liturgical structure creates a theological vision of what it means to "stand aright" and live by hope, charity and faith. The law of belief rests upon its fundament, the kingdom, and the reign of God is symbolized, manifested and epiphanized in liturgy. Here the kingdom of God happens. The world is done the way it was meant to be done, under God's reign.

## TRADITION

In liturgy, God's speech resonates in the Church's grammar, namely Tradition. It continues as a present force. "Tradition is not the past; it is the Church's self-consciousness *now* of that which has been handed on to her not as an inert treasure but as a dynamic inner life. Theology must be reflection on the whole of that reality. . . . [T]radition is not the past, but the present understood genetically, in continuity with that which produced it."[8] The reason for leafing through the pages of history, Fr. Taft continues, is to understand the present, not the past, like a psychiatrist investigates a childhood in order to understand the adult.

Vladimir Lossky uses a spatial image to describe Tradition. The vertical line of Tradition unpacks itself on a horizontal line. It is projected onto a public horizontal line (proclaimed and written),

8. Taft, "The Liturgical Year: Studies, Prospects, Reflections," *Worship* 55 (1981) 2–3.

namely Scripture, icon, liturgy, dogma or exegesis. Though these belong to the world of *logoi* (words), by his Holy Spirit God's own *logos* is projected through horizontal *logoi*.

"If the Scriptures and all that the Church can produce in words written or pronounced, in images or in symbols liturgical or otherwise, represent the differing modes of expression of the Truth, Tradition is the unique mode of receiving it. . . . [Tradition] is not the content of Revelation, but the light that reveals it; it is not the word, but the living breath which makes the word heard at the same time as the silence from which it came."[9]

Tradition is the Holy Spirit living in the church, giving to each the faculty of hearing, receiving and knowing. Tradition is not the expression itself, the *logoi* of Scripture, icon, dogma, exegesis, liturgical rite, yet in these horizontal projections the inexpressible is expressed. We have been trying to refer to this with our use of the concept grammar: grammar is not the words, it is what holds the words together rightly, meaningfully and intelligibly. One speaks according to a grammar, as one paints an icon according to Tradition, or interprets Scripture or formulates dogma according to Tradition. A dogma, Lossky says, is "an intelligible instrument which makes for adherence to the Tradition of the church. A doctrine is traitor to Tradition when it seeks to take its place. . . ."[10] It is a witness to its external limit. Development of dogma is not the augmentation of Tradition but a means for adherence to it.

We might compare the role of Tradition in intellectual form (dogma, exegesis, and creed) with its presence in pictorial form (icon) and in ritual form (liturgy). In every case, the content of the horizontal line must be interpreted in light of the vertical. This means, in the case of icons, that completely excluded is "any possibility of painting icons of Christ or of the saints according to the painter's imagination. . . ."[11] We could expand the thought. Artists can no more paint an icon according to their painters' im-

9. Vladimir Lossky, "Tradition and Traditions," in *The Meaning of Icons*, edited by Lossky and Ouspensky (New York: St. Vladimir's Press, 1983) 15.
10. Ibid., 19.
11. Leonid Ouspensky, *Theology of the Icon* (New York: St. Vladimir's Press, 1978), 165.

agination, than story tellers could tell the life of Jesus according to their poetic imagination, or preachers preach the gospel according to their ideology, or theologians theologize according to their philosophical imagination. Icon, catechesis, homily, and doctrine must all be Traditional, composed according to a grammar which derives from the Holy Spirit. Ouspensky argues that a priest, in order to be priest to a people, should be capable of distinguishing between icon and secular image. "A priest should simply know how to 'read' an icon as well as the liturgy,"[12] to know if it is orthodox.

It is the Holy Spirit who capacitates the primary theologian. To distinguish icon from secular art, symbol from sign, mystagogy from allegory, and liturgical gesture from pontifical showmanship is more than a science, it is pneumatic art. If so, it is not true that the first of the terms in the above pairings (icon, symbol, mystagogy and gesture) can only be recognized by the educated upper tier while the second of the terms (crude art, sign, allegory and pageantry) are usually embraced by the vulgar lower tier. Mrs. Murphy also becomes capable of "reading" an icon, a liturgy, a scriptural exegesis, and even a doctrine (if it is taken out of the elite jargon in which doctrines are normally cast and made intelligible to her) because she hears the Christian grammar and sees the Christian mystery epiphanized every eighth day. Tradition, Lossky said, is the unique mode of receiving the Scriptures and all that the Church has produced in words, images, and symbols (liturgical or iconic); liturgy capacitates Mrs. Murphy for such reception because it is precisely here that sources function as sources. She becomes theologian when she is capacitated to read an icon and distinguish it from secular image, Scripture and distinguish exegesis from ideology, liturgical rite and distinguish it from sentimentality or pontificalism, theology and distinguish it from religious kitsch. Liturgical theology is not corporate devotional opinion. Not anything and everything floats just because it is popular devotion, but it is possible that the lower tier can identify that which deserves to be sunk without the help of the upper tier.

12. Ibid., 18.

A liturgical theologian exercises another obligation as well, a macrocosmic task: the Christian is capacitated to "read" the world. In liturgical confrontation with the kingdom, one discovers what it means to "stand aright," or what a "good place" would be like, or how the world was meant to be done. If theology is like a grammar, then learning theology is not an end in itself. One learns a grammar in order to say something and Christians learn kingdom grammar in the liturgy in order to tell the world the truth about itself. Theology used only microcosmically, within the Church and for Church business alone, becomes the rational version of cult, perpetuating isolation from an allegedly profane world. The body of Christ does not assemble to do Church, it assembles to do the world, redeemed. The objective is for the hearer to become godly in order to draw an ungodly world back to its source. The principle meaning of the existence of the world is its participation in building the kingdom of God, and the principle meaning of the existence of the Church in this world is the work of drawing the world into the fullness of the revelation—its salvation.[13] Liturgy is the Church's work in the world on the world's behalf. What is celebrated within the temple shines beckoningly through the lives of the faithful to those who do not live in the kingdom of faith, hope and love but in the hell of sin, despair and hate. Liturgy's theology is a form, grammar, or shape which should become the form, grammar or shape of each liturgist's life.

So we suggest that one consequence of liturgical theology is a heightened sense of appreciation for and obligation of the laity's capacity to theologize. That the laity are assumed capable of discerning Tradition in the horizontal modes they experience (preaching, ritual, scriptural use, episcopal authority, etc) would impact the authority structure of the Western ecclesiastical institution, a point made by many Orthodox theologians.[14] And this indirectly

13. Ouspensky, "The Meaning and Language of Icons," 28.
14. See, for instance, John Meyendorff's discussions about differing Eastern and Western expectations of authority in *Living Tradition* (New York: St. Vladimir's Seminary Press, 1978) especially "Historical Relativism and Authority in Christian Dogma," "What is an Ecumenical Council," "Rome and Orthodoxy: Is 'Authority' Still the Issue?" and also Dumitru Staniloae *Theology and the Church* ch. 2, "The Holy Spirit and the Sobornicity of the Church."

leads us to a second consequence of liturgical theology: its potential for ecumenicity.

It is important to immediately clarify that we do not mean an ecumenical potential which is the result of theology becoming fuzzier—a conclusion we fear might be drawn by some theologies from worship. Liturgical theology's contribution to the ecumenical dialogue does not consist of descending from an upper tier where thinking is sharp and disciplined, to a lower tier where there is none at all, as though one can sidestep hard theological issues if one deals with them in inchoate form at the level of faith feelings (allegedly liturgy).

Nevertheless, liturgical theology does provide a way of thinking about how Tradition establishes theology which is not dead-ended by propositional categories. By way of illustration, consider Ouspensky's description of what makes an icon orthodox. It is not by virtue of copying a particular historical style. "An Orthodox iconographer faithful to Tradition always speaks the language of his time, expressing himself in his own manner, following his own way. . . . In the Church there is only one criterion: Orthodoxy. Is an image Orthodox or not? Does it correspond to the teaching of the Church or not? Style as such is never an issue in worship."[15] Tantamountly, doctrinal formulation will speak the language of its time, be expressed in its own manner, follow its own way, but nevertheless can be subject to the criterion of Tradition: orthodoxy. "To preserve the 'dogmatic tradition' does not mean to be attached to doctrinal formulae: to be within the Tradition is to keep the living truth in the Light of the Holy Spirit, or rather—it is to be kept in the Truth by the vivifying power of Tradition."[16] Tradition is inwardly changeless, but constantly assumes new forms which supplement the old without superseding them.[17] To renew does not mean to replace ancient expressions with new ones; the development of dogma does not equal augmentation. It does mean applying the mystery and meaning of Christ to the *sitz im leben* of today. The theological craft is practiced at the intersection of tradition and contemporary culture (Fr. Taft).

15. Ouspensky, *Theology of the Icon,* 14–15.
16. Lossky, "Tradition and Traditions," 19.
17. Timothy Ware, *The Orthodox Church,* 260.

George Lindbeck's reflections upon the nature of doctrine yields similar sounding conclusions. For this reason we find the categories he created in order to account for ecumenical concordance on doctrinal matters friendly to describing liturgical theology's character. He notes that ecumenical agreement has often been greeted with suspicion due to either of two inadequate assumptions. On the one hand, it is assumed that one doctrine must be right and the other wrong, and therefore agreement can be achieved only when someone admits error. This perspective Lindbeck identifies as a propositional theory of religion, i.e., doctrine is essentially cognitive content. On the other hand, it is assumed that doctrines don't really matter anyway since they're only peepholes from various perspectives upon the same shared reality, so ignore ecumenical theological discussion in favor of ecumenical shared experiences. This perspective he identifies as an expressive-experiential theory of religion, i.e., doctrine is essentially only an idiosyncratic expression, a sort of style peculiar to a group but not incumbent on all. Lindbeck's intention is to steer a middle course between these alternatives with a third option: what he calls a cultural-, linguistic theory of religion.

He suggests that religion finds its significance not in propositionally formulated statements alone, nor in inner experiences alone. Rather, its abiding and doctrinally significant aspect is located "in the story it tells and in the grammar which informs the way the story is told and used."[18] There is, in other words, an underlying shape to doctrines which is more important for understanding the point of the doctrine than is the particular formulation. "On this view, doctrines acquire their force from their relation to the grammar of a religion. . . . Faithfulness to such doctrines does not necessarily mean repeating them, but rather requires adherence to the same directives which were involved in their formulation in the making of any new formulations."[19] In its own way, the cultural-linguistic theory accommodates the strengths of both the propositional and the experiential theory,

18. George Lindbeck, *The Nature of Doctrine* (Philadelphia: Westminster Press, 1984), 80.
19. Ibid., 81.

while correcting their weaknesses. Like the propositional theory, the cultural-linguistic theory considers the external beliefs primary. The "givenness" of the religion is significant; not any feeling will meet the established criteria. But, correcting the propositional theory, these are known in the form of story, not in statable propositions. Like the experiential theory, the cultural-linguistic theory does justice to the unreflective dimension of human existence. The aesthetic and nondiscursive elements in theology are not taken as mere ornamentation. Yet due to its external grounding it can discriminate between objectifications of religion.

This tightrope may at first be difficult to walk, as Lindbeck admits.

"It may be more difficult to grasp the notion that it is the framework and the medium within which Christians know and experience, rather than what they experience or think they know, which retains continuity and unity down through the centuries. Yet this seems to make more empirical, historical, and doctrinal sense. . . . [T]he permanence and unity of doctrines . . . is more easily accounted for if they are taken to resemble grammatical rules rather than propositions or expressive symbols."[20]

In one sense, we are dealing with a less tangible factor here in the framework, viz. the grammar, the rules of doctrine; and yet it is the more common factor in another sense. The grammar of faith weekly exercised in liturgical rhythms establishes itself in a life, even if one cannot put it in second-order propositions. One's life will have been steeped in the Christian lexicon, formed by the Christian story, and one can exercise the Christian grammar even if one cannot reflectively articulate it. Liturgical experience will have capacitated a theological grammar. To use another phrase from Lindbeck, one can understand the *code* even if not how it has been *encoded*. "This stress on the code rather than the (e.g. propositionally) encoded, enables a cultural linguistic approach to accommodate the experiential-expressive concern for the unreflective dimensions of human existence far better than is possible in a cognitivist outlook."[21] Liturgy is ontological to both theology and piety.

20. Ibid., 84.
21. Ibid., 35.

We suggest that Fr. Schmemann's desire to find the Ordo behind the 'rubrics' or that element of the Typicon which is presupposed by its whole content is the same grammar, code or story which Lindbeck discusses. The meaning of the liturgy, its *lex orandi*, is ultimately the Church's faith enacted, i.e., symbolized, but it does not exist in naked vertical form, either as proposition or as emotion. Vertical, pneumatic Tradition projects itself onto the historical horizontal line and is manifested in Scripture, liturgies, icons, and dogmas where these sources function precisely as sources. Liturgical theology searches for the code presupposed by the whole content of what is encoded in liturgy. It searches for the *lex orandi* code which establishes *lex credendi* encodements.

Under the propositional model, liturgy looks like soft experience, of little help to the hard discipline of theology; under the experiential-expressivist model, liturgy hasn't sufficient shape to make theological claims. The cultural-linguistic theory takes liturgy seriously as a locus for theology.

"To become religious—no less than to become culturally or linguistically competent—is to interiorize a set of skills by practice and training. One learns how to feel, act, and think in conformity with a religious tradition which is in its inner structure far richer and more subtle than can be explicitly articulated. The primary knowledge is not *about* the religion, nor *that* the religion teaches such and such, but rather *how* to be religious in such and such ways. Sometimes explicitly formulated statements of the beliefs or behavioral norms of a religion may be helpful in the learning process, but by no means always. Ritual, prayer, and example are normatively much more important."[22]

As we have argued all along, liturgy has a more significant role to play regarding doctrine than just being mystical ornamentation of a concept. If liturgy is a *ruled activity*, not just a fuzzy experiential exercise, then the following are miscast as antagonists: prayer-belief, faith–doctrine, liturgy–theology, law of prayer–law of belief. These are not alternative, opposite sorts of activities for the very reason that the former term in the pairing also names ruled activi-

22. Ibid.

ties, their ruled grammar being the very womb from which the latter activities arise. Liturgical theology strives to grasp liturgy's theology in the womb, so to speak. To do this one must begin with the Ordo. One cannot separate liturgical theology from its ritual life and keep it alive by artificial academic respirators. The structure, the code, the grammar is discovered, not invented. The Church's leitourgia, said Fr. Schmemann, is the full and adequate epiphany of that in which the Church believes. If this is true, then all theology ought to be liturgical, not in the sense of making liturgy an exclusive subject matter for study (as did our samples of theology of worship and theology from worship) but in the sense of theology having its ultimate term of reference in what the Church epiphanizes liturgically.

Liturgy has a theological structure, we claim, and is an embodiment of Christianity's interpretive schema; heavily ritualized, it is not just a raw experience of God which then spins off rites and theologies. This grammar is the subject matter of the special discipline, liturgical theology. Ecumenical concord might then be recovered when a commonly shared code can be perceived despite differences of encodement. Then our unity would lie in orthodoxy (right worship; *doxa* means glory) rather than uniform orthodidascalia (right teaching) or fuzzy orthopistis (right believing). Such would be the power of Pentecost. Gregory of Nazianzus says the curse of the tower of Babel was to make a variety of tongues a cause of disarray and incoherence, but Pentecost corrects Babel, not by squeezing out uniformity, but by making the same variety of tongues a means of harmony. Dumitru Staniloae comments upon Pentecostal existence:

"We might say that the Church was founded precisely through the infusion into all believers of a common understanding, an understanding which was shared by faithful and Apostles alike. In this way the Church is the opposite of the Tower of Babel. . . . This common mind which belongs to those who have entered into the Church does not, however, mean uniformity in all things. The fact that all those who received the same understanding preserved their distinct languages is a symbol of this unity in variety."[23]

23. Dumitru Staniloae, "The Holy Spirit and the Sobornicity of the Church," in *Theology and the Church*, 53.

302

Theology wonders what happened—what happened as God passed through Ur of Chaldees, or the burning bush on Sinai, or the barn behind a Bethlehem inn. Liturgical theology wonders what happened after a believer has known God to pass sacramentally through his or her life. The Church's Pentecostal unity lies in its gathering every eighth day to celebrate and be transformed by a Mystery which capacitates theological vision so the *laos* can tell the world its true identity until Christ comes and knowledge is perfected.

# Bibliography

Adam, Adolf. *The Liturgical Year*. New York: Pueblo Publishing Company, 1981.

Adam, Karl. *The Spirit of Catholicism*. New York: Image Books, 1954.

Alexander, J. Neil, ed. *Time and Community*. Washington, D.C.: The Pastoral Press, 1990.

Althaus, Paul. *The Theology of Martin Luther*. Philadelphia: Fortress Press, 1966.

Arseniev, Nicholas. *Russian Piety*. New York: St. Vladimir's Seminary Press, 1964.

Atiya, Aziz. *A History of Eastern Christianity*. London: Methuen & Co, 1968.

Aulen, Gustaf. *Eucharist and Sacrifice*. Philadelphia: Muhlenberg Press, 1958.

_____. *The Faith of the Christian Church*. Philadelphia: Fortress Press, 1960.

Aune, Michael B. " 'To Move the Heart': Word and Rite in Contemporary American Lutheranism." *Currents in Theology and Mission* 10 (1983) 210–221.

Austin, Gerard. *The Rite of Confirmation: Anointing with the Spirit*. New York: Pueblo Publishing Company, 1985.

Baldovin, John. *City, Church & Renewal*. Washington, D.C.: The Pastoral Press, 1991.

Baumstark, Anton. *Comparative Liturgy*. Maryland: The Newman Press, 1958.

Beasley-Murray. *Baptism in the New Testament*. Grand Rapids: William Eerdmans Publishing Company, 1962.

Bell, Richard, ed. *The Grammar of the Heart*. San Francisco: Harper & Row, 1988.

304

Benz, Ernst. *The Eastern Orthodox Church.* New York: Doubleday & Company, 1963.

Bishops' Committee on the Liturgy. *Environment and Art in Catholic Worship.* Washington, D.C.: Publications Office, U.S. Catholic Conference, 1978.

Bobrinskoy, Boris. "The Icon: Sacrament of the Kingdom" *St. Vladimir's Theological Quarterly* 31 (1987) 287–296.

Boehringer, Hans. "Liturgical Minimalism—A Second Look." *Response* 11 (1971) 89–95.

Bouley, Alan. *From Freedom to Formula.* Washington, D.C.: The Catholic University of America Press, 1981.

Bouyer, Louis. *Eucharist.* Notre Dame: University of Notre Dame Press, 1968.

_____. *Introduction to Spirituality.* Collegeville: The Liturgical Press, 1961.

_____. *Liturgical Piety.* Notre Dame: University of Notre Dame Press, 1955.

_____. *Liturgy and Architecture.* Notre Dame: University of Notre Dame Press, 1967.

_____. *Rite & Man.* Notre Dame: University of Notre Dame Press, 1963.

_____. *Spirit and the Forms of Protestantism.* Maryland: The Newman Press, 1957.

_____. "The Two Economies of Divine Government," in *God and His Creation,* ed. A. M. Henry, O.P. Chicago: Fides Publishers Association, 1955.

_____. *The Meaning of the Monastic Life.* London: Burns & Oates, 1955.

Bradshaw, Paul F. *Daily Prayer in the Early Church.* New York: Oxford University Press, 1982.

Brand, Eugene. "Ceremonial Forms and Contemporary Life." *Response* 8 (1966) 91–99.

Braso, Gabriel M. *Liturgy and Spirituality.* Collegeville: The Liturgical Press, 1971.

Brilioth, Yngve. *Eucharistic Faith and Practice, Evangelical and Catholic.* London: S.P.C.K., 1930.

Brown, Peter. *The Cult of the Saints.* Chicago: The University of Chicago Press, 1981.

_____. *The World of Late Antiquity.* London: Harcourt Brace Jovanovich, Inc., 1971.

_____. "Eastern and Western Christendom in Late Antiquity: A Parting of the Ways." *Studies in Church History,* ed. Derek Baker. Oxford: Basil Blackwell, 1976.

Brunner, Peter. "Die Bedeutung des Altars fur den Gottesdiest der christlichen Kirche." *Kerygma und Dogma* 20 (1974) 218–244.

_____. "Divine Service in the Church." *Scottish Journal of Theology* 7 (1954) 270–283.

_____. "Eschata." *Dialogue* 15 (Spring 1976) 131–140.

_____. "Salvation and the Office of the Ministry." *Lutheran Quarterly* 15 (May 1963) 99–117.

_____. "Theologie des Gottesdienstes?" *Kerygma und Dogma* 22 (April/June 1976) 96–121.

_____. *Worship in the Name of Jesus.* St. Louis: Concordia Publishing House, 1968.

Burghardt, Walter J. "A Theologian's Challenge to Liturgy." *Theological Studies* 35 (1974) 233–248.

Burkhart, John E. *Worship: A Searching Examination of the Liturgical Experience.* Philadelphia: The Westminster Press, 1982.

Cabasilas, Nicholas. *A Commentary on the Divine Liturgy.* London: S.P.C.K., 1960.

_____. *The Life in Christ.* New York: St. Vladimir's Seminary Press, 1974.

Casel, Odo. *The Mystery of Christian Worship and Other Writings.* Maryland: The Newman Press, 1962.

Childs, Brevard. *Memory and Tradition in Israel.* London: SCM Press, 1962.

Collins, Mary. "Liturgical Methodology and the Cultural Evolution of Worship in the United States." *Worship* 49 (1975) 85–106.

Corbon, Jean. *The Wellspring of Worship.* New York: Paulist Press, 1988.

Crichton, J. D. *Christian Celebration: The Sacraments.* London: Geoffrey Chapman, 1973.

Cullmann, Oscar. *Early Christian Worship.* London: SCM Press Ltd., 1953.

Cullmann, Oscar and Leenhardt, F. J. *Essays on the Lord's Supper.* Atlanta: John Knox Press, 1958.

Cullmann, Oscar. *Baptism in the New Testament.* London: SCM Press, 1950.

Dalmais, Irenee-Henri. *Eastern Liturgies.* New York: Hawthorn Books, 1960.

Daly, Robert J. *The Origins of the Christian Doctrine of Sacrifice.* Philadelphia: Fortress Press, 1978.

Daniélou, Jean. *The Bible and the Liturgy.* Notre Dame: University of Notre Dame Press, 1956.

_____. *From Shadows to Reality.* London: Burns & Oates, 1960.

Davies, J. G. *The Architectural Setting of Baptism.* London: Barrie and Rockliff, 1962.

_____. "The Disintegration of the Christian Initiation Rite." *Theology* 50 (November 1947) 407–412.

_____. ed. *The New Westminster Dictionary of Liturgy and Worship.* Philadelphia: The Westminster Press, 1986.

Debuyst, Frederic. *Modern Architecture and Christian Celebration.* London: Lutterworth Press, 1968.

Deiss, Lucien. *God's Word and God's People.* Collegeville: The Liturgical Press, 1976.

_____. *Early Sources of the Liturgy.* Collegeville: The Liturgical Press, 1967.

de Lubac, Henri. *Catholicism: Christ and the Common Destiny of Man.* San Francisco: Ignatius Press, 1988.

Delumeau, Jean. *Catholicism between Luther and Voltaire: A New View of the Counter-Reformation.* Philadelphia: Westminster Press, 1977.

Dix, Gregory. *The Shape of the Liturgy.* London: Dacre Press, 1945.

Douglas, Mary. *Natural Symbols.* New York: Random House, 1973.

Dugmore, C. W. *The Influence of the Synagogue Upon the Divine Office.* London: Oxford University Press, 1944.

Ebeling, Gerhard. *Luther, An Introduction to His Thought.* Philadelphia: Fortress Press, 1970.

Eisenhofer, Ludwig and Lechner, Joseph. *The Liturgy of the Roman Rite.* London: Nelson, 1953.

Elert, Werner. *The Structure of Lutheranism.* St. Louis: Concordia Publishing House, 1962.

Emminghaus, Johannes. *The Eucharist: Essence, Form, Celebration.* Collegeville: The Liturgical Press, 1978.

Erickson, Craig Douglas. *Participating in Worship: History, Theory and Practice.* Louisville: Westminster/John Knox Press, 1989.

*Eucharistic Theology Then and Now.* London: S.P.C.K., 1968.

Evdokimov, Paul. *The Sacrament of Love.* New York: St. Vladimir's Seminary Press, 1985.

Fink, Peter. "Three Languages of Christian Sacraments." *Worship* 52 (1978) 561–575.

_____. "Towards a Liturgical Theology." *Worship* 47 (1973) 601–609.

Fisch, Thomas, ed. *Liturgy and Tradition.* New York: St. Vladimir's Seminary Press, 1990.

Fisher, J. D. C. *Christian Initiation: Baptism in the Medieval West.* London: S.P.C.K., 1965.

FitzGerald, Thomas. "The Orthodox Rite of Christian Initiation." *St. Vladimir's Theological Quarterly* 32 (1988) 309–328.

Forde, Gerhard and Jenson, Robert. "A 'Great Thanksgiving' for Lutherans?" *Response* 15 (1975) 49–62.

Gallen, John, ed. *Christians at Prayer.* Notre Dame: University of Notre Dame Press, 1977.

Gingras, George, ed. *Egeria: Diary of a Pilgrimage.* New York: Newman Press, 1970.

Grabar, Andre. *Christian Iconography: A Study of Its Origins.* New Jersey: Princeton University Press, 1968.

Grelot, P., and Pierron, J. *The Paschal Feast in the Bible.* Baltimore: Helicon, 1966.

Guardini, Romano. *The Church and the Catholic and The Spirit of the Liturgy.* New York: Sheed & Ward, 1953.

Hahn, Ferdinand. *The Worship of the Early Church.* Philadelphia: Fortress Press, 1973.

_____. "Zum Stand der Erforschung des urchristlichen Herrenmahls." *Evangelische Theologie* 35 (1975) 553–563.

Hatchett, Marion J. *Sanctifying Life, Time and Space.* New York: The Seabury Press, 1976.

Holmer, Paul. *The Grammar of Faith*. New York: Harper & Row, 1978.

_____. "About Liturgy and Its Logic." *Worship* 50 (January 1976) 18–28.

Holmes, Urban T. "Theology and Religious Renewal." *Anglican Theological Review* 62 (1980) 3–19.

_____. "Liminality and Liturgy." *Worship* 47 (1973) 386–397.

Hopko, Thomas. "Criteria of Truth in Orthodox Theology." *St. Vladimir's Theological Quarterly* 15 (1971) 121–129.

Hovda, Robert. *Dry Bones*. Washington, D.C.: The Liturgical Conference, 1973.

Huizinga, J. *Homo Ludens: A Study of the Play-Element in Culture*. Boston: The Beacon Press, 1950.

Idelsohn, A. Z. *Jewish Liturgy and Its Development*. New York: Schocken Books, 1960.

Jasper, R. C. D., and Cuming, G. J. *Prayers of the Eucharist Early & Reformed*. London: Collins Publishers, 1975.

Jenson, Robert. *Visible Words: The Interpretation and Practice of Christian Sacraments*. Philadelphia: Fortress Press, 1978.

Jeremias, Joachim. *The Eucharistic Words of Jesus*. Philadelphia: Fortress Press, 1966.

Jordahl, Leigh D. "Liturgy and Ceremony: Catholic-Protestant Cross Currents." *Worship* 44 (1970) 171–181.

Jones, Wainwright and Yarnold, eds. *The Study of Liturgy*. New York: Oxford University Press, 1978.

_____. *The Study of Spirituality*. New York: Oxford University Press, 1986.

Jungmann, Joseph. *Announcing the Word of God*. New York: Herder & Herder, 1967.

_____. *Christian Prayer Through the Centuries*. New York: Paulist Press, 1978.

_____. *The Early Liturgy to the Time of Gregory the Great*. Notre Dame: University of Notre Dame Press, 1959.

_____. *The Mass, An Historical, Theological and Pastoral Survey*. Collegeville: The Liturgical Press, 1976.

_____. *The Mass of the Roman Rite, Its Origins and Development*. Westminster: Christian Classics, 1951.

_____. *The Place of Christ in Liturgical Prayer*. London: Geoffrey Chapman, 1965.

Kavanagh, Aidan. *On Liturgical Theology*. New York: Pueblo Publishing Company, 1984.

_____. *Elements of Rite: A Handbook of Liturgical Style*. New York: Pueblo Publishing Company, 1982.

_____. *Confirmation: Origins and Reform*. New York: Pueblo Publishing Company, 1988.

_____. *The Shape of Baptism: The Rite of Christian Initiation*. New York: Pueblo Publishing Company, 1978.

_____. "Response: Primary Theology and Liturgical Act." *Worship* 57 (1983) 321–324.

_____. "Thoughts on the Roman Anaphora." *Worship* 39 (1965) 515–529.

_____. "How Rite Develops." *Worship* 41 (1967) 334–347.

Keifer, Ralph A. "Liturgical Text as Primary Source for Eucharistic Theology." *Worship* 51 (1978) 186–196.

Kelly, J. N. D. *Early Christian Doctrines*. New York: Harper & Row, 1960.

Kilmartin, Edward. *Christian Liturgy: Theology and Practice*. Kansas City: Sheed & Ward, 1988.

_____. "Sacramental Theology: The Eucharist in Recent Literature." *Theological Studies* 32 (1971) 233–277.

Klauser, Theodor. *A Short History of the Western Liturgy*. New York: Oxford University Press, 1979.

Lampe, G. W. H. *The Seal of the Spirit*. New York: Longmans, Green & Co., 1951.

Lathrop, Gordon W. "A Rebirth of Images: On the Use of the Bible in Liturgy." *Worship* 58 (1984) 291–304.

_____. "Pastoral Liturgical Theology and the Lutheran Book of Worship: A Reconnaissance." *Dialog* 18 (1978) 108–113.

_____. "The Prayers of Jesus and the Great Prayer of the Church." *The Lutheran Quarterly* 26 (1974) 158–175.

Ledogar, Robert J. "The Eucharistic Prayer and the Gifts over Which it is Spoken." *Worship* 41 (1967) 578–596.

Lindbeck, George. *The Nature of Doctrine*. Philadelphia: The Westminster Press, 1984.

Lindemann, Herbert. "Contemporary Worship: A Report from the Lutherans." *Worship* 48 (1974) 153–163.

*The Liturgy Documents: A Parish Resource.* Chicago: Liturgy Training Publications, New York: 1985.

*The Living God, A Catechism.* New York: St. Vladimir's Seminary Press, 1989.

Lossky, Vladimir. *The Mystical Theology of the Eastern Church.* New York: St. Vladimir's Seminary Press, 1976.

_____. *Orthodox Theology, An Introduction.* New York: St. Vladimir's Seminary Press, 1978.

_____. *In the Image and Likeness of God.* New York: St. Vladimir's Seminary Press, 1974.

_____. *The Vision of God.* New York: St. Vladimir's Seminary Press, 1983.

Luther, Martin. *Luther's Works* vol. 36: Word and Sacrament. Philadelphia: Fortress Press, 1959.

*Lutherans and Catholics in Dialogue IV: Eucharist and Ministry.* Washington, D.C.: US Catholic Conference, 1970.

Macy, Gary. *The Theologies of the Eucharist in the Early Scholastic Period.* Oxford: Clarendon Press, 1984.

*Made, Not Born.* The Murphy Center for Liturgical Research. Notre Dame: University of Notre Dame Press, 1976.

Mantzaridis, Georgios. *The Deification of Man.* New York: St. Vladimir's Seminary Press, 1984.

Martimort, A. G., ed. *Introduction to the Liturgy.* New York: Desclee Company, 1968.

_____. ed. *The Eucharist.* Ireland: Irish University Press, 1973.

_____. ed. *The Church at Prayer: New Edition* 4 vol. Collegeville: The Liturgical Press, 1987.

Martos, Joseph. *Doors to the Sacred.* New York: Image Books, 1982.

Marxsen, Willi. *The Lord's Supper as a Christological Problem.* Philadelphia: Fortress Press, 1970.

Mathews, Thomas F. *The Early Churches of Constantinople: Architecture and Liturgy.* University Park: Pennsylvania State University Press, 1971.

Mazza, Enrico. *Mystagogy.* New York: Pueblo Publishing Co., 1989.

Meyendorff, John. *Christ in Eastern Christian Thought.* New York: St. Vladimir's Seminary Press, 1975.

_____. *Byzantine Theology, Historical Trends and Doctrinal Themes.* New York: Fordham University Press, 1974.

_____. *A Study of Gregory Palamas.* New York: St. Vladimir's Seminary Press, 1964.

_____. *Catholicity and the Church.* New York: St. Vladimir's Seminary Press, 1983.

_____. *Living Tradition.* New York: St. Vladimir's Seminary Press, 1978.

_____. *The Byzantine Legacy in the Orthodox Church.* New York: St. Vladimir's Seminary Press, 1982.

Meyendorff, Paul, ed. *St. Germanus of Constantinople On the Divine Liturgy.* New York: St. Vladimir's Seminary Press, 1984.

Mitchell, Nathan. *Cult and Controversy: The Worship of the Eucharist Outside Mass.* New York: Pueblo Publishing Company, 1982.

Mitchell, Leonel. *Baptismal Anointing.* Notre Dame: University of Notre Dame Press, 1966.

_____. *The Meaning of Ritual.* New York: Paulist Press, 1977.

_____. "Response: Liturgy and Theology." *Worship* 57 (1983) 324–325.

Moule, C. F. D. *Worship in the New Testament.* England: Grove Books, 1977.

Newman, David R. "Observations on Method in Liturgical Theology." *Worship* 57 (1983) 377–384.

Oesterley, W. O. E. *The Jewish Background of the Liturgy.* Massachusetts: Peter Smith, 1965.

Olson, Oliver K. "Luther's 'Catholic' Minimum." *Response* 11 (1970) 17–98.

_____. "The St. Olaf–St. John's Interim." *Response* 9 (1968) 167–171.

Ostrogorsky, George. *History of the Byzantine State.* New Jersey: Rutgers University Press, 1969.

Ouspensky, Leonid. *Theology of the Icon.* New York: St. Vladimir's Seminary Press, 1978.

_____. "Iconography of the Descent of the Holy Spirit." *St. Vladimir's Theological Quarterly* 31 (1987) 309–348.

Ozolin, Nicholas. "The Theology of the Icon." *St. Vladimir's Theological Quarterly* 31 (1987) 297–308.

Pascoe, Louis B. *Jean Gerson: Principles of Church Reform*. Leiden: E. J. Brill, 1973.

Pelikan, Jaroslav. *Spirit Versus Structure: Luther and the Institutions of the Church*. New York: Harper & Row, 1968.

Pieper, Josef. *In Tune with the World, A Theory of Festivity*. Chicago: Franciscan Herald Press, 1965.

_____. *Leisure, the Basis of Culture*. New York: The New American Library, 1952.

Power, David N. *Unsearchable Riches: The Symbolic Nature of Liturgy*. New York: Pueblo Publishing Company, 1984.

_____. *The Sacrifice We Offer: The Tridentine Dogma and Its Reinterpretation*. New York: Crossroad, 1987.

_____. *Gifts that Differ: Lay Ministries Established and Unestablished*. New York: Pueblo Publishing Company, 1980.

_____. "Response: Liturgy, Memory and the Absence of God." *Worship* 57 (1983) 326–329.

_____. "Cult to Culture: The Liturgical Foundation of Theology." *Worship* 54 (1980) 482–494.

_____. "Unripe Grapes: The Critical Function of Liturgical Theology." *Worship* 52 (1978) 366–399.

Power, David and Luis Maldonado, eds. *Liturgy and Human Passage*. New York: The Seabury Press, 1979.

Power, David and Herman Schmidt, eds. *Liturgical Experience of Faith*. New York: Herder & Herder, 1973.

Powers, Joseph M. *Eucharistic Theology*. New York: The Seabury Press, 1967.

Prenter, Regin. *Theologie und Gottesdienst*. Denmark: Vandenhoeck & Ruprecht, 1977.

_____. *Spiritus Creator*. Philadelphia: Fortress Press, 1953.

_____. *Creation and Redemption*. Philadelphia: Fortress Press, 1968.

_____. "Tradition and Renewal in the Liturgy." *Response* 8 (1966) 5–11.

_____. "Worship and Creation." *Studia Liturgica* 2 (1963) 82–95.

_____. "The Doctrine of the Real Presence." *The Lutheran Quarterly* 3 (1951) 156–166.

_____. "Secularization as a Problem for Christian Dogmatics." *Lutheran World* 13 (1966) 357–365.

Quenot, Michel. *The Icon: Window on the Kingdom*. New York: St. Vladimir's Seminary Press, 1991.

Rahner, Hugo. *Man At Play*. New York: Herder & Herder, 1972.

_____. "The Christian Mysteries & the Pagan Mysteries," in *The Mysteries, Papers from the Eranos Yearbooks*. New York: Pantheon Books, 1955.

Reed, Luther D. *The Lutheran Liturgy*. Philadelphia: Fortress Press, 1947.

Regan, Patrick. "The Fifty Days and the Fiftieth Day." *Worship* 55 (1981) 194–218.

Riley, Hugh M. *Christian Initiation*. Washington, D.C.: The Catholic University of America Press, 1974.

Roguet, A.-M. *The Liturgy of the Hours*. Collegeville: The Liturgical Press, 1971.

_____. *Christ Acts Through the Sacraments*. Collegeville: The Liturgical Press, 1954.

*Roles in the Liturgical Assembly*, New York: Pueblo Publishing Company, 1981.

Rordorf, Willy. *The Eucharist of the Early Christians*. New York: Pueblo Publishing Company, 1978.

_____. *Sunday*. London: SCM Press, 1968.

Rorem, Paul. *The Medieval Development of Liturgical Symbolism*. Grove Liturgical Study 47, Nottingham: Grove Books, 1986.

Roth, Robert. "Work, Leisure, and Worship." *Response* 17 (1977) 21–32.

_____. *Story and Reality*. Michigan: Eerdmans Publishing, 1973.

_____. *The Theater of God: Story in Christian Doctrines*. Philadelphia: Fortress Press, 1985.

Rouillard, Philippe. "From Human Meal to Christian Eucharist." *Worship* 52 (1978) 425–439.

Rowley, H. H. *Worship in Ancient Israel: Its Forms and Meaning*. London: S.P.C.K., 1967.

Rutherford, Richard. *The Death of a Christian: The Rite of Funerals.* New York: Pueblo Publishing Company, 1980.

Salaville, Severien. *An Introduction to the Study of Eastern Liturgies.* London: Sands & Co., 1938.

Saliers, Don. *The Soul in Paraphrase.* New York: The Seabury Press, 1980.

_____. "Language in the Liturgy: Where Angels Fear to Tread." *Worship* 52 (1978) 482–488.

_____. "Prayer and the Doctrine of God in Contemporary Theology." *Interpretation* 30 (1980) 265–278.

_____. "On the 'Crisis' of Liturgical Language." *Worship* 44 (1970) 399–411.

_____. "Theology and Prayer: Some Conceptual Reminders." *Worship* 48 (1974) 230–235.

Sasse, Hermann. *This is My Body.* Adelaide S.A.: Lutheran Publishing House, 1959.

Schillebeeckx, E. *Christ the Sacrament of the Encounter with God.* New York: Sheed & Ward, 1963.

_____. *The Eucharist.* New York: Sheed & Ward, 1968.

_____. "Transubstantiation, Transfinalization, Transignification." *Worship* 40 (1966) 324–338.

Schlink, Edmund. *The Doctrine of Baptism.* St. Louis: Concordia Publishing House, 1972.

_____. *Theology of the Lutheran Confessions.* Philadelphia: Fortress Press, 1961.

_____. *The Coming Christ and the Coming Church.* Philadelphia: Fortress Press, 1967.

Schmemann, Alexander. *Church, World, Mission.* New York: St. Vladimir's Seminary Press, 1979.

_____. *The Eucharist.* New York: St. Vladimir's Seminary Press, 1988.

_____. *For the Life of the World.* New York: St. Vladimir's Seminary Press, 1973.

_____. *Great Lent, Journey to Pascha.* New York: St. Vladimir's Seminary Press, 1974.

_____. *Historical Road of Eastern Orthodoxy.* New York: St. Vladimir's Seminary Press, 1977.

_____. *Introduction to Liturgical Theology*. New York: St. Vladimir's Seminary Press, 1966.

_____. *Liturgy and Life: Christian Development Through Liturgical Experience*. New York: Department of Religious Education, OCA, 1974.

_____. *Of Water and the Spirit*. New York: St. Vladimir's Seminary Press, 1974.

_____. "The Problem of the Church's Presence in the World of Orthodox Consciousness." *St. Vladimir's Theological Quarterly* 21 (1977) 3–17.

_____. "Theology and Liturgical Tradition." in *Worship in Scripture and Tradition* ed. M. Shepherd, 165–178.

_____. "Liturgy and Theology." *The Greek Orthodox Theological Review* 17 (1972) 86–100.

_____. "Liturgical Theology, Theology of Liturgy, and Liturgical Reform." *St. Vladimir's Theological Quarterly* 13 (1969) 217–224.

_____. "Prayer, Liturgy and Renewal." *The Greek Orthodox Theological Review* 16 (1969) 7–16.

_____. "Theology and Eucharist." *St. Vladimir's Theological Quarterly* 5 (1961) 10–23.

Schmidt, Herman. "Language and its Function in Christian Worship." *Studia Liturgica* 8 (1971) 1–19.

Schoonenberg, Piet. "Presence and the Eucharistic Presence." *Cross Currents* Winter (1967) 39–54.

Schweizer, Eduard. *The Lord's Supper According to the New Testament*. Philadelphia: Fortress Press, 1967.

Schulz, Hans-Joachim. *The Byzantine Liturgy*. New York: Pueblo Publishing Company, 1986.

Scott, R. Taylor. "The Likelihood of Liturgy." *Anglican Theological Review* 57 (1980) 103–120.

Searle, Mark, ed. *Sunday Morning: A Time for Worship*. Collegeville: The Liturgical Press, 1982.

Seasoltz, R. Kevin. *Living Bread, Saving Cup*. Collegeville: The Liturgical Press, 1982.

Senn, Frank C. *Christian Worship and Its Cultural Setting*. Philadelphia: Fortress Press, 1983.

_____. "Response: The Relation Between Theology and Liturgy." *Worship* 57 (1983) 329–332.

_____. "Contemporary Liturgical Theology." *Response* 14 (1974) 10–16.

_____. "Review of *Lutheran Book of Worship*." *Dialog* 18 (1979) 301–305.

_____. "Liturgia Svecanae Ecclesiae: An Attempt at Eucharistic Restoration during the Swedish Reformation." *Studia Liturgica* 14 (1980/81) 20–36.

Shaughnessy, James D. *The Roots of Ritual*. Michigan: Eerdmans Publishing Company, 1973.

Shepherd, Massey. *Worship in Scripture and Tradition*. New York: Oxford University Press, 1963.

Srawley, J. H. *The Early History of the Liturgy*. London: Cambridge University Press, 1957.

Staniloae, Dumitru. *Theology and the Church*. New York: St. Vladimir's Seminary Press, 1980.

Stevenson, Kenneth. *Eucharist and Offering*. New York: Pueblo Publishing Company, 1986.

Stevick, Daniel B. "The Language of Prayer" *Worship* 52 (1978) 542–560.

Taft, Robert. *The Great Entrance*. Rome: Pont. Institutum Studiorum Orientalium, 1978.

_____. *Beyond East and West: Problems in Liturgical Understanding*. Washington, D.C.: The Pastoral Press, 1984.

_____. *The Liturgy of the Hours in East and West*. Collegeville: The Liturgical Press, 1986.

_____. "The Liturgy of the Great Church." *Dumbarton Oaks Papers* 34/35 (1980–1981) 47–75.

_____. "Historicism Revisited." *Studia Liturgica* 14 (1982) 97–107.

_____. "The Structural Analysis of Liturgical Units: An Essay in Methodology." *Worship* 52 (1978) 314–328.

_____. "How Liturgies Grow: The Evolution of the Byzantine 'Divine Liturgy'." *Orientalia Christiana Periodica* 43 (1977) 355–378.

_____. "Liturgy as Theology." *Worship* 56 (1982) 113–116.

_____. "Ex Oriente Lux? Some Reflections on Eucharistic Concelebration." *Worship* 54 (1980) 308–325.

_____. "The Liturgical Year: Studies, Prospects, Reflections." *Worship* 55 (1981) 2–23.

Talley, Thomas J. *The Origins of the Liturgical Year.* New York: Pueblo Publishing Company, 1986.

_____. *Worship: Reforming Tradition.* Washington, D.C.: The Pastoral Press, 1990.

_____. "From Berakah to Eucharistia: A Reopening Question." *Worship* 50 (1967) 115–136.

Tappert, Theodore G., ed. *The Book of Concord.* Philadelphia: Fortress Press, 1959.

Taylor, Michael J., ed. *The Sacraments.* New York: Alba House, 1981.

Tegels, Aelred. "A Viable Structure." *Response* 11 (1970) 32–36.

*Thinking about the Eucharist,* Essays by the Archbishops' Commission on Christian Doctrine. London: SCM Press, 1972.

Thompson, Bard. *Liturgies of the Western Church.* New York: Collins, 1961.

Thurian, Max. *The Eucharistic Memorial,* 2 vols. Richmond: John Knox Press, 1960.

_____. "The Present Aims of the Liturgical Movement." *Studia Liturgica* 3 (1964) 107–114.

Toporoski, Richard. "The Language of Worship." *Worship* 52 (1978) 489–508.

Turner, Victor. *The Ritual Process.* New York: Cornell University Press, 1969.

Ugolnik, Anthony. *The Illuminating Icon.* Grand Rapids: Eerdmans Publishing Company, 1989.

Vagaggini, Cipriano. *The Canon of the Mass and Liturgical Reform.* New York: Alba House, 1967.

Vajta, Vilmos. *Luther on Worship.* Philadelphia: Muhlenberg Press, 1958.

_____. "Creation and Worship." *Studia Liturgica* 2 (1963) 29–46.

van Olst, E. H. *The Bible and Liturgy.* Michigan: Eerdmans Publishing, 1991.

Vasiliev, A. A. *History of the Byzantine Empire.* Wisconsin: University of Wisconsin Press, 1952.

Verghese, Paul. *The Joy of Freedom, Eastern Worship and Modern Man.* London: Lutterworth Press.

Volz, Carl. "Lex Orandi, Lex Credendi." *Response* 14 (1974) 17–22.

_____. "Concepts of Salvation in Early Christian Worship." *Dialog* 18 (1979) 258–264.

von Allmen, J.-J. *Worship: Its Theology and Practice.* New York: Oxford University Press, 1965.

_____. "Worship and the Holy Spirit." *Studia Liturgica* 3 (1963) 124–135.

_____. "A Short Theology of the Place of Worship." *Studia Liturgica* 3 (1964) 155–171.

Vonier, Anscar. A Key to the Doctrine of the Eucharist. Maryland: The Newman Press, 1948.

Wainwright, Geoffrey and Wiebe Vos, eds. *Liturgical Time.* Rotterdam: Liturgical Ecumenical Center Trust, 1982.

Wainwright, Geoffrey. *Eucharist and Eschatology.* London: Epworth Press, 1971.

_____. *Doxology: The Praise of God in Worship, Doctrine, and Life.* New York: Oxford University Press, 1980.

_____. "A Language in Which We Speak to God." *Worship* 57 (1983) 307–321.

_____. "Eucharist and/as Ethics." *Worship* 62 (1988) 123–137.

_____. "Review of *On Liturgical Theology*." *Worship* 61 (1987) 183–86.

Wakefield, Gordon, ed. *The Westminster Dictionary of Christian Spirituality.* Philadelphia: The Westminster Press, 1983.

Ware, Timothy. *The Orthodox Church.* England: Penguin Books, 1963.

Ware, Kallistos. *The Orthodox Way.* New York: St. Vladimir's Seminary Press, 1986.

Wegman, Herman. *Christian Worship in East and West.* New York: Pueblo Publishing Company, 1985.

White, James F. *Introduction to Christian Worship.* Nashville: Abingdon Press, 1980.

_____. *Sacraments as God's Self-Giving.* Nashville: Abingdon Press, 1983.

_____. *Protestant Worship, Traditions in Transition.* Louisville: Westminster/John Knox Press, 1989.

_____. "Traditions of Protestant Worship." *Worship* 49 (1975) 272–283.

Wilken, Robert L. "Liturgical Piety and the Doctrine of the Trinity." *Dialog* 18 (1978) 114–120.

Willimon, William H. *The Service of God: How Worship and Ethics are Related*. Nashville: Abingdon Press, 1983.

Wingren, Gustaf. *Gospel and Church*. London: Oliver & Boyd, 1964.

_____. *Luther on Vocation*. Philadelphia: Muhlenberg Press, 1957.

_____. *The Living Word*. Philadelphia: Fortress Press, 1960.

Wittgenstein, Ludwig. *Culture and Value*. Chicago: University of Chicago Press, 1980.

_____. *On Certainty*. New York: Harper Torch Books, 1969.

_____. *Philosophical Investigations*. New York: The Macmillan Company, 1958.

Wolterstorff, Nicholas. "Liturgy, Justice, and Holiness." *The Reformed Journal* 39, Issue 12 (Dec 1989) 12–20.

World Council of Churches, *Baptism, Eucharist and Ministry*. Geneva: World Council of Churches, 1982.

Yarnold, Edward. *The Awe Inspiring Rites of Initiation*. Maryland: Christian Classics, 1971.

Zhivov, V. M. "The Mystagogia of Maximus the Confessor and the Development of the Byzantine Theory of the Image." *St. Vladimir's Theological Quarterly* 31 (1987) 349–376.

# Index

creed, 121
cross, 41, 89
crucifixion, 79
cult, 45, 62, 80, 153–54, 161, 166–68, 186, 203, 215, 224, 226, 280–81, 297
cult of saints, 212ff.
cultural-linguistic theory of religion, 299
Cyprian, 125

**D**

deacons, 235, 250–51, 254, 268, 273
death, 271
democracy, pseudo, 264
*Deutsche Messe*, 101, 129
devil, 35, 58, 271
*diakonia*, 226
dichotomy, 13, 148
Dionysius, 229–32, 243–44, 248–49
discipleship, 278
discos, 250–51
disunity, 117
Divine Liturgy, 220, 223, 226, 234, 257–58, 263, 269, 272, 280, 290
divinity school, 219
divine-human love, 271
Dix, Gregory, 197, 218, 238
doctrine, 12, 71, 90, 97, 99, 103, 105, 112, 120, 130, 140, 197, 220, 257, 262, 270, 298, 299
  as guard over worship, 125–127, 131
  doctrinal formulae, 298
dogma & Tradition, 295, 298
dogmatics, 23–26, 31, 37, 72–73, 76–78, 86, 88, 90, 97, 130, 160, 183, 198, 217, 285
dogmatic
  agnosticism, 24
  prolegomena, 23, 25, 33
dominical liturgy, 27
Donatists, 125
doxological acclamation, 96
doxological theology, 107, 132
doxology, 102, 130, 182, 195, 200, 207, 287
dramatization, 261
dramatic reenactment, 278
dynamic monarchianism, 110

# E

gospel book, 262
*Gottesdienst* (worship service), 97, 99, 135
grace, 194, 217, 269
grammar, 19, 108, 203, 208, 210, 222, 252, 289, 294–95, 297, 299–302
Great Entrance, 191, 250, 267, 269
Great Litany, 260–61, 291
Gregory of Nazianzus, 302
Gregory of Nyssa, 219, 223
Gregory of Thaumaturgus, 241
Guardini, Romano, 218

**H**
Hagia Sophia, 231, 241, 244
Hahn, Ferdinand, 186, 194
handlaying, 292
*he kyriake hemera*, 225
heavenly
    altar, 253
    Christ, 278
    creatures, 82
    hierarchy, 230
    liturgy, 225, 240, 268
    priesthood, 235, 237
    offering, 253
heaven on earth, 281
Hellenism, 112
hermeneutics, 120, 126, 205–06
High Priest, Christ, 39–40, 235
hierarchy, 264
hieratic duties, 288
*historia*, 245, 248
historical
    analysis, 170–71
    community, 105, 135
    Jesus, 242, 249, 251
    reduction, 276–77
historicizing, 252
hocus pocus, 280, 282
Holmer, Paul, 201, 207
Holy Communion, 29, 36, 84, 89–92, 98, 101, 191
Holy Gifts, 247, 279
Holy Oblation, 272

Holy Spirit, 24, 26, 34, 41, 56–57, 83, 92, 113–114, 152, 164, 256, 263, 271, 279, 282, 292, 295–96
holy table, 250–51
Holy Week, 238
homily, 200, 262, 296
*homo adorans*, 158, 226, 269, 274
*homo religiosus*, 215
*homologia*, 30, 94
*homoousion*, 110, 219
horizontal projections, 295
Hovda, Robert, 189
Huizinga, J., 14
Hume, David, 213ff.
Hunter, A. M., 111
Hussites, 128
hymnody, 87, 122
hypostatized theology, 73
hypostatic church, 199

I
icon, 200, 220, 232, 243, 270, 295–96
  Eucharist is not icon, 246
  image of person, not nature, 247
  rank of images, 244
iconoclasm, 240, 242–48, 285
iconoclastic Council of 754, 240
iconophiles, 243
iconography, 232, 258
iconostasis, 254, 261–62
idolatry, 44, 51, 54, 58, 62, 80
identity, 121
Ignatius, 125, 225
illocutionary speech, 137–39
image of God, 107–108
imminent trinitarianism, 114
incarnation, 55, 89, 92, 237, 242, 247–49, 269
incense, 231, 250–51, 291
individualism, 45, 117, 176, 283
Innocent I, Pope, 292
institution (linguistic), 138
institution narrative, 279
instrumental error, 185

old Adam, 61
Old Testament, 116, 118, 119, 253–54, 283, 291
omnipresence of God, 54
*On the Freedom of a Christian,* 64
Optatus of Melevis, 125
*opus operatum, opus operantis,* 50
ordination, 57, 113, 115, 264
Ordo, 150, 169, 171, 173, 176–79, 194, 277, 283, 293, 301–02
*ordo salutis,* 33
organic definition, 144, 181, 211
Origen, 110, 226, 229
original sin, 158
orthodox, 298, 302
Ouspensky, Leonid, 246–48, 298

**P**
Palestine, 239
Pantocrator, 251
paradise, 274–75
parousia, 34, 199, 237, 254–55, 259
Pasch, 236
paschal grammar, 221
paschal mystery, 290
passage, 159, 166, 260
Passion, 239
passivity of persons, 59, 62
Patriarch of Constantinople, 239, 242
patristic tradition, 145–46, 240
Paul of Samosata, 110
pedagogical school of worship, 46, 59
penitents, 115
Pentecost, 81, 302
performativity of liturgical language, 136
personal salvation, 263
phases of salvation, four, 236
phelonia, 250
phenomenology of ritual, 116
philanthropy, 268
piety, 174, 176, 187, 263
pietism, 287
pilgrims, 238, 279
Pius XII, Pope, 123, 134, 141

proskomide, 250, 265, 268–69
Prosper of Aquitaine, 124, 141, 198
Protestant reform of worship, 128–29, 276
prothesis, 244
prototype, 246, 248
psalmody, 87
pulpit, 53
Puritan, 46
puritanism, 287


## R

rationalism, 287, 293
real presence, 37, 40, 53, 56, 89–90, 163–64, 257, 276
realistic representation
  in iconography, 243
  in liturgy, 244–45
*redditio symboli,* 121
*regula fidei,* 125
reductionism, 181, 185
Reformation, 42, 97, 100–101, 112, 128, 206
regeneration, 34
religion, 158, 169, 266, 299
religious ritual, 116, 301
religious history, 214
remembrance, 256, 270, 275, 277, 282
resurrection, 33, 52, 125, 157, 224, 235, 253–54, 262, 290
revelation, 26, 45, 54, 76, 201, 249, 252, 289, 295
rhetoric, classic, 234
Ricoeur, Paul, 205
righteousness, 48, 51, 206
Riley, Hugh, 229
rite, 19, 27, 69, 116, 141, 162, 184–85, 193, 210, 255, 284, 290–91
ritual, 106, 152, 160, 203, 225, 253, 287
  logistics, 195, 216
  celebration, 205
  grammar, 210
  words, 206
ritualism, 28, 186, 216, 293
Roman Canon, 101, 110
rubrics, 20, 67–68, 151, 177, 181, 265, 284, 301
ruled acts, 222, 301–02

## S

Sabbath, 109, 157, 174, 189
sacraments, 110, 159, 165, 223, 230, 257
  as *sui generis*, 163–64
  seven, 280
Sacrament of
  Anaphora, 256, 272–273, 278
  Assembly, 256–57, 278
  Communion, 256, 283–84
  Entrance, 256, 260–61, 279
  the Faithful, 256, 264–65
  the Holy Spirit, 279–82
  the Kingdom, 256, 258–60, 278
  Offering, 256, 265–270, 278
  Remembrance, 256, 275–78, 278
  Thanksgiving, 256, 274–75, 278
  Unity, 256, 271–72, 278
  the Word, 256, 261–63
sacramentology, 71, 165, 257
sacred-profane, 157–58, 189–90, 226, 281, 285
sacred topography, 238
sacrifice, 27, 29, 32–42, 49, 50, 61, 92, 191, 265–67, 276, 278
  repetition of, 50, 266
  & sacrament, 85, 88–89, 96, 270, 276
  self-sacrifice, 267
*sacrificium*, 43, 46, 51, 70
saints, 114, 244, 269
Saliers, Don, 202
salvation, 90, 110, 156, 254, 264, 273–74
salvation-history symbolism, 239, 270
sanctification, 34–35
Sanctus, 96
saving event, 155
Schleiermacher, Friedrich, 25
Schlink, Edmund, 129–31
Schmemann, Alexander, 9–10, 12, 20, 104, 135, 180, 191, 212, 216, 218, 221–22, 224–25, 227, 256ff., 291, 293, 302
scholasticism, 146, 161–64, 257, 276, 285
Schulz, Hans-Joachim, 230ff., 244, 249
Scott, R. Taylor, 185
Scripture, 24, 53, 87, 98, 117–121, 233, 252, 289, 295
  & sacrament, 261

theology from worship, 12, 78, 105, 116, 133, 180
theology of worship, 11, 30, 33, 42, 67, 76, 99, 102–103, 173, 180, 228, 298
*theoprepeis logoi*, 281
*theoria*, 244
Theotokos, 251, 261
thirst for God, 266
tomb, 250–51, 253
Tower of Babel, 302
*traditio symboli*, 121
Tradition, 176, 192, 200, 212, 222, 255, 294–98, 301
transfiguration, 273
transfigured earth, 273
transformation of holy gifts, 279–80
transformative ritual, 116
*transitus*, 82, 89, 94
transubstantiation, 55, 71, 165, 276, 278, 282, 291
Trent, Council of, 38, 125
Trinity, 24–26, 82, 92, 95, 113, 127, 217, 220, 230, 253
Triumph of Orthodoxy, 230
tropological meaning, 233
Trullan Synod, 243
Turner, H. E. W., 111
two-tier model, 212–15, 222, 225, 289, 296, 298
*Typicon*, 171, 177–78, 184, 301
typological approach, 230, 249, 255

U
Unitarian, 113
unlettered believers, 217
*usus* of worship, 77, 84, 86, 97–100, 102, 134, 140, 183

V
Vajta, Vilmos, 12, 42–66, 97, 104, 129, 133, 148, 173, 181, 183
Venerable Bede, 239
*verbum vocale*, 35
vestments, 68, 181–82, 250
vicarious, 50
visible signs of church, 41
vocation, 275
von Rad, Gerhard, 118
Vonier, Anscar, 163
vulgar religion, 213ff., 221